AF790755

COMPARING ONLINE LEGAL EDUCATION

Ius Comparatum – Global Studies in Comparative Law

Founding Editors
Jürgen Basedow, Max Planck Institute for Comparative and International Private Law, Hamburg, Germany

George A. Bermann, Columbia University, New York, USA

Former Series Editors
Katharina Boele-Woelki, Bucerius Law School, Hamburg, Germany

Diego P. Fernández Arroyo, Institut d'Études Politiques de Paris (Sciences Po), Paris, France

Series Editors
Giuditta Cordero-Moss, University of Oslo, Oslo, Norway

Gary Bell, National University of Singapore, Singapore

Series Assistant Editor
Philippine Blajan, IACL, Paris, France

Editorial Board Members
Ewa Baginska, Gdansk University, Gdansk, Poland

Vivian Curran, University of Pittsburgh, Pittsburgh, PA, USA

Nicolás Etcheverry, Universidad de Montevideo, Montevideo, Uruguay

Makane Moise Mbengue, Université de Genève, Geneva, Switzerland

Marilda Rosado de S. Ribeiro, Universidade do Estado do Rio de Janeiro, Rio de Janeiro, Brazil

Marilyne Sadowsky, Université Paris 1 Panthéon-Sorbonne, Paris, France

Dan Wei, University of Macau, Macau, China

COMPARING ONLINE LEGAL EDUCATION

Past, Present and Future

Edited by
Luke NOTTAGE
Makoto IBUSUKI

INTERSENTIA
Cambridge – Antwerp – Chicago

Intersentia Ltd
8 Wellington Mews
Wellington Street | Cambridge
CB1 1HW | United Kingdom
Tel: +44 1223 736 170
Email: contact@larcier-intersentia.com
www.larcier-intersentia.com

Distribution for the UK and
Rest of the World (incl. Eastern Europe)
NBN International
1 Deltic Avenue, Rooksley
Milton Keynes MK13 8LD
United Kingdom
Tel: +44 1752 202 301 | Fax: +44 1752 202 331
Email: orders@nbninternational.com

Distribution for Europe
Lefebvre Sarrut Belgium NV
Hoogstraat 139/6
1000 Brussels
Belgium
Tel: +32 (0)2 548 07 13
Email: contact@larcier-intersentia.com

Distribution for the USA and Canada
Independent Publishers Group
Order Department
814 North Franklin Street
Chicago, IL 60610
USA
Tel: +1 800 888 4741 (toll free) | Fax: +1 312 337 5985
Email: orders@ipgbook.com

Comparing Online Legal Education. Past, Present and Future
© The editors and contributors severally 2023

The editors and contributors have asserted the right under the Copyright, Designs and Patents Act 1988, to be identified as authors of this work.

No part of this book may be reproduced, stored in a retrieval system, or transmitted, in any form, or by any means, without prior written permission from Intersentia, or as expressly permitted by law or under the terms agreed with the appropriate reprographic rights organisation. Enquiries concerning reproduction which may not be covered by the above should be addressed to Intersentia at the address above.

Artwork on cover: © Erica Kobayashi Nottage

ISBN 978-1-83970-348-5
ISSN 2214-6881
D/2023/7849/65
NUR 828

British Library Cataloguing in Publication Data. A catalogue record for this book is available from the British Library.

FOREWORD

A long time ago I experienced the mixed joys of both undergraduate and postgraduate law lectures and tutorials delivered directly in the classroom among fellow students. In my final undergraduate year in 1973, however, I studied part-time entirely remotely by reading lecture notes with references to the relevant texts and cases. Luckily, I had access to an excellent law library and was the associate of a judge in a final appellate court where there were other such judges with associates who were recent graduates. I could bounce ideas off them and learn from the cases argued before the court. I hate to think what that experience of remote learning would have been like had I not had that environment around me. I admire greatly those lawyers who have successfully educated themselves solely through distance or online education.

I recognise the advantages that modern technology can provide to remote learning not only through video-conferencing of lectures and tutorials but by direct access to relevant primary materials online. That early experience, however, has biased me in favour of live teaching in a class full of students actually present. As the general rapporteurs recognise in their General Report, even interactive video-conferencing makes it more difficult for remote students 'to engage in classroom discussions … where picking up on nuances can be harder than in physical interactions, even for native speakers'. Common experience of video-conferencing outside the academic environment backs up those conclusions.

There is so much to be learned also in informal discussion with lecturers and other students and from an environment where the social interaction and physical facilities are focused on what you are studying. As the special rapporteurs say about the experience of online education in Macao, 'law is rooted in human interactions, benefiting not only from direct student–teacher contact but also from student learning among peers, through classroom teaching but also other personal contacts on campus'. This personal contact is recognised as a continuing advantage particularly in aspects of courses where students need to learn practical or 'soft' skills.

The period leading up to the International Academy of Comparative Law's 2022 Congress in Paraguay coincided with the spread of the COVID-19 virus and the curtailment of normal legal education in very many jurisdictions. So the decision to examine the topic of online legal education at the Congress proved to be very 'timely', as Professors Nottage and Ibusuki say in their General Report. Suddenly online legal education had become frighteningly necessary and common. It can also provide access to courses otherwise practically too expensive or unavailable to less privileged students. What, therefore, may be the consequences of greater use of online legal education for the future of the profession and the teaching of law around the world?

This useful volume examines those issues relevant to online legal education in 13 jurisdictions representative of the major common law and civilian traditions as well as some hybrid jurisdictions. It makes some tentative predictions for the future of such education. The examples also carry the advantage of having been drawn from countries with widely varying economies, unequal access to technology for online teaching and differing traditions in the teaching of law.

The general and special rapporteurs link legal education to the legal profession and main legal traditions of each jurisdiction covered, and include pre- and post-admission education for law graduates. The focus is mostly on university-level legal education but practical professional training in some jurisdictions is also addressed. Online education for such practical training can be more effective than may be the case for young undergraduates. It is also notable that the topic shows the typical tensions between continuity and change often found in comparative studies.

Some of the main general conclusions reached are that developments in online legal education in the 13 jurisdictions examined should be influenced by the nature of the jurisdiction's legal tradition and legal profession, its level of public funding for universities, its level of economic development, including its infrastructure for information and communications technology, and the particular impact of the COVID-19 pandemic. The work as a whole will be especially useful for those considering how to deploy online legal education in a particular jurisdiction, using that analysis, with a view to setting up a properly nuanced regime for that style of education for that jurisdiction.

Those charged with these significant responsibilities in jurisdictions and universities around the world will derive great benefit from studying the insights contained in this volume.

The Hon. James Douglas KC
Royal Commissioner
Former Judge of the Supreme Court of Queensland
Associate Member of the International Academy of Comparative Law
Member of the Senate of the Australian Catholic University

CONTENTS

LIST OF ABBREVIATIONS

AAM	Macao Association of Lawyers
ABA	American Bar Association
ADSL	Asymmetric Digital Subscriber Line
AGC	Attorney General's Chambers
AI	Artificial Intelligence
AITI	Authority for Info-communications Technology Industry of Brunei Darussalam
ALEP	Advanced Legal Education Programme
ANVUR	Agenzia di Valutazione del Sistema Universitario e della Ricerca
AQF	Australian Qualification Framework
ASEAN	Association of Southeast Asian Nations
AU	African Union
AZVO	Agency for Science and Higher Education
BAS	Bar Association of Seychelles
BSB	Bar Standards Board
BVC	Bar Vocational Course
C3L	Centre for Lifelong Learning
CALD	Council of Australian Law Deans
CARNET	Croatian Academic and Research Network
CBA	Cyprus Bar Association
CFU	Italian University Credits
CGS	Commonwealth Grants Scheme
CityU	City University of Macau
CJEU	Court of Justice of the European Union
CLE	Continuing Legal Education
CLP	Certificate in Legal Practice
CMS	Case Management System
CMS	Class Management System
CMS	Course Management System

CNF	Italian National Bar Council
CoE	Council of Europe
CommTLE	Committee on Teaching and Learning Enhancement
CPD	Continuous/Continuing Professional Development
CPLE	Centre for Professional Legal Education
CPLED	Canadian Centre for Professional Legal Education
CRUI	Italian University Rectors' Conference
CSP	Commonwealth Supported Places
CTLE	Centre for Teaching and Learning Enhancement
CYQAA	Cyprus Agency of Quality Assurance
DAD	Didattica a Distanza (distance learning)
DAI	Degree Awarding Institution
DESI	EU's Digital Economy and Society Index
DORH	Croatian State Attorney's Office
DSES	MSAR Higher Education Bureau
EFS	Electronic Filing System
EIU	Economist Intelligence Unit
EJS	European Justice Scoreboard
EJTN	European Judicial Training Network
ELFA	European Law Faculties Association
ERA	Academy of European Law
EU	European Union
FFO	Ordinary Financing Fund
FLC	Faculty Learning Community
FLL	Federal Legislative List
FLSC	Federation of Law Societies of Canada
FT	Full Time
GAP	General Adjournment Period
GDP	Gross Domestic Product
GPA	Grade Point Average
HE	Higher Education
HEC	Higher Education Commission
HECO	Higher Education Commission Ordinance
HECS/HELP	Higher Education Contribution Scheme/Higher Education Loan Program
HESF	Higher Education Standards Framework

HKU SPACE	HKU School of Professional and Continuing Education
HR-ZOO	Croatian Scientific and Educational Cloud
iCMS	Integrated Course Management System
ICON	In-Class Optional Niche
ICT	Information and Communications Technology
ICTO	Information and Communication Technology Office
IIUM	International Islamic University of Malaysia
IMF	International Monetary Fund
IPC	Integrated Practice Curriculum
IT	Information Technology
ITSP	Information Technology Strategy Plan
IVLE	Integrated Virtual Learning Environment
JCMS	Judiciary Case Management System
JD	Juris Doctor
KUPUSB	Seri Begawan Religious Teachers University College
LACC	Law Admissions Consultative Committee
LAT	Law Admission Test
Law-GAT	Law Graduate Assessment Test
LBA	Lahore Bar Association
LC	Legal Council
LEC	Legal Education Committee
LHCBA	Lahore High Court Bar Association
LLB	Bachelor of Laws
LLD	Doctor of Laws
LLM	Master of Laws
LPA	Legal Practitioners Act
LPBCA	Legal Practitioners and Bar Councils Act 1973 (Pakistan)
LPC	Legal Practice Course
LPP	Law Practice Program
LSAT	Law School Admission Test
MBL	Macao Basic Law
MEXT	Japanese Ministry of Education, Culture, Sports, Science and Technology
MIB	Malay Islamic Monarchy
MMU	Multi-Media University
MOEC	Cypriot Minister of Education, Culture, Sports, and Youth

MOOC	Massive Open Online Course
MSAR	Macao SAR
MSC	Multimedia Super Corridor
MUR	Italian Ministry of Universities and Research
MUST	Macau University of Science and Technology
NCA	National Committee of Accreditation
NRRP	National Recovery and Resilience Plan
NUS	National University of Singapore
ODR	Online Dispute Resolution
OECD	Organisation for Economic Co-operation and Development
OUM	Open University Malaysia
PBC	Pakistan Bar Council
PBCLER	Pakistan Bar Council Legal Education Rules
PBS	Pakistan Bureau of Statistics
PC	Personal Computer
PCLL	Postgraduate Certificate of Laws
PhD	Doctor of Philosophy
PHEC	Punjab Higher Education Commission
PLPBCR	Pakistan Legal Practitioners and Bar Councils Rules
PLT	Practical Legal Training
PRC	People's Republic of China
PSLMS	Pakistan Social and Living Standards Measurement Survey
PT	Part Time
PTA	Pakistan Telecommunication Authority
QA	Quality Assurance
QMS	Queue Management System
SAC	Superior Advocacy Council
SADC	Southern African Development Community
SAEH Act	Act on Scientific Activity and Higher Education
SAR	Special Administrative Region
SCLET	Standing Committee on Legal Education and Training
SCS	Space Collaboration System
SeyLII	Seychelles Legal Information Institute
SHEC	Sindh Higher Education Commission
SIDS	Small Island Developing State
SMS	Short Message Service

SMU	Singapore Management University
SQA	Seychelles Qualifications Authority
SRCE	E-learning University Computing Centre
SUSS	Singapore University of Social Sciences
TA	Teaching Assistant
TEQSA	Tertiary Education Quality and Standards Association
UBD	University of Brunei Darussalam
UGC	University Grants Committee
UiTM	Universiti Teknologi MARA
UKM	National University of Malaysia
UM	University of Macau
UNESCO	United Nations Educational, Scientific and Cultural Organization
UniSey	University of Seychelles
UNISSA	Sultan Sharif Ali Islamic University
UNODC	United Nations Office on Drugs and Crime
UOL	University of London
USJ	University of St. Joseph
USKOK	Croatian Office for the Suppression of Corruption and Organised Crime
UTB	University of Technology Brunei
VCF	Video-Conferencing Facilities
WHO	World Health Organization
WTO	World Trade Organization

LIST OF RAPPORTEURS

Syed Imad-ud-Din Asad
Lawyer and academic based in Lahore, Pakistan, and the first elected associate member from Pakistan for the International Academy of Comparative Law.

Rossella Esther Cerchia
Full Professor of Comparative Law, University of Milan, Italy.

Salim Farrar
Associate Professor, University of Sydney, Australia.

Adrien Habermacher
Assistant Professor of Law, Université de Moncton, Canada.

Makoto Ibusuki
Professor of Law, Seijo University, Tokyo, Japan.

Nyasha Noreen Katsenga
Legal Researcher in the Supreme Court of Seychelles, and LLD Candidate, University of the Western Cape, South Africa.

Alice Lee
Associate Professor, Faculty of Law, University of Hong Kong, and Senior Fellow of the UK Higher Education Academy.

Demetra Loizou
Lecturer in International Criminal Law and Humanitarian Law and LLM Deputy Course Leader, University of Central Lancashire, Cyprus.

Wilson Lui
Pre-Doctoral Fellow and Lecturer, Faculty of Law, University of Hong Kong.

Trish Mundy
Professor and Dean of Law, University of Wollongong, Australia.

Rostam J. Neuwirth
Professor of Law, Head of Department of Global Legal Studies, Faculty of Law, University of Macau, Macao (China).

Luke Nottage
Professor of Comparative and Transnational Business Law, University of Sydney, Australia, titular member of the International Association of Comparative Law, and founding co-director of the Australian Network for Japanese Law.

Lida Pitsillidou
Lecturer in Company Law and Corporate Governance and LLB Course Leader, University of Central Lancashire, Cyprus.

Muruga P. Ramaswamy
Associate Professor, Coordinator of Services Teaching, Faculty of Law, University of Macau, Macao (China).

Alexandr Svetlicinii
Associate Professor, Programme Coordinator of the Master of International Business Law, Faculty of Law, University of Macau, Macao (China).

Nobumichi Teramura
Assistant Professor of ASEAN and Asia-Wide Regionalisation, Institute of Asian Studies, University of Brunei Darussalam.

William van Caenegem
Professor of Law, Bond University, Australia.

Barbara Vari
Assistant Professor of Comparative Law, University of Milan, Italy.

Ken'ichi Yoneda
Professor of Law and Director, Education and Research Center on Judicial Policy, Kagoshima University, Japan.

Mirela Župan
Associate Professor and Director of the PhD program in the Faculty of Law, J. J. Strossmayer University of Osijek, Croatia.

GENERAL REPORT

Comparing Online Legal Education

Luke NOTTAGE and Makoto IBUSUKI*

Résumé

Ce rapport général compare l'éducation juridique en ligne dans des juridictions représentatives avant et après la pandémie, couvrant principalement l'éducation de niveau universitaire, mais aussi la formation juridique continue pour la profession. La partie 2 explique des éléments de contexte importants et pertinents,

* We are grateful to for excellent research and editorial assistance provided by Amelia Frey through the University of Wollongong's Transnational Law and Policy Centre (where Nottage is affiliated as an Honorary Professor, and which provided some funding for excellent editorial and research assistance by Amelia Frey), and by James Tanna and Xinghan (Chris) Li through the Centre for Asian and Pacific Law at the University of Sydney (CAPLUS). For helpful feedback on earlier drafts, we also thank participants at seminar presentations mentioned below and hosted by Griffith University's Law Futures Centre (Brisbane, 20 July 2022) and at the Congress of the International Academy of Comparative Law (Paraguay, 24 October 2022), as well as Peng Guo, Alan Koh and the rapporteurs who have authored the ensuing special reports (especially Adrien Habermacher). Any errors or misconceptions remain of course our sole responsibility.

que les rapporteurs spéciaux ont été invités à prendre en compte pour leurs rapports sur les différentes juridictions. La partie 2.1 se concentre sur la taille et la nature de la profession juridique, y compris ses principaux « gardiens » (tels que le gouvernement, la profession elle-même ou le marché) permettant la qualification en tant qu'avocats, procureurs, juges et autres professionnels du droit. Cette question peut également être liée à la tradition juridique prédominante dans cette juridiction, les pays historiquement plus influencés par la tradition de la common law ayant tendance à avoir un plus grand nombre d'avocats (mais pas toujours). À son tour, l'étendue et les caractéristiques de la profession juridique peuvent influencer ce qui est enseigné dans les facultés de droit universitaires et la manière d'enseigner. Par exemple, une grande profession liée à de nombreux programmes d'écoles de droit et à des exigences de formation juridique continue peut permettre une plus grande expérimentation de l'enseignement juridique en ligne, bien qu'elle puisse également exercer des pressions supplémentaires sur les instructeurs, ce qui entrave de telles initiatives.

La partie 2.2 identifie ensuite la structure et le financement des universités comme un autre facteur contextuel potentiel ayant un impact sur le besoin et les aspects pratiques de l'enseignement juridique en ligne. Comme autre facteur, la partie 2.3 souligne l'environnement général des technologies de l'information et des communications (TIC), y compris les questions relatives à la place d'Internet dans les universités, la profession juridique et la population générale. Ce facteur est en partie lié à la richesse d'une économie, bien que certains pays en développement aient atteint un taux élevé de pénétration de l'Internet avant la pandémie, tandis que le développement des TIC peut également être corrélé au nombre et à la densité des populations. Comme résumé dans la partie 2.4, ces facteurs, ainsi que l'impact diversifié de la COVID-19 dans les juridictions (mesuré par exemple par le nombre d'infections et de décès), devaient avoir un impact sur l'important mouvement vers l'enseignement juridique en ligne provoqué par les restrictions de mobilité liées à la pandémie pour les étudiants, les enseignants et les administrateurs.

La partie 3 décrit certaines des grandes questions associées au développement de l'enseignement juridique en ligne, à la fois avant et surtout après la pandémie, en tant que thèmes communs aux chapitres suivants. Ces rapports spéciaux portent sur neuf juridictions de la région Asie-Pacifique (Australie, Canada, Malaisie, Brunei, Singapour, Hong Kong, Macao, Japon et Pakistan), ainsi que sur quatre autres juridictions (Seychelles, Croatie, Chypre et Italie), ce qui permet d'illustrer la diversité des tailles et des niveaux de revenus. La quatrième partie présente les points forts des 13 juridictions, identifiant à la fois des thèmes communs et des divergences intrigantes.

En conclusion, la partie 5 affirme que l'enquête sur les juridictions représentatives suggère que les facteurs contextuels élaborés dans la partie 2 aident à expliquer les expériences plus variées de l'enseignement juridique en ligne, en particulier avant la pandémie, et les développements de l'enseignement en ligne provoqués par les limitations de mobilité communément rencontrées depuis 2020. Cependant, même dans les juridictions qui avaient moins de COVID-19 et n'imposaient pas de verrouillages sanctionnés par la loi (comme le Japon), l'enseignement s'est souvent déplacé volontairement en ligne. De plus, certaines des caractéristiques favorisant la transition étaient dues à des circonstances tout à fait fortuites, telles que des réformes plus larges de l'enseignement du droit (Japon), des expériences passées en matière de pandémies (Singapour) et les règles des associations du barreau (Pakistan). En outre, certaines juridictions et certains groupes au sein de celles-ci ont eu plus de difficultés que d'autres.

Au fur et à mesure de la progression de la pandémie, nous avons également observé un « retour à la normale » (c'est-à-dire des pratiques typiques d'avant la pandémie). Bien que les expériences de l'enseignement juridique en ligne induites par la pandémie aient généralement amélioré l'environnement pour de nouvelles initiatives et des discussions plus informées entre les parties prenantes, la prise de conscience des inconvénients ainsi que les progrès du « e-learning » rendent prévisible le fait que seules certaines juridictions (principalement à revenu élevé) continueront à développer de manière significative l'enseignement juridique en ligne. Même dans ce cas, il reste à voir si ces nouveaux changements s'avéreront vraiment optimaux pour les étudiants et les enseignants, plutôt que pour les administrateurs.

1. INTRODUCTION

The COVID-19 pandemic declared by the World Health Organization on 11 March 2020 generated immense personal, economic and political turmoil, extending to the legal community.[1] The public health and related crises generated many challenges, including those focusing on higher education, and some opportunities.[2] Domestic and international travel as well as other restrictions forced many legal education providers to move their teaching and learning activities completely or partly online, sometimes for extended periods. Some jurisdictions had already been experimenting with online or hybrid delivery methods, or were better prepared to make this transition, but others struggled more as COVID-19 spread worldwide.[3]

---

1 See e.g. J. Grogan and A. Donald (eds), *Routledge Handbook of Law and the COVID-19 Pandemic*, Routledge, New York 2022.

2 See e.g. R. Chan, K. Bista and R. Allen (eds), *Online Teaching and Learning in Higher Education During COVID-19: International Perspectives and Experiences*, Routledge, New York 2002.

3 International Association of Law Schools (ed.), *Transitioning to Online Legal Education: The Student Voice* (August 2020) and *Transitioning to Online Legal Education: The Faculty Voice* (November 2020), both available via https://www.ialsnet.org/.

After COVID-19 was temporarily eliminated in some jurisdictions, or effective vaccines were developed and administered from late 2020 (initially mostly in the harder-hit Europe and North America and then other developed economies), restrictions were relaxed and some jurisdictions quickly reverted to more traditional means of delivering legal education. Yet educators, administrators and policymakers everywhere have become much more aware of the possibilities as well as the problems associated with online delivery. Therefore, it was very timely for the International Academy of Comparative Law to nominate 'online legal education' as a topic for comparative research.[4] This project was also able to build on earlier research by the Academy into somewhat related topics, such as the internationalisation of legal education and bilingualism in legal research and studies.[5]

This report compares online legal education across fairly representative jurisdictions before and after the pandemic, covering mainly university-level education but also continuing legal education for the profession. Section 2 explains arguably relevant important background, which special rapporteurs were asked to consider for their jurisdictional special reports. Section 2.1 focuses on the size and nature of the legal profession, including its primary 'gatekeepers' allowing qualification as practising lawyers, prosecutors, judges and other core legal professionals. This question may also be linked to the predominant legal tradition in that jurisdiction, with those historically more influenced by the common law tradition for example tending to have larger numbers of lawyers. In turn, the scope and features of the legal profession may influence what is taught in university law schools and in what ways.[6]

Section 2.2 then identifies the structure and funding of universities[7] as another potential contextual factor impacting on the need for and practicalities of online legal education. As a further factor, section 2.3 highlights the general environment for information and communications technology (ICT),[8] including

4 By 'online legal education', we mean primarily remote teaching and learning mediated through the internet (asynchronous and synchronous). However, to varying extents, the special reports also touch on the wider digitalisation of in-person teaching and learning.

5 C. Jamin and W. van Caenegem (eds), *The Internationalisation of Legal Education*, Springer, Cham/New York 2016; N. Etcheverry Estrázulas (ed.), *Bilingual Study and Research*, Springer, Cham/New York 2022.

6 Compare generally e.g. W. P. Alford (ed.), *Raising the Bar: The Emerging Legal Profession in East Asia*, Harvard University Press, Cambridge 2007; C. Sampford and H. Breakey (eds), *Law, Lawyering and Legal Education: Building an Ethical Profession in a Globalizing World*, Routledge, New York 2017.

7 See E. Bennetot Pruvot, A. Claeys-Kulik and T. Estermann (eds), *Strategies for Efficient Funding of Universities in Europe*, Springer, Cham/New York 2015 and S. Babones, *Australia's Universities: Can They Reform?*, Ocean Reeve, Brisbane 2021.

8 A few years before the pandemic, see e.g. World Bank, *The Little Data Book on Information and Communication Technology 2018*, World Bank, Washington DC 2018, available at https://data.worldbank.org/products/data-books/little-data-book-on-info-communication-tech.

issues around internet penetration in universities, the legal profession and the general population. This partly overlaps with how wealthy an economy is, although even some developing countries had achieved high internet penetration before the pandemic, while ICT developments may also correlate with population numbers and density. As summarised in section 2.4, these factors as well as the diverse impact of COVID-19 across the jurisdictions (measured for example by infections and deaths) are expected to impact on the large shift towards online legal education prompted by pandemic-related mobility restrictions for students, teachers and administrators.

Section 3 outlines some of the broad issues associated with the development of online legal education, both before and especially after the pandemic, as common themes across the ensuing chapters. Those special reports encompass nine jurisdictions in the Asia-Pacific region (Australia, Canada, Malaysia, Brunei, Singapore, Hong Kong, Macao, Japan and Pakistan),[9] as well as four elsewhere (Seychelles, Croatia, Cyprus and Italy), providing an illustrative mix of sizes and income levels.[10] Section 4 presents highlights from all 13 jurisdictions, identifying both common themes and intriguing divergences.

In conclusion, section 5 argues that the survey of representative jurisdictions suggests that the background factors elaborated below do help explain the more varied experiences of online legal education, particularly before the pandemic, and the developments in online education prompted by the commonly found mobility limitations since 2020. Some of the features assisting the transition, however, were due to quite fortuitous circumstances. Various jurisdictions and groups within them struggled more than others. As the pandemic progressed, we saw more or less 'reversion to the mean' (typical pre-pandemic practices). Although the pandemic-induced experiences of online legal education have generally improved the environment for further initiatives, and ongoing more informed discussions among stakeholders, the awareness of the disadvantages as well as advances in e-learning make it foreseeable that only some (mostly higher-income) jurisdictions will keep significantly expanding online legal education. Even then, whether such further shifts will prove truly optimal for students and teachers, rather than administrators, remains to be seen.

---

9 For a webinar recording involving presentations of draft reports for most of the covered Asia-Pacific jurisdictions, see https://japaneselaw.sydney.edu.au/2021/12/asia-pacific-online-legal-education-before-and-after-the-covid-19-pandemic/.

10 For a webinar and materials following presentations of draft reports for covered jurisdictions outside the Asia-Pacific region, see https://japaneselaw.sydney.edu.au/2021/03/online-legal-education-compared-australia-japan-and-far-beyond/.

2. BACKGROUND: LEGAL PROFESSION, UNIVERSITIES, ICT AND PANDEMIC IMPACT

To provide context and hypotheses for the development of online legal education, we first consider the nature and extent of a jurisdiction's legal profession, which is arguably quite closely related to its main legal tradition – at least historically (section 2.1). Then we consider university structures and funding (section 2.2); ICT infrastructure (section 2.3); and the impact of COVID-19 across jurisdictions (section 2.4, including Table 2 summarising these factors across the covered jurisdictions).

2.1. LEGAL PROFESSION AND LEGAL TRADITION

A useful way to grasp the contours of a jurisdiction's legal profession is to ascertain who are its main 'gatekeepers': what institutions determine who is allowed to qualify and be licensed to practise law in various forms? Primary candidates are the legal profession itself, the government, universities or the market, although most jurisdictions have a mixture of these, which can evolve over time.[11]

One possible gatekeeper is the existing legal profession, setting training requirements or qualifying examinations, including sometimes especially a cap on the number allowed to enter the profession each year. This may create a type of cartel limiting access to the profession, tending to protect incumbents from potentially 'excessive' competition undermining minimum standards for legal services. An example of such a gatekeeper institution is the Federation of Bar Associations in Japan, whose modern legal system in the 19th century was influenced by the European civil law tradition (France and especially Germany), although after World War II there has been a growing influence from Anglo-American law.[12] However, following recommendations of the Justice System Reform Council in 2001, there have been steady growth in the numbers allowed each year to pass the National Legal Examination to qualify as practising lawyers able to provide full legal services, including litigation services, or (if hired) public prosecutors or career judges.[13] This is because the Federation of Bar

---

[11] K. Anderson and T. Ryan, 'Gatekeepers: A Comparative Critique of Admission to the Legal Profession and Japan's New Law Schools' in S. Steele and K. Taylor (eds), *Legal Education in Asia*, Routledge, New York 2009, pp. 183–212. Compare also e.g. E. Katvan, C. Silver, N. Zi and A. Sherr (eds), *Too Many Lawyers? The Future of the Legal Profession*, Routledge, New York 2019.

[12] L. Nottage, 'The Development of Comparative Law in Japan' in M. Reimann and R. Zimmerman (eds), *The Oxford Handbook of Comparative Law*, 2nd edn, Oxford University Press, Oxford 2019, pp. 201–227.

[13] M. Abe and L. Nottage, 'Japanese Law' in J. Smits (ed.), *Encyclopedia of Comparative Law*, Edward Elgar, Cheltenham 2012, pp. 157–168, with forthcoming new edition manuscript at https://papers.ssrn.com/sol3/papers.cfm?abstract_id=3672112.

Associations is not the sole gatekeeper. Rather, it negotiates for the quota allowed to pass the Legal Examination, each year, with the Ministry of Justice (responsible for public prosecutors) and the judiciary (which, although an independent branch for administration of justice, derives much of its budget from the executive and legislative branches of government).[14]

In some jurisdictions other than Japan, the government may play a more direct or significant role as 'gatekeeper' to the profession, by setting such quotas. In Australia before 2011, for example, this was more evident by the government limiting the number of students allowed to be enrolled in university law schools. Even after further deregulation of universities from 2011, allowing them to compete more to attract law or other students and associated government funding, the government retains an indirect and loose gatekeeper role. This derives from the government capping the number of 'Commonwealth Supported Places' for funding of domestic students taking qualifying LLB or JD law degrees, and/or by the government providing access to cheap student loans.[15]

However, Australia's experience could also be argued to be an example of universities emerging as the bigger gatekeeper to the legal profession. Each university, mainly public but a few private ones, can decide how many law students to enrol for the LLB degree or (after another non-law degree) the JD degree. The legal profession correspondingly started losing its control over entry to the profession from the 1960s, although it still requires university law schools to teach many compulsory courses (and topics) within the LLB or JD degree programme. The legal profession also still supports an alternative 'night school' to teach equivalents to such qualifying law degrees, at least in some parts of the country. It also has input into a post-graduation short practical training course for those wanting to enrol and practise as lawyers.[16] Because almost all

---

14 See also K.-W. Chan, 'Setting the Limits: Who Controls the Size of the Legal Profession in Japan?' in E. Katvan, C. Silver, N. Ziv and A. Sherr (eds), *Too Many Lawyers? The Future of the Legal Profession*, Routledge, New York 2019.

15 With effect from 2021, for example, the Commonwealth (federal) government increased the annual fees that domestic law students need to pay universities for LLB or JD students, although those fees can still then be covered by a student loan administered by the government (involving a low interest rate and no repayment obligation until and unless the graduate starts earning a minimum salary amount). Although the government maintained the subsidy additionally provided to law schools for each such Commonwealth Supported Place (provided to all LLB students, plus some JD students studying law after a non-law degree), this government adjustment indirectly creates some financial disincentive to commencing the LLB or JD degree, which is the predominant route to then qualify and practise as a lawyer. The adjustment was part of a broader attempt by the government to encourage students to study more in some disciplines involving perceived better employment prospects and national benefit, such as science and technology, teaching and foreign languages. See generally e.g. https://www.abc.net.au/news/2020-06-19/university-fees-tertiary-education-overhaul-course-costs/12367742.

16 See e.g. respectively https://www.lpab.justice.nsw.gov.au/Pages/diploma-law-course/diploma-law-course.aspx and https://www.collaw.edu.au/programs/plt/c-24/c-78.

pass that training course, and even the LLB or JD degrees once admitted into the programmes by the universities, this had led to a large and growing legal profession, especially over the last few decades.[17]

This current situation for Australia also points to yet another gatekeeper to the profession: the market for legal services. What ultimately determines how many students enrol for LLB and JD degrees is the job prospects after graduation from university and completion of the short practical training course needed to then practise as lawyers. If the student can only get into a less well-regarded law school and/or achieves poor marks, s/he will find fewer opportunities to secure the necessary position as a trainee lawyer, or even work in-house in government or corporations providing legal services internally without registering as a lawyer.

This situation is even more apparent in the United States, for example, where moreover there is a much higher proportion of private rather than state-funded law schools. Although there the states do retain a separate Bar examination with a significant fail rate, even in the toughest jurisdictions (California and New York) a very high proportion of those sitting the examinations pass on second or third attempts. They can then qualify as US lawyers, although, again, if they required multiple attempts and/or had poor course marks, especially from less-regarded law schools, there may be only a limited market for their services as lawyers. The even more market-driven US system nonetheless generates a very large legal profession, although its growth slowed particularly after the global financial crisis of 2007–8.[18]

These differences in the legal profession can also be roughly mapped onto differing major legal traditions, at least historically. Common law jurisdictions like the US, Australia or England tend to have much larger legal professions compared to those more influenced by the civil law tradition like Japan, or indeed the socialist law tradition. Of course, comparative lawyers have long pointed out differences within such traditions and transformations or 'hybridisation' over time, reflected for example in much higher per capita lawyers in Germany (with no cap set on the number allowed to pass the qualifying National Legal Examinations each year) compared to in France.[19] Nonetheless, these differences remain quite striking, as Table 2 in section 2.4 below indicates, and they also correlate often to different civil lawsuit filing rates per capita and related aspects of what sort of legal work is then done by legal professionals across the different

---

17 M. McNamara, 'University Legal Education and the Supply of Law Graduates: A Fresh Look at a Longstanding Issue' (2018) 20 *Flinders Law Journal* 241, 255.

18 S. Harper, *The Lawyer Bubble: A Profession in Crisis*, Basic Books, New York, 2016, and generally B. Green, 'The Flood of US Lawyers: Natural Fluctuation or Professional Climate Change?' in E. Katvan, C. Silver, N. Ziv and A. Sherr (eds), *Too Many Lawyers? The Future of the Legal Profession*, Routledge, New York 2019.

19 See generally J. Merryman, D. Clark and J. Haley (eds), *The Contemporary Civil Law Tradition: Europe, Latin America, and East Asia*, Carolina Academic Press, Durham 2015.

jurisdictions.[20] Thus, the still comparatively few practising lawyers in Japan (*bengoshi*) still mainly specialise in litigation, but various 'quasi-lawyers' (like judicial or administrative scriveners) are accredited under specific legislation to assist usually with more transactional or advisory legal services.[21]

Such differences in the size and nature of the legal profession, especially the socio-economically influential practising lawyers (permitted to provide all types of legal services, including litigation), therefore often derive from the extent and influence of university-level legal education in different jurisdictions. In turn, the variations in the legal profession can impact back on the contents and format of legal education in universities. If there is a large profession, for example, universities will often have many law students and accordingly be more open to experimenting with more 'efficient' teaching methods such as online legal education. We might therefore expect (and indeed partly find) more moves towards online education in say Australian law schools than in Japan, where there are far fewer students graduating particularly from the postgraduate law schools to enter the legal profession, but even (per capita) when we include all the graduates from the LLB programmes. However, that same aspect of large numbers of law students and then practising lawyers, as in Australia, may put law teachers under extra strain, especially if the budget from central universities for law schools is tight. Where law faculties lack good funding, they may therefore be less able to experiment with online teaching methods, unless pressed strongly by university administrators and/or jolted by external shocks like the COVID-19 pandemic.

2.2. FUNDING UNIVERSITIES AND LAW FACULTIES

How universities are funded, and specifically law faculties, is therefore another important factor to consider when trying to assess the current and prospective situation for online legal education. One aspect is the amount of government funding for tertiary education, although that may be spread beyond universities, and such funding may not trickle down proportionately to law faculties. For example, Australia has one of the higher proportions of public funding for tertiary education relative to gross domestic product (GDP: 35%) among nations of the Organisation for Economic Co-operation and Development (OECD), although the funding becomes closer to that in Japan (21%) when limited to direct grants using World Bank data reproduced in Table 2 in section 2.4 below.[22]

---

20 C. Wollschlager, 'Historical Trends of Civil Litigation: Japan, Arizona, Sweden and Germany' in H. Baum (ed.), *Economic Success and Legal System*, De Gruyter, Berlin 1997, pp. 89–142. Disentangling cause and effect, of course, is difficult.

21 M. Abe and L. Nottage, 'Japanese Law' in J. Smits (ed.), *Encyclopedia of Comparative Law*, Edward Elgar, Cheltenham 2012, pp. 157–168.

22 S. Babones, *Australia's Universities*, Ocean Reeve, Brisbane 2021, pp. 32–35. The OECD data considers all government support: direct grants, subsidised student loan schemes, etc.

This variation reflects another aspect: whether the universities are mostly public (as in Australia) or have a considerable proportion of private universities (as in Japan). In addition to reducing dependence on taxpayers or future generations for funding tertiary education generally, private universities may be more incentivised to try novel and potentially more efficient teaching methods, including online delivery.

However, such aspects also play out in complex ways when it comes to their impact on both conventional and online legal education initiatives. For example, Australian public universities have increasingly started to act like private organisations. Babones observes that Australian government funding rose steadily until 2012, before levelling off, generating a more than corresponding increase in full fee-paying international student enrolments and revenue. This correlated with a declining Australian dollar, which had boosted international student enrolments during earlier periods since the turn of the 21st century. The extra total revenue for Australian universities was primarily directed to standalone researchers and new facilities particularly in the sciences, to move Australian universities up in various international rankings, then marketed to attract even more students from abroad, rather than to support teachers/scholars and improve the student learning experience generally.[23] Further bolstering this private-sector mindset among Australian universities, as mentioned in section 2.1 above, in 2011 the government deregulated the numbers of domestic students that universities could enrol, allowing them to charge full fees if not Commonwealth Supported Places.

Such growing fee revenue in Australia combined with ongoing comparatively high levels of government funding should give university teachers more opportunity to experiment with and invest in online teaching methods. Yet, because this system also entails a burgeoning number of students and related administrative burdens or new systems, teachers in most universities were typically too pressed to be able to pursue such opportunities until the pandemic hit from 2020. Japanese universities have not seen such dramatic growth in law student numbers, and so can retain more emphasis on research. However, the new postgraduate law schools required extra attention to be given to teaching. Further, even in the undergraduate law faculties, individual law professors sometimes took opportunities to experiment with online or other innovative forms of delivery.[24]

---

23 S. Babones, *Australia's Universities*, Ocean Reeve, Brisbane 2021, pp. 35–66 (especially Figures 1 and 3). He argues further that the Australian government funding is based on an average cost formula, whereas international students were charged by universities on a marginal cost approach that did not sufficiently account for the universities' fixed costs (campus facilities, etc.).

24 See e.g. M. Ibusuki, 'Joho Gijutsu to Hogaku Kyoiku ni kansuru Jittai Chosa Hokoku' [Report of an Empirical Survey on Information Technology and Legal Education] (2002)

As a further complication, even quite high levels of funding at the university level may not necessarily flow down proportionately to the law faculties, which instead can end up cross-subsidising faculties with more fixed costs (such as science, engineering or medicine). In addition, if law faculties increasingly attract non-native speakers, as in Australia much more say than in Japan, this can have mixed effects on conventional as well as online legal education. On the one hand, it could encourage more use of ICT to help such students (for example, by requiring all lectures to be recorded). On the other hand, it may be more difficult for such students to engage in classroom discussions if held through video-conferencing – where picking up on nuances can be harder than in physical interactions, even for native speakers.[25] Babones observes that by 2018 after two decades, Australian universities – as highlighted in Table 1 below – were enrolling remarkably high levels of students from abroad (mostly from Nepal, India and especially China from around 2013), arguably well beyond the proportions useful for pedagogical benefits for all students in the classroom.

Table 1. Top 8 destination countries for international students (2018)[26]

Country	Number of international students	Percent of world total	International students per 1,000 people	Ratio of inbound to outbound students
United States	987,314	17.7%	3.0	11.7
United Kingdom	451,079	8.1%	6.7	11.6
Australia	444,514	8.0%	17.9	33.4
Germany	311,738	5.6%	3.8	3.5
Russia	262,416	4.7%	1.8	N/A
France	229,623	4.1%	3.5	2.3
Canada	224,548	4.0%	6.1	4.6
Japan	182,748	3.3%	1.4	5.7

2.3. ICT IN GENERAL

Another obvious factor impacting on the uptake and features of online legal education is the access to good-quality and affordable ICT, including both hardware (computers and other devices) and software. A crucial aspect is

74(3) *Horitsu Jiho* 58, 60; N. Kashiwagi, 'Creation of Japanese Law Schools and Their Current Development' in S. Steele and K. Taylor (eds), *Legal Education in Asia*, Routledge, New York 2009, pp. 191–192.

25 E. Dhawan, *Digital Body Language: How to Build Trust and Connection, No Matter the Distance*, St. Martin's Press, New York 2021.

26 S. Babones, *Australia's Universities*, Ocean Reeve, Brisbane 2021, pp. 66–81, adapting Table 7 (Top 10 Destination Countries).

internet access, which still differs significantly across populations, as shown in Table 2 in section 2.4 below. That also illustrates that variations correlate mostly also to the jurisdiction's wealth or GDP. Yet there are also some more developing economies that had achieved high levels of internet penetration overall before the pandemic, and which have accelerated subsequently.[27]

Another influence, also mentioned in Table 2 below, is population scale and density (per capita). Geographically dispersed populations (as in Australia or Canada) can face extra challenges in installing high-speed broadband, compared to micro-states (like Singapore or Brunei). However, micro-states can also face barriers from economies of scale if their GDP and resources are fewer (like Seychelles, also covered in this book).

In addition, even if a jurisdiction achieves high internet penetration and good ICT overall, this may not necessarily map onto positive outcomes for law students and teachers. For example, the pandemic exposed that internet and ICT resources in Japan were quite good for lawyers but less so for judges and the court system. They were also quite variable for university teachers, and often quite poor for law students in the undergraduate law faculties, although better for the (more practice-oriented) postgraduate law schools inaugurated from 2004.[28]

2.4. COVID-19 IMPACT, SUMMARY AND PROSPECTS

Focusing on the impact from the pandemic on legal education, the comparative extent of disruption caused by COVID-19 generally is obviously a key factor. This can be measured in various ways, including numbers of infections (limiting mobility for patients, but also typically their household members), deaths (a salient proxy for socio-economic disruption), economic impact (influencing GDP and ICT capacity), and public health measures that require or encourage operations to move online.[29] The first two indicative measures are listed in Table 2 below, giving cumulative COVID-19 numbers as at the end of

---

27 See e.g. Thailand: https://datareportal.com/reports/digital-2022-thailand.

28 See the special report on Japan by Yoneda and Nottage in this volume; R. Grayson-Morrison and S. Steele, 'Judicial Responses to COVID-19' (2020) *Asian Legal Conversations – COVID-19*, https://law.unimelb.edu.au/centres/alc/engagement/asian-legal-conversations-covid-19_old/covid-19-original-articles/judicial-responses-to-covid-19-japanese-and-victorian-courts-use-of-technology.

29 For comparative analyses of these trends, including related legal aspects, see e.g. V. Ramraj (ed.), *COVID in Asia*, Oxford University Press, Oxford 2021.

2020 and (after vaccines became more widely available) the end of 2021. The higher the numbers of infections and deaths in a jurisdiction, relative to population, particularly during the first year of the pandemic, the more pressure we would expect for university-level and continuing legal education to move online.

However, because all jurisdictions have experienced COVID-19 waves since early 2020, these aggregate figures may be somewhat misleading, and more developing countries tend to have under-reporting of COVID-19 cases. Even jurisdictions with few infections and deaths overall may still have had periods with numbers high enough to prompt shifts to online legal education, and indeed we find such shifts in almost all jurisdictions covered (except Pakistan). An alternative metric, pushing legal education online, might be mobility restrictions in each jurisdiction. Yet those are not easy to calculate and compare, especially 'in action' as well as 'in books'. Japan never imposed lockdowns, for example, but the social norms against risk-taking and congregating during the pandemic also pushed the universities to move courses online in 2020.

Despite such caveats, Table 2 provides a preliminary summary of the COVID-19 spread and other major key factors identified above as likely to be relevant to promoting online legal education, both before and after the COVID-19 pandemic. In addition, the last two columns of Table 2 below sketch some subjective assessments for the past, present and future of online legal education. Based on key findings uncovered by the special reports in the ensuing chapters in this book (summarised also in section 3 below), one column assesses the situation for online legal education before 2020, ranging from poor (X) through moderate (XX) and good (XXX) to very good (XXXX, being a superlative pre-COVID-19 assessment not achieved by any jurisdiction covered in this book).

The other (last) column assesses the situation during or in the short term after the pandemic hit from 2020. It also includes, more speculatively, the prospects for future development given the background factors identified above for each jurisdiction as well as the details provided in the special reports. Identifying some jurisdictions with more positive outcomes or possibilities should be useful especially for those which have had more trouble transitioning to this form of delivery, with its many benefits (such as efficiencies, mentioned above), but also many challenges (as outlined next in section 3). In addition, such prospects may benefit certain groups (university and professional association administrators, or only some subsets of law students or teachers) over others. Future prospects may also be impacted by changes to the wider political economy and institutions in the jurisdictions covered, especially changes to the main gatekeepers to the profession, which are difficult to anticipate.

Table 2. Summary of background factors and assessments for online legal education

Jurisdiction	Population (millions)	GDP per capita (USD) [PPP][30]	Lawyers per million[31]	Legal system[32]	Public spending on tertiary education (%)[33]	Individuals' internet usage (%)[34]	Cumulative COVID-19 infections per million as of 31.12.20 (and 31.12.21)	COVID-19 deaths per million as of 31.12.20 (and 31.12.21)[35]	Pre-pandemic online legal education[36]	Post-pandemic: short-term (and long-term potential)
Australia	25.7	$51,680 [$53,317]	3,620	CL	18	89	1,102 (15,322)	35.6 (87)	XXX	XXXX (XXXX)
Brunei	0.44	$27,493 [$65,613]	300	CL and Syariah	19	95	356 (35,037)	6.8 (222)	X	XXX (XXX)
Canada	38.2	$43,258 [$46,572]	3,360	CL and some CVL	36	91	15,505 (57,287)	438 (803)	XX	XXX (XXX)
Croatia	3.9	$14,132 [$28,780]	1,595	CVL	22	78	51,654 (173,870)		X	XX (XXX)

30 Population (2021) and GDP (2021) in US dollars and purchasing power parity (PPP) via https://data.worldbank.org.

31 Based on lawyer numbers given in the special reports (mostly including 'trainee' lawyers).

32 CL = common law, CVL = civil law. Based on the University of Ottawa's http://www.juriglobe.ca/eng/index.php and this volume's special reports.

33 Government expenditure per tertiary student (% of GDP per capita) via https://data.worldbank.org/indicator/SE.XPD.TERT.PC.ZS (various years 2016–19, plus 2013 for Pakistan). Compare also https://data.oecd.org/eduresource/spending-on-tertiary-education.htm.

34 See https://data.worldbank.org/indicator/IT.NET.USER.ZS (2020). Most jurisdictions have recorded an increase in internet use since 2019, related to the pandemic.

35 See https://ourworldindata.org/covid-cases (including comparative charts, etc. at https://ourworldindata.org/covid-cases?country=AUS~BRN~CAN~HRV~CYP~HKG~ITA~JPN~MAC~MYS~PAK~SYC~SGP). However, particularly in more developing countries with poorer testing facilities, the numbers of infections and even deaths from COVID-19 may be considerably higher than reported: compare e.g. 'Tracking Excess Deaths Across Countries', *The Economist* (2021) https://www.economist.com/graphic-detail/coronavirus-excess-deaths-tracker.

36 X = minimal, XX = moderate, XXX = considerable, XXXX = extensive.

Cyprus	1.2	$27,528 [$39,373]	(around) 4,500	CL and CVL	21	91	24,940 (180,556)	134 (712)	X	XX (XXX)
Hong Kong	7.41 (7.51 in 2019)	$46,324 [$59,234]	1,835	CL	24	92	1,171 (1,672)	19.6 (28)	XX	XXXX (XXXX)
Italy	59.1	$31,770 [$41,902]	(over) 4,000	CVL	19	76	34,517 (101,473)	1228 (2,276)	X	XX (XXX)
Japan	125.7	$40,193 [$42,390]	343	CVL	20	93	1,870 (13,740)	233 (146)	XX	XXX (XXX)
Macao	0.66	$39,403 ($86,197 in 2019) [$60,895]	892	CVL	19	86	70 (120)	N/A	XX	XXX (XXX)
Malaysia	32.8	$10,412 [$17,131]	634	CL and Shariah	24	90	3,448 (84,040)	14.4 (961)	X	XX (XXX)
Pakistan	225.9	$1,189 [$4,813]	(at least) 1,000	CL	67	17	2,141 (5,752)	45.2 (128)	X	X (X)
Seychelles	0.099	$10,764 ($16,213 in 2019) [$25,768]	590	CL and CVL	71	59	2,285 (250,612)	N/A (1,355)	XX	XXX (XXX)
Singapore	5.45	$59,798 [$98,520]	1,113	CL	23.5	76	10,745 (51,170)	5.3 (152)	XXX	XXXX (XXXX)

3. ONLINE LEGAL EDUCATION GENERALLY BEFORE AND AFTER THE COVID-19 PANDEMIC

The special reports in this volume's next 11 chapters, underpinning our more subjective comparative assessments in the final two columns of Table 2 contained in section 2.4 above, first examine initiatives in university-level education before 2020. The chapters also outline some moves towards online delivery for continuing legal education for lawyers, especially in jurisdictions with large legal professions. In addition, since the pandemic struck in 2020, these reports trace the often-dramatic shifts towards online legal education, especially for universities, followed by some moves back towards more traditional forms of teaching and learning. An interesting empirical question linked to such considerable 'reversion to the mean' is whether employers perceive law graduates who had completed much of their legal education online, especially over 2020–21, as less well trained and therefore offer them fewer opportunities (in hiring or career development) than those who enjoyed or will enjoy more face-to-face education. Answers may take some years to emerge.

When COVID-19 spread from early 2020, firstly, course and programme goals had to be reconsidered due to the pandemic-induced shift to online legal education in almost all jurisdictions. Promoting 'soft skills', including the capacity of students to debate legal issues, often had to be downplayed due to the move to virtual classrooms, leading to more traditional content-focused law courses. Secondly, and relatedly, assessment methods frequently changed. In particular, in-room examinations became impossible or complicated. This encouraged teachers to move to more take-home assignment or essay tasks, but this created more risks of student dishonesty. Such plagiarism and the like are especially problematic in jurisdictions in which completing a law degree (like the LLB or JD in Australia) is the main hurdle to qualifying as a lawyer. A response of some law teachers to this challenge was to expand assessment tasks that required and rewarded creative thinking, rather than tasks more susceptible to cheating (with answers easier to look up or share among students). However, the capacity to do this, and the associated redesign of course content, was subject to resource and other constraints from the pandemic.

Thirdly, teachers needed to consider and implement diverse delivery methods. Sometimes they were required by their university- or faculty-level administrators to switch between methods even mid-course. Alternative delivery methods ranged from purely online delivery (either live or pre-recorded classes), through to various forms of hybrid delivery (such as 'Zoom in the room', where some students access the class via video-conferencing while others attend in person). These methods were deployed especially in jurisdictions where existing or new students faced legal or practical impediments to travelling domestically, or especially from abroad, to attend classes.

Fourthly, the special reports considered various broader impacts on students. Many struggled to keep engaged in classes, and to remain motivated in completing readings and assessment tasks on time. Anticipating such problems, some jurisdictions, universities or teachers required or strongly encouraged students to keep their video feed on for Zoom or other video-conferenced classes; but others deferred to student concerns about privacy or stress from being observed. Students often found it difficult to develop the support groups, social networks and extra-curricular activities characteristic of physical campus life before the pandemic. Despite efforts from administrators and teaching staff, survey and anecdotal evidence across jurisdictions was often quite mixed concerning law students' experience of the enforced moves to greater online education.[37] Fewer surveys and studies have been published regarding the views and experiences of law teachers, but the pandemic-induced shift towards online legal education also seems to have generated both pros and cons.[38]

Overall, as in other law-related fields affected by the COVID-19 pandemic, the special reports reveal both continuities and changes, and some significant moves back towards more traditional teaching methods. Some (especially high-income) jurisdictions have stronger prospects for continuing to expand online legal education, but this may not necessarily be welcomed by students, teachers, employers of law graduates and other stakeholders. Law teachers have benefited from developments in technology, such as running joint courses or guest lectures with colleagues far afield (particularly useful for comparative or international law studies), and some interesting new experiments continued to emerge as the pandemic abated in 2022.[39] Yet there clearly remain challenges as well as opportunities with this still novel pedagogical approach.[40]

37 More generally among undergraduate students in Australia, for example, there was a considerable drop in student satisfaction from 2019 to 2020, especially regarding 'learning engagement'. See S. Babones, *Australia's Universities*, Ocean Reeve, Brisbane 2021, pp. 145–150.

38 See e.g. International Association of Law Schools (ed.), *Transitioning to Online Legal Education: The Student Voice* (August 2020) and *Transitioning to Online Legal Education: The Faculty Voice* (November 2020), both available at https://www.ialsnet.org/surveyreports/.

39 See e.g. 'virtual reality mooting' initiatives reported at two Canadian law schools: https://www2.uottawa.ca/about-us/media/newsroom/uottawas-faculty-law-takes-moot-trials-metaverse and https://allard.ubc.ca/about-us/news-and-announcements/2022/you-may-approach-virtual-bench-taking-anxiety-out-first-year-law-mooting. However, highlighting these innovations, special rapporteur Adrien Habermacher observes that they were accelerated (rather than simply triggered) by the pandemic experience, along with the perceived shortcoming of recreating moot court experiences in the 2D Zoom or other video-conferencing environment.

40 For a critique that the pandemic has allowed Australian university administrators to push through further a neo-liberal agenda, see P. Burdon '"Never Let a Crisis Go to Waste": The Impact of COVID-19 on Legal Education' (2022) 8 *Canadian Journal of Comparative and Contemporary Law* 1 (in a special issue on 'Charting the Future of Legal Education').

4. REGIONAL AND JURISDICTIONAL SUMMARIES

Section 4.1 below considers special reports from the Asia-Pacific region, beginning with Australia as a representative state in the common law tradition with many law faculties and lawyers. The summaries then compare five other (predominantly) common law jurisdictions (Canada and Malaysia, plus the small jurisdictions of Singapore, Brunei and Hong Kong), followed by another micro-jurisdiction (Macao) and a much larger Asian jurisdiction historically influenced instead by the civil law tradition (Japan). Pakistan is then compared as a developing economy, distinguished by particular challenges preventing a transition to greater online delivery of legal education. Section 4.2 compares highlights from Europe and the rest of the world (Italy, Croatia, Cyprus and Seychelles). Overall, the reports cover a rich variety of jurisdictions in terms of geography, size of population and legal profession, economic development and ICT infrastructure and COVID-19, to allow useful comparisons and some further generalisations in the concluding section 5.

4.1. ASIA-PACIFIC REGION

Australia is a high-income economy with very pervasive levels of internet penetration and ICT infrastructure, despite its moderately large but geographically dispersed population. There is also comparatively extensive government support for legal education in universities, once a loan scheme is added to direct grants. The universities serve as the main gatekeepers (along with the market for law graduates) to the legal profession, which is very large and still growing. The then Gillard government's decision in 2011 to allow law schools to enrol as many domestic students as desired paralleled the increase of law schools offering fully online legal education. This volume's special report by Trish Mundy and William van Caenegem notes that that first to do so was Charles Darwin University from 2010 to 2011, in the lightly populated Northern Territory, while the University of New England (in rural New South Wales) was another early mover. Before the pandemic, eight of Australia's (mostly public) 38 law schools offered fully online legal education. However, legislation prevented them from delivering a course exclusively online to students overseas, and from delivering more than a third of courses by online or distance learning to them, which may have further underpinned the growth of international students arriving in Australia.

The pandemic led to relaxation of these rules, and the loose residual controls exercised by the legal profession mainly over the basic content and some assessment methods for the compulsory law courses that universities teach for the qualifying LLB and JD degrees. Australia closed its borders internationally (and even internally) and got close to eliminating COVID-19 by late 2020, before new waves struck generating new mobility restrictions, maintained until the population reached very high levels of vaccination in late 2021. Law schools were generally able to pivot to online delivery from 2020, but experienced challenges including growing concerns about student honesty in completing assessments. The pandemic-induced move online has resulted in blended delivery of legal education becoming widely accepted, although law schools by 2022 were resuming more in-person teaching, especially for classes and activities involving development of practical or 'soft' skills.

Canada bears many similarities with Australia in background factors. These include a large legal profession (even in Quebec, built on the civil rather than common law tradition), with a lawyer density of 3,360 per million inhabitants in Canada in 2017 (3,620 per million in Australia in 2020). However, there are roughly only half the number of law schools.[41] This appears connected to the government still imposing caps on the numbers of law students that can be accepted by law schools for the qualifying degrees, making the government a second main gatekeeper to the profession. Because this generates far greater demand than supply for spots in law schools, there is less competition among them and few newly established law schools, even in the larger cities, compared to Australia.

Canadian universities have (more gradually) increased tuition fees for domestic students as there has been a gradual decline in government funding, although that remains high by World Bank standards. However, they have not sought to supercharge the influx of students from abroad, as in Australia especially since 2013. Indeed, Adrien Habermacher's special report observes that 20% of newly admitted lawyers in Canada over recent years instead did their first degrees abroad (mostly in the US, also recently in Australia), although they then must complete foundational courses in Canadian law – often offered by Canadian universities, and sometimes online even before the pandemic. However, such online courses were not made available to Canadian law students. Generally, there were few initiatives in online legal education across Canadian universities, except by individual teachers, or to make course materials available online, etc. The law societies' federation since 2015 had allowed law school graduates seeking qualification to have at least one year of in-person instruction (over the three-year qualifying law degree) if the distance education component was interactive, or a minimum of two years in person otherwise. Yet no Canadian law school innovated by allowing say a year of online legal education, perhaps because of less competition among the (all public) law schools. In addition, a fully online law degree (as in Australia even before the pandemic) was not permitted.

---

41 For further background on legal education in Canada, focusing on its internationalisation, see also A. Grenon, H. Glenn and H. Dedek, 'The Global Challenge in Common and Civil Law Contexts: A Canadian Perspective' in C. Jamin and W. van Caenegem (eds), *The Internationalisation of Legal Education*, Springer, New York 2016, pp. 75–93.

After the pandemic struck Canada harder from 2020, its law schools seem to have experienced more challenges moving education online, as fewer instructors initially had experiences to share as best practices, and most expected the shift to be temporary so did not substantially reinvent curricula and pedagogies. Canadian universities' lower dependence on international students, generally, may also have generated less sense of crisis and push for change compared to Australian counterparts. Surrounding circumstances (enforced working or studying from home, with ICT challenges evident especially for more rural or disadvantaged homes, etc.) were anyway not conducive to developing and introducing effective online legal education. Nonetheless, stripping away such circumstantial factors, Habermacher's emerging survey evidence suggests that Canadian law students' experience of online delivery was generally quite positive.[42]

Online learning methods arguably produce significant benefits for content delivery and even building up general skills, such as critical and case method analysis, but less so for other aspects of legal education. Habermacher adds that that in-person education is also important, especially for early-year law students, to facilitate wider socialisation into future professional careers. This may be particularly so for those who are the first in their families ever to go to law school or from disadvantaged communities, even though remote delivery seems at first blush to promise better accessibility for such students. He further highlights how the pandemic-related shift to online legal education likely exacerbated mental health issues, growing among law students and the legal profession for many years (as also in Australia).[43] Nonetheless, the moves even before 2020 towards online education for law graduates as part of mandatory training before being admitted as practising lawyers, and for mandatory continuing legal education after admission, may bolster university-level online legal education initiatives. Admittedly, instructors have reverted mostly to more traditional delivery methods as pandemic restrictions have eased, while appreciation has grown about the often-overlooked benefits of campus-based education, sliding the measure of hybridity (mix with online education) back overall in 2022 to close

---

42 Cf. a survey in early 2021, attracting responses from around 10% of the approximately 4,000 students in Canadian law schools (but mostly from those in Manitoba, Calgary and Alberta, with half of respondents being first-year students), finding that the students seemed to strongly favour in-person over online learning methods. See, also with useful background on some individual professors' attempts over 2010–19 to develop the 'flipped classroom' (pre-recording material for students to access before more interactive in-person classes), M. Murchison et al., 'Remote Learning in Law School During the Pandemic: A Canadian Survey' (2022) 8 *Canadian Journal of Comparative and Contemporary Law* 148.

43 See e.g., before the pandemic, N. Skead and S. Rogers, 'Stress, Anxiety and Depression in Law Students: How Student Behaviors Affect Student Wellbeing' (2014) 40(2) *Monash University Law Review* 1. Compare e.g., since the pandemic, E. Fah, 'Wellbeing and Resilience: Perfectionism, Excessive Workloads and Lack of Senior Support: Survey reveals mental and wellbeing challenges for SA lawyers' (2021) 43(7) *Bulletin: Law Society of South Australia* 22.

to where it was before 2020. In future years, however, we may see for example an innovative three-year qualifying law degree allowing one or two semesters of purely online legal education (especially perhaps for later-year courses).

The next special report in this volume, by Nobumichi Teramura and Salim Farrar, covers three states in Southeast Asia retaining many similarities and linkages as former British colonies, including a shared common law tradition. *Singapore* is another high-income economy with very strong ICT and services, but it is small and densely populated state. Its per capita lawyer population is about a third of that for Canada and Australia.[44] For Singaporean citizens and permanent residents, who are permitted to join the Bar, the main gatekeeper is the three law schools awarding the qualifying LLB or JD degrees. Another is the government, which sets annual caps on such law student enrolments. In addition, the legal profession itself has become increasingly concerned about a perceived over-supply of lawyers, so is emerging as a stronger gatekeeper by for example raising the (currently close to 100%) pass rate for Part B of the Bar examinations needed before law graduates can start practice. For foreigners, the legal profession is already the main gatekeeper, by setting a tougher (approximately 70%) pass rate for the extra Part A, along with the legal services market. Practising lawyers in Singapore also have had mandatory continuing legal education since 2017, but this includes reviewing recordings, not necessarily more interactive forms of online delivery (as required partly in Canada before the pandemic).

Singapore's three law schools (all public) benefit from reasonable direct government funding by World Bank standards, supplemented by growing numbers of higher fee-paying LLM students (mainly from abroad).[45] They have maintained smaller class sizes than Canada and especially Australia. There are very few LLB or JD students from abroad as foreigners are more interested in practising their home country's or international law in Singapore than qualifying to practise local law. The law schools were also advantaged by quite extensive digital learning platforms introduced after the 2003 SARS epidemic, although some were proprietary systems.[46] These circumstances allowed a comparatively smooth transition to fully online learning after the COVID-19

44 There were 6,333 lawyers registered in 2021 (but only 5,191 in 2017), according to https://www.lawsociety.org.sg/news-media/statistics/ (including foreign lawyers registered in Singapore with more limited rights to legal practice).

45 For further background on legal education and practice in Singapore, focusing on its internationalisation, see also G. Bell, 'Global Lawyers for a Global City: Legal Education in Singapore' in C. Jamin and W. van Caenegem (eds), *The Internalisation of Legal Education*, Springer, New York 2016, pp. 233–254. On the make-up of the law student body and academic staff, see A. Koh, 'Legal Monolingualism in a Multilingual State: Whither Bilingual Legal Education in Singapore?' in N. Etcheverry Estrázulas (ed.), *Bilingual Study and Research*, Springer, Cham/New York 2022, pp. 267–286.

46 As classes at the National University of Singapore started meeting again in person, Professor Walter Woon conducted a small-scale survey of his students that suggested they found Zoom classes to be somewhat more convenient, easier to ask questions and see shared materials

pandemic, with low levels of deaths and infections, although there were differences between the two main law schools (for example around providing the option of Pass/Fail grades).[47] Many instructors also offered virtual office or coffee hours, particularly for international (mostly LLM) students, recognising their extra challenges. By contrast, the large numbers of (undergraduate as well as postgraduate) law students from abroad in Australia made such tailored support more difficult.

Brunei is another high-income micro-state, but with less than a tenth of Singapore's population, and only 129 practising lawyers for its 440,000 people (so around 300 per million, less than a third of the lawyer density rate for Singapore and a tenth of the rate for Australia or Canada). The main gatekeeper for lawyers practising in the common law courts is formally the Chief Justice, but this function is essentially outsourced as admission is possible for any lawyer from the UK, Singapore, Malaysia or Australia, or Brunei permanent residents with alternative qualifications. No full LLB or JD degree is provided by the four universities, enjoying comparatively high direct government funding, although one university offers some common law-related courses and another a postgraduate law master's degree or qualification in Shariah law (for practice in local Shariah courts). Another contrast with Singapore is worse ICT and internet infrastructure, especially for low-income households, although public legal sectors had good facilities even before the pandemic.

The universities (all public) nonetheless offered some degrees via blended learning, including some law-related courses, and had quite good e-learning infrastructure. This again allowed a quite smooth transition to fully online law teaching when the pandemic struck Brunei, where there are moreover very few non-exchange students, but internet accessibility and psychological wellbeing were problematic. The virus was essentially eliminated by late 2020, whereupon face-to-face teaching resumed, but another wave from mid-2021 meant further lockdowns and online teaching. There is likely to be comparatively little long-term impact from these experiences on legal education, as it is limited in universities (as most study law and qualify abroad) and preferably conducted face-to-face for continuing legal education (underpinned by a very small legal profession, and market for legal services, compared to say a regional hub like Singapore).

---

in, easier to hear the instructor in, and (to a lesser degree) less inhibiting for participation: see https://www.todayonline.com/commentary/why-online-university-classes-herald-better-way-forward-not-temporary-fix-1799926 (26 January 2022). He subsequently moved to Singapore Management University's law school.

47 For an early report from one Singaporean law school, see E.I. Ong, 'The Year of COVID-19' in A. Gurrea-Martínez, M. Findlay and G. Yihan (eds), *Law and COVID-19*, Singapore Management University, Singapore 2020, pp. 177–184, available at https://ssrn.com/abstract=3686357. Compare its early history, established in 2000 (after the National University of Singapore's predecessor, the University of Malaya, started teaching the LLB degree from 1957) in K. Yang Low, 'Legal Education in Singapore and the Introduction of a New Law School at the Singapore Management University' in S. Steele and K. Taylor (eds), *Legal Education in Asia*, Routledge, New York 2009, pp. 156–168.

Malaysia's population is much larger, similar to Canada's but much more densely populated. It is a middle-income country with a significant divide (socio-economic and digital) between urban and rural areas. There is also lower direct government funding for the tertiary sector, with the proportion of grants decreasing considerably over the last 15 years for the public universities, and correspondingly quite a few private universities. Lawyer density (634 per million)[48] lies less than midway between Brunei and Singapore. However, most are in small legal practices that had less extensive ICT systems until the pandemic hit Malaysia more severely in 2020. This is despite courts in Malaysia (as in Singapore and Brunei) having operated e-filing systems for many years previously.

Although universities had responded to government encouragement by developing some micro-credentialing and massive open online courses (MOOCs) by 2013, and some (especially private) universities had developed online learning infrastructure, courses at the nine law schools offering qualifying degrees remained overwhelmingly face-to-face before 2020. Teramura and Farrar suggest this was (and is) due to some regulatory requirements but also because of a traditional learning culture plus budgetary austerity. When COVID-19 prompted hard lockdowns, some private universities were well set up to transition to online learning. However, teachers and students struggled in the public universities, especially if they returned to rural hometowns with poor internet accessibility. As pandemic restrictions eased from 2021, staff morale was low due to the extra stress of moving suddenly online, with teachers and students keen to revert to more traditional delivery methods, which also characterise practical training for the profession after graduation. The future prospects for online legal education therefore seem quite limited, less favourable than Brunei, with Singapore showing the most potential.

Turning from Southeast to North Asia, *Hong Kong* as a Special Administrative Region (SAR) of China is another high-income island economy in the common law tradition, but with a population (7.4 million) somewhat higher than Singapore, and almost double the density of lawyers (13,585 including trainees, so 1,835 per million). Universities are quite well funded by the government, including the three law schools offering qualifying degrees, attracting significant numbers of mainland Chinese and some other international students.[49]

48 There were 20,556 registered lawyers in 2022 (but only 16,524 in 2017), according to https://www.malaysianbar.org.my/article/about-us/malaysian-bar-and-bar-council/about-us/figures/general-statistics.

49 For further background on legal education in Hong Kong, see also C. Jones, 'Legal Education in Hong Kong: Producing the Producers' in S. Steele and K. Taylor (eds), *Legal Education in Asia*, Routledge, New York 2009, pp. 107–136; F. Leng, 'Legal Education at a Turning Point: A Case Study of Hong Kong' in C. Jamin and W. van Caenegem (eds), *The Internalisation of Legal Education*, Springer, New York 2016, pp. 131–154.

The special report by Wilson Lui and Alice Lee explains that the primary gatekeeper to the legal profession is the Postgraduate Certificate in Laws programme, following a qualifying LLB or JD degree. This is similar to the Legal Practice Course in the UK or Malaysia, or equivalent post-degree training in Australia, but with a notable difference: only around half of applicants are admitted into the one-year programme, and only about 75% pass the final examinations on the first attempt. Although most succeed on the second attempt, their employability will be impacted, meaning the market is also a gatekeeper. The government also plays a gatekeeper role by funding only some students in the Certificate programme, as well as only some of the places for students in the preceding law school degrees.

Despite comparatively advanced ICT infrastructure society-wide and in universities, LLB, JD and postgraduate law degree teachers did not innovate much with e-learning before the pandemic. Nor did the courts, being quite slow to develop e-procedures but revitalising initiatives from 2020, or the Certificate programme delivered through the law schools. The latter programme is criticised for still not being offered purely online, as with some providers of equivalents (albeit with much higher admission and pass rates) in Australia and New Zealand. This is despite the switch to proctored online exams during pandemic restrictions addressing student integrity concerns, and even though maintaining an online delivery option would increase accessibility to the legal profession.

Lui and Lee argue further that law schools should maintain the interest in online education prompted by the pandemic, as this would mesh with the profession's engagement with e-learning through continuing education requirements (allowing for online delivery since 2020, as long as interactive), as well as the increasingly hi-tech world of court and legal practice. They also point to some survey evidence that due to commuting time savings and peer influence law students quite often preferred online attendance even when in-person classes resumed in hybrid arrangements after Hong Kong largely eliminated COVID-19, before its resurgence in early 2021 prompting renewed lockdowns. However, this may be due to insufficient functionality for 'Zoom in the room' classes, and respondents also favoured in-person teaching for tutorials and skills-based sessions. Lui and Lee suggest that, even though Hong Kong law schools seem to have more resources (compared say to more stretched Australian law schools) to shift towards more sustained online education, the scholars still lack incentives as the focus of universities in Hong Kong and elsewhere (including say Australia) has become increasingly research-oriented and audit-driven. Nonetheless, their special report suggests that the future for online legal education in Hong Kong is comparatively bright.

Macao is another high-income SAR of China, with an even smaller land mass and population than nearby Hong Kong, and a legal system rooted instead in the civil law tradition (as a former colony of Portugal). Since becoming an SAR from the late 1990s, like Hong Kong, Macao was formally guaranteed considerable autonomy in its legal system. Perhaps reflecting the continuing influence of the civil law tradition, and/or less legal work than in an economy heavily dependent on gaming and related services, lawyer density is around half (892 per million) that of Hong Kong. This is so even though the main gatekeeper is the university sector rather than the legal profession itself, as explained in the special report by Rostam J. Neuwirth, Muruga P. Ramaswamy and Alexandr Svetlicinii. Three of the eight universities provide comprehensive legal education, although only the programme from the public University of Macau (established in 1981) allows for local admissions to the Bar. The Macao courts have also rendered significant judgments favouring foreign-educated jurists seeking to join the post-degree internship programme which must be completed before legal practice.

The universities receive government funding that is somewhat lower than other jurisdictions surveyed, by World Bank standards. In addition, pandemic-related travel restrictions hit the economy very hard, so tuition fees were raised significantly for local students, who comprise the large majority of undergraduate law students. The University of Macau is also planning to boost the numbers of postgraduate students, where for legal studies a small majority of students are already from abroad – particularly from China, with courses available in Chinese (with larger class sizes) as well as in English and Portuguese. With Macao comparatively less impacted by COVID-19 in the early stages, although classes were moved online, exceptions were made for law students in their final stages. After COVID-19 was essentially limited in the second half of 2020, classes resumed in person for groups of up to 100 students, with the option of online attendance. However, waves of the Omicron variant from mid-2021 led to mass testing and restrictions, forcing law courses into and out of online mode.

The University of Macau had adopted the Moodle platform, but law teachers were relatively slow in deploying it until the pandemic restrictions, which also led to the use of Zoom from 2020. Various technical/logistical and pedagogical challenges have been revealed, albeit less so for smaller classes (such as the postgraduate law courses taught in English and Portuguese). More general surveys have highlighted mental health issues and growing concerns about online education generally. Although the pandemic-induced switch to periods of online or blended delivery of law courses has increased familiarity with the main platforms and their potential, the on-off switches have been stressful. The experience has also highlighted that law is rooted in human interactions, benefiting not only from direct student–teacher contact but also from student learning among peers, through classroom teaching but also other personal contacts on campus.

Japan is a populous country (with 125 million inhabitants), albeit quite compact geographically, enjoying high levels of GDP per capita and ICT infrastructure generally. It also is rooted primarily in the civil law tradition, and still has a very low per capita proportion of lawyers (only 343 *bengoshi* per million in 2021) due partly to the existing legal profession itself being a primary gatekeeper to legal practice. The special report by Ken'ichi Yoneda and Luke Nottage explains how universities, which receive relatively low public funding and include many private universities, gradually began improving their ICT systems to allow some law teachers to experiment with online education from the mid-1990s through to the mid-2000s.

A significant improvement came from 2004, when wider justice system reforms resulted in the addition of a new postgraduate law school profession-oriented programme aimed at increasing the numbers and quality of lawyers. Some of the resultant ICT and e-learning facilities were adapted also for the (more extensive) undergraduate LLB degree programmes. This happenstance helped Japanese law teachers and students to transition better to widespread online delivery after the 2020 pandemic, although the government unusually did not impose mobility restrictions on its residents, and some law students struggled with ICT capacity and other stresses. Lessons learned and facilities expanded in Japanese universities should position them well for ongoing development of hybrid legal education, although fatigue is currently quite pervasive and Japanese law faculties maintain a strong focus on research (as reported in some of the other jurisdictions covered in this book).

Pakistan stands out as an indicative low-income developing economy, with the largest population of all the jurisdictions covered in this book (225 million, the fifth most populous country in the world). The special report by Syed Imad-ud-Din Asad highlights how Pakistan has very many public (solely government-funded) as well as private (fee-based) tertiary education providers, but an additional 32 public providers established over the period 2017–21 did not generate extra public funding for the sector. (The high level of government funding for the tertiary sector recorded by the World Bank in 2013, in Table 2 above, therefore appears anomalous.) In addition, Pakistan suffers from poor ICT and internet connectivity in universities, offices and homes, even for mobile phones – with problems exacerbated by income and gender disparities.

The legal profession is very large in absolute numbers, although lawyer density is (at least) 1,000 per million inhabitants. Leading lawyers are often quite politically active, so Bar associations are not well focused on regulatory matters or training (still not setting continuing legal education requirements), while most law firms are small and/or family based. The main gatekeeper to the legal profession comprises the (53) law schools providing the qualifying LLB degree. Because of their proliferation and perceived poor quality overall, the Pakistan Bar Council in 2015 promulgated detailed rules that such law schools had to comply with to continue awarding the LLB. These range from upper limits on class size, through to requirements to hold classes at least five days a week but only in the mornings, and minimum requirements for classrooms and other physical facilities for accredited law schools.

Such new requirements meant that after the first of several serious waves of COVID-19 struck Pakistan in early 2020, prompting lockdowns and the government ordering universities to switch to online classes, even the law schools and students with more ICT and other resources could no long function effectively. Some tried to continue online, but the Pakistan Bar Council remained silent about this possibility, so university-level legal education was essentially suspended. Internships in law firms, required during the LLB, partly continued but such internships anyway do not provide much opportunity for serious legal training. Overall, this experience provides a 'reality check' for other middle- and high-income economies covered in this book: they certainly faced problems developing online legal education both before and after the pandemic, but on a much-reduced scale compared to a developing country like Pakistan.

4.2. AFRICA AND EUROPE

Seychelles is an African island micro-jurisdiction in the Indian Ocean, with only around 100,000 inhabitants. The World Bank records it as a high-income country with comparatively high direct government funding per capita for tertiary education. However, Seychelles is borderline (upper-)middle-income, with per capita GDP of US$15,000–16,000 (2013–19), before a large drop to under US$11,000 (2020),[50] due to reduced tourism related to the pandemic. In 2017, Seychelles ranked second in Africa for ICT development, but internet penetration is significantly lower than in most other developed economies covered in this book, and internet cost is high relative to other African states.

Formerly a colony of the UK and France, it has a mixed legal system, impacting on the legal profession, as explained in the special report by Nyasha Noreen Katsenga. The main routes to becoming a Seychelles lawyer involve (1) being admitted to practise in a Commonwealth jurisdiction, or (2) obtaining an eligible law degree – currently from the UK, France or Mauritius (another mixed-tradition island state) – and passing Bar examinations set in the UK, Mauritius or locally, plus undergoing pupillage (traineeship) in an approved local legal practice. The main formal gatekeeping mechanisms are the local Bar examination (with a comparatively low pass rate) and obtaining a pupillage position. Practical impediments include the high cost of studying for a law degree from a recognised jurisdiction, and of the optional but useful Bar Vocational Course in preparation for the local admission examination (although the course

50 See https://datahelpdesk.worldbank.org/knowledgebase/articles/906519-world-bank-country-and-lending-groups and https://data.worldbank.org/indicator/NY.GDP.PCAP.CD?locations=SC (with GDP on a PPP basis, furthermore, similar to the US dollar basis).

cost was halved from 2021 when taught by the Supreme Court rather than the Bar itself). The net result is a low lawyer density (59 for its population of around 100,000, or around 590 per million), even compared to some other micro-states.

In 2009, the private University of Seychelles was established and began offering an eligible law degree through the University of London, with 68 graduates over the period 2013–20. The partnership ended in mid-2020, but the University of Seychelles planned its own law degree that should be recognised for the purpose of admission as a lawyer. Before the pandemic, law students had access virtually to University of London materials but the courses were taught on the University of Seychelles campus, and the Bar Vocational Course was also taught only in person. The latter course was suspended after the first lockdown in April 2020, whereas the University of Seychelles continued classes online via Microsoft Teams and switched to online exams. Fewer LLB exam questions were set, because the high internet costs (and unreliability) resulted in shorter classes and therefore less coverage. University law teachers also had limited ability to adjust the curriculum and assessment, as they were set by the University of London. Despite such challenges, and comparative quick reversion to on-campus classes as COVID-19 was brought under control, the pandemic-induced shift to online delivery provided useful experiences as the University of Seychelles embarked on its own new LLB degree from late 2022. It may also encourage more online delivery for the Bar Vocational Course, and prompt the development of (currently non-existent) structured continuing legal education after admission. This could further expand, diversify and upskill the legal profession in Seychelles.

Turning to Europe, *Croatia* is a similarly classified (borderline) high-income state that joined in the EU over the period 2004–13, also having comparatively low public spending on tertiary education, but with a very long history of legal education, a much larger population (around four million) and better ICT infrastructure than Seychelles (albeit somewhat below the EU average for internet usage as of 2019). Although part of socialist Yugoslavia until independence in 1999, Croatia has a legal system following the civil law tradition. Nonetheless, it has quite a high lawyer density (1,595 per million) as well as a very high proportion of judges.

The special report by Mirela Župan explains that four public universities offer legal education in a five-year programme essentially combining an undergraduate and master's degree, as in most other continental European countries nowadays, with almost no foreign students as the courses are taught in Croatian. Entry into the programme is unrestricted (as in Italy, mentioned below), fluctuating around 10,000 entrants annually over the last two decades, but only around 900 graduate each year lately – making universities an important gatekeeper to the profession. However, the legal profession plays somewhat of a gatekeeper role too. This is because prospective lawyers also need to intern for 18 months and then pass the Bar examination, although this is an aptitude test (as in Germany), meaning no limit on the numbers permitted to pass (in contrast say to Japan).

Before the pandemic, a fully online law degree programme was possible under regulations but none was sought to be accredited. Although the Croatian government followed EU pushes to promote e-learning generally, these were not systematically implemented at the level of universities (unlike in schools). Universities cherish and retain autonomy, while higher expectations are put on academics for research compared to teaching. Although some individual law teachers took advantage of universities introducing platforms like Moodle or Merlin, the high numbers of students enrolling (especially in the early years of the law programme) limited capacity and enthusiasm to innovate with online or hybrid legal education. This was despite some calls from employers to boost computer literacy among law students, connecting also perhaps to greater opportunities to develop English language skills. A related growing influence on legal education in Croatia was the importance of EU law domestically, and more lawyer mobility regionally.

Soon after the pandemic struck in early 2020, law faculties switched to mainly hybrid classes, but often reverted to in-person classes from later in the year – albeit with some options to livestream classes, meaning hybrid delivery. Early surveys indicated positive student responses to the online learning initiatives, but this could be due to the lack of suitable alternatives given lockdown measures in 2020. Overall, it remains unclear whether pandemic-boosted online education, long promoted by the EU, will result in significant long-term changes in Croatia. Advantages include more flexibility for student learning and academics prioritising teaching versus research, as well as possible new revenue streams for universities reaching new audiences, and greater scope to explore the interaction of law with technology across various evolving fields. Disadvantages include less connected teachers and students, costs in implementing and updating ICT skills and facilities, and more potential for cheating and plagiarism. A key development will be supporting digital competencies for legal academics, encouraging (and resourcing) a shift towards more student-centred learning using the new ICT tools made more broadly available since 2020.

Cyprus, an EU member state but located close to the Middle East, has a higher GDP per capita than Croatia, with a population of 1.2 million. It has better internet penetration but a similar (average) proportion of public funding for tertiary education. Following largely the common law tradition, the special report by Demetra Loizou and Lida Pitsillidou indicates that Cyprus had the highest lawyer density among EU states in 2020 (over 4,500 per million), although many qualify as lawyers but then engage in other careers. This very large legal profession is paralleled by delays in expanding ICT and digitalisation to make court proceedings more efficient, as well as in continuing education for judges, although the latter (including some online training) improved more during the pandemic. Mandatory continuing legal education for lawyers was phased in from 2017, and the pandemic has resulted in online offerings being permitted.

The (weak) gatekeeper to becoming a lawyer in Cyprus is the legal profession itself. It requires graduates with a recognised law degree from a university (in Cyprus, but also in an EU or third-country state) to join the Bar Association and sit examinations in various fields of law. Bar examination training was available online even before the pandemic. However, classes could be attended in person and the examinations were traditionally conducted face-to-face.

Before 2020, e-learning platforms in local universities were mostly used to deliver information (like course readings). Innovations were few as they were perceived as time-consuming, training in new technologies was limited, and traditional face-to-face learning was favoured. However, as the law schools in Cyprus itself (including some affiliated with overseas universities) were relatively few, and with smaller class sizes, the transition to online learning due to pandemic restrictions was quite smooth. Nonetheless, a key technological impediment was internet accessibility for law students, especially from socio-economically deprived environments. Another problem was a lack of training. Even when this was provided, say for Microsoft Teams, time and resource constraints meant insufficient opportunity to explore other video-conferencing platforms. Pedagogically, the requirement to record lectures was welcomed by students, although some instructors were concerned about related inattention or lack of participation in classes. Students (and teachers) were also able to access a wider array of online seminars and resources. However, a serious challenge identified was a lack of student engagement. With most students keeping their video feed and microphones turned off, it was also more difficult for teachers to assess student performance and gaps in comprehension. In addition, the biggest problem created by the initial 'emergency' online teaching phase was psychological, with mental health issues and lack of motivation emerging among law students. The hybrid delivery mode since late 2020 helped by allowing the option of in-person and on-campus attendance.

Italy is a populous high-income country built on the civil law tradition, with a strong engagement in comparative law.[51] For its mix of many state and non-state (including 'telematic' or distance learning) universities, the special report by Rossella Cerchia and Barbara Vari indicates that the government

---

51 R. Sacco and A. Gianola, 'The History and Importance of Comparative Law in Italy' in C. Jamin and W. van Caenegem (eds), *The Internalisation of Legal Education*, Springer, New York 2016, pp. 175–183. For some further background and aspects regarding legal education in Italy, see also E. Ioratti, 'Bilingual Legal Education in Italy: Translating Languages into Teaching Methods' in N. Etcheverry Estrázulas (ed.), *Bilingual Study and Research*, Springer, Cham/New York 2022, pp. 209–229.

provides relatively low funding (although more reasonable by World Bank standards), badly impacted by the global financial crisis of 2007-8. Data in 2019 also showed a considerable 'digital divide', with more disadvantage in the south, in smaller localities and among families without younger members. Analysis in 2020 ranked Italy 20th out of 27 EU states for digital economy and society, despite a notable upturn in broadband connections and government initiatives since the pandemic.

University law faculties offer no barriers to student enrolment in the three-year law degree aimed at more general careers or the five-year course aimed at careers in the legal profession, resulting in quite large classes. Candidates as lawyers also need to complete an 18-month apprenticeship and pass a Bar examination, but the latter is an aptitude test (with no limit on the numbers allowed to pass) and is far easier than the qualifying examinations for notaries or judges. The main gatekeeper is therefore the market for law firm jobs, which seems to be becoming saturated after years of increases. This has resulted for example in limited extra lawyers joining the profession or average income growth in 2019, as well as declining enrolments in university law courses. Nonetheless, Italy is left with one of Europe's highest lawyer density rates (around 4,000 per million).

This situation provided little incentive to experiment with offering online legal education before the pandemic. Exceptions were some offerings by individual professors or via the telematic universities. Other factors impeding more usage of ICT in higher education were the traditional focus of universities and law faculties on research rather than teaching, and the quite high average age of professors.

Italy was the one of the first countries to be hit by the pandemic, overwhelming the public health system and triggering lockdowns, forcing law faculties to teach online. After this emergency teaching period, when the first wave of COVID-19 abated, from the next semester in September 2020 the law faculties reverted to more on-campus classes with hybrid delivery. A University of Trento survey in the previous semester found that only 15% of students had previously experienced (generally limited) online classes and overwhelmingly preferred in-person teaching, while appreciating online education given the lack of alternatives in that first stage of the pandemic. Major problems they reported related to concentration, motivation and lack of engagement. A University of Pisa survey, in mid-2020, highlighted the advantages of online education for those say with some physical disabilities, but the disadvantages for those with learning impediments. Another problem was less digitalised law libraries compared to some other European countries. Meanwhile, due to the pandemic, the Bar Council suspended its rule for mandatory continuing legal education that limited accredited training to 40% online courses in which lawyer participation could be verified.

Debates over the modalities as well as the pros and cons of online education have become mainstream. However, there remain considerable obstacles to developing it extensively, given Italian universities' traditional didactic approach and expectation that subject-matter expertise is sufficient for teachers, with correspondingly little weight given to teaching for career progression. However, the recent experiences may belatedly lead to interest in (EU-supported) MOOCs as well as some other e-learning innovations, if law professors are given sufficient ongoing technical training and incentives.

5. GENERAL CONCLUSIONS

Overall, this survey of 13 jurisdictions does confirm the usefulness of locating developments in online legal education in the multi-factor context elaborated in section 2 above. This includes the nature of the jurisdiction's respective legal tradition and profession of lawyers; its levels of public funding for universities, of economic development and ICT infrastructure; and, to a lesser extent, the differential impact of the COVID-19 pandemic. Even in states that had comparatively few infections and deaths, a shift to online legal education in universities was required in early 2020. Across all jurisdictions, this led to an 'emergency teaching' phase where law teachers raced to adopt quite unfamiliar e-learning platforms, which were fortunately more available in high-income countries compared to low-income countries (like Pakistan). Some jurisdictions were also more advantaged than others by having introduced such platforms or other e-learning resources in response to the shock of an earlier epidemic (like SARS in Singapore), or thanks to wider gradual improvements in university infrastructure (as in Brunei), or broader reforms to legal education (such as Japan's new postgraduate law school programmes).

Nonetheless, a common pattern before 2020 was only sporadic uptake of online legal education opportunities across law faculties. This contrasted sometimes with online education options for graduates seeking to pass Bar examinations (as in Cyprus) or in continuing legal education for qualified lawyers (increasingly being made mandatory, although not yet for example in Seychelles). Some frequently mentioned reasons for the sporadic uptake included a traditional focus on research in universities (especially perhaps in civil law tradition jurisdictions such as Italy and Croatia, but also increasing say in Australia as its university administrators sought to improve their international rankings), as well as a traditional focus on in-person classes and even occasionally (more often in civil law tradition universities) oral examinations. Law teachers with big classes and large numbers of students, especially those from different countries and language backgrounds necessitating more care, also typically lacked the time and resources to experiment with online legal education. Some training programmes for prospective or qualified lawyers may also have favoured in-person education to further help socialise them as a profession (as in Hong Kong).

Because of such hesitancy, it is less surprising to see how online delivery and assessment prompted by initial pandemic-related mobility restrictions started to revert to more traditional in-person mechanisms after the first COVID-19 waves subsided, typically from late 2020. Surveys and anecdotal evidence had started to reveal a mixed picture about the net benefits of the enforced shift to purely online education, allowing more flexibility but also generating concerns about digital and socio-economic divides (highlighted for example in the special report for Canada), paucity of student engagement, and mental health issues. Nonetheless, the ongoing pandemic meant that hybrid delivery became typical, leaving the option for law teachers and students to maintain online components.

Although vaccines have been developed and administered, and jurisdictions have increasingly learned to 'live with COVID' since the latter half of 2021, universities and professional bodies have partly reverted to past practices. Yet discussion has continued about the pros and cons of different types of online legal education, no longer limited to a few pioneering professors or practitioners. The discussion is instead informed by widespread experiences with at least some aspects of online teaching, even if derived from 'emergency teaching' periods – often in multiple iterations (as in Malaysia, and later Macao). Because universities and legal professions are large organisations, and universities are mostly publically funded institutions with large bureaucracies, they are perhaps less likely to shift as significantly towards online legal education than other law-related fields driven by commercial suppliers (like international arbitration) that were forced to adopt new technologies (like virtual hearings).[52] Nonetheless, online legal education has clearly achieved a big step-up over 2020–21, and should continue to develop strongly, particularly in jurisdictions with high GDP and good ICT infrastructure combined with large numbers of law students in universities and in legal practice. Even so, this may not necessarily be ideal for students and teachers, as opposed to administrators and other stakeholders.[53]

---

52 L. Nottage, *International Commercial and Investor-State Arbitration: Australia and Japan in Regional and Global Contexts*, Edward Elgar, Cheltenham 2021, pp. 378–385.

53 Compare e.g. P. Burdon '"Never Let a Crisis Go to Waste": The Impact of COVID-19 on Legal Education' (2022) 8 *Canadian Journal of Comparative and Contemporary Law* 1.

PART I

ASIA-PACIFIC

ONLINE LEGAL EDUCATION IN AUSTRALIA

Pandemic Pitfalls and Promises

William van Caenegem and Trish Mundy

1. INTRODUCTION

This report considers the position of online legal education in Australia, both before and after the COVID-19 pandemic. Australia was an early adopter of integration of online aspects in legal education, but Australia's first provider of fully online legal education began only in 2010/2011 at Charles Darwin University,[1] arguably reflecting a cautious and conservative approach to legal

[1] See M. Kirby, 'Online Legal Education in Australia: The New CQU Law Degree' (2011) 34 *Australian Bar Review* 237.

pedagogy and practice, at least as far as the legal profession accrediting bodies are concerned. Since this time, a small but growing number of online providers have emerged across Australia with eight of the 38 law schools offering fully online legal education,[2] while others offer elements of their courses in online formats such as through flipped classes, blended learning and recorded lectures.[3] Adopting online education and embracing digital literacy within the legal profession has been equally slow and cautious over that period.[4]

Of course, in March 2020, the COVID-19 pandemic necessitated the urgent and rapid move to online delivery by all Australian law schools and, for many, this situation continued while several states in Australia experienced subsequent outbreaks of the virus and various levels of 'lockdown'.[5] With COVID-19 still prevalent as at the end of 2022, many universities have not fully transitioned back to pre-COVID-19 in-person course delivery. When the pandemic started, many 'traditional' on-campus legal education providers, teaching academics and school leaders were challenged to quickly engage with new technologies, design online learning resources, redesign assessment, and consider ways to support and facilitate student learning in an online environment, all while taking into consideration such matters as accreditation bodies' requirements, academic integrity, resourcing constraints, and staff and student wellbeing.

The sudden and difficult circumstances flowing from COVID-19 made already pressing questions for law schools take on acute importance. These included the benefits, challenges and potential of online legal education in Australia, managing substantive constraints such as how we best teach, learn

---

2 Fully online degree offerings were as follows: the University of New England by 2015 was offering a fully online law course; Southern Cross University by 2015 was offering a fully online law course; University of Southern Queensland by 2015 was offering a fully online law course; Central Queensland University by 2015 was offering a fully online law course; Deakin University as at 2013 developed a fully online learning offering; by 2015 Edith Cowan University was offering a fully online law course; RMIT (through Open Universities Australia) by 2015 was providing a fully online law course; and Australian National University in 2010 introduced a GDLP course component that is run through a completely simulated online environment.

3 For example, Griffith University offered individual subjects in an online flipped learning format in 2015, and LaTrobe University was openly providing legal education resources online and free to the public at large through iTunes U (as at 2013).

4 See e.g. B. May and H. Veldre, 'Where Are We Going? New Media, Technology and the Law' (2016) 29 *Law Society Journal* 92, 93; M. Thomas, 'Econveyancing: From Growing Pains to One Giant Leap?' (2018) 38(10) *Proctor* 29; S. McKeith, 'The Must-have Legal Technology Tools for 2021' (2021) 74 *Law Society Journal* 34, 36.

5 See e.g. C. Kelly, 'Victoria Covid Update: State on Track to Reopen Despite Record 2,297 Cases, Daniel Andrews Says', *The Guardian* (14.10.2021), https://www.theguardian.com/australia-news/2021/oct/14/victoria-covid-update-state-on-track-to-reopen-despite-record-case-numbers-says-daniel-andrews; S. Stewart and A. Radford, 'What Restrictions Ease in Each Stage of the ACT's Phased Path Out of COVID-19 Lockdown', *ABCNews* (27.09.2021), https://www.abc.net.au/news/2021-09-27/act-lockdown-path-forward-revealed/100494524.

and assess legal skills in an online environment, and regulatory constraints imposed by various gatekeepers that arguably prefer traditional models of legal education and assessment. Many law schools are now reviewing what aspects of the adoption of online legal education might become permanent features of their teaching approach.

This report provides an overview of the key gatekeepers to the legal profession in Australia, considers domestic and international funding arrangements and outlines the evolution of online legal education in Australia while considering current and future prospects for online legal education as well as the challenges and lessons from the transition to online education in the context of the pandemic.

2. BACKGROUND

2.1. GATEKEEPERS TO THE LEGAL PROFESSION

2.1.1. Overview

There are four gatekeepers to the legal profession operating in Australia: law schools responsible for delivering the academic requirements; Practical Legal Training (PLT) providers; admitting authorities in each state or territory; and the relevant professional bodies responsible for regulating practising privileges upon admission. Each of these represent a regulatory requirement in the process to practise as a lawyer and all engage with and view online education in different ways, reflecting different 'tensions and uncertainties' as to the role and purpose of legal education.[6] Each of these gatekeepers are considered below.

2.1.2. Legal Professional Bodies

A person is eligible for admission as a lawyer if they are 18 years or over, have attained approved academic qualifications and satisfactorily completed approved PLT requirements.[7] Applicants must then seek admission to the Supreme Court via the relevant admitting body in their state or territory. The legal profession in Australia operates in a federated system, meaning there are eight separate admitting bodies; however, with the adoption of national uniform admission

---

6 P. Collins, T. Brackin and C. Hart, 'Rocky Rhetoric and Hard Reality: The Academic's Dilemma Surrounding Assessment' (2010) 20 *Legal Education Review* 157, 177.

7 Legal Profession Act 2006 (NT), s. 29; Legal Profession Uniform Law (NSW) No. 16a of 2014, ss. 16, 17; Legal Profession Act 2006 (ACT), s. 21; Legal Profession Act 2007 (Qld), s. 30; Legal Practitioners Act 1981 (SA), s. 15(1); Legal Profession Act 2007 (Tas), s. 25; Legal Profession Act 2008 (WA), s. 22(2); Legal Profession Uniform Admission Rules 2015, r. 5, r. 6.

laws, the requirements of admission are largely the same across the country. The judges of the Supreme Court in each state and territory, by virtue of their inherent jurisdiction, act as the ultimate gatekeeper to the profession insofar as they must be satisfied of both the academic and character requirements for admission, including that the applicant be of 'good fame and character' and a 'fit and proper person'.[8]

Once admitted, a person may choose to practise as a solicitor or barrister and must apply to their relevant professional body for a practising certificate. There are currently 83,643 practising solicitors in Australia,[9] with 53% practising in city-based locations, 34% in suburban and 10% in rural locations. In 2023, there were approximately 9,200 barristers in Australia.[10] The use of technology within the legal profession has developed slowly and unevenly. In recent years the profession has increased its use of technology, for example through adoption of practice management software, innovative models of legal service delivery such as 'virtual firms' and in the context of the pandemic has adapted to the courts' use of Microsoft Teams to facilitate court appearances. The pandemic has seen rapid upskilling and adoption of technology and online platforms by the legal profession like never before. However, literature suggests that in the light of technological advancements priority should now be given to skill development and instilling ethical values/dispositions rather than increasing further technological skills for future practice.[11]

2.1.3. *Universities and PLT Providers (Education)*

There are 38 legal education providers in Australia offering accredited law degrees, along with two non-university providers.[12] There are 11 accredited

---

8 Legal Profession Act 2006 (NT), s. 30; Legal Profession Uniform Law (NSW) No. 16a of 2014, s. 17(1)(c); Legal Profession Act 2006 (ACT), s. 22; Legal Profession Act 2007 (Qld), s. 31; Legal Practitioners Act 1981 (SA), s. 15(1)(a); Legal Profession Act 2007 (Tas), s. 26; Legal Profession Act 2008 (WA), s. 22.

9 Urbis, '2020 National Profile of Solicitors' (01.07.2021), p. 2, https://www.lawsociety.com.au/sites/default/files/2021-07/2020%20National%20Profile%20of%20Solicitors%20-%20Final%20-%201%20July%202021.pdf.

10 JobOutlook, 'Barristers' (2020), https://labourmarketinsights.gov.au/occupations/occupation-search?keyword=barristers. Note: the Australian Bar Association represents over 6,000 barristers, see Australia Bar Association, 'Member Information' (01.2021), https://austbar.asn.au/for-members/member-information.

11 See e.g. L.B. Moses, 'Artificial Intelligence in the Courts, Legal Academia and Legal Practice' (2017) 91 *Australian Law Journal* 561; T. Hutchinson, 'Legal Research in the Fourth Industrial Revolution' (2017) 43(2) *Monash Law Review* 567; K. Galloway et al., 'The Legal Academy's Engagements with Lawtech: Technology Narratives and Archetypes as Drivers of Change' (2019) 1(1) *Law, Technology and Humans* 27; J. Webb, 'Information Technology and the Future of Legal Education: A Provocation' (2019) 7(1) *Griffith Journal of Law and Human Dignity* 72.

12 Legal Profession Admission Board and Top Education Institute, Sydney City School of Law.

PLT providers.[13] To satisfy professional admission requirements, a Bachelor of Laws (or JD) degree must be the equivalent of at least three years' full-time study. Beyond this requirement, law schools must seek accreditation of their law course from the relevant admitting authority in their state or territory. While these bodies vary across jurisdictions, the requirements are largely uniform, due to the efforts of the Law Admissions Consultative Committee (LACC) and the Council of Australian Law Deans (CALD).[14]

Accreditation standards require that law schools teach certain prescribed areas of academic knowledge known as the 'Priestley 11'.[15] In 2017, LACC Accreditation Standards were developed which address elements beyond the Priestley 11 to include areas such as mode of delivery and assessment.[16] Elements of these standards have been criticised as being intrusive into the work of law schools and law curricula. While not necessarily dictating how courses are taught, scholars argue that they are overly restrictive and go far beyond prescribing subject matter because they also predetermine the number of hours which must be allocated to prescribed areas, methods generally employed in their teaching and qualifications of teachers, etc.[17] However, the standards do not prevent online learning; rather they require that the 'methods employed when teaching prescribed areas of knowledge (whether face-to-face, online or in a blended format) enable students to acquire appropriate knowledge and competence in each area of knowledge'.[18] CALD accreditation standards for law schools provide standards relating to curriculum and content but, similarly, are also largely concerned with aligning curriculum design and educational methods rather than addressing specific issues for online contexts.[19]

Admitting authorities have traditionally been very cautious about online law courses and online learning more generally, seeking to monitor in their

13 University of New South Wales, University of Technology Sydney, University of Newcastle, Flinders University, University of Adelaide, University of Tasmania, Australian National University, Bond University, Queensland University of Technology with non-university providers of the College of Law Australia and Leo Cussen Institute.

14 J. Littrich and K. Murray, *Lawyers in Australia*, 4th edn, Federation Press, Sydney 2019, pp. 31–32.

15 See Law Admissions Consultative Committee, 'Prescribed Academic Areas of Knowledge' (12.2016), https://legalservicescouncil.org.au/documents/prescribed-academic-areas-of-knowledge.pdf.

16 See Law Admissions Consultative Committee, 'Accreditation Standards for Australian Law Courses' (07.2018), https://legalservicescouncil.org.au/documents/accreditation-standards-for-law-courses.pdf.

17 O. Rundle and L. Griggs, 'Law Schools and the Burden of Bureaucracy: Release the Yoke (A Plea from the Coalface). Part 1: Over-regulation in Australia' (2019) 93 *Australian Law Journal* 389, 400–401.

18 Law Admissions Consultative Committee, 'Accreditation Standards for Australian Law Courses' (07.2018) p. 11, standard 4.5, https://legalservicescouncil.org.au/documents/accreditation-standards-for-law-courses.pdf.

19 See Council of Australian Law Deans, 'Australian Law School Standards with Guidance Notes' (30.07.2020), https://cald.asn.au/wp-content/uploads/2020/07/Australian-Law-School-Standards-v1.3-30-Jul-2020.pdf.

accreditation the ratio of online and face-to-face that takes place in a law course. Further, accrediting authorities require notification of any change to an accredited law course, including modes of delivery, which means that change can be slow and arguably embeds a culture and practice that inhibits innovation. However, it should be noted that state and territory accrediting bodies were reported to have been very accommodating of law schools doing what needed to be done to support the rapid shift to online during the pandemic. In particular, most accrediting bodies have stipulated that all law schools will be deemed to meet accreditation standards provided they document and report any and all changes made in response to the pandemic and continue to ensure the volume of learning and topics covered are maintained. It will be interesting to see what, if any, lasting changes might remain in place post-pandemic, for example online examinations. At the time of writing, some accrediting bodies are actively reviewing pandemic arrangements relating to course delivery modes and supervision of online examinations.

In addition to professional standards, legal education providers must also comply with the Higher Education Standards Framework, enforced by the Tertiary Education Quality and Standards Association (TEQSA), when providing online education. During the COVID-19 pandemic, when all education providers moved to online delivery, TEQSA reduced their regulatory burdens to assist with the necessary transition to online education.[20] TEQSA also published 'Key Considerations for Providers'[21] in relation to online delivery to ensure continued compliance with the Higher Education Standards Framework (HESF).[22]

---

20 Tertiary Education Quality and Standards Agency, 'Reducing Regulatory Burden During COVID-19 – Important Update from TEQSA' (26.03.2020), https://www.teqsa.gov.au/reducing-regulatory-burden-during-covid-19-important-update-teqsa.

21 Tertiary Education Quality and Standards Agency, 'Online Delivery – Key Considerations for Providers' (08.04.2020), https://www.teqsa.gov.au/latest-news/publications/online-delivery-key-considerations-providers.

22 See e.g. Higher Education Standards Framework (Threshold Standards) 2021 (Cth) (HESF). Standard 1.4.3 requires methods of assessment that are consistent with the learning outcomes being assessed and that are capable of confirming that all specified learning outcomes are achieved and that grades awarded reflect the level of student attainment (online education would need to meet this standard). HESF Standard 2.1.3 requires that the learning environment, whether physical, virtual or blended, and associated learning activities support academic interactions among students outside of formal teaching. HESF Standard 2.3.4 requires that providers promote and foster a safe environment, including by advising the students and staff on actions they can take to enhance safety and security on campus and online. HESF Standard 3.1.1 necessitates that each course of study is specified and specifications include matters such as the modes of delivery and the methods of assessment. HESF Standard 3.1.5 is specifically relevant to legal education as the course also requires professional accreditation and this standard states that where professional accreditation is required for graduates to be eligible to practise, that course of study must be accredited and continue to be accredited by the relevant professional body. HESF Standard 3.3.3 states that access to learning resources must not present unexpected barriers, costs or technology requirements for students, including those with special needs and those who study off campus.

There is no formal limit on the number of places that can be afforded at law schools in Australia. There has long been a suggestion that Australia has been graduating too many lawyers, resulting in a 'dumbing down' of the curriculum and concern that 'anyone is let through'.[23] However, this has been contested by the CALD and others.[24] Kim Economides points to the fact that, in Australia, regardless of whether standards have been relaxed not, there remains considerable unmet legal needs in many areas of the 'legal market', including in those serving the public interest and those serving diverse legal needs, including people living in regional, rural and remote areas.[25] The Gillard government in 2011 deregulated the university sector to allow individual institutions to decide how many domestic students to admit. This allowed universities to attract government funding per student (according to a recently amended schedule). Maximum contributions chargeable to domestic students are specified, and by limiting the subsidies by discipline some brake is put on expanding law school admissions. Generally it is felt that law graduates readily find employment,[26] although many outside the traditional confines of law practice.[27]

2.2. FUNDING

University education is largely funded through the Commonwealth Grants Scheme (CGS) based on the number of full-time equivalent domestic students in Commonwealth Supported Places (CSP), which are in turn funded by a mix of Commonwealth and student contributions. The level of both CSP and student funding provided varies according to the field of study and 'funding cluster',[28] with law sitting in the highest fee cluster for

---

23 E. Ryan, 'Frustration Grows over Unis "Cashing In" on Law Grad Oversupply', *Lawyers Weekly* (19.02.2018) https://www.lawyersweekly.com.au/sme-law/22768-frustration-grows-over-unis-cashing-in-on-law-grad-oversupply.

24 See Council of Australian Law Deans, '2018 Data Regarding Law School Graduate Numbers and Outcomes' (2019), https://cald.asn.au/wp-content/uploads/2019/07/Updated-Factsheet-Law_Students_in_Australia-20-04-2019.pdf.

25 K. Economides, 'Strategies for Meeting Rural Legal Needs: Lessons from Local, Regional and International Experience' (2011) 16(1) *Deakin Law Review* 47.

26 According to data in 2017, around 75% of law graduates had secured full-time employment within four months of graduating (although the data does not identify whether employment is in the legal sector), see Council of Australian Law Deans, '2018 Data Regarding Law School Graduate Numbers and Outcomes' (2019), https://cald.asn.au/wp-content/uploads/2019/07/Updated-Factsheet-Law_Students_in_Australia-20-04-2019.pdf.

27 See Law Society of Western Australia, 'The Future of the Legal Profession' (12.12.2017), p. 1, https://www.lawsocietywa.asn.au/wp-content/uploads/2015/10/2017DEC12-Law-Society-Future-of-the-Legal-Profession.pdf.

28 Commonwealth Department of Education, Skills and Employment, 'Funding Clusters and Indexed Rates', https://www.dese.gov.au/higher-education-loan-program/approved-hep-information/funding-clusters-and-indexed-rates#toc-funding-clusters.

student contribution but being the least supported in terms of government contribution.[29] Student loans operate under the HECS/HELP scheme, to be repaid once students enter the workforce. The CGS does not distinguish in terms of online or on-campus providers.

International student fees are considerably higher than for domestic students, although fees vary across higher education providers. Higher education providers are governed by the Education Services for Overseas Students Act 2000 (Cth) (ESOS) and related legislation. Of relevance to this report is the ESOS requirement that a registered provider must not deliver a course exclusively online to an overseas student nor deliver more than one-third of the units by online or distance learning to an overseas student.[30]

Government funding to support online education initiatives was sparse prior to the pandemic. However, as a response to the displacement of workers due to the pandemic, the Australian government introduced a Higher Education Relief Package involving the provision of subsidies for selected online Higher Education Certificate courses (in teaching, nursing, health, IT and the sciences) for up to 20,000 students in May 2020.[31] In 2021, the Australian government continued to provide additional CSP places for undergraduate and graduate certificates across a range of national priority areas, temporarily integrating these certificate courses into the Australian Qualification Framework (AQF), which may be delivered online, face to face or in a combination of these modes. The government has since reviewed its support for this initiative as part of the 2021–22 Commonwealth budget and, at the time of writing, has committed to fund 5,000 short-course places through non-university providers and committed AU$9.4 million to an Innovation Fund, which would help providers with grants to shift to offshore and online delivery. Encouragement and funding support for the integration and enhancement of online, blended and e-learning has been a progressively growing feature of the university landscape in recent years. Law schools and law faculties in particular have been keen to encourage the uptake of e-learning and enhance digital literacy amongst staff and students.[32] Examples of support for e-learning include a project funded by the Australian Office for Learning and Teaching that produced a set of flexible delivery modules designed to help prepare lawyers and other legal professionals for careers in rural and regional Australia,[33] and a 'flipped classroom' initiative

---

29 Ibid.

30 National Code of Practice for Providers of Education and Training to Overseas Students 2018 (Cth), 8.18, 8.19.

31 See Open Universities Australia, 'Higher Education Relief Package: Discounted Online Higher Education Certificates', https://www.open.edu.au/study-online/higher-education-relief-package.

32 M. Nehme, 'E-Learning and Students' Motivation' (2010) 20 *Legal Education Review* 223.

33 A. Kennedy et al., 'Preparing Law Graduates for Rural and Regional Practice: A New Curriculum-based Approach' (2013) 93 *Procedia – Social and Behavioral Sciences* 317.

undertaken at Griffith University,[34] to name just two. As noted by Rogers, 'universities are changing their models in favour of digitisation, or online or blended learning; a development recently accelerated by COVID-19'.[35]

2.3. IT SYSTEMS

While there are obvious benefits from online learning, including flexibility and greater access for rural, regional and remote students, increased use of technology may also be a challenge for students unable to access laptops, computers or the internet (at all or with sufficient data capacity). Broadly, access to IT hardware by students in Australia is high but there are equity issues for some students who are unable to access hardware, software and internet connectivity, especially in 'non-traditional' student cohorts.[36] During the pandemic, many institutions provided loan computers to students to support their access during remote study. Further, for students in rural, regional and remote parts of Australia there have been reports of internet access problems, especially when public libraries were inaccessible during the most stringent periods of lockdown.

As noted above, the pandemic has accelerated the pace of technological change for many universities, evidenced by some institutions trialling online invigilation software for examinations and permanently shifting some courses and subjects to online or blended delivery. Online examinations can also create access and equity challenges as their use assumes students have compatible levels of software and hardware to match the software's requirements.

3. MOVES TOWARDS ONLINE EDUCATION

3.1. ACHIEVEMENTS BEFORE THE PANDEMIC

Before the pandemic the most common development in law schools in Australia was the adoption of blended learning.[37] Some universities had also

---

34 K. Burns et al., 'Active Learning in Law by Flipping the Classroom: An Enquiry into Effectiveness and Engagement' (2017) 27(1) *Legal Education Review* Art. 14, http://www5.austlii.edu.au/au/journals/LegEdRev/2017/9.pdf.

35 J. Rogers, 'Teaching Soft Skills Including Online: A Review and Framework' (2020) 30(1) *Legal Education Review* 1, 2.

36 J. Willems et al., 'The Increasing Significance of Digital Equity in Higher Education: An Introduction to Digital Equity Special Issue' (2019) 35(6) *Australasian Journal of Educational Technology* 1.

37 See G. Torrisi-Steele and S. Drew, 'The Literature Landscape of Blended Learning in Higher Education: The Need for Better Understanding of Academic Blended Practice' (2013) *International Journal for Academic Development* 1.

started offering purely online courses: the University of New England and Charles Darwin University (NT), for instance, in part due to the deregulation of the tertiary sector under the Gillard government in 2011 and in part due to intensifying competition between universities. Some universities also experimented with wholly online delivery of postgraduate courses in law. An interesting innovation in that regard was the Melbourne Law Masters online programme for competition and (some) consumer law developed from around 2017, set up by Prof. Caron Beaton-Wells and now coordinated by Prof. Julie Clark.[38] The courses were structured so students would actively read modules/topics online. These courses were well thought out pedagogically and were innovative rather than having been quickly developed under pandemic conditions.[39]

However, blended learning remains the most common form of integration of online technology in legal education. Colbran and Gilding in their 2013 survey of Australian law schools reveal the already widespread adoption of blended learning that incorporates elements of both distance education and e-learning.[40] Such online approaches are generally used to supplement on-campus, face-to-face delivery.[41] Blended learning combines traditional face-to-face delivery of education with the use of online technologies.[42] The traditional method of teaching law courses generally includes a lecture and a tutorial. In a blended learning environment these are largely retained but sometimes in a modulated form, where additional elements are included to provide a better learning environment and more effective systems. A 'flipped classroom' approach is a good example – the materials that are generally used during a lecture are made available online and instead of a tutorial, a two- to three-hour seminar/workshop is employed. Blended learning can also occur within traditional classroom settings: for example, the teacher could incorporate an online poll, videos or a game in the lecture. Elphick focuses on adopting transformative teaching methods in law lectures and how effective this has been for improving attendance and engagement.[43] The implications

---

38 University of Melbourne, 'Competition and Consumer Law', https://law.unimelb.edu.au/study/masters/specialist-legal-areas/competition-and-consumer-law.

39 Ibid. It is understood the course contains many interactive elements, including links to further readings, short video interviews with experts, links to relevant webinars as well as Discussion Boards embedded with pre-set questions which link to subject assessment.

40 See S. Colbran and A. Gilding, 'E-Learning in Australian Law Schools' (2013) 23(1) *Legal Education Review* 201.

41 Ibid.

42 See ibid., p. 202 citing G. Torrisi-Steele and S. Drew, 'The Literature Landscape of Blended Learning in Higher Education: The Need for Better Understanding of Academic Blended Practice' (2013) *International Journal for Academic Development* 1.

43 L. Elphick, 'Adapting Law Lectures to Maximise Student Engagement: Is it Time to "Transform"?' (2018) 28(1) *Legal Education Review* Art. 5.

of this research are that the traditional 'information transfer' lecturing, while it is still necessary in some contexts, is failing to engage many students and therefore use of online methods of legal education must move away from pure information transfer, otherwise it just replicates the issue in an online setting. Blending technology into learning has many modalities and rich potential that is still being realised. It consists of more than simply delivering traditional reading materials and reflection tasks through the internet rather than in the traditional format. There is considerable experimentation and reflection in Australian law faculties on these matters.

Corbin and Budgen point out that the term 'online' can be used to mean both the support activities that are used for face-to-face teaching and teaching solely online.[44] It could be said that there is almost universal adoption of blended learning in Australian law schools, predating COVID-19 but accelerated by the pandemic because of the rapid transition it required to online delivery. Additional online elements and further experimentation will undoubtedly remain part of the mix post-pandemic. COVID-19 has resulted in a realisation that technology offers many possibilities that are worth adopting or at least trying out. There is considerable tolerance at faculty managerial levels for experimentation with online delivery and interaction.

The adoption of blended learning is also well supported by the law libraries attached to the various universities. Most Australian universities maintain a separate law library, although this is not a regulatory requirement as it is for accreditation of law degrees/schools in the United States. Recent times have seen very considerable evolution in the role of law libraries, and in their physical infrastructure – from providing only books and journals in paper form, to providing a mix of paper and online, to the most common situation now where books and monographs are still made available in paper form, but judgments and journals are almost exclusively offered online. A number of paying proprietary services are offered in Australia (e.g. LexisNexis and Westlaw), and most courses integrate access to relevant online sources (whether annotated versions of legislation or more textbook-style tracts) via links contained in course websites. Some legal publishers also offer more interactive forms of access to and study of legal materials. The pandemic only accelerated the integration online of legal source materials, which is also manifest in the profession and court libraries, which are an important resource for practitioners in Australia.[45] Before the pandemic there had been

---

44 L. Corbin and L. Budgen, 'Online Teaching: The Importance of Pedagogy, Place and Presence in Legal Education' (2018) 28(1) *Legal Education Review* 1.

45 See J. Botherway, 'Changing Times – High Court of Australia Library During COVID-19' (2021) 42(4/5) *Library Management* 261.

a discernible trend towards turning law libraries into livelier places allowing co-study, group work, discussion, and with varied spaces tailored to particular needs (including occasional classes). Although the pandemic put a temporary stop to this development,[46] it can be anticipated that this trend will continue apace in Australia: far from disappearing in favour of pure online availability of source materials, law libraries will continue to transmogrify into more social and interactive spaces for learning.[47]

3.2. REGULATORY EFFECTS ON ONLINE LEGAL EDUCATION

According to Colbran, Beattie and Gilding, the regulation of education in Australia is overly restrictive in a manner that prohibits law schools from taking full advantage of modern technology.[48] For overseas students, regulation stipulates that no more than one-third of legal education can be delivered remotely. For domestic students, the HESF includes AQF and Threshold Learning Outcomes which address curriculum content and minimum learning outcomes but do not prescribe suitability of learning and teaching activities that develop, support or achieve such academic standards.[49]

Corbin and Budgen point out that, in contrast, the legal profession presses educators to incorporate more digital technologies into legal education so that graduates are tech-savvy and have relevant workplace skills.[50] There is universal acceptance that increased adoption of technology in practice should be reflected in legal education, but how and to what extent is not clear. There is concern amongst law lecturers about loss of focus on traditional substantive content, of disconnection between student and lecturer and of skills-based training, and also about the constantly evolving landscape of technology and practice which is difficult to reflect in education. These concerns seem to be reflected in the regulators' insistence that online delivery be limited – but this is in part also inspired by the fact that a considerable industry and income stream is built around the presence of international students on domestic campuses.

---

46 See T. Sneed, 'The Effect of COVID-19 on Law Libraries: Are These Changes Temporary or a Sign of the Future?' (2020) 60 *Washburn Law Journal* 107.

47 See B. Masters, 'Academic law libraries post covid-19 pandemic' (2020) 28(4) *Australian Law Librarian* 236.

48 S. Colbran, S. Beattie and A. Gilding, 'Legal Education xMOOCs – A Mirage in the Australian Regulatory Environment' (2018) 28(1) *Legal Education Review* 1, 1.

49 Ibid., p. 17.

50 L. Corbin and L. Budgen, 'Online Teaching: The Importance of Pedagogy, Place and Presence in Legal Education' (2018) 28(1) *Legal Education Review* 1, 3.

4. TECHNOLOGY, LEARNING AND ASSESSMENT

Steel et al. point out the connection between using technology for learning and for assessment.[51] The issue of appropriateness of online assessment, and its integrity, has become a key question in terms of evolving towards a more complete online environment. There has always been a disconnect between assessment and learning because handwritten two- or three-hour exams (the pre-pandemic norm) are not reflective of actual study and workplace practices (which generally involve use of technology, use of resources and more time). Online examinations where students have 24 hours to complete the assessment better reflect real-life situations in practice, although this is perhaps less self-evident in the light of the integrity problems we discuss below. They allow students' problem-solving skills and understanding of principle to be tested rather than memory retention. Steel et al. highlight that because of the changing workplace, university and faculty mission statements are being modified to focus on more technology-integrated learning to ensure that graduates are technologically literate and ready for the modern workplace, as we note above.[52] There is considerable debate in Australia concerning how far this takes law schools in relation to assessment: in terms of academic integrity and in terms of the modalities for testing student capability that an online environment newly provides. However, the latter has also given rise to debate about over-assessment and trivialisation of assessment tasks. One option that has attracted support is 'formative assessment' where assessment tasks are better integrated with learning, and not purely focused on grading students. Students submit work that is graded throughout a semester, but then select a 'portfolio' of pieces to submit for the final assessment grade.

During the pandemic itself, relatively drastic changes to normal assessment practices were sometimes adopted. The response of Australian universities to the impacts of COVID-19 on student learning, assessment and performance resulted in many introducing temporary adjustments to grading regimes as a means of easing pressure on students during 2020 and periods of 2021, often in response to student demands for such consideration. For example, at a number of universities, fail grades were not recorded on academic transcripts where students demonstrated a 'genuine attempt' at a subject, and where the failure did not involve academic misconduct. Further, where students considered that their mark did not reflect their true capabilities, they could opt to replace it with a 'Satisfactory' grade that would not count towards their weighted average mark. Similar arrangements (in effect) were implemented at various institutions across Australia during the height of the pandemic.

[51] A. Steel et al., 'Use of E-Exams in High Stakes Law School Examinations: Student and Staff Reactions' (2019) 29(1) *Legal Education Review* 1.

[52] Ibid., p. 2.

The fact is that in Australia e-exams have become more common with the pandemic whatever the academic integrity issues might be, and howsoever they are addressed. They have obvious pedagogical advantages and also simulate the problem-solving environment graduates will experience in the workplace better than the assessment methods pre-pandemic, as we say above. However, there are variables that affect the utility of e-exams. Steel et al., relying on the results of a survey of students, identify that assessment items are more valid if students are assessed in an online format that is comfortable and familiar to them. That is so because students found that it shifted their focus from the 'mechanics of production' to the content of their work. However, while some students found that 'the ability to edit increased writing quality', other students may find that the ability to 'cut, paste and delete detracted from the flow of their thoughts, rather than facilitated meaningful engagement with their writing'.[53] Steel et al. point to a significant problem other than academic integrity with deploying technology both in assessment and in testing students, that is, e-exams and the like may unfairly advantage students who are more computer proficient, although the same can be said for students who are able to write faster.[54] The same can be said for access to digital services, etc. Most students in Steel et al.'s study reported that they would use electronic means to type notes during the semester and prepare for the exam; however, there was a relatively balanced response between favouring typing or handwriting in the exams. Many students also reported that they are faster at typing than at handwriting, and therefore perceived e-exams as better because more marks could be gained. From the perspective of markers, one difficulty that arises from e-exams is that examination papers become excessively long, which makes marking extremely onerous. However, some faculties adopt word limits for e-exams to alleviate this problem, and strict time limits on e-exams will have a similar effect.

The debate about e-exams and about assessment more generally from an academic and pedagogical perspective, and from an integrity perspective, remains live in Australia. There has been extensive reporting concerning the prevalence of online services that assist students to cheat, in particular in relation to written research assignments and essays.[55] The Commonwealth government has moved to attach serious penal consequences to 'contract cheating'.[56] Moving the weight of assessment away from high-integrity exams to research papers is controversial in a general pedagogical sense, but exactly also because of the

---

53 Ibid., p. 4.

54 Ibid., p. 5.

55 A. Steel, 'Contract Cheating: Will Students Pay for Serious Criminal Consequences?' (2017) 42(2) *Alternative Law Journal*; [2017] *University of New South Wales Faculty of Law Research Series* 73.

56 E. Cosenza, 'New Laws Passed Could See Cheaters Who Sell Services to University Students Jailed', *News.com* (04.09.2020), https://www.news.com.au/lifestyle/parenting/school-life/new-laws-passed-could-see-cheaters-who-sell-services-to-university-students-jailed/news-story/599e268e4e5ff39e0766544688274092.

integrity risks adhering to research papers. Universities are trialling different methods of dealing with the apparent rise of assisted cheating.[57]

The debate is further complicated by the role admitting authorities play in the various states, and the different attitudes and rules adopted in each. Some states' admission authorities leave the question of academic integrity of online examination to law faculties to resolve, whereas others are more interventionist. This seems to be the case in South Australia where active review of online examinations is undertaken in collaboration with law schools.[58]

5. PRACTICAL LEGAL TRAINING

The debate about the adoption of e-learning also focuses on PLT and in particular how far it can go in departing from traditional face-to-face methods while still delivering on the acquisition of face-to-face skills. In 2009, Lansdell formulated the traditional position: there are certain legal skills that are better taught face to face, for example advocacy and negotiation.[59] Lansdell sounded a warning note about the adoption of e-learning, but despite that the evolution has been towards more delivery online, so that now there are a number of providers who offer purely online PLT (including for example Bond). It is not clear that online PLT is ineffective, and it has obvious advantages for students who have already started work. However, issues of depersonalisation do arise in this context, as they do in law programmes generally. Lansdell stresses that the expanding uses of technology 'arguably threaten any deep learning of material and development of a professional ethos, particularly where traditional face-to-face material is converted into online modules.'[60] Even so, Lansdell admits that e-learning does have the potential to promote deep learning because it allows the individual to work in their own time in a way that is most suitable to their own learning needs. However, a non-law study has found that face-to-face delivery is still the best way to meet student expectations.[61]

---

57 See C. Ribeiro, 'The push and pull of cheating at university: "No one knows what cheating is any more"', *The Guardian* (26.11.2022), https://www.theguardian.com/australia-news/2022/nov/27/the-push-and-pull-of-cheating-at-university-no-one-knows-what-cheating-is-any-more: 'The pandemic's disruption to students and education has given rise to contract cheating.'

58 Internal e-mail from Prof. Melissa de Zwart, (then) Dean of Law and Head of School, Adelaide Law School in response to request for information via the LEAD network (22.07.2021); she stated: 'Online examination has been permitted. This position is currently under review, with a joint paper to be provided from the three law schools to LPEAC at its September meeting.'

59 G.T. Lansdell, 'Have We Pushed the Boat out Too Far in Providing Online Practical Legal Training: A Guide to Best Practices for Future Programs' (2009) 19(1) *Legal Education Review* 149.

60 Ibid., p. 156.

61 Ibid., p. 157 citing A. Smith, P. Ling and D. Hill, 'Adoption of Multiple Modes of Delivery in Australian Universities' (2006) 3(2) *Journal of University Teaching and Learning Practice* 67.

Where Lansdell refers to 'deep learning' concerns, Rogers focuses on another significant aspect of the debate within the Australian academy, concerning so-called 'soft skills'.[62] When it comes to balancing the 'soft skills' of a more interpersonal and relational kind, with traditional academic or substantive learning in law, Rogers stresses how important the soft skills in fact are. She identifies five 'core skills' – self-awareness; self-management and self-development; social proficiency; leadership; and professionalism and ethics – and also provides a framework and a set of strategies to teach soft skills to law students in a digital format.[63] Rogers points out that blended learning can support the development of soft skills. She identifies that blended learning is receiving growing attention in the legal education literature as a method for 'efficient, engaging instruction, offering potentially greater learning outcomes than either purely online or purely in-class modes'.[64] The potential of blended learning has certainly received a lot of attention in the literature, which has then impacted the practice of the teaching of law in most, if not all, law faculties. In some cases that process has been driven by the necessities of COVID-19. Hewitt and Stubbs describe a project at Adelaide Law School, a case in point.[65] The project inter alia evaluated the efficiency of online skills development modules in assisting students to acquire legal skills. The authors say that online learning can be more efficient and effective in developing legal skills in law students and addressing law student distress, which there is increasing evidence of, provided online learning is designed in a way that promotes resilience and wellbeing.[66] However, it would be fair to say that it remains controversial to claim that online education is better for the acquisition of soft skills, and most law faculties retain person-to-person teaching in some form or another, or intend to return to it post-COVID-19, inter alia to deliver effective skills education.

More generally, the debate is open about online learning in Australian law schools, both in the substantive part of the degree and in PLT – it clearly has advantages and disadvantages. A blended learning environment is generally perceived as offering the best of both worlds. In some law schools that have migrated much content delivery and learning online, the interpersonal part of legal education is delivered in intensive formats – students and lecturers come

---

62 See J. Rogers, 'Teaching Soft Skills Including Online: A Review and Framework' (2020) 30(1) *Legal Education Review* 1.

63 Ibid., pp. 5–6.

64 Ibid., p. 3 citing W.R. Slomanson, 'Blended Learning: A Flipped Classroom Experiment' (2014) 64(1) *Journal of Legal Education* 93.

65 See A. Hewitt and M. Stubbs, 'Supporting Law Students' Skills Development Online – A Strategy to Improve Skills and Reduce Student Stress?' (2017) 25 *Research in Learning Technology* 1.

66 See ibid.

together for a number of multi-day intensive sessions, where the practical and communication skills inherent in law studies can be rehearsed. One aspect that has influenced the debate is the increased interest in lifelong learning and micro-credentialing. The online format lends itself particularly well to offering lawyers (or those members of the public interested in the law) continuous education outside or above what is required to maintain a practising certificate. Some law faculties offer courses freely online to any person interested; others offer courses for consideration, sometimes with certificates attached if the interested party wishes to undertake assessment.

It seems that where fully online degrees are offered, the advantages in convenience and reduction of the cost of delivery (not requiring all the traditional physical infrastructure of classrooms, etc.) could outweigh the pedagogical drawbacks. Because the legal education landscape in Australia is quite varied and competitive, it is a matter for individual students to decide whether this is acceptable to them, and to choose where to study. The availability of the option is generally seen as a useful piece in the law education puzzle, while the legal profession and the academy are aware of its pros and cons.

6. TECHNOLOGY IN EDUCATION AND TECHNOLOGY IN THE PRACTICE OF LAW

It has not escaped commentators and teachers that there is a connection between technology in legal education and technology in practice. We have averted to it above. Smith considers how integrating technology into modern legal education is effective for law students preparing for modern legal practice.[67] He says technology has shaped contemporary legal practice and this has meant that employers are seeking broader skillsets, including a capacity to practise in both online and partially automated settings and to work collaboratively.[68]

However, there are considerable difficulties in Australia in this regard. Integration between practice and law schools remains at a fairly low ebb in comparison with other jurisdictions. In other words, practitioners and law firms play a limited role in the delivery of legal education. Firms provide little financial support or sponsorship, and the same goes for providers of technology in law practice. It is also the case that the adoption of technology in practice varies, both in law firms and in the courts and tribunals, of which there are many in Australia (at state and Commonwealth levels). Since the adoption of technology is not universal and the providers of proprietary tech solutions are very varied,

---

67 M. Smith, 'Integrating Technology in Contemporary Legal Education' (2020) 54(2) *The Law Teacher* 209.

68 Ibid.

it is difficult for law schools to translate tech practice in the courts and law firms to the educational environment.

Aspects of the common law adversarial system, with witnesses being called to testify and be cross-examined in Australia, also mean that adoption of technology in the courts has its limits.

Case Study 1: Southern Cross University

Southern Cross University (SCU) Law & Justice had a head start over most other Australian institutions in providing online teaching during the pandemic because SCU had already specialised in distance education for nearly three decades previously. Initially, printed study guides and readings were provided to students by post and later replaced by the CD, while in the last half-decade, items are now available for download from the SCU learning website (MySCU).

Since circa 2005, a typical Law & Justice unit features each week (over 12 teaching weeks):

(a) one two-hour lecture, always recorded and available to be viewed/downloaded from MySCU. Before the 2020 lockdowns, some staff also delivered their lectures in person to students on campus at regular times (SCU teaching spaces being equipped with video facilities to beam classes live between SCU's Gold Coast and Lismore campuses, and to record them to MySCU). Other lecturers delivered their lectures online via Collaborate (an interactive web-conferencing tool) – some with students sitting in, and others recorded their lectures with no students present, allowing for irregular recording times that best suited the lecturer.

(b) one two-hour online tutorial, again delivered via Collaborate at, of course, a scheduled time, usually in the evening, and invariably recorded to MySCU.

(c) on-campus tutorials – these have been the most changeable of all. Before 2020, Law & Justice traditionally ran weekly two-hour tutorials on both the Lismore and Gold Coast campuses for all core (Priestley 11) units. When COVID-19 and the lockdowns hit, for the first time in Session One 2020 and for the Delta variant sequel in Session Two 2021, these were also immediately migrated to Collaborate. In the interlude of Session One 2021, when on-campus teaching resumed to some extent, budgetary constraints led SCU senior executive to cancel all Law & Justice classes at Lismore, so that only the Gold Coast tutorials were resumed on campus. While rationalised on the basis of continuity, this raised some questions – for example, it seemed futile for the same staff member to conduct a second tutorial addressing the same questions and in the same medium. It also meant that some of the more diligent students felt obliged to watch four hours of recorded tutorials per week, not just two, for fear that they might miss key information. In some instances, this led to the decision that the 'on campus' tutorial would not be recorded.

Thus, COVID-19 only really affected the third of SCU's three venues of teaching to a large extent for all staff (and to some extent for some staff as to the first venue).

As for assessment, SCU had already used electronically submitted assignments for most of the last decade, run through Turnitin to check for suspicious similarities. When COVID-19 hit in March 2020, the university immediately announced that invigilated attendance exams would be suspended, and they have remained suspended since. In their place online electronic exams are run. These are not "take-home" exams in the traditional sense since students have only a short timeframe (usually 3.5 hours) to complete the questions. No additional academic integrity mechanisms have been adopted (other than running submitted exams through Turnitin, which has caught a few too-close matches so far), such as online proctoring services, but these may be introduced in the near future at the insistence of legal professional accreditation bodies.

One perhaps unintended disadvantage of this move to completely online teaching is that SCU can no longer resource incarcerated students. Prison inmates typically have extremely restricted (or even no) internet access. Before circa 2020 this could be accommodated by printing out study guides and burning CDs, which could be posted to the relevant jail's education offer for vetting. However, with the new SCU model, this will no longer be possible and SCU has had to regretfully inform groups like the Justice Action Coalition that it cannot accept incarcerated persons as students, given the current (and likely for the foreseeable future) corrections policy on web access.[69]

7. ACHIEVEMENTS AND CHALLENGES AFTER THE PANDEMIC

In terms of achievements, it seems that the pandemic has accelerated the adoption of online elements in legal education, in particular reinforcing the advantages and feasibility of blended learning. It has not resulted in a wholesale move to 'pure' online delivery, for the various reasons debated above. Most law faculties

69 The rapporteurs thank Tom Round and Bee Chen Goh of SCU for supplying this case study; some edits were for the sake of brevity.

intend to return to blended learning so that traditional lectures are retained, as well as in person tutorials, and also 'live' consultation and participation in skills exercise and other aspects of the life of a law school. However, it remains to be seen at this point how far some aspects of the COVID-19 adoption of technology and online learning will be pegged back – one area where there is considerable concern over the potential retention of pandemic-inspired practices is in relation to exam-style high-integrity assessment online.

Certain common elements of integrated online legal education (e.g. course materials, video content, online exercises, bulletin boards, discussion forums, etc.) have found a permanent place in law teaching, with increased experimentation during COVID-19. It remains to a large extent a matter for individual lecturers in Australia to what extent they adopt any or all of these disparate techniques, in terms of both content delivery and assessment. It could be said that there has been a shift from online 'delivery' to online 'learning' during the period of the pandemic, and that this will continue to be the focus post-COVID-19.

However, there are significant remaining challenges, not least being how to make online learning most effective: there are many options and individual components that remain controversial. There is little consolidation around common elements across law schools. In part this reflects the varied and competitive environment of law teaching in Australia, and in part also the latitude given to individual lecturers concerning pedagogy and technology. However, in terms of intervention in technological choices, two issues continue to be at the forefront of debate in faculties: the integrity of particular forms of online assessment; and how to synchronise adoption of technology in practice with adoption of technology in legal education. Some of the difficulty lies in the awareness that there are new technological developments on the horizon, particularly in the sphere of AI in legal practice, problem solving, etc. These developments will affect legal education but at present it is difficult to gauge how and to what extent.[70] Therefore it is difficult to make effective and useful decisions as to what technologies to adopt and to instruct students about.

In the broader context the debate in Australia has to some extent flipped from 'What are the uses of online in law education?' to 'What are the continuing uses of a campus for law students and studies?'. Most universities and thus law faculties remain rooted in physical campuses with large lecture theatres and similar facilities. Some campuses are evolving to focus more on co-curricular facilities, communal learning and working spaces, more social law library spaces, and a greater focus on support delivery. This has had and will continue

---

[70] See e.g. M. Legg and F. Bell, 'Artificial Intelligence and the Legal Profession: Becoming the AI-Enhanced Lawyer' [2020] *University of New South Wales Law Research Series* 63; M. Bailes, 'An End to Lawyers? Implications of AI for the Legal Profession', Speech, Law Council of Australia, 24.10.2018.

to have an important effect in law libraries, whose roles have strongly evolved with a move from physical books to online resources, and to more active support of students' research needs.

In this regard there is also a broader question concerning future integration of online learning in law with university online management systems (Blackboard, Moodle, etc.). Often it is not faculty-based but university management-based decisions that drive adoption of technology and online delivery in Australian universities, which are marked by a strong managerial culture. Indirectly, choices are therefore often provider-driven rather than driven by teachers and academics from their own needs and experiences.

Finally, there is a remaining challenge – although perhaps better viewed as an opportunity – in relation to online delivery and the growing interest in lifelong learning, and in the case of law, compulsory skills maintenance in practice (CPLE). Many Australian law faculties are experimenting with new options for lifelong learning, and non-law professional learning in relation to the world of the law, micro-credentialing and reaching out to other professions with a need for some legal learning. There is considerable potential in this regard, and online delivery is an obviously suitable model. It remains to be seen to what extent this post-university world will remain isolated from what happens during primary legal education.

Case Study 2: Bond University

A number of years ago Bond moved to using an integrated online management system for all its courses. This enabled all aspects of teaching to be delivered through a single platform and therefore encouraged standardisation as between courses. The main features of this system were focused on information delivery (course materials, PowerPoints, short introductory videos, perhaps some quizzes and the occasional online forum or chatroom). Some key aspects of Bond's delivery model remained largely unaffected by the adoption of an online backbone for course delivery.

Bond has traditionally been a very on-campus-focused university and the Law Faculty has been a prime exponent of the face-to-face philosophy. The campus experience is seen as central to students' socialisation and general development, and in terms of law also to developing some key interpersonal skills in future law graduates. Personal interaction with teachers was always considered very important. These core settings of education at Bond present some challenges to online delivery of legal education, but this was a limitation accepted in light of the benefits of on-campus student presence.

The Law Faculty's courses have also been skills-integration-based. In other words, practical legal skills were uniquely integrated into course delivery – for example evidence or criminal law courses commonly included a mooting exercise; procedural courses a client-interviewing component. Therefore integration of online elements had until the pandemic been partial only and mainly focused on course management, certain aspects of assessment, and backroom tasks such as grade compilation. The most unique and typical aspect of Bond teaching and learning in law is the 'live' tutorial, with a maximum number of 11 students, weekly for one hour in each course, and assessed. This has been standard practice for the whole history of the university, and a core point of distinction from other education providers. Skills assessments and then in particular mooting have always been central also to the learning experience in Bond. For that purpose, the Faculty designed and built very advanced and technologically supported moot courts in its Legal Skills Centre.

The arrival of COVID-19 therefore necessitated fairly radical changes to key delivery aspects of Bond law courses. Tutorials moved online and were delivered by individual academics from their desktops as opposed to being conducted in tutorial rooms. Assessment remained an integral component of online tutorials. Because of the interactive quality of tutorials (being student-driven) this involved the challenge of maintaining interactivity and something analogous to the 'live' experience online. That is less demanding for traditional lectures as they tend to be uni-directional – a move to online delivery is a less fundamental departure. Nonetheless, adaptation to the online environment for tutorials, via the Collaborate system, has been generally experienced as having some advantages, in particular in the management of student participation – certain features allow a more ordered approach than is possible in a classroom. Some important elements of the classroom experience are lost, however, since the system does not allow the same direct student-to-student interaction and lacks the more subtle queuing and cluing that a real classroom permits. However, adaptation was fairly rapid and although challenging in some respects initially (e.g. occasional system failures), well accepted in time. The general sentiment, however, is that such delivery remains second-best to actual in-class presence, and falls short in developing certain inter-personal skills and abilities in law students. The university has recently resolved to return to only on-campus education from January 2023, a decision generally supported by staff. Examinations will not return to a paper in-person format, however, instead most likely adhering to the three-hour online approach developed in the latter stages of the pandemic.

As far as such exercises as mooting are concerned, these also moved online fairly swiftly and technological challenges were readily overcome. Here again, however, it was challenging to replicate some key aspect of live mooting in a court or moot court. The student mooting online perhaps from home or office is in a less stressful situation than the 'real' mooter, and online mooting thus does not replicate the real-life challenges of court and tribunal experiences as faithfully as traditional law school mooting exercises do. However, it remains to be seen when and to what extent courts themselves return to live appearances before judges and magistrates – one effect of the pandemic might be that some permanent adaptation to more online advocacy will follow. In terms of Bond University, it still disposes of excellent physical and in-person facilities which now await their re-adoption post-pandemic. What aspects of pandemic online delivery will become permanent features remains to be seen.

8. CONCLUSIONS

The Australian legal education sector is a patchwork quilt of different law faculties that are adapted to the particular state regulatory environment, the size and nature of the universities they form part of, different pedagogical and research philosophies, and different markets. Suffice it to say that this even before COVID-19 had resulted in a sector that experimented quite actively with online delivery in legal education. This ranged from faculties that offered a purely online degree, although those were relatively few, to ones with a great focus on in-class experience and skills exercises, with many different models in between.

Much of the practice of education in the substantive degrees came to adopt various iterations of blended learning – i.e. a mix of in-person and online delivery methods. In-person education generally remained in the form of lectures and tutorials and in skills exercises and training such as mooting and client interviewing. Online education centred primarily around content delivery from various documentary sources but also more dynamic content such as video-recorded lectures, PowerPoint presentations, audio recordings, and visual representations of subject matter. Additionally, more interactive uses of the internet were becoming more commonplace, such as bulletin and discussion boards, quizzes, online tutorials, individual online meetings, and participation in third-party events, talks and clinics. Law libraries also stepped up to the mark to make more sources available digitally – the libraries transmogrifying more into learning and social spaces, areas for group work and chat, etc.

With the pandemic, much of the previously in-person delivery moved online, and delivery became almost entirely 'remote', i.e. students were not required to attend campus at all. Although this has proven to be a passing state of affairs, it has resulted in greater acceptance and above all familiarity with online delivery across the whole gamut of learning experiences, including skills education. If nothing else, lecturers and faculties have accepted that it can be done and to a reasonably satisfactory extent. Questions remain, however, as to what moving online means for soft skills and elements of socialisation, inter-personal skills and general wellbeing. There seems little appetite for a wholesale move to online even if the pandemic has revealed to many what the possibilities of online education actually are.

It seems therefore that blended learning is here to stay, perhaps enhanced with some additional flexibilities and learning tools that had remained the province of just a few more innovative lecturers and faculties. The delivery mode of legal education has become far more flexible, varied and mixed again than it already was before the pandemic. The general attitude in Australian legal education circles could be described as adopting some of the modalities forcefully acquired during the period of pure online delivery, while retaining core in-person teaching and skills training, but further enhanced with all the options that the more sophisticated course management software packages can deliver. In the meantime, the perennial debate about optimising legal education with all its varied demands remains as active as ever.

It seems that there has been little permanent impact on the broader world of legal practice resulting from the pandemic. Admission authorities have shown themselves to be largely unconcerned about the extent to which faculties adopt online learning and teaching. They have demonstrated little interest even in the new assessment environment, which presents one of the principal challenges to further deployment of online technologies. There is still little flow-through from the adoption of digital technology and online delivery and collaboration in practice and the courts to legal education and educators. Quite a divide remains between the academy and the profession of law – it does not seem that moving online, and the imperatives of the pandemic, have made much of an impact on this separation. Perhaps an opportunity lost; but in any case, varied as the law schools are in Australia, they do not by any means agree on the extent law schools should involve the profession or the more professional aspects of legal education. The faculties vary greatly in their philosophical outlook, as they do in many other aspects. In terms of the student body, that means that in Australia there are many different options to choose from – including making a choice between more or less online content. The post-COVID-19 balance in that regard has not yet been found, as the pandemic trails on. However, we know the picture will not be uniform but rather a patchwork quilt of attitudes, philosophies, technologies and a varied attitude to online legal education. We leave to one side the impact COVID-19 has had on delivery of legal education to international students, and what the future might look like if such students do not return to Australian shores in anything like the numbers that existed before the pandemic.

ONLINE LEGAL EDUCATION IN CANADA

Just a Short-Lived Anomaly?

Adrien HABERMACHER

1. INTRODUCTION

An examination of Canada's legal education system first requires a general understanding of the structure of Canadian federalism, as regulation of access to the legal professions remains a provincial matter despite recent developments toward a national regime. This is all the more important since all but one of the provinces[1] follow the common law tradition, whereas Quebec is a mixed jurisdiction where the (French) civil law tradition imbues many aspects of the legal order.[2] However, as this report will outline, structural differences in legal tradition and legal education in the country have not impacted the general outlook of online legal education prior to the pandemic and thereafter; in fact, the experience with online legal education, whether at the initial stage (qualifying education) or at the professional development stage (continuing education) has been quite similar across Canada. Online education was nearly absent at the initial stage before the pandemic but was already starting to gain presence at the continuing stage. The pandemic forced all legal education to move online for more than a year, with similar modalities across the country. As it abates, the online or hybridity sliders are largely reversing to their pre-pandemic levels in all regions as well.

Canada is a federal state in which the Constitution allocates legislative powers between the ten provinces and the federal government.[3] In addition, three territories located in the North are jurisdictions where the federal government delegated powers to local authorities. The provinces and the territories regulate legal education and the legal professions within their respective boundaries. Each province and territory features its own regulating body or bodies tasked with overseeing who can practise law within the jurisdiction.

The common and civil law traditions do not only differ as to their respective substantial rules, sources, institutions and modes of reasoning; they also each have a historically distinct approach to legal education. In common law provinces, the legal education tradition is that inherited from England with major American influences, whereas in Quebec, the legal education regime follows the French tradition. Besides these two official legal traditions, Indigenous Peoples' legal traditions continue to exist across Turtle Island (the way many Indigenous societies refer to North America); despite the long-lasting impact of the cultural genocide,[4] recent efforts from and within Indigenous communities,

---

1 Alberta, British Columbia, Manitoba, New Brunswick, Newfoundland and Labrador, Nova Scotia, Ontario, Prince Edward Island and Saskatchewan.

2 In Quebec, the substance of the private law is based on the French civil law tradition whereas public law is based on the common law tradition.

3 Constitution Act, 1867, ss. 91–92.

4 As an integral part of Indigenous cultures, Indigenous legal traditions (as well as Indigenous spiritualities, languages and ways of life) have greatly suffered, and sometimes disappeared, as a result of the cultural genocide perpetrated by the colonial authorities of Canada. See generally Truth and Reconciliation Commission of Canada, *Honouring the Truth, Reconciling for the Future* (2015), https://nctr.ca/records/reports/.

supported by cultural shifts in mainstream Canadian society, have led the legal community to recognise that Indigenous legal orders are part of the fabric of Canada and ought to be part of a Canadian lawyer's education.[5]

This report is based on a variety of sources, including academic publications, institutional websites, regulations and unformal information. Wherever possible, I sought to provide references to publicly available sources to corroborate statements as well as offer readers avenues to explore primary sources; alas, this was not always possible. In addition to the general paucity of empirical reports and research in Canada, the novelty of online legal education in this country means that research is currently limited; in fact, this very report presents an original summary of recent practices and emerging research. I also contacted numerous institutions across Canada[6] and consulted with many colleagues whose own ongoing research inform this report.[7]

2. BACKGROUND

2.1. THE LEGAL PROFESSIONS

2.1.1. Structure of the Legal Professions

In Quebec, the professions providing legal advice are divided between *avocats* and *notaires* following the heritage of the French legal system. *Avocats* are

---

5 Truth and Reconciliation Commission of Canada, *Calls to action* (2015), nos. 27–28, https://nctr.ca/records/reports/.

6 Law schools, law societies and others; mostly by phone or e-mail queries (no uniform questionnaire); I thank Jacob Gauthier, JD 2022, for his tremendous help with this endeavour.

7 Here are the main research projects on legal education in Canada during the pandemic that I am relying on in this report: J. Bliss and D. Sandomierski, 'Learning Without Grade Anxiety: Lessons from the Pass/Fail Grading Experiment in North American JD Programs' (2022) 48 *Ohio Northern University Law Review* 555 and J. Bliss, D. Sandomierski and T. Collesso, 'Pass for Some, Fail for Others: An Equity Analysis of Law School Grading Changes in the Early COVID-19 Pandemic' (forthcoming 2023) *UBC Law Review* (based on a survey of nearly 2,000 law students across Canada and the United States focused on the impact of and attitudes toward the temporary changes to the grading schemes); A. Fried, 'Lessons from Online Pandemic Pedagogy in North American Law Schools: Toward Law Student Wellbeing' in E. Jones and C. Stevens (eds), *Wellbeing and Transitions in Law: Legal Education and the Legal Profession*, Palgrave Macmillan, London (forthcoming) (based on a survey and interviews with 36 law school instructors regarding their attitudes toward online pedagogies); A. Habermacher and S. Giwa, 'Online legal education: empirical findings regarding the development of professional competencies and professional identity in the Fall 2020' (unpublished to date, submitted to the FLSC National Requirement Review Committee in January 2023) (based on a survey of law students at three Canadian law schools

regulated by the *Barreau du Québec*; they typically represent the interests of their clients in transactions and dispute settlements. On the other hand, *notaires* are primarily in charge of real estate transactions, wills and estates and other situations where the law requires certified documents; they are regulated by the *Chambre des notaires du Québec*. In the common law jurisdictions across Canada, the traditional division between barristers and solicitors has long been abolished. The result is a unitary legal profession regulated by a single law society in each province. In Ontario, the most populous province, paralegal professionals can also give legal advice and represent clients in court proceedings in limited circumstances; the provincial law society regulates this profession alongside lawyers. Debates exist in other provinces as well on whether to follow the same model.

Furthermore, there is a national organisation called the Federation of Law Societies (FLSC); it is a coordinating body tasked with developing of national standards and harmonising rules across the local law societies. The FLSC most notably developed national standards concerning the recognition of common law degrees earned in Canada and a common process for admission of foreign-trained lawyers, mobility agreements allowing easier moves across provincial borders for lawyers, and a model code of professional conduct. Just like the provincial law societies from which it exercises delegated authority, the FLSC's official mandate includes regulating the professions in the public interest; advocacy for and promotion of the interests of lawyers belongs in the hands of voluntary associations like the Canadian Bar Association.

The law societies are regulatory bodies whose authority derives from enabling legislation in each province. The common law societies have traditionally enjoyed greater autonomy from government intervention in the regulation of access to and practice of the legal professions than their counterparts in Quebec. For instance, in Quebec, there are governmental regulations determining the professional training and continuing education requirements for members of the *Barreau* and *Chambre*,[8] whereas such matters are squarely within the law societies' self-regulation mandate in other provinces.

Despite such differences in the structure of the legal professions between the civil law province and its common law counterparts, the ratio of lawyers per capita is largely similar in the two regions (see Table 1).

---

regarding the development of legal competencies in an online environment); M. Murchison, R. Jochelson, D. Ireland, T. Ciyiltepe and S. Koulack, 'Remote Learning in Law School During the Pandemic: A Canadian Survey' (2022) 8 *Canadian Journal of Comparative and Contemporary Law* 148 (based on a survey of 422 law students at 13 Canadian law schools).

8 See e.g. By-law respecting the professional training of advocates, under Act respecting the Barreau du Québec c B-1, s. 15, para. 2, subpara. b.

Table 1. Membership of law societies and new admissions in 2019

	Active membership (2019)	Active membership per million inhabitants (Q4 2019)	New admissions (2019)
Québec (*avocats* only)	27,298	3,195	1,068
Québec (*notaires* only)	3,899	456	139
Common law provinces and territories (lawyers only)	74,656	2,551	3,668
Canada (lawyers, *avocats, notaires*)	105,853	2,800	4,875

Sources: Statistics Canada, *Table 17-10-0009-01* 'Population estimates, quarterly', https://doi.org/10.25318/1710000901-eng (population estimates in Q4 2019); FLSC, *2019 Statistical Report of the Federation of Law Societies of Canada* (2022), https://flsc.ca/resources/resource-library/?resource-category=statistics.

2.1.2. *Access to the Legal Professions*

Across Canada, joining the legal professions (lawyers, *avocats* and *notaires*) requires obtaining a university law degree from a recognised institution, then completion of the educational courses offered by the local law society and finally a period of professional experience (*stage* or articling) ranging from six to 12 months.

Law students in Quebec, whether they aspire to become an *avocat* or *notaire*, first need to obtain an undergraduate degree in civil law at one of the six universities offering such a programme.[9] Typically, students enrol immediately after completing their *CEGEP* (a universal two-year college programme unique to Quebec), at around 19 years old, and the programme takes three years of full-time studies to complete. The curriculum is primarily designed for students to acquire theoretical knowledge. Students seeking admission to the *Barreau du Québec* will then complete classes focusing on practical abilities offered by l'*École du Barreau* over four to eight months before spending at least six months working under the supervision of a registered *avocat*. Students seeking to join the *Chambre des notaires* take a different route after obtaining their first degree in civil law: they need to complete an additional year of studies at one of the four universities offering a master's degree in *droit notarial*,[10] complete the professional training offered by the *Chambre*, and spend at least 14 weeks working under the supervision of a registered *notaire*.

9 Université Laval, Université McGill, Université de Montréal, Université d'Ottawa, Université du Québec à Montréal and Université de Sherbrooke. A new qualifying programme is opening at Université du Québec en Outaouais in 2023.

10 Université Laval, Université de Montréal, Université d'Ottawa and Université de Sherbrooke.

Outside of Quebec, students need to earn a JD degree at one of the 18 institutions recognised by the FLSC.[11] Even though this degree is considered an undergraduate degree, as it is the first in the discipline, candidates need to have completed several years of university studies before applying. Typically, they join the programme after completing a first bachelor's in another discipline. There is no specific requirement as to which discipline or courses they should have completed prior to starting law school. The JD programmes typically require three years of full-time studies. Upon completion, the aspiring lawyers need to complete the admission course delivered by their local law society (a series of training modules and examinations) and article for eight to 12 months under the supervision of a practising lawyer.

This articling requirement is the main feature distinguishing common law legal education in Canada from its counterpart in the United States. It is now under severe pressure, at least in Ontario – the most populous province. Both as a result of the mobility of individuals and ideas across the 49th parallel border and concerns regarding the availability of articling positions for all law graduates, the Law Society of Ontario has approved alternatives in the past decade. One such alternative is the Law Practice Program (LPP) offered at two universities:[12] this programme consists of a four-month training course followed by a four-month work placement. The other alternative takes the form of increased practice-oriented content in the JD programmes at two universities in the province (Integrated Practice Curriculum, IPC),[13] such that graduates from these programmes are exempt from further professional experience requirements before admission. The LLP and the IPC still concern a minority of new lawyers; if no longer universal, the articling requirement remains the norm in Ontario and the only option in other common law provinces. Debates are raging on within the Law Society of Ontario as to the fate of articling, with critics pointing to a shortage of available placements compared to the number of candidates, the persistence of barely paid positions, the inconsistency of training and feedback across positions, as well as the incidence of harassment, abuse and sometimes discrimination during placements.[14] Law societies in the other provinces are watching closely the fate of articling and pilot alternatives

---

11 University of Alberta, University of British Columbia, University of Calgary, Dalhousie University, Lakehead University, University of Manitoba, Université de Moncton, University of New Brunswick, University of Ottawa, Queen's University, University of Saskatchewan, Thomson Rivers University, Toronto Metropolitan University (formerly Ryerson University), University of Toronto, University of Victoria, University of Western Ontario, University of Windsor, York University. Memorial University of Newfoundland has worked on a proposal for a new Faculty of Law since 2012 (see https://www.mun.ca/law/).

12 Toronto Metropolitan University (in English) and University of Ottawa (in French).

13 Toronto Metropolitan University and Lakehead University.

14 See e.g. Law Society of Ontario, Professional Development and Competence Committee, *Experiential Training Enhancements* (26.11.2021).

in Ontario; it remains to be seen whether they will follow the emerging Ontario model.

Several universities offer a one-year programme enabling students trained in Canada in one legal tradition to obtain a degree in the other tradition. Students who earned a law degree outside of Canada and seek to practise law in a common law province need to apply to the National Committee of Accreditation (NCA, an emanation of the FLSC) for their credentials to be assessed; depending on the results, they will have to pass several examinations administered by the NCA or complete equivalent courses in an approved law school. A similar but independent process exists within Quebec's regulatory bodies.

2.2. THE LAW FACULTIES AND UNIVERSITIES

With only one exception, qualifying law programmes are offered through a dedicated academic unit within their university typically called the Faculty of law (colloquially referred to as law schools). Although they are typically smaller than other faculties in their own university, faculties of law typically operate in their own separate building and enjoy their own library. Faculties of law range in size from just a dozen to 70 full-time professors. Most law professors are full-time academics whose job descriptions include teaching, research and community services (e.g. university committees, contributions to non-governmental organisations). Law professors typically hold an undergraduate degree in law and at least one graduate degree in the same discipline or related field; most new hires now also hold a doctoral degree. They may or may not have practising experience. In addition, law schools also employ occasional instructors, often local practitioners, to teach a portion of their courses.

2.2.1. Market Considerations and Gatekeeping

The main gatekeepers of access to the legal professions are the faculties of law, rather than the law societies. If the latter formally set the criteria for and allow new persons to practise law in their jurisdiction, it is the law school admission process which is most determinative in selecting future lawyers.

All qualifying university law programmes are subject to caps as to the number of students they can accept, as determined by the provincial governments and/or the universities themselves. For common law schools, the number of first-year places has remained between 10% and 15% of the number of applications since 1985.[15] For civil law programmes, the admission rate varies between

15 B. Cotter, 'Report on Canadian Common Law Admissions Information And Statistics: 2012, 2013 And Historical Perspective 1985–2013' (04.2014), https://ccld-cdfdc.ca/wp-content/uploads/2019/10/CLASSIREPORT2014.pdf.

20% and 30%. Moreover, at least 90% of students admitted in qualifying law programmes end up graduating with the coveted degree; the same proportion of law graduates seeking admission in their local law society are eventually called to the bar.[16]

Thus, in both systems, the number of applicants greatly outweighs the available places, and the law schools' admission process is the main determinant of who will join the professions.

Law schools set their own admission criteria, within the broad parameters set by the FLSC. Common law schools typically rely on a combination of previous academic performance (GPA) and performance on the American-based Law School Admission Test (LSAT) to rank applications and make offers to the highest-ranking individuals; the respective weight given to each metric varies from institution to institution. Since there is no French-language equivalent to the LSAT, French-language programmes in either tradition do not require it.[17] There, admission is determined almost exclusively by previous academic performance. A few law schools rely on more holistic evaluations of the applicants' background and performance,[18] and most require candidates to submit personal essays to complete their file.

All law schools have special admission processes for certain categories of applicants for whom the usual factors (GPA and LSAT scores) are less relevant, for instance mature students with professional experience in a relevant field or Indigenous applicants, against whom current metrics of academic performance are skewed due to the history of discrimination.

Except for Canada's two biggest cities, Montréal and Toronto, there is only one university with a law school per metropolitan area in the country. Three provinces count only one law school; two provinces and all three territories have no permanent law programme. Many law schools are therefore alone in their region. While in the past decade it has become much easier to transfer from one law society to the next (among common law jurisdictions), some law schools thus remain the near-singular point of entry for geographically vast legal markets. This situation does not seem to foster competitive innovation among law schools, such as experiments with new formats of delivery in legal education. The emphasis on pedagogic innovation at Toronto Metropolitan University's law school, established only a few years ago in a city where two legacy law schools already existed, shows how increased competition among law

---

16 Approximations obtained by comparing the number of available first-year places with that of yearly graduating students at the different law schools, and by comparing the number of students enrolled in law societies' admission programmes with that of new admissions.

17 Moncton, uOttawa, McGill and other programmes in Quebec.

18 For instance at Windsor, where the 'Holistic Admission Process' assesses candidates in light of their work experience, community involvement, personal accomplishments, career objectives and personal considerations in addition to previous university achievements and LSAT scores (see https://www.uwindsor.ca/law/343/our-admissions-criteria).

schools (for students, faculty, but mostly for scarce public funding) could foster a more innovative environment.

An historical review shows that lawyers regularly complain that law schools admit too many students, on the basis that many law graduates struggle to find articling positions or employment once admitted to the bar. Whether such perception truly comes from a 'numbers problem' or from the way in which the profession has organised and distributed the work among practitioners,[19] this trope highlights that gatekeeping is truly in the hands of law faculties.

Periods of economic downturn affect the availability of law jobs, including articling positions, at the national scale (e.g. in the late 2000s) or even more at the regional scale (e.g. in Alberta in the mid-2010s). While perennial, the recent iterations of this problem have led to innovations in the pathway to bar admission. In Alberta, for instance, it led to the possibility of 'composite articles': the required eight-month work experience can be completed by working in different settings for various lengths of time, including with interruptions in between each. In Ontario, it led the profession to seriously consider whether to abolish the articling requirement altogether or to make the LPP universal. Instead, the current compromise is the coexistence of several alternative pathways, including traditional articling, but also the LPP and IPC at two Ontario law schools.

In recent years, the FLSC has come to play an increasing role in gatekeeping. First, since 2015, qualifying law programmes for common law jurisdictions in Canada must comply with the FLSC's National Requirement; although much less detailed than the American Bar Association's (ABA) equivalent,[20] the former nonetheless imposes minimal admission requirements.[21] The National Requirement came about as new law schools were opening in the 2010s, a first since the 1970s, and as a complement to the lifting of most obstacles to lawyers' mobility across provinces. While the National Requirement concerning admission, length and format of study and other institutional elements were initially designed to preserve the status quo,[22] the FLSC has now entrenched its regulatory power in this area (although not uncontested) and could make changes in the future. Second, approximately 20% of newly admitted lawyers in Canada in recent years had earned their first law degree abroad. These candidates had to go through the assessment process set up by the NCA, which

---

19 See e.g. R.K. Wilkins, 'The Person You're Supposed to Become: The Politics of the Law School Experience' (1987) 45(1) *University of Toronto Faculty of Law Review* 98, 147; see also R.L. Abel, 'What Does and Should Influence the Number of Lawyers' (2012) 19(2–3) *International Journal of the Legal Profession* 131.

20 American Bar Association, *Standards and Rules of Procedure for Approval of Law Schools*, 2021–22 (ranging to approximately 124 pages compared to four in the Canadian equivalent).

21 FLSC, *National Requirement* (01.01.2018), https://flsc.ca/law-schools/.

22 FLSC, Task Force on the Canadian Common Law Degree, *Final Report* (10.2009), pp. 38–41, https://flsc-s3-storage-pub.s3.ca-central-1.amazonaws.com/Apprtaskforcereportoct2009.pdf.

is a branch of the FLSC. In 2015, for instance, the NCA approved 900 out of 1,700 applications.[23] The increased mobility of students and young professionals across provincial and international borders and the regulatory responses to such mobility (whether to genuinely protect the public against insufficiently competent lawyers or as a form of legal protectionism) have thus eroded Canadian law schools' previously unchallenged gatekeeping and carved out a solid role for the FLSC in this phenomenon.

The new role that the FLSC gave itself could have prevented innovation in the field regarding online legal education. Indeed, the National Requirement mandates that qualifying programmes consist 'primarily of in-person instruction and learning and/or instruction and learning that involves direct interaction between instructor and students'.[24] As interpreted by the NCA when assessing foreign-earned credentials, this rule means that a three-year programme must include at least one year of in-person instruction if the distant education component is interactive, and a minimum of two years in person otherwise. Prohibiting purely online programmes, even interactive or synchronous ones, created logistical and financial obstacles to innovation in this regard: any new law school willing to offer some form of online legal education needs to invest both in the physical facilities required for the substantial in-person components and in the online education infrastructure. On the other hand, one could think that the rule still provided ample room for existing law schools to experiment with chunks of online education in their curriculum. As we will see later, there had been hardly any steps in that direction before the pandemic.

Lastly, the 'numbers problem' and perceived oversupply of law graduates mentioned above concern large urban centres only. Indeed, in most rural areas lawyers are few and far between. Out of seven recent proposals for new law programmes (some now implemented, others abandoned or still in development), six featured arguments about preparing lawyers to work in rural areas.[25] Moreover, even in urban centres access to legal services remains difficult

---

23 Cambridge Professional Development, *Program Review of the National Committee on Accreditation for the Federation of Law Societies of Canada* (29.05.2017), https://flsc.ca/wp-content/uploads/2014/10/NCA-Program-Review-Report-FINAL-May-31-2017-GenDistRED.docx.pdf.

24 FLSC, *National Requirement* (2018), s. C.1.2; note that while the competencies requirements set by the FLSC derive from a study of the necessary knowledge and skills for entry-level lawyers, institutional requirements (among which features the 'in-person' item) are mainly based on preserving the status quo; see also FLSC, Task Force on the Canadian Common Law Degree, *Final Report* (10.2009), pp. 38–41, https://flsc-s3-storage-pub.s3.ca-central-1.amazonaws.com/Apprtaskforcereportoct2009.pdf.

25 Including at Lakehead University, Thompson Rivers University and the Nunavut law programme, all of which came to light in early 2010s, and at Université du Québec en Outaouais, opening in 2023; similar arguments were included in Trinity Western University's proposal, which did not succeed in establishing a new law school, and in Memorial University of Newfoundland's ongoing project. Among all the recent proposals, projects and newly established law schools, the only exception is that created at Toronto Metropolitan University, in downtown Toronto.

for a significant portion of the population due to financial obstacles, but also sometimes cultural and linguistic ones. Access to legal services is a key component of access to justice, and the public needs are far from met in this domain. If there is a need for more law schools in Canada, it is mostly to help provide legal professionals in low-density regions and for low-income communities. Physical presence in the target region or within the target communities seems crucial to foster connections likely to encourage graduates to stay and practise locally.

In short, the structure of university legal education in Canada does not promote experiments with online legal education.

2.2.2. Universities and Law Schools Funding

Despite sometimes omnipresent testimonies of gratitude toward private donors in certain law schools (e.g. classroom names, or even sometimes the name of the school itself), law schools in Canada form part of public universities and most of their revenues come from government funding and student fees.

Even as they are typically a distinct academic unit within their university, law faculties are financially integrated within them. This means that central university administrations receive public funding and tuition fees and redistribute them across their different units. Law faculties generate and retain only a small portion of their budget on their own, through tuition add-ons specific to the law programmes or private fundraising from alumni or wealthy law firms.

All universities offering qualifying law programmes are public institutions. This means that they do not aim to make profits and are largely funded by governments. However, the share of government revenues in universities' budgets across Canada has shrunk steadily over the past decades. On average, government funding amounted to over 70% of Canadian universities' revenues in the early 1980s; nowadays, the same source represents just over 45%.[26] While this number may remain high in comparison with many other jurisdictions, the sharp decline in just a few decades has not been painless for Canadian higher education institutions, and may very well have impaired their ability to invest in pedagogic innovation.

In order to make up for this sharp decline in public revenues, universities have had to increasingly rely on private revenues. Student fees are the source that most grew in proportion within universities' budget over the same period, rising from less than 10% of universities' revenues in the early 1980s to more than 25% nowadays.

The cost of tuition varies greatly across Canada and across universities. In Quebec, tuition fees are set by the provincial government close to

26 H.W. Arthurs, 'The Political Economy of Canadian Legal Education' (1998) 25(1) *Journal of Law & Society* 24, 28; Statistics Canada, *Table 37-10-0110-01* 'University revenues by source, as a percentage of total revenue' (2019), https://doi.org/10.25318/3710011001-eng.

CA$3,800 per year for undergraduate law programmes. In other provinces, each university sets its own tuitions fees, usually within some parameters determined by the province. Moreover, several universities apply some fees specific to the law programme on top of the normal tuition rate based on law students' greater capacity to obtain loans for their education as their expected income once in professional life is higher than for most other fields of undergraduate study. The Canadian average tuition for undergraduate law programmes is around CA$17,000, with more than a fourfold difference between the lowest (CA$8,150) and the highest (CA$34,800).

The above figures are for local students. International students face much higher tuition fees in the same programmes: slightly under twice as much in most common law provinces and a staggering 7.4 times higher in Quebec. However, international students represent only a near-negligible percentage of undergraduate law students across Canada.

As public funding has decreased, tuition fees have increased steadily across the country since the 1990s. For instance, in Ontario, average tuition costs for undergraduate law programmes have nearly doubled in the past 15 years. As qualifying law programmes generally require three years of full-time studies, composed of two terms each, students usually work during summers but have had to increasingly rely on debt to finance their education. As of 2015, 69% of law students graduated owing more than CA$30,000 in debt either to government-sponsored student loans or other sources.[27] The median debt owed at the time of graduation was CA$60,000.

This level of debt can explain in part several attitudes on the part of students. First, the pursuit of private practice jobs in large firm settings upon graduation, where salaries are notably higher than in public service or solo practice. This fuels the perception of an oversupply of lawyers even when access to legal services remains difficult for a large part of the population (see above). Second, a somewhat consumerist attitude of students toward law schools, characterised by expectations on the part of students as to what the law school offers in connection with the high price of attending.

Law schools have also relied on fundraising campaigns to finance specific infrastructure projects (e.g. renovating their building) or when changes in government policies made cuts to public funding suddenly acute. This has been more possible for law schools than other academic units of the universities thanks to the relatively higher socio-economic status of many law graduates willing to engage in philanthropic giving to their *alma mater* or local law school.

Since the 1970s, and even more so since the early 2010s, law schools have come under increasing pressure from diverse stakeholders to provide experiential

---

27 Statistics Canada, *Table 31-10-0200-01* 'Student debt of postsecondary graduates from all sources, by province of study, level of study, field of study and sex' (2020), https://doi.org/10.25318/3710020001-eng.

learning opportunities so that their students can develop practical skills as well as theoretical understanding in the field of law. Experiential learning takes to the form of clinics (where students work with, and sometimes represent, actual clients under the supervision of a licensed instructor), moot court competitions (usually involving preparation of written and oral submissions on a hypothetical case and a series of pleading matches against other teams), externships (work placement with a legal professional, like a prosecutor or a judge), or even practical courses in negotiation and mediation. Because they require more intense teaching and learning on an individual basis, experiential learning opportunities weigh more heavily in law schools' budgets than the traditional combination of large groups in lecture halls (typically in the first year and for required upper-year courses) and smaller seminar-style classes (typically for optional upper-year courses).

On the eve of the pandemic, most Canadian law schools did not have much leeway to make large investments in personnel or equipment in order to adapt to a new mode of teaching. They mostly coasted on existing pedagogies, with innovation taking the form of mostly marginal tweaks.

2.3. ACCESS TO IT EQUIPMENT AND ADOPTION OF TECHNOLOGY

Canada is a developed country with generally very good access to high-quality IT. Nearly all Canadian households have internet access at home. However, average figures hide significant disparities between rural and urban areas, and also between socio-economic groups.

As of 2019, 87.4% of Canadians enjoyed the minimal connection speeds (50 Mbps download/10 Mbps upload, or 50/10) recognised as adequate to fully engage in online activities, including online learning and video-conferences; only 45.6% of rural households had the same access, compared to 98.6% for urban households. The rate was even lower among Indigenous communities: 34.8%.[28] Moreover, among households in the lowest quartile for revenues, 63% had less than one connecting device in the home per family member and 24.1% only used mobile devices (smartphones or tablets) to access internet resources (compared to 8% in the highest quartile).[29] In short, despite the overall good

---

28 Canadian Radio-television and Telecommunications Commission, *Communications Monitoring Report* (2020), https://crtc.gc.ca/eng/publications/reports/policyMonitoring/2020/cmr4.htm.

29 Innovation, Science and Economic Development Canada, *High-Speed Access For All: Canada's Connectivity Strategy* (2019), p. 5, https://www.ic.gc.ca/eic/site/139.nsf/vwapj/ISEDC_19-170_Connectivity_Strategy_E_Web.pdf/$file/ISEDC_19-170_Connectivity_Strategy_E_Web.pdf; Statistics Canada, *COVID-19 Pandemic: School Closures and the*

connectivity to IT in Canada, disadvantaged segments of the population do not have access to the infrastructure or the devices to fully engage in online learning activities.

The price for home and mobile internet services at the mentioned speed in Canada is much higher than in most developed countries.[30] The average monthly price for a 50/10, unlimited internet plan was around CA$69 in 2019, and ranges from CA$40 to CA$140 depending on the region and the service provider; unlimited data plans were not available in a number of low-density areas, including the territories in Canada's North.[31]

It is fair to assume that the above portrait applies to university students.[32] University teachers on the other hand all have access to an individual computer and high-speed internet provided by their employers, at least on campus. Nearly all classrooms are equipped with a computer and projector; however, only a small number of classrooms were equipped with cameras and microphones allowing for live exchanges between those inside and those outside of the physical classroom.

While mastery of information technology is now part of the national competency standard set by the FLSC,[33] the level of IT to which legal professionals have access and the extent to which they adopt it in their practice varies according to the practice setting. Nearly all legal professionals routinely used basic technology such as communicating by e-mails and conducting legal research in online databases before the pandemic. Only the large law firms had started using emerging legal technology such as management systems (e.g. for potential conflicts of interests) and automated task systems (e.g. AI for document review). Use of IT in the administration of courts (e.g. scheduling, filing of

---

Online Preparedness of Children (15.04.2020), https://www150.statcan.gc.ca/n1/pub/45-28-0001/2020001/article/00001-fra.htm; Statistics Canada, *Canadians' Well-being in Year One of the COVID-19 Pandemic* (15.04.2021), https://www150.statcan.gc.ca/n1/pub/75f0002m/75f0002m2021003-eng.htm.

30 Wall Communications Inc., *2019 Price Comparison Study of Telecommunications Services in Canada and with Foreign Jurisdictions*, https://www.ic.gc.ca/eic/site/693.nsf/eng/00182.html.

31 Canadian Radio-television and Telecommunications Commission, *2019 Year-End Monthly Prices for Internet, Mobile, Landline and TV Services* (2020), https://crtc.gc.ca/eng/publications/reports/policyMonitoring/2020/cmr5.htm#a2.

32 See also Top Hat, 'Lessons From a Year of Pandemic Learning: Survey of 3,052 Higher Ed Students Reveals Their Expectations for Instruction and Educational Value in the Fall 2021 Academic Term' (30.04.2021), https://tophat.com/press-releases/lessons-from-pandemic-learning-survey/ (reporting that 27% of students missed the internet and computer access provided by their university on campus, based on a survey of 3,000+ university students in Canada and the United States); V. Sutton, 'Perceptions of Online Learning and COVID-19 Countermeasures Among Law Students in a One-year Follow-up Study' (2021), https://ssrn.com/abstract=3865262 (reporting that 40% of surveyed law students declared in May 2020 that their home internet connection was not reliable).

33 FLSC, *Model Code of Professional Conduct* (19.10.2019), Art. 3.1–2 (commentary 4A–4B), https://flsc.ca/national-initiatives/model-code-of-professional-conduct/.

documents, payment of fees) and in court proceedings (e.g. remote hearings) remained very sparse before the pandemic.

Very few courses in law schools across the country focus on teaching how to best use technology in legal services beyond basic legal research in online databases (e.g. e-discovery and e-litigation). The two newest law schools in Canada stand out, as one requires all its students to take several courses related to digital technology literacy,[34] and the other includes mastering the digital resources specific to the practice of law in its learning objectives.[35]

3. MOVES TOWARDS ONLINE EDUCATION

3.1. SUMMARY ACHIEVEMENTS BEFORE THE PANDEMIC

3.1.1. Online University Legal Education before the Pandemic

Before 2020, online education was nearly absent in Canadian law schools. By design, it existed only at the margins of qualifying law programmes.

The FLSC requires qualifying programmes to consist 'primarily of in-person instruction and learning and/or instruction and learning that involves direct interaction between instructor and students'.[36] While this leaves some room for experimentation in Canadian law schools, none has come even close to this mark.

Prior to the pandemic, a handful of law schools had implemented pedagogical designs that required no presence on site, but those were restricted to programmes other than their initial qualifying degree programme. For instance, UBC Law's Online Learning programme offered some of the foundational courses required for JD students (public law, criminal law, tort law, property law, administrative law, contracts, business organisations); these courses, however, were only open to foreign-trained lawyers seeking to fulfil the topics that the NCA had assigned to them in order to obtain accreditation. JD students at UBC Law could not earn credits toward their degree from any of these online courses online even as this option was open to LLM students. A different law school, Osgoode Hall, also offered online options aimed at NCA candidates, LLM students and professionals seeking continuing legal education and professional development but did not make them available to its own JD students. In Quebec,

34 Toronto Metropolitan University's JD's programme includes the following required courses: Technology Innovation Intensive, Coding Intensive, Data, Code and Social Innovation, Access to Justice and Technology.

35 Université du Québec en Outaouais, see 'Baccalauréat en droit, Compétence visées par le programme', https://etudier.uqo.ca/programmes/8308.

36 FLSC, *National Requirement* (2018), s. C.1.2.

a similar trend could be observed: for example, Université Laval offered short undergraduate programmes in law for future legal technicians but would not recognise credits thus earned toward a LLB degree. Moreover, some universities also offered online law courses in non-law specific programmes.

In sum, while they were starting to embrace the possibility of online education in a variety of programmes, including non-qualifying undergraduate programmes, re-qualifying bridge programmes, graduate programmes and non-law degrees, Canadian law schools willingly and specifically excluded online education from the initial qualifying education of future lawyers. This was despite the interactive possibilities of modern online education and the possibility to experiment with it under the FLSC National Requirement for approved law degrees. Although absent at the institutional level, elements of online or hybrid pedagogy were nonetheless implemented by individual instructors as part of their regular pedagogies or ad hoc initiatives (flipped classrooms,[37] co-teaching through video-conferences,[38] etc.). This is in addition to the well-established presence of digital technologies in support of in-person education (e-mail communication, digital readings, online legal research, intentional use of digital technologies to enhance in-person classroom experience, etc.).

Online education was however more systematically present in a law student's journey to admission at later stages. First of all, for those opting for the LPP at Toronto Metropolitan University: the programme consists in 17 weeks of training, including 14 taking place online in an interactive format and three separate weeks occurring in person, before a 16-week work placement. The training part consists in immersion in a simulated online law firm.

Second, several provincial law societies' admission programmes consisted at least in part of online modules for students-at-law to complete during their articling period. In particular, four provinces (Alberta, Saskatchewan, Manitoba, Nova Scotia) relied on the Canadian Centre for Professional Legal Education's (CPLED) Practice Readiness Education Program as an admission course; this programme lasts about 300 hours over a nine-month period and takes place mostly online except for two four-day sessions (about 25% of the total hours). The remaining law societies, including the large *Barreau du Québec*, offered no portion of their respective admission course in an online format or did not administer an admission course, such as in Ontario.

Post-law school pre-admission education thus existed in online formats in several parts of the country before the pandemic, but it concerned only a

37 See e.g. P. Sankoff, 'Taking the Instruction of Law Outside the Classroom: How the Flipped Classroom Can Make Learning More Productive and Enjoyable (for Professors and Students)' (2014) 51(4) *Alberta Law Review* 891.

38 See e.g. D. Harris et al., '"Community without Propinquity": Teaching Legal History Intercontinentally' (1999) 10(1) *Legal Education Review* 1; B. Atwood et al., 'Franchir Les Limites de la Salle de Classe: Une Expérience en Droit Comparé de la Famille' (2008) 24(1) *Canadian Journal of Family Law* 65.

minority of aspiring lawyers. Indeed, less than 20% of new lawyers in Canada every year went through the CPLED and only about 10% of new Ontario lawyers went through the LPP instead of the traditional articling experience.

3.1.2. *Online Continuing (Post-Admission) Legal Education before the Pandemic*

Canadian law societies require registered lawyers to complete a minimum number of hours of continuing legal education every year (12–15 depending on the province, including 1.5–2 in ethics and professional responsibility). Several methods can be employed to meet this requirement, ranging from attending courses or conferences to teaching or even publishing books or articles. Some eligible events are organised by law societies themselves, while events organised by third parties (e.g. academic conferences) can also be recognised. This system has been in place for about a decade in most Canadian jurisdictions and is currently under review, at least in Ontario, where it does not seem to have reduced the amount of claims against lawyers.[39]

Before the pandemic, a number of continuing legal education opportunities were already offered remotely. Some law societies and other providers (e.g. Osgoode Hall Professional Development) had already built a virtual library of content (e.g. archived recordings) and regularly offered live events to this end (e.g. webinars).

Interestingly, the interactive aspect discussed above for initial legal education finds an echo in this section as well. The Law Society of Ontario capped to 50% (six hours) the amount of continuing legal education hours that could be completed in a format that did not include interactions with colleagues (e.g. watching an archived programme on one's own rather than attending a live event in person or by video-conference). Similarly, the Law Society of British Columbia specified that reading or reviewing recorded material on one's own ('self-study') did not count toward meeting the required hours.

3.2. ACHIEVEMENTS AND CHALLENGES AFTER THE PANDEMIC

3.2.1. *Continuing Legal Education*

Lawyers in diverse situations faced a wide range of challenges through the pandemic. Many in private practice saw a sharp decline in business, especially

[39] See e.g. Law Society of Ontario, Competence Task Force, *Renewing the Law Society's Continuing Competence Framework* (23.06.2021), https://lawsocietyontario.azureedge.net/media/lso/media/about/convocation/2021/convocation-june-2021-competence-taskforce-report.pdf.

in the first few months of the pandemic, or had to curtail their hours for other reasons (e.g. more caregiving responsibilities at home with the closure of schools). On the other hand, many others worked (and billed) significantly more hours than in previous years. This is why some law societies adopted provisional measures to allow affected individuals to defer or decrease annual fees owed to them.

In response to the varying challenges faced by lawyers across Canada, most law societies also made temporary changes to their continuing legal education requirements. These changes intended to recognise that lawyers, like all members of society, faced new pressing concerns and challenges in their professional and personal lives when the pandemic hit; they also allowed the law societies themselves to focus their time and resources on addressing new challenges in regulating the disrupted practice of law. In some provinces, all continuing legal education requirements were temporarily lifted (e.g. Alberta, New Brunswick); a few others made no official changes. In addition, between the two ends of this spectrum, some adapted the requirements to make them easier to comply with in the circumstances. For instance, Ontario temporarily lifted the restriction on self-study or watching recorded materials on one's own (previously capped at 50% of eligible hours). In addition, some law societies lifted registration fees for the events or content they offered. Generally, all law societies strived to make continuing legal education content and opportunities more accessible online.

3.2.2. University Qualifying Legal Education

During the pandemic, all law schools in Canada turned primarily, and most often exclusively, to online delivery to offer their programmes. The switch was sudden in March 2020 as the authorities across the provinces took drastic measures to fight the pandemic. This occurred as the winter/spring 2020 term was underway (from early January to late April). In most universities, all courses were suspended for a week or two in order to let students and teachers adjust their personal lives (e.g. closure of university residences and schools) and prepare to finish the term and examinations remotely.

Most teachers faced new challenges at home as they had to juggle caregiving and schooling responsibilities for their own children, the continued presence of family members in the home-turned-office, increased demand on their home internet capacities, and so forth. Many did not have good-quality webcams and microphones at home. In addition to these widespread challenges, the near-universal lack of prior exposure, training or practice with online pedagogy left law professors also wholly unprepared for transitioning to an online format. This was a consequence of the general lack of innovation for decades in the delivery of university legal education across Canada. Thus, each individual teacher finished the term as they could through a diversity of delivery methods, including live video lectures and guided readings, depending on what they could achieve.

At that time, few institutions, if any, imposed rules as to the modes of delivery. Teachers also modified as they saw fit the assessment methods in light of the disruption to the course.

Universities made significant changes to their grading policies for the winter/spring 2020 term. Whereas law students were typically graded on an alphabetical scale (A+, A, A-, B+, B, B-, etc.), and whereas in most law schools there were rules as to the distribution of the grades within the group (through bell-curve distribution or imposed average), nearly all law schools adopted some variation of a Pass/Fail or Credit/No Credit grading scheme for the winter/spring 2020 term. The details of the policy greatly varied from one institution to the next, as to whether the Pass/Fail scheme was imposed on all students or optional for students who opted for it, and that in latter case as to when students had to make that choice (i.e. before taking the exams, soon after writing it or even after reviewing their final grade for the course). Such variation shows the absence of an established standard or even data pointing to best practices in this regard, thus leaving each group of university administrators to design what they saw as the best policy in the circumstances based on their own intuitions.

Universities' main motivation was to ensure greater fairness among students in light of the pandemic, as many new burdens could impact students' academic performance (illness, relocation in a living space with suboptimal study conditions, new caregiving responsibilities, financial stress, mental health challenges, and so forth) and would be unevenly distributed among all students. While well intentioned, such policies were received differently across the student population. In particular, students from communities historically underrepresented in the legal professions feared that the absence of grades would harm their professional prospects as employers would revert to making hiring decisions on the basis of social capital rather than academic merit.[40] This fear was heightened in situations where the schools did not impose a universal switch to the Pass/Fail grading scheme but let students choose to opt in or out of it; in such cases, students whose grades were neither at the top nor at the bottom of their school's ranking were left to guess whether future employers would look at a chosen Pass grade as hiding a poor performance. Despite ample evidence to the contrary,[41] grades are largely perceived as a neutral and commensurable way to signal academic merit. In the legal environment in particular, law school grades play a major role in sorting students for the benefit of potential employers in a very competitive market, but also for scholarship committees and other academic institutions.

---

40 J. Bliss and D. Sandomierski, 'Learning Without Grade Anxiety: Lessons from the Pass/Fail Grading Experiment in North American JD Programs' (2022) 48 *Ohio Northern University Law Review* 555.

41 See e.g. S.D. Blum (ed.), *Ungrading: Why Rating Students Undermines Learning (and What to Do Instead)*, West Virginia University Press, Morgantown 2020.

For the 2020/21 academic year, law schools largely reinstated their usual grading policies. Rather than the unexpected shortcomings of the Pass/Fail schemes mentioned above, the main reason for this was the sentiment that as universities had announced well in advance that the year would take place primarily online, on the whole students had had time to adjust their living and study conditions accordingly. Unforeseen changes such as illness could be handled on an individual basis with the usual accommodation mechanisms. Most law schools maintained much lighter changes to their policies, such as postponing by several weeks the deadline to withdraw from a course without a failing grade or even the possibility to apply the Pass/Fail grading scheme to a single course.

Online education remained the primary modality in all Canadian law schools throughout 2020–21. In a majority of law schools, all teaching activities took place online; nonetheless, a few of them attempted to maintain some in-person teaching.

The few law schools that took this route prioritised their efforts on offering an in-person experience to first-year students. This took the form of convening small groups of students in large classrooms where sufficient distancing was possible, with the option for students to attend remotely. Depending on the size of the groups (which vary in each law school according to the total size of the cohort and the number of sections offered for the same course), in-person attendance was offered to all students (e.g. Western, Queen's) or to a smaller group on a rotating basis (e.g. UBC, Université de Montréal). In the latter cases, the design was for hybrid courses allowing equal participation from students whether they were on site or attending remotely. The first year of law school is commonly perceived as foundational not only in terms of the knowledge it imparts, but also on the socialisation of students into the legal community. The first year of law school is key for students to form friendships and networks that will help them acquire the social norms of the legal community as well as overcome the challenges of the demanding curriculum. This is what students missed the most in their online legal education in 2020–21.[42] Moreover, law schools are more willing to invest significant resources for first-year students (e.g. to plan and deliver even limited in-person options), in part because they are already subject to a competitive admission process to enter the programme and very few of them will fail or drop out.[43]

In very rare instances, some schools attempted to maintain other in-person teaching activities; the target activities were never mandatory courses and

---

42 See A. Habermacher and S. Giwa, 'Online legal education: empirical findings regarding the development of professional competencies and professional identity in the Fall 2020' (unpublished to date, submitted to the FLSC National Requirement Review Committee in January 2023).

43 The very high tuition fees at several law schools may also fuel the sentiment that students are akin to clients whose satisfaction is a high priority.

concerned mainly pleadings in preparation for moot court competitions and clinical placements.

All in-person experiments had to stop through the fall term as new cases soared again across the country and severe public health restrictions were reinstated. All schools thus conducted nearly all teaching activities online for most of the 2020/21 year.

Regarding the pedagogies deployed by law teachers in 2020–21, those varied greatly according to the teacher and the nature of the course: live lectures, Socratic questioning, interactive activities with small or large groups, recorded video or audio materials, guided readings, etc. While pedagogies were far from uniform before the pandemic, except perhaps in first-year courses where variations of the Socratic method are still often in use, the online format led most teachers to experiment with new strategies rather than simply delivering their usual teaching through video. The only common feature across the range of practices is that courses were never purely asynchronous: they all retained regular synchronous interactions between teacher and students in one form or another, usually through video. Thus, even when teachers relied on pre-recorded material to convey information, they also met with students on a weekly basis for other learning activities (e.g. using the flipped classroom model).

In most cases, synchronous lectures were recorded and made available to students until the end of the term. This was meant to accommodate not only the technological difficulties one could experience during these periods but also other challenges that could impact focus or even attendance.

All universities offered opportunities to their personnel to educate themselves on online pedagogies in the summer of 2020, for instance through presentations by and exchanges with education and technology experts. Some law schools set up internal committees to help teachers design and implement adequate pedagogies. A 'Redesign for online' course designed for law teachers across the country was also offered online by Osgoode Hall Law School.[44] There were however major obstacles to an optimal experience with online education. First, rare were the law teachers in Canada who had previously taught or taken a course even partially online. They had thus no point of reference in terms of best practices for it. A few law teachers had experimented with some forms of online pedagogies even as they also taught in person (e.g. pre-recorded video modules for flipped classroom pedagogy) and a few had been involved in the rare non-qualifying programmes offered online; those teachers had usually been eager to share their experience before the pandemic.[45] A small amount of

44 See A. Fried, 'Using a Community of Inquiry Framework to make the Transition to Teaching Law Online' (2021) 70(2–3) *Journal of Legal Education* 274.

45 See e.g. P. Sankoff, 'Taking the Instruction of Law Outside the Lecture Hall: How the Flipped Classroom Can Make Learning More Productive and Enjoyable (for Professors and Students)' (2014) 51(4) *Alberta Law Review* 891; several presentations by F. Brochu on the

research had also already been published on Canadian law students' attitudes toward online technology in legal education.[46] However, their audience was limited by the perception that such practices were marginal and deemed to remain so. Second, the pandemic has been perceived as a parenthesis at the end of which old habits could resume with in-person teaching. This could have limited the investment of time in training, design and implementation that some teachers were willing to do for the 2020/21 year. Note however that many teachers discovered pedagogical tools and strategies due to the online context that they would like to deploy in the future even in non-online courses.[47]

Overall, law schools made no major changes to their curricula in 2020/21. Only on very rare occasions did law schools temporarily lift some requirements in their programmes, for instance for an oral advocacy class if it was deemed that this course could not be effectively delivered online. They also continued to offer experiential opportunities such as moot court competitions, clinical placements, and even field courses,[48] even as those were overwhelmingly conducted online as well.

The aspect of the typical law school experience that was most impacted was the social element. Law school in Canada is oriented, even if implicitly, as much toward the acquisition of legal knowledge as toward the development of social skills and attitudes specific to the legal community. As lawyers form a profession, a distinct social group in society, legal education is the cradle of the professionalisation of future members, i.e. their socialisation into the norms of the legal community. While most schools and student associations attempted to offer social events, conferences, networking opportunities and the like, which normally take place in person, online interactions by nature feel curated and impersonal. In addition, with all learning opportunities happening online and from home, attending social events in the same conditions did not give students the flavour of novelty and relaxation compared to the rest of the experience.

---

topic in 2018 and 2019 (see https://www.fd.ulaval.ca/notre-faculte/repertoire-du-personnel/francois-brochu).

46 See R. Jochelson and D. Ireland, 'Law Students' Responses to Innovation: A Study of Perspectives in Respect of Digital Knowledge Transmission, Flipped Classrooms, Video Capsules and Others Means of Classroom Dissemination' (2018) 41(1) *Manitoba Law Journal* 131; R. Jochelson, J. Gacek and D. Ireland, 'Reconsidering Legal Pedagogy: Assessing: Assessing Trigger Warnings, Evaluative instruments, and Articling Integration in Canada's Modern Law School Curricula' (2021) 44(2) *Manitoba Law Journal* 87.

47 A. Fried, 'Lessons from Online Pandemic Pedagogy in North American Law Schools: Toward Law Student Wellbeing' in E. Jones and C. Stevens (eds), *Wellbeing and Transitions in Law: Legal Education and the Legal Profession*, Palgrave Macmillan, London (forthcoming).

48 See e.g. Canadian Urban Institute, 'The Non-field Field School: Community-Immersed Learning in COVID times' (28.10.2021), https://www.youtube.com/watch?v=FFiZkeAGmdc (University of Victoria's law school's Indigenous-focused field school experience during the pandemic).

Lastly, law students' mental health deserves some mention here. Law schools had started to acknowledge the widespread mental health issues among law students prior to the pandemic, fostered in part by the competitive atmosphere, demanding curriculum in law school and some pedagogies themselves. Mental health issues are also widespread among lawyers more generally.[49] The pandemic has heightened them since March 2020 as students faced new worries about their health and that of their loved ones, social isolation, financial stress in the short term (as many could not work during the summer as initially planned) and in the long term (worse job prospects due to the state of the economy), as well as screen exhaustion. Some schools attempted to adapt their course schedule and organise events in order to alleviate some of these difficulties; the results were sometimes counterproductive, for instance as mandated screen breaks could be perceived as wasted time during which no real relaxing or productive activities could take place.[50]

During the 2021/22 year, more schools were able to offer more in-person learning for longer periods, although all remained subject to changing circumstances. All had to contend with at least a few weeks of online teaching, whether they had hoped to teach entirely in person for the whole year or whether they had planned a gradual return to pre-pandemic modalities. In all cases, in-person activities remained heavily affected by the pandemic, as masking, physical distancing, vaccine requirements and other protective measures were in place. For many, the 2021/22 year illustrated that short periods of online teaching are now part of the universities' toolkits to respond to extenuating circumstances, including but perhaps not limited to public health conditions. It is further evidence that online teaching has become part of the modalities of legal education and will remain so after the pandemic subsides, even if compelled and in small doses; the hybridity slider has moved and legal educators must continue to develop their abilities to offer quality teaching in such circumstances for the long term instead of longing for the good old times, in the hope that they will soon merely wake up from a bad dream.

---

49 See e.g. I. Reid, *Survey of Lawyers on Wellness Issues* (2012), https://www.cba.org/CBAMediaLibrary/cba_na/PDFs/CBA%20Wellness%20PDFs/FINAL-Report-on-Survey-of-Lawyers-on-Wellness-Issues.pdf and N. Cadieux et al., *Research report (preliminary version): Towards a Healthy and Sustainable Practice of Law in Canada National Study on the Psychological Health Determinants of Legal Professionals in Canada, Phase I (2020–2022)*, Université de Sherbrooke, 2022, https://flsc.ca/wp-content/uploads/2022/10/EN_Preliminary-report_Cadieux-et-al_Universite-de-Sherbrooke_FINAL.pdf.

50 See A. Habermacher and S. Giwa, 'Online legal education: empirical findings regarding the development of professional competencies and professional identity in the Fall 2020' (unpublished to date, submitted to the FLSC National Requirement Review Committee in January 2023).

4. CONCLUSIONS

4.1. LESSONS LEARNED FROM THE SHIFT TO ONLINE LEGAL EDUCATION

The shift to online legal education as a result of the pandemic has been a journey of contrasts. It has undoubtedly questioned long-held assumptions in legal education and forced many to experiment with tools and pedagogies that they had no previous exposure to; it has also been marked by challenges and accentuated many concerns. While it is still too early to draw definitive conclusions from this unprecedented experience in Canadian legal education, especially as research findings on the phenomenon take time to come out and percolate, I will venture this treacherous exercise here.

First of all, one needs to keep in mind that online academic legal education set up in the first few weeks of the pandemic was an emergency solution to salvage the then-ongoing activities and avoid either cancelling the spring 2020 term altogether or bestowing credits when only half the intended learning had taken place. In the same vein, online education throughout the 2020/21 academic year (and onward in some places) was a temporary solution as well. University legal educators expected activities to go back to in-person formats within a few months; despite their best intentions to provide quality education at all times, they most often altered their usual ways of doing things as little as possible rather than reinventing curricula and pedagogies as they would if online education had been perceived to be the new norm for the long term.

Second, the conditions surrounding online education were far from ideal for instructors and students alike: legal prohibitions on physical gatherings, interruption of children's schooling, confinements in small quarters, worries about one's own and one's loved ones' health (to name only a few) made it much harder than would otherwise be the case to work and study online and to live a healthy and social life outside of classes. Ideal online education is very different from emergency or temporary variations on this idea. All these factors need to stay top of mind when assessing the outcomes of online legal education since early 2020.

For instance, online education is often thought to be a promising way to close the gap in access to education. Freedom from the necessity for students to find accommodation in expensive urban areas close to their law school, the possibility to remain close to their pre-law support network of family and friends, greater flexibility to reconcile part-time work and family life with law school: given all of these factors, one might think that students from marginalised communities, lower socio-economic backgrounds and mature students had the most to benefit from online legal education. However, they were more adversely affected by the pandemic situation than their peers as many businesses providing part-time work opportunities closed their doors, all members of the household spent all day in the same crowded dwelling, being geographically close to loved ones meant nothing when social gatherings were banned, and so forth. In addition, the same law students, who are also often the first in their family to attend law school, could no longer benefit from socialisation into the legal community and networking with peers and future employers to make up the gap in cultural capital that distinguishes them from more fortunate peers. As counterintuitive as it may seem, similar lessons emerged from the well-intentioned changes to grading schemes in the early stages of the pandemic.[51]

Furthermore, mental health is notably worse among law students and lawyers than the general population[52] and the pandemic further worsened this dimension of wellbeing across all segments of society.[53] In these circumstances, it is not surprising that many, regardless of their background, had a negative experience with online legal education. If we filter out reasons unrelated to the online character of education itself, i.e. the sources of discontentment having more to do with the pandemic situation and public health restrictions, the opinions are less critical. It is most surprising that even in such circumstances, some students and educators thrived.[54] This ambivalent picture reminds us that learning styles and preferences can vary greatly even within the legal community, and that legal education could gain from offering a variety of options for students to become competent lawyers.

4.2. FUTURE PROSPECTS FOR ONLINE LEGAL EDUCATION IN CANADA

First of all, the online character of legal education is a variable on a spectrum and will never be a binary proposition. Pre-COVID-19, education was already hybrid as it included some online components, even as innocuous as e-mail

51 J. Bliss and D. Sandomierski, 'Learning Without Grade Anxiety: Lessons from the Pass/Fail Grading Experiment in North American JD Programs' (2022) 48 *Ohio Northern University Law Review* 555.

52 S. Nemeth, 'Addressing the Elephant in the Legal Profession: The Lawyer's Struggle with Mental Health' (2019) *Saskatchewan Law Review Comments*, https://sasklawreview.ca/comment/addressing-the-elephant-in-the-legal-profession-the-lawyers-struggle-with-mental-heath-.php.

53 Statistics Canada, 'Self-perceived mental health and mental health case needs during the COVID-19 pandemic' (08.09.2021), https://www150.statcan.gc.ca/n1/pub/45-28-0001/2021001/article/00031-eng.htm.

54 A. Habermacher and S. Giwa, 'Online legal education: empirical findings regarding the development of professional competencies and professional identity in the Fall 2020' (unpublished to date, submitted to the FLSC National Requirement Review Committee in January 2023).

communications and the availability of readings online. During the pandemic, the hybridity slider moved sharply upwards, with almost everything happening online.[55] As the public health situation improves and has become more stable, the slider has come back down, close to its initial position, at least in the short term. The lessons from the forced and temporary experience with universal online teaching during the pandemic will take some time to percolate and bring durable changes to legal education in Canada.

Many educators intend to retain some of the pedagogical techniques they deployed for online education even when returning to in-person teaching.[56] Institutional and individual inertia, and perhaps some good reasons too, nevertheless caused all law schools in Canada to largely return to old practices as soon as possible. No existing law school will start offering a significant portion of its JD programme online in the short term after the pandemic. While the FLSC would allow up to one year out of three to take place online in the current regulatory framework, it is questionable if the investment would be worthwhile for what might appear to be a small difference with competitors. Moreover, the FLSC has now established its authority on the regulation of qualifying programmes in common law Canada, and it is unimaginable that a new school could open for that market without its approval.[57] The conversation on the future of online university legal education in Canada will thus need to happen at the FLSC level. The FLSC will undoubtedly observe with attention developments in the United States (unaccredited fully online JD programmes or accredited programmes happening primarily online with some in-person activities throughout the course of studies) and research findings from the pandemic period. There is already evidence that the FLSC is reconsidering its requirement regarding mode of study in Canadian common law programmes, but at the time of writing the outcome remains unknown.[58]

In each individual law school, the slider will move slightly, with some courses to be delivered online on an ad hoc basis: for instance, to accommodate a faculty member for medical reasons, to avoid cancelling classes when the instructor has

---

[55] I thank Professor David Thomson, Sturm College of Law, University of Denver, for the helpful slider metaphor ('The Future is Hybrid: Actually, It Already Is', keynote address delivered online at UNSW Legal Education Research Conference, 26.11.2021).

[56] A. Fried, 'Lessons from Online Pandemic Pedagogy in North American Law Schools: Toward Law Student Wellbeing' in E. Jones and C. Stevens (eds), *Wellbeing and Transitions in Law: Legal Education and the Legal Profession*, Palgrave Macmillan, London (forthcoming).

[57] FLSC's approval is required, but not sufficient, as testifies the fate of Trinity Western University's proposed law school; see *Trinity Western University v. Law Society of Upper Canada*, 2018 SCC 33.

[58] FLSC, 'Communiqué: Update on Review of National Requirement' (27.02.2023), https://flsc.ca/wp-content/uploads/2023/03/National-Requirement-2.pdf (indicating 'mode of study provisions – how much in-person instruction is required' as the no.1 priority in the ongoing review of the National Requirement).

to travel during the term or even to bring in experts who live far away without the cost of travel. This will probably affect first-year activities the least, as they are considered the bedrock of legal education, where Socratic interactions and networking set law students on the right track to becoming lawyers.[59]

Physical presence in the same space seems to be most valuable in legal education for the social professionalisation of future lawyers. In-person education does not seem to be demonstrably better at developing students' legal knowledge and technical skills;[60] however, it matters greatly to form networks of peers and pass on the implicit norms of the profession. First-generation law students and those from disadvantaged backgrounds may benefit the most from these aspects of the typical law school experience, even as it can create an alienating experience for some. While all law programmes would help these students succeed by making explicit the otherwise implicit goals and norms they aim to impart to them, law schools considering significant online components in their curriculum would have to pay the most attention to such elements of their students' experience.

Today, the most blatant needs for legal education in Canada are with regards to rural areas and marginalised communities; some law schools have decided to focus on addressing these needs. The physical distance that is characteristic of online education would run counter to the objective of creating genuine and sustainable connections between law students and the communities they would aim to serve as practitioners. Other law schools primarily serve linguistic minorities.[61] For them, the physical presence of students in the same unilingual space and proximity with other community institutions is key to the sociolinguistic elements of their mission.[62] We can therefore also see that long-term online education may come with special challenges in the pursuit of certain law schools' social goals.

Paradoxically, the forced and universal experiment with online education in Canadian law schools serves to reveal the often-forgotten benefits of campus-based education, especially for social and linguistic considerations. On this front, as for other learning objectives, law schools need to examine what their priorities are and what the available literature tells us about the best methods to achieve them. Law schools making different choices as to where to allocate their

---

59 A. Habermacher and S. Giwa, 'Online legal education: empirical findings regarding the development of professional competencies and professional identity in the Fall 2020' (unpublished to date, submitted to the FLSC National Requirement Review Committee in January 2023).

60 A. Petzold, M.E. Deo and C. Christensen, *LSSSE 2022 Annual Report: Success With Online Education* (2022), https://lssse.indiana.edu/annual-results/ (measuring that online law students studying reported learning crucial legal skills at the same level as in-person students).

61 Moncton and uOttawa's JD programme in French serve primarily the French-speaking minorities outside of Quebec.

62 R. Landry, *Éducation postsecondaire bilingue et francophonie minoritaire*, Canadian Institute for Research on Linguistic Minorities, Moncton 2017.

resources and how much to hybridise their education offerings will reinforce Canadian legal education's ability to serve the needs of all segments of the population, as long as law schools' strategic choices are based on the best data and analysis on the effectiveness of different modalities of education to achieve specific goals.

We can imagine that in a majority of law schools, online components in the law school experience will increase over time after the expected post-pandemic *retour à la normale*. Research shows that 80% of those who experienced working from home during the pandemic would like to continue in that vein for at least half of their working hours.[63] There is thus a clear demand for possibilities to work, and study, at least in part remotely. Moreover, as law schools are now much better equipped with hardware allowing hybrid teaching experiences, they may be more willing, or even required, to offer this option on an ad hoc basis, for example to accommodate a student's inability to attend in-person classes due to a medical condition. A mainstream law school could even see an opportunity to distinguish itself and attract students (or even instructors) most interested in this possibility. Online education for one or two terms of studies could become a market positioning strategy for an innovative law school. While improbable in the current context, it may not be completely unrealistic in a few years if there is a clear advantage to gain from it.

Canadian law schools face a number of big challenges, and pedagogic innovation in the form of online or even digital-heavy teaching may not be on top of the list. The FLSC is in the process of revamping its competency profile, including defining in much greater detail the competencies it will require law graduates to demonstrate for admission to practise. This alone may force law schools to invest resources and focus their attention on addressing new requirements from the regulator, even as they are fighting the FLSC's attempts to play a greater role in setting law school curricula. Other pressing issues would have an equally significant impact on university legal education in Canada, such as whether the articling requirement will disappear or even whether a law school degree will remain a requirement to be admitted to the bar.[64] Those issues will probably weigh heavily on the ability and willingness of Canadian law schools to consider fully or partially online education as a possible modality to offer their services in the future.

In the field of continuing education, the outlooks are more favourable. Webinars and other online learning activities, synchronous or asynchronous,

---

63 Statistics Canada, T. Mehdi and R. Morissette, 'Working from home: Productivity and preferences' (01.04.2021), https://www150.statcan.gc.ca/n1/pub/45-28-0001/2021001/article/00012-eng.htm.

64 See e.g. J. Furlong, 'A Competence-Based System for Lawyer Licensing in British Columbia, Interim Report submitted to the Law Society of British Columbia' (10.05.2022), https://www.lawsociety.bc.ca/Website/media/Shared/docs/publications/reports/Furlong_Report_-_A_Competence-Based_System_for_Lawyer_Licensing_in_BC.pdf.

were already on the rise before the pandemic. The pandemic led all providers to invest in software and hardware to keep offering opportunities for lawyers to update or enhance their competence remotely. Regulators adapted their rules on the matter to allow more distance learning. Law societies invested in producing asynchronous modules for bar admissions courses. All of these are here to stay and will likely keep growing in the next few years. This does not mean that training courses or continuing education activities will all be online and asynchronous; instead, resources will be invested in in-person activities where that format proves truly advantageous.

ONLINE LEGAL EDUCATION IN MALAYSIA, BRUNEI DARUSSALAM AND SINGAPORE

Comparing the Members of the Commonwealth in Southeast Asia

Nobumichi TERAMURA and Salim FARRAR*

* The rapporteurs are grateful for inputs from (mostly anonymous) interviewees teaching law in Malaysia, Brunei and Singapore. For research and editorial assistance, we thank Joseph Black, former JD student intern at the Centre for Asian and Pacific Law at the University of Sydney (CAPLUS). Moreover, Teramura is appreciative of comments on the Brunei Legal System from Pg Nina Jasmine Binti PLKDR Pg Hj Bahrin and Pg Siti Rosanidah Binti Pg Hj Idris. Responsibility for any errors in the resulting work remains our own.

1. INTRODUCTION

This report considers Malaysia, Brunei Darussalam and Singapore, three geographically proximate Southeast Asian nations sharing similar features in their legal systems. As former British protectorates, the three jurisdictions maintain laws based on English common law and equity.[1] At the same time, the impact of Shariah law[2] is also salient in those countries as Islam has been practised in Maritime Southeast Asia since the ninth century, long before the arrival of the British Empire and other Western colonial powers in the region.[3] Thus, the development of their legal systems has been affected by common law and Islamic law, albeit to a lesser degree regarding the latter's influence in Singapore where Muslims comprise a minority,[4] unlike Brunei and Malaysia whose constitutions designate Islam as their state religion.[5] This report discusses similarities and differences in (online) legal education in these three closely

---

1 Generally see documents on legal systems in Malaysia, Brunei Darussalam and Singapore available via ASEAN Law Association, 'Legal System in ASEAN' (2019), https://www.aseanlawassociation.org/legal-system-in-asean/.

2 The spelling provided in the text refers to the most commonly used spelling internationally for Islam's religious law. Southeast Asian Bahasa-speaking states – Brunei, Indonesia, Malaysia and Singapore – all use the alternative spelling 'Syariah' (though not consistently) with 'Sy' signifying 'Sh' to avoid confusion with the Arabic letter 'Saad'. The latter is transliterated in Bahasa Indonesia as 'Sh'. Malaysian and Bruneian courts which apply this rule are termed and spelt 'Syariah courts'. Both international and regional spellings will be used in this report.

3 K. Steiner, 'Branding Islam: Islam, Law and Bureaucracies in Southeast Asia' (2018) 37 *Journal of Current Southeast Asian Affairs* 27; R.M. Feener, 'Islam in Southeast Asia to c. 1800' (2019) *Oxford Research Encyclopedias*, https://oxfordre.com/asianhistory/view/10.1093/acrefore/9780190277727.001.0001/acrefore-9780190277727-e-40#notes; K. Steiner, 'Comparative Law in the Syariah Courts: A Case Study of Singapore, Malaysia, and Brunei' in M. Andenas and D. Fairgrieve (eds), *Courts and Comparative Law*, Oxford University Press, Oxford 2015, pp. 595–612.

4 Department of Statistics (Singapore), 'General Household Survey (GHS) 2015' (2015), p. 23, https://www.singstat.gov.sg/-/media/files/publications/ghs/ghs2015/ghs2015.ashx.

5 Article 3 of the Federal Constitution (Malaysia); Article 3 of the Constitution (Brunei).

related jurisdictions. By online legal education we mean (a)synchronous remote law teaching mediated through the internet.

While COVID-19 equally hit Malaysia, Brunei Darussalam and Singapore in early 2020, these countries have experienced the pandemic in different ways. At the time this report was first contemplated, 27 August 2021, Malaysia was still struggling to control the spread of the virus, recording a total of 1,616,244 confirmed infections and 14,818 deaths. An average of 1,500 new community transmissions took place every day.[6] Singapore and Brunei Darussalam fared relatively better than Malaysia in containing the disease: 66,812 confirmed cases and 52 deaths in Singapore, and 2,159 confirmed cases and six deaths in Brunei Darussalam.[7] In both countries, community transmission was under control, thanks to the strict measures taken by the governments during the early stages of the pandemic.[8] Schools and universities in Brunei and Singapore started resuming face-to-face classes in mid-2020,[9] followed by disruptions caused by the spread of the Delta variant until June 2021 in Singapore and May 2022 in Brunei,[10] while many tertiary education institutions in Malaysia remained under lockdown until March 2022.[11] The three jurisdictions have produced distinct online legal education programmes, linked to their divergent pandemic experiences and disparities in their legal training systems.

---

6 World Health Organization, 'WHO Coronavirus (COVID-19) Dashboard: Malaysia' (2021), https://covid19.who.int/region/wpro/country/my.

7 World Health Organization, 'WHO Coronavirus (COVID-19) Dashboard: Singapore' (2021), https://covid19.who.int/region/wpro/country/sg (note that the number in Singapore was caused by a substantial increase in infections among migrant workers in dormitories in late 2020); World Health Organization, 'WHO Coronavirus (COVID-19) Dashboard: Brunei Darussalam' (2021), https://covid19.who.int/region/wpro/country/bn.

8 N.A. Hamdan and W. Case, 'Behind Brunei's COVID-19 Success Story', *East Asia Forum* (28.01.2021), https://www.eastasiaforum.org/2021/01/28/behind-bruneis-covid-19-success-story/; C.Y. Kwan, 'Singapore's Uncertain Economic Recovery in 2021', *East Asia Forum* (08.01.2021), https://www.eastasiaforum.org/2021/01/08/singapores-uncertain-economic-recovery-in-2021/.

9 S. Han, 'Brunei to Partially Reopen Schools on June 2 As Coronavirus Concerns Ease', *The Scoop* (21.05.2020), https://thescoop.co/2020/05/21/brunei-partially-reopens-schools-on-june-2-as-coronavirus-concerns-ease/; J. Ang, 'Singapore Schools to Open in Phases from June 2 after Covid-19 Circuit Breaker: How This Will Work', *The Straits Times* (19.05.2020), https://www.straitstimes.com/singapore/schools-to-open-in-phases-from-june-2-after-covid-19-circuit-breaker-how-this-will-work.

10 L. Lai and M. Menon, 'Schools in S[inga]pore Reopen with Covid-19 Safe Management Measures in Place for Students Returning to Class', *The Straits Times* (28.06.2021), https://www.straitstimes.com/singapore/schools-in-spore-reopen-with-safe-management-measures-in-place-for-students-returning-to; Ministry of Education, 'All Systems Go', *Borneo Bulletin* (14.05.2022), https://borneobulletin.com.bn/all-systems-go/.

11 Bernama, 'Public Higher Learning Institution Students to Return to Campus in Stages Beginning March 1', *New Straits Times* (09.02.2022), https://www.nst.com.my/news/nation/2022/02/770115/public-higher-learning-institution-students-return-campus-stages.

2. MALAYSIA

Malaysia is a pluralist and democratic country in Southeast Asia comprising 13 states with a total population of approximately 32 million people, divided between the rural east (Sabah and Sarawak) and the more urbanised west Malaysia (or Peninsular Malaysia). The World Bank has described Malaysia as an 'upper middle income' economy on an upward trajectory, expected to soon achieve 'fully developed' status. This was until the COVID-19 pandemic hit Malaysia in March 2020.[12] Although the country is still projected to become a 'high income' economy by 2024, income inequality is currently high, with the COVID-19 pandemic pushing an increasing number of Malaysian households into poverty.[13]

2.1. BACKGROUND FOR MALAYSIA

Similar to Singapore and Brunei, Malaysia has a parallel legal system, consisting of statutory laws, Shariah law and customary law, and is enforced in a plural legal structure.[14] East and West Malaysia have civil courts[15] of coordinate jurisdiction (the High Courts of Malaya and of Sabah and Sarawak have equal status), which enforce statutes, common law and equity. They are divided into subordinate and superior courts, with the Federal Court at the top applying rules of precedent. Appeals to the Privy Council were abolished in 1985. The Shariah courts have separate jurisdiction and their own court hierarchy.[16] Customary law has dwindling significance, but is important in Sabah and Sarawak, where it is enforced in the native courts and has generally been codified.[17]

Reflecting Malaysia's diversity and plurality, each of the 13 states have their own statutory laws as well as their own statutory versions of Shariah law, on top of Federal law. Jurisdiction is delimited by the Federal Constitution, which restricts the operation of Shariah law to matters defined in the 'State List';

---

12 The World Bank, 'The World Bank in Malaysia' (2021), https://www.worldbank.org/en/country/malaysia/overview.

13 Ibid.

14 On the complexities of pluralism in Malaysia, see A. Harding and D.A.H. Shah (eds), *Law and Society in Malaysia: Pluralism, Religion and Ethnicity*, Routledge, Abingdon 2019.

15 Malaysians categorise all common law courts as 'civil courts' (i.e. not Islamic).

16 For details on the Shariah courts, see F.S. Shuaib, T.A.A. Bustami and M.H. Mohd Kamal, *Administration of Islamic Law in Malaysia*, 2nd edn, LexisNexis (Kuala Lumpur), Kuala Lumpur 2010, pp. 385–433.

17 For an overview and critical discussion of Malaysia's court system and legal institutions, see T.H. Tey, 'Malaysia: The Undermining of Its Fundamental Institutions and the Prospects for Reform' in E.A. Black and G. Bell (eds), *Law and Legal Institutions of Asia: Traditions, Adaptations and Innovations*, Cambridge University Press, Cambridge 2011, pp. 212–261.

most criminal law matters are thus punished in accordance with the federal Penal Code, and commercial disputes are determined through legislation. In practice, Shariah law is confined mostly to family law, and even then is applied only to Muslims.[18] Education, including higher education, is a federal matter, and is overseen by the federal government.[19] The federal government sets national curricula, including approaches to online education. Federal legislation also determines legal qualification to practise in the civil courts.[20] State enactments and state rules, however, lay down the rules to practise as a lawyer (*Peguam Syarie*) in the Shariah courts.[21]

2.1.1. Malaysia's Legal Profession

Under the Legal Profession Act (LPA) 1976,[22] the High Court may admit a 'qualified person' to practise as a barrister and solicitor, so long as they are at least 18 years old, of good character, a citizen or permanent resident of Malaysia, and have served their nine months' pupillage.[23] A 'qualified person' needs to have obtained a qualifying law degree at one of the nine local (eight public, one private) universities specified in the LPA or have been admitted as a 'barrister-at-law' in England.[24] Malaysians who have studied law elsewhere need to take the Certificate in Legal Practice (CLP).[25]

Malaysia has more than 20,000 lawyers, with the vast majority in small to medium-sized firms.[26] While the big firms, like Zaid Ibrahim & Co., have sophisticated information and communications technology (ICT) and their own operating systems, and provide online training,[27] approximately 80% of the firms are small (one to five persons) and do not have sufficient capital to

---

18 See A. Harding, 'Sharia and National Law in Malaysia' in J.M. Otto (ed.), *Sharia Incorporated: A Comparative Overview of the Legal Systems of Twelve Muslim Countries*, Leiden University Press, Leiden 2010, pp. 510–520.

19 The governing framework is framed by the Education Act 1996 and the Private Higher Education Institutions Act 1996.

20 See the Legal Profession Act 1976.

21 See further F.S. Shuaib, T.A.A. Bustami and M.H. Mohd Kamal, *Administration of Islamic Law in Malaysia*, 2nd edn, LexisNexis (Kuala Lumpur), Kuala Lumpur 2010, pp. 507–551.

22 Legal Profession Act 1976, section 11.

23 Legal Profession Act 1976, section 12(2).

24 See further Legal Profession Qualifying Board, 'Qualifications To Be A "Qualified Person"' (2021), http://www.lpqb.org.my/index.php?option=com_content&view=article&id=131&Itemid=77.

25 Ibid.

26 Bar Council Malaysia, 'General Statistics | Members and Law Firms (as at 28 Feb 2021)' (2021), https://www.malaysianbar.org.my/article/about-us/malaysian-bar-and-bar-council/about-us/figures/general-statistics.

27 Interview with Paul Subramaniam, 10.07.2021. See further section 2.2.1 below.

invest in the necessary technology or software.[28] The financial difficulties caused by the COVID-19 pandemic for local lawyers have made further investment in technology quite problematic, notwithstanding increased usage of ICT by the courts. A rapid transition to online education across Malaysian law firms, therefore, is unlikely in the short term.

Admission procedures for Shariah lawyers (*Peguam Syarie*) are determined by a special committee (the *Majlis*) formed at the state level to advise their executive on Islamic matters.[29] The procedures for legal admission[30] are much the same as for the civil courts,[31] though in addition prospective practitioners must be Muslim and demonstrate 'sufficient knowledge of Islamic law'. The latter is satisfied either by obtaining a Bachelor of Shariah Law from one of the local universities, or, as in the case of an already qualified advocate and solicitor, by taking a supplementary written examination in Shariah law.[32] Some states also require interviews and a nine-month pupillage with a legal firm specialising in Shariah law.[33]

2.1.2. Universities in Malaysia

In Malaysia, there are currently 20 public universities, 47 private universities, 34 private university colleges and 10 foreign universities with branches in Malaysia,[34] with 29 of these offering a law course.[35] These include undergraduate, graduate (LLM) and doctoral programmes. Both the International Islamic University Malaysia[36] and the Islamic Science University Malaysia[37] offer

---

28 Daniel Lui, 'The Current State of Legal Innovation in Malaysia. An interview with Daniel Lui, Co-Founder, LawTech Malaysia', *Asia Law Portal* (01.03.2020), https://asialawportal.com/2020/03/01/the-current-state-of-legal-innovation-in-malaysia-an-interview-with-daniel-lui-co-founder-lawtech-malaysia/. This was confirmed by the interview with Paul Subramaniam.

29 See A. Whiting, 'The Training, Appointment, and Supervision of Islamic Lawyers in the Federal Territories of Malaysia' (2012) 21 *Pacific Rim Law & Policy Journal* 133, 136.

30 As set out in the relevant state enactment. For example, see the Administration of Islamic Law (Federal Territories) Act 1993.

31 A. Whiting, 'The Training, Appointment, and Supervision of Islamic Lawyers in the Federal Territories of Malaysia' (2012) 21 *Pacific Rim Law & Policy Journal* 133, 135.

32 Ibid., p. 137.

33 Ibid. For the most up-to-date requirements and information on the Islamic judiciary and Syariah lawyers, see Department of Syariah Judiciary Malaysia, 'E-Syariah Official Portal' (2011), http://www.esyariah.gov.my/portal/page/portal/Portal%20E-Syariah%20BI/E-Syariah%20Main%20Portal.

34 StudyMalaysia.com, 'List of Universities in Malaysia' (24.06.2020), https://www.studymalaysia.com/education/top-stories/list-of-universities-in-malaysia.

35 See Afterschool Higher Education Advisor.my, 'Courses: Law Courses' (2021), https://afterschool.my/law-courses.

36 See further International Islamic University Malaysia, 'Bachelor of Laws (Shariah) (Honours): Undergraduate' (2021), https://www.iium.edu.my/programme/show/bachelor-of-laws-shariah-honours.

37 See further the University's website available at Islamic Science University Malaysia, 'USIM Bachelor of Laws and Syariah Degree Programme Obtained Full Recognition from LPQB'

a double degree, the Bachelor of Laws and Shariah programme, which are accredited by the Legal Profession Qualifying Board, enabling graduates to practise in both the civil courts and Shariah courts. Programmes with combined law and Syariah units are also offered by Universiti Malaya,[38] the National University of Malaysia (UKM) and Universiti Teknologi MARA (UiTM).

The capacity of these universities and colleges to offer efficient and effective online education is impacted by their funding sources and structures. The formula for the funding of Malaysian public universities has changed over the years. In 2007, 90% of the operating budgets of the 20 public universities came from the government purse, with the remaining 10% covered by tuition fees and self-generated income.[39] Since that time, the contribution ratio has been reduced to 70%/30%, respectively. In 2017, the government also introduced stringent budget cuts of approximately 20% to university funding, reflecting austerity measures across government.[40] In turn, this has forced the public universities to cut costs (including spending on infrastructure), reduce inefficiencies and to consider ways to generate more income,[41] such as developing more executive and continuing education courses and hiking tuition fees (where possible). Notwithstanding the cost-cutting, the push to innovate and look for alternative income streams accelerated a trend towards more online learning even before the pandemic.

More than a year after the pandemic, the federal government indicated its intention to focus on education and allocated 20% of the 2021 budget to it (approximately AU$21 billion), including almost AU$5 billion for higher education alone.[42] More than AU$16 million has been ring-fenced for upgrading university internet infrastructure and a further AU$16 million for upgrading lecture rooms and laboratories for remote learning.[43] The federal government allocated a slightly higher proportion to education in its 2022 budget.[44] While questions remain as to whether these amounts are adequate for

(2021), https://www.usim.edu.my/news/usim-bachelor-of-laws-and-syariah-degree-programme-obtained-full-recognition-from-lpqb/.

38 See University of Malaya Centre for Continuing Education, 'Universiti Malaya's Open Channel: Bachelor of Shariah & Law' (2021), https://umcced.edu.my/programme/satu/bsl.

39 D. Abdullah, 'Public Universities and Budget Cuts in Malaysia' (2017) *International Higher Education* 15, 17.

40 Ibid.

41 Ibid., p. 16.

42 J. Lau, 'Malaysian Universities Given Funds to "Weather the Pandemic"', *Times Higher Education* (01.12.2020), https://www.timeshighereducation.com/news/malaysian-universities-given-funds-weather-thepandemic.

43 Ibid.

44 'Largest Allocation in 2022 Budget for the Education Ministry at RM52.6 Billion', *New Straits Times* (29.10.2021), https://www.nst.com.my/news/nation/2021/10/740917/largest-allocation-2022-budget-education-ministry-rm526-billion-nsttv.

the necessary investment,[45] the funding bodes well for government support of online education in the future.

2.1.3. *ICT in Malaysia*

According to the ICT Use and Access by Individuals and Household Survey Report 2019,[46] approximately 90% of Malaysian households have access to the internet, more than 98% to a mobile phone and 71% to a computer (either a laptop, desktop or iPad device). The Network Readiness Index, which measures and ranks countries globally on the digitalisation of their economies, positions Malaysia 34th globally and seventh in the ASEAN region, indicating that the country punches above its weight as a middle-income country.[47] The ICT sector is one of the fastest-growing sectors in the Malaysian economy and has strong support and investment from the Malaysian government.[48] With the prevalence of ICT use and the government's wish to make Malaysia a hub for innovative multimedia technology,[49] the future of online education in Malaysia appears bright.

However, these figures hide the digital divide that exists between the rural and urban areas and the problems of getting internet access outside Peninsular Malaysia, especially in Sabah.[50] Telecoms operators are required to reach 95% of the population, but not 95% of geographical areas, meaning that the more sparsely populated rural areas are either left without internet service or have very poor connectivity.[51] Some Universiti Malaysia Sabah students, for example, have resorted to constructing makeshift wooden platforms in the trees to secure better WiFi.[52] The situation in Sarawak, where the terrain presents similar obstacles, is better as its telecoms infrastructure provider (SACOFA) has pushed the innovation envelope by deploying solar-powered drones to reach remote

---

45 J. Lau, 'Malaysian Universities Given Funds to "Weather the Pandemic"', *Times Higher Education* (01.12.2020), https://www.timeshighereducation.com/news/malaysian-universities-given-funds-weather-thepandemic.

46 Department of Statistics Malaysia, 'ICT Use and Access by Individuals and Households Survey Report 2019' (10.04.2020), https://www.dosm.gov.my/v1/index.php?r=column/pdfPrev&id=SFRacTRUMEVRUFo1Ulc4Y1JlLzBqUT09.

47 Portulans Institute, 'Network Readiness Index: Malaysia 2020' (2021), https://networkreadinessindex.org/countries/malaysia/.

48 See GlobalData, 'ICT Spending in Malaysia to Reach US$25.2bn 2023, Says GlobalData', *GlobalData* (16.03.2020), https://www.globaldata.com/ict-spending-in-malaysia-to-reach-us25-2bn-2023-says-globaldata/. Note that these figures were compiled immediately before the COVID-19 crisis hit.

49 Ibid.

50 J. Jacobs and P. Subramaniam, 'Cover Story: The Digital Divide and Disconnection', *The Edge Malaysia Weekly* (19.10.2020), https://www.theedgemarkets.com/article/cover-story-digital-divide-and-disconnection.

51 Ibid.

52 Ibid.

areas and pulling transmission from neighbouring telecoms towers. Providing *all* of Malaysia with internet coverage, however, remains a logistical and financial challenge.[53]

The Malaysian court system, including its Shariah courts,[54] began operating an e-filing system in March 2011, and since December 2017 has required all legal firms to file their court documents online so as to streamline court processes.[55] When the system was rolled out, the courts provided weekly training sessions for lawyers throughout Peninsular Malaysia.[56] In addition to the e-filing system, courts are increasingly embracing ICT through the introduction of video-conferencing, a new case management system and auto alerts.[57] There are also moves to introduce artificial intelligence to reduce disparities in sentencing when punishing in similar types of cases.[58]

Notwithstanding the enthusiasm of the government and courts for using ICT, the adoption of ICT by legal firms, especially smaller firms, has been slower and has lagged behind the use of technology by Malaysia's neighbours.[59] Nevertheless, ICT is extensively used for legal training within Malaysian firms,[60] a trend accelerated by the lockdowns caused by COVID-19.

2.2. MALAYSIA'S MOVES TOWARDS ONLINE EDUCATION

The first cases of COVID-19 were detected in Malaysia on 25 January 2020 but remained at low levels until 14 March 2020 when there was a sharp spike in infections.[61] This prompted the Malaysian government to act, announcing

---

53 Ibid.

54 See further, W.S.W.M. Saman and A. Haider, 'E-Shariah in Malaysia: Technology Adoption within Justice System' (2013) 7 *Transforming Government: People, Process and Policy* 256. The E-Syariah Portal, which links together all of the 110 Syariah courts and which acts as a virtual one-stop shop for all matters related to the Islamic judiciary, was launched in April 2007. See further, N.A. Siddiquee, 'Public Service Innovations, Policy Transfer and Governance in the Asia-Pacific Region: The Malaysian Experience' (2007) 2(1) *Journal of Administration & Governance* 81, 86.

55 I. Lim, 'Lawyers Required to Go Digital by 2018', *Malay Mail* (11.08.2017), https://www.malaymail.com/news/malaysia/2017/08/11/lawyers-required-to-go-digital-by-2018/1440087.

56 Ibid.

57 Tech Wire Asia, 'Malaysia Courts Get Tech Savvy and Lawyers Must Follow Suit', *Tech Wire Asia* (18.02.2019), https://techwireasia.com/2019/02/malaysian-courts-get-tech-savvy-and-lawyers-must-follow-suit/.

58 Ibid.

59 Ibid.

60 The bigger firms either have their own learning management system, like the universities (see section 2.2.2.1 below), or use Microsoft Teams. As for the smaller firms, training is generally conducted through Zoom or Webex: interview with Paul Subramaniam, 10.07.2021.

61 K.H.D. Tang, 'Movement Control as an Effective Measure against Covid-19 Spread in Malaysia: An Overview' (2020) *Journal of Public Health* 1.

the 2020 Movement Control Order (MCO) on 16 March (which ran from 18 March 2020 to 12 May 2020). This prohibited mass movements and gatherings everywhere and locked down all business premises and learning institutions, including the universities.[62] Only essential services (energy, electricity, telecoms, food, finance and banking, etc.) were allowed to remain open.[63] This was a shock to the system for private and public universities in Malaysia, with some (particularly the private and West Coast/urban-based universities) more prepared than others for the shift to online education.[64] Due to poor internet connectivity, universities on Malaysia's East Coast were especially unprepared.[65]

On 27 May 2020, the Higher Education Ministry of Malaysia declared that all teaching and learning activities had to be conducted through online platforms until 31 December 2020.[66] Specified exceptions, included activities for students needing to attend practical classes,[67] such as professional practice classes that Malaysian law students study in their final year or those studying for the conversion course (the CLP) for non-qualifying law degrees. While some university students and campuses[68] returned to mixed forms of teaching in March 2021, on 10 May 2021 the government announced a third lockdown following a large spike in active cases and reported deaths, re-instituting online

62 Prime Minister's Office of Malaysia, 'The Prime Minister's Special Message on COVID-19 – 16 March 2020' (16.03.2020), https://www.pmo.gov.my/2020/03/perutusan-khas-yab-perdana-menteri-mengenai-covid-19-16-mac-2020/.

63 Ibid.

64 S. Imitiaz, 'East Asia Watch: How Are Malaysian Universities Adapting during Covid-19', *Insights Blog* (26.06.2020), https://education-services.britishcouncil.org/insights-blog/east-asia-watch-how-are-malaysian-universities-adapting-during-covid-19 (interview with Professor Perry Hobson, Pro-Vice Chancellor for Engagement at Sunway University, Malaysia).

65 See A.J.A. Tajuddin et al., 'Lecturers' Readiness and Emotional Presence on Online Teaching Data in a Malaysian University During COVID-19' (2021) 536 *Advances in Social Science, Education and Humanities Research* 548, 554.

66 Y. Palansamy, 'Higher Education Ministry: All University Lectures to Be Online-only until End 2020, with a Few Exceptions', *Malay Mail* (27.05.2020), https://www.malaymail.com/news/malaysia/2020/05/27/higher-education-ministry-all-university-lectures-to-be-online-only-until-e/1869975.

67 See Malaysian Ministry of Health, 'Covid-19 Standard Operating Protocols (SOPs) for Higher Education', http://covid-19.moh.gov.my/faqsop/sop-pkp-pemulihan/03SOP-Sektor-Pengajian-Tinggi-8-Julai-2020.pdf.

68 The picture is not uniform across Malaysia. Variability exists, for example, depending on the course, location, approach of a particular university, as well as the particular student activity. Even the foreign universities with branches in Malaysia differ, with Monash University keeping its campus closed to students and all classes online (see Monash University, 'Malaysia: Covid-19 Updates' (2021), https://www.monash.edu.my/COVID19-updates) and the University of Reading Malaysia keeping its campus open (see University of Reading Malaysia, 'Covid-19 Update' (2021), https://www.reading.edu.my/covid-19-update).

learning for the majority of students.[69] Classes remained online until the government-announced return to campus on 1 March 2022.[70]

2.2.1. *Achievements before the Pandemic*

The strategic direction and structural transformation of Malaysia under the leadership of Tun Mahathir Mohamed in the 1990s facilitated the reception and development of ICT networks and online education in Malaysia.[71] With the launching of the Multimedia Super Corridor (MSC) and Cyberjaya in 1999, Malaysia was well placed to act as a future regional ICT hub and innovative education provider.[72] From 2001, the Open University Malaysia (OUM) offered online and distance learning and before the start of the pandemic the online network had expanded to nine educational institutions providing online courses and programmes.[73] Operating in tandem with national strategic plans (such as the 11th Malaysia Plan 2015–2020, the National Economic Model and the Economic Transformation Programme), public and private universities had begun to deliver micro-credentials and massive open online courses (MOOCs) by 2013.[74] Figuring prominently in the government's 2015 Blueprint for Higher Education,[75] MOOCs were to enable Malaysian public universities to develop niche areas of expertise, such as Islamic banking and finance, and to participate in international forums. Through MOOCs, substantial investment and the country roll-out of the necessary cyber infrastructure, the government hoped that online learning would become an integral component of all higher

---

69 J. Ross, 'Universities Shuttered across Malaysia as Third Covid Wave Hits: Lockdown Comes Days before Eid Religious Festival', *Times Higher Education* (11.05.2021), https://www.timeshighereducation.com/news/universities-shuttered-across-malaysia.

70 See Bernama, 'Public Higher Learning Institution Students to Return to Campus in Stages Beginning March 1', *New Straits Times* (09.02.2022), https://www.nst.com.my/news/nation/2022/02/770115/public-higher-learning-institution-students-return-campus-stages.

71 For detail of this structural transformation, see J.K.S. and S.N. Wong (eds), *Law, Institutions and Malaysian Economic Development*, NUS Press, Singapore 2008.

72 See M. Sarimin and T. Yigitcanlar, 'Planning for Knowledge Based Urban Development in Malaysia: Cyberjaya @ Multimedia Super Corridor' in A.C. Fachinelli and T. Yigitcanlar (eds), *Summit Proceedings of the 4th Knowledge Cities World Summit*, The World Capital Institute and Ibero-American Community for Knowledge Systems, Brazil 2011, pp. 342–349.

73 See Malaysian Investment Development Authority, 'Evolution of e-Learning in the Malaysian Higher Education Institutions' (08.02.2021), https://www.mida.gov.my/mida-news/evolution-of-e-learning-in-the-malaysian-higher-education-institutions/.

74 M. Fadzil, L.A. Latif and T.A. Munira, 'MOOCs in Malaysia: A Preliminary Case Study', E-ASEM Forum: Renewing the Lifelong Learning Agenda for the Future, Bali, Indonesia, 10–11 March 2015, https://core.ac.uk/download/pdf/298087393.pdf.

75 See Ministry of Education Malaysia, 'Executive Summary Malaysia Education Blueprint 2015–2025 (Higher Education)' (2015), https://www.um.edu.my/docs/um-magazine/4-executive-summary-pppm-2015-2025.pdf.

education and lifelong learning courses and that up to 70% of all undergraduate programmes would use blended learning by 2025.[76]

While the Malaysian government gave general support for and promoted online education,[77] the vast majority of law programmes were still taught traditionally (two-hour lecture mode) and 'in person' before the pandemic arrived (with the exception of single law units in non-law degrees, such as business and engineering, which were delivered online).[78] Even the private Multi-Media University (MMU), the most high-tech of the Malaysian law schools, only used online learning to complement rather than replace traditional lectures. Before the pandemic, even income-generating short courses for professional lawyers and annual judicial training were still taught in person.[79] In-person training was (and still is) dictated by the requirements of the Malaysian Legal Qualifying Board as well as by a traditional learning culture that favours extensive contact hours between staff and students.[80] Complications caused by budgetary austerity further exacerbated the problem.[81]

2.2.2. *Achievements and Challenges after the Pandemic*

2.2.2.1. Managing the Swift Transition

Private universities, like MMU, were well set up before the pandemic hit and staff in 2018 were already using Google Classrooms, Google Meet and G-Suite to conduct some of their classes and to set and submit coursework, although examinations remained in person. All staff generally had excellent internet connectivity,[82] access to all necessary equipment and were well trained in the

---

76 Ibid., p. 28.

77 Especially following the much publicised shift toward the technology-based industries and the re-direction of government attention towards Cyberjaya and the Multi-Media Super Corridor in August 2018, see further the interview with then Prime Minister Tun Mahathir Mohamed: 'Dr Mahathir to Revive Cyberjaya and Multimedia Super Corridor (MSC)', *The Star* (27.08.2018), https://www.thestartv.com/v/dr-mahathir-to-revive-cyberjaya-and-multimedia-super-corridor-msc.

78 For a current example, see UTM's micro-credential course in building laws, available at: UTM, 'Building Development Laws and Legislations' (2021), https://mooc.utm.my/courses/building-development-laws-and-legislations/?cl=1.

79 MMU interview, 03.07.2021; interview with Paul Subramaniam, Zico Holdings, 10.07.2021.

80 See comments of Professor Perry Hobson in S. Imitiaz, 'East Asia Watch: How Are Malaysian Universities Adapting during Covid-19', *Insights Blog* (26.06.2020), https://education-services.britishcouncil.org/insights-blog/east-asia-watch-how-are-malaysian-universities-adapting-during-covid-19.

81 See J. Henderson, 'Budget Cuts Ahead as Enterprise Swings Tech Axe in Malaysia', *Channel Asia* (03.08.2020), https://www.channelasia.tech/article/681856/budget-cuts-ahead-enterprise-swings-tech-axe-malaysia/. See also section 2.1.2 above.

82 MMU is a subsidiary of Telecom Malaysia, Malaysia's main internet provider: see MMU, 'Telekom Malaysia Was Given the Distinction by the Ministry of Education to Set up the

technologies and software and thus able to operate the system effectively.[83] When the pandemic hit, the transition to full online delivery, assessment and marking was relatively straightforward for MMU staff, subject to the common problems of internet connectivity, identity verification and ease of plagiarism.[84] In-person professional short courses were also easily converted to 'webinars'.[85]

Other universities, particularly in the public sector, were less well prepared for the sudden move to working from home, with some staff having to use their own mobile phones to deliver classes or even compete with their children for use of the only available laptops.[86] The switch was so sudden following the first MCO on 18 March 2020 that some law academic staff were initially locked out from their offices on campus and could not access their equipment or research.[87] The working culture of 'needing to be seen at your desk' meant few academic staff worked from home before the pandemic.[88] In addition, in terms of teaching, many were only familiar with conventional delivery and had not been properly inducted into the new online modes of instruction.[89] While the public universities had started online learning prior to the pandemic, at UKM, for instance, online platforms were used predominantly by young lecturers[90] and generally limited to uploading lecture notes.[91]

At the International Islamic University of Malaysia (IIUM), the technology, lab facilities and equipment were available to teach law courses online from 2017 and staff were invited for training courses throughout 2017 and 2018;[92] however, fewer than approximately 10% of staff had chosen to do so. This meant that at the start of the first wave of the pandemic, from mid-March to

---

First Private University in Malaysia' (2021), https://www.mmu.edu.my/cool_timeline/telekom-malaysia-was-given-the-distinction-by-the-ministry-of-education-to-set-up-the-first-private-university-in-malaysia/.

83 In 2018, it was mandatory for all MMU staff to complete their online training modules. The rapporteur is grateful to MMU academics for sharing this information.

84 Ibid.

85 Ibid.

86 See interview with Perry Hobson in S. Imitiaz, 'East Asia Watch: How Are Malaysian Universities Adapting during Covid-19', *Insights Blog* (26.06.2020), https://education-services.britishcouncil.org/insights-blog/east-asia-watch-how-are-malaysian-universities-adapting-during-covid-19, and confirmed in interview with IIUM academic, 11.07.2021. The problem of device sharing, particularly in large families, was also mentioned by Paul Subramaniam in his interview on 10.07.2021.

87 IIUM interview, 11.07.2021.

88 See S. Imitiaz, 'East Asia Watch: How Are Malaysian Universities Adapting during Covid-19', *Insights Blog* (26.06.2020), https://education-services.britishcouncil.org/insights-blog/east-asia-watch-how-are-malaysian-universities-adapting-during-covid-19.

89 This included legal trainers in law firms; interview with Paul Subramaniam, 10.07.2021.

90 UKM interview, 09.08.2021.

91 The rapporteurs are grateful to a former UKM academic for this information.

92 IIUM interview, 11.07.2021. The other points in this paragraph and the next three derive from this interview.

mid-April 2020, the *Kulliyyah* (Faculty) had to spend considerable time training the staff on how to use the new software and make full use of its own learning management system (*I-Ta'lim*) as well as how to use other programs, such as Google Classrooms, Google Meet, Zoom and WhatsApp. Apart from uploading the teaching modules, assignments and examinations to IIUM's learning management system, it was left up to individual staff to decide which platform to use for online classes. While some staff welcomed the flexibility, with the delegation to staff clearly a pragmatic response in these peculiar circumstances, this may have given an impression to other staff, especially those not so familiar with IT, that they were being left to fend for themselves when a dangerous disease was so rife. On top of the time spent in extra training, staff also had to prepare, upload and deliver these classes in the new format, substantially adding to staff workloads and stress.

Regarding students, their experiences of this transition differed depending on whether they stayed on campus at the start of the pandemic or had returned to their *kampung* (village). The former had access to good internet facilities and strong internet coverage enabling them to access the online classes with little problem. But for the latter, it was difficult to access classes because of poor internet coverage in their rural areas or because of no internet access at all in some cases. Such students had no choice but to travel to the nearest town to find an internet shop, café or some other public internet facility. Where unable to do so, students were forced to apply for study leave from the university.

2.2.2.2. Challenges

Over the course of the pandemic, much improved as staff and students became used to the online system and the convenience of WhatsApp. The university also responded to the concerns of poorer students by providing free meals, free equipment and more on-campus accommodation during the semester. However, there were numbers of challenges. Law assessment at IIUM, before the start of the pandemic, used to be in the form of essays and problem questions. But owing to the risks of plagiarism in the online environment, staff no longer set essay questions, relying almost exclusively on long and elaborate problem questions. This shift in the approach of question setting was problematic, with lower-quality student responses.

After more than a year of teaching and assessing online, staff morale was also a problem. Staff were 'fed up with the whole thing' and wanted to return to their teaching methods pre-pandemic. They missed the interactions and felt Muslim students were deprived of the close teacher–student relationships customarily associated with Islamic approaches to education.

Staff and students also complained of the volume of assessments and the additional time taken to set, complete and submit assessments for multiple subjects, especially given connectivity issues, adding to workloads and stress.[93] For some students, coupled with the social distancing measures and family pressures, these issues led them to drop out of the university or, in extreme cases, even contemplate suicide, despite attempted suicide being a criminal offence in Malaysia and carrying religious taboos.[94] The IIUM central administration and the Faculty recognised this and responded with new courses for students on how to manage stress, and facilitated student-led peer support groups to assist law students facing such difficulties.[95]

In terms of teaching professional practice subjects, although advocacy skills were taught efficiently and conveniently on Zoom, with the added bonus of part-time staff from the Bar better able to commit to teaching as they no longer had to travel across Kuala Lumpur to the campus, the move to online education did not successfully replicate the practical lessons learned from pupillages and attachment programmes.[96] The concern is that 'pandemic graduates' will not have the same practical understanding of the law as the law students who graduated before the pandemic hit.[97]

The Malaysian government is now prioritising the digitalisation of the economy and the promotion of high-tech industries. The provision of micro-credentials is seen as an important element in this policy and is stated explicitly in the 12th Malaysia Plan.[98]

3. BRUNEI DARUSSALAM

Brunei Darussalam is a small state located on the north coast of Borneo Island, surrounded by the South China Sea and the Malaysian state of Sarawak. The Sultanate follows the national tradition of the Malay Islamic Monarchy (*Melayu Islam Beraja*, MIB), embedded into its constitution, and maintains one of the

93 IIUM interview, 11.07.2021.

94 Ibid. This reflects an increasing phenomenon amongst Malaysian youth since the pandemic began. See H. Hassan, 'Malaysia Sees Rise in Suicides and Calls to Helplines Amid Covid-19 Pandemic', *The Straits Times* (12.07.2021), https://www.straitstimes.com/asia/se-asia/malaysia-sees-rise-in-suicides-and-calls-to-helplines-amid-covid-19-pandemic. See also L.P. Wong et al., 'Escalating Progression of Mental Health Disorders during the COVID-19 Pandemic: Evidence from a Nationwide Survey' (2021) *PLoS One*, https://journals.plos.org/plosone/article?id=10.1371/journal.pone.0248916.

95 IIUM interview, 11.07.2021.

96 Ibid.

97 Ibid.

98 See the Malaysian Government website: Smart Partnership with Malaysian Administrative Modernisation and Management Planning Unit (MAMPU) Economic Planning Unit, 'Twelfth Malaysia Plan: Garis Panduan Penyediaan RMKe-12, 2021–2025' (2019), http://rmke12.epu.gov.my/about-us. The 12th Malaysia Plan represents national government strategic planning for the period 2021–25.

highest living standards in the world brought about by revenue from its oil reserves.

3.1. BACKGROUND FOR BRUNEI

Brunei Darussalam is governed by a dual legal system consisting of statutory laws and Syariah law.[99] The statutory laws are an amalgam of diverse legal systems, such as English law, Singaporean law, Malaysian law, Indian law and Bruneian law that reflects the Sultanate's customs and traditions.[100] The statutory laws apply to matters including commercial activities and disputes between private individuals, while Syariah law regulates personal matters of Muslims (and occasionally non-Muslims), such as marriage, divorce, inheritance, maintenance of dependents and the estates of deceased Muslims.[101] The dual system is maintained in the judiciary, too. On the one hand, there is the civil justice system that deals with both civil and criminal matters, comprising the Subordinate Court (consisting of the Magistrate's Court, the Juvenile Court and the Small Claims Tribunal), the Intermediate Court, the High Court and the Court of Appeal as the final appellate court.[102] In exceptional cases, certain civil matters may be appealed from the Supreme Court of Brunei to the Judicial Committee of the Privy Council in England,[103] although the Privy Council has

---

99 See generally A. Haji Majid, 'Duality of the Brunei Legal System: Effectiveness of Legislative Drafting Process of Syariah Legislation' (2014), https://sas-space.sas.ac.uk/5902/; Council of ASEAN Chief Justices, 'Overview of Brunei Legal System' (2021), https://cacj-ajp.org/brunei/legal-system/introduction-to-the-legal-system/overview/. As for Syariah law practised in Brunei, see A.R.A. Haqqi, 'Islamic Law in State Life of Brunei Darussalam' (2017) 1 *Journal of Malay Islamic Studies* 81.

100 Teramura's interview with local senior legal officers in the government sector. See also section 2 of the Application of Laws Act, stating, 'the common law of England and the doctrines of equity, together with statutes of general application, as administered or in force in England at the commencement of this Act, shall be in force in Brunei Darussalam … [p]rovided that the said common law, doctrines of equity and statutes of general application shall be in force in Brunei Darussalam so far only as the circumstances of Brunei Darussalam and of its inhabitants permit and subject to such qualifications as local circumstances and customs render necessary'.

101 Oxford Business Group, 'Breakdown of Legal Environment in Brunei Darussalam' (2016), https://oxfordbusinessgroup.com/overview/law-land-breakdown-country%E2%80%99s-legal-environment.

102 See generally State Judiciary Department, 'About Us' (2019), https://www.judiciary.gov.bn/SJD%20Site%20Pages/Subordinate%20Court.aspx.

103 The exceptional cases are where the Sultan of Brunei gives leave; the amount or value of the subject matter is beyond 200,000 Brunei dollars; the case is fit for appeal; and 'the parties to the proceedings have at any time before the hearing of the case on appeal by the Supreme Court consented in writing to be bound by an appeal to [the Sultan and the Judicial Committee of the Privy Council]': Article 2 of the Brunei (Appeals) Order 1989 (UK) and Article 2 of the Brunei (Appeals) (Amendment) Order 1998 (UK).

no jurisdiction over criminal or constitutional matters. On the other hand, there is the Shariah justice system, the framework of which largely mirrors the civil justice system. The Islamic judiciary's jurisdiction extends to personal status matters (e.g., family, inheritance and trusts), enforcement of Muslims' obligations and Islamic criminal offences.[104] As demonstrated in the subsections that follow, the dual system is also maintained for legal qualification and law education in Brunei Darussalam.

3.1.1. Brunei's Legal Profession

For the common law courts, the Chief Justice acts as the main gatekeeper to the legal professions, and s/he may, at his/her discretion, admit as an advocate and solicitor any qualified person who is over 21 years old, is of good character and has completed his/her pupillage satisfactorily.[105] Admission to the Brunei Bar is regulated by the Legal Professions Act, which defines the qualified person as: a barrister-at-law or a solicitor of England, Northern Ireland, or Scotland; an active advocate and solicitor in Singapore or in any part of Malaysia; 'a barrister, solicitor or who is a barrister and solicitor of a Supreme Court of any Australian State or Territory'; or a citizen or a permanent resident of Brunei Darussalam holding any alternative qualification,[106] which is prescribed by the Legal Profession (Alternative Qualifications) Rules as: '(a) the Certificate of Legal Practice issued by the Qualifying Board pursuant of section 5 of the Legal Profession Act, 1976 of Malaysia; (b) [a] degree in law conferred by the Universiti Islam Antarabangsa of Malaysia';[107] '(c) [a] degree in law conferred by the Universiti Kebangsaan Malaysia';[108] and '(d) [a] degree in law conferred by the Universiti Islam Sultan Sharif Ali'.[109] Therefore, the number of lawyers admitted to the Bar in Brunei is arguably influenced by the gatekeepers to the legal profession in the foreign Commonwealth jurisdictions, although the real influence is not discernible due to Brunei being a small jurisdiction maintaining only 129 active lawyers and 36 active law firms as of May 2021.[110]

It is unclear whether the nature of the Brunei civil legal profession may contribute to facilitating a transition to online legal education in the country. Bruneian lawyers might not feel the necessity for such reform in their home

---

104 Sections 15–16 of the Shariah Courts Act, Cap 184 of the Laws of Brunei (Revised Edition 2011).

105 Section 4 of the Legal Profession Act, Cap 132 of the Laws of Brunei (Revised Edition 2022).

106 Section 3 (1)–(2) of the Legal Profession Act. Note that for a person who is neither a citizen nor a permanent resident to apply for admission, s/he must have been an active practitioner in practice in the respective jurisdiction: section 3(3) of the Legal Profession Act.

107 Rule 2 of the Legal Profession (Alternative Qualifications) Rules (Revised Edition 2006).

108 Rule 2 of the Legal Profession (Alternative Qualifications) (Amendment) Rules, 2007.

109 Rule 2 of the Legal Profession (Alternative Qualifications) (Amendment) Rules, 2014.

110 The Law Society of Brunei Darussalam, 'Home' (2017), https://www.bruneilawsociety.com/.

jurisdiction because the majority have been trained abroad in foreign law schools and institutions, and because some elite practitioners might find online law courses offered by British institutions the most attractive.

For the Shariah courts, the Chief Shariah Judge is responsible for deciding the admission of Shariah lawyers.[111] He may admit a person to be a Shariah lawyer if the person is a Muslim who: has passed the final examination of a bachelor's degree in Shariah from any university or educational institution recognised by the government; is a qualified advocate or solicitor admitted under the Legal Profession Act and has passed the Shariah Lawyer Certificate examination; has served as a Shariah Judge, *Kadi* (magistrate) or Shariah Prosecutor for not less than three years; has received a government-recognised professional training in Islamic judicial matters; or has knowledge in the laws of Islam (*Hukum Syara'*).[112] In addition, the person must be over 21 years old, of good behaviour, and have no convictions or any adjudged bankruptcy and suspension in his capacity as a legal practitioner in any other country.[113]

3.1.2. Universities in Brunei

With a population of 0.43 million, the country only has four universities: the University of Brunei Darussalam (UBD), University of Technology Brunei (UTB), Sultan Sharif Ali Islamic University (UNISSA), and Seri Begawan Religious Teachers University College (KUPUSB) – all publicly funded. As of 2021, only UNISSA offers non-Islamic law degrees at its Faculty of Shariah and Law, such as Master of Laws, Master of Laws in Intellectual Property Law and Master of Laws in International Law.[114] The UBD offers several common law courses at its School of Business and Economics, including Business Law and International Trade Law. Degrees in Shariah, such as Bachelor of Shariah (Fiqh and Usul) and Master of Shariah are offered by UNISSA only, although students at UBD can undertake research in Islamic law to obtain a Master of Arts (MA) or Doctor of Philosophy (PhD) in Arts degree.

Those public universities are not dependent on international student revenues, in contrast to their competitors in Australia and England. For example, UBD fixes annual tuition fees for most bachelor's degrees (apart from laboratory-based degrees and medical degrees) at 3,000 BND (around US$2,270), regardless of a student's background.[115] However, Australian universities often set tuition

111 Rule 9 of the Syariah Courts (Syar'ie Lawyers) Rules, 2002.
112 Rule 10(a) of the Syariah Courts (Syar'ie Lawyers) Rules.
113 Rule 10(b)–(c) of the Syariah Courts (Syar'ie Lawyers) Rules.
114 UNISSA, 'List of Programmes Offered For BDGs' (2021), http://www.mfa.gov.bn/PublishingImages/Pages/bdgs2021/UNISSA%20PROGRAMMES%202021-2022.pdf.
115 UBD, 'Fees & Funding' (2016), https://ubd.edu.bn/admission/undergraduate/gennext-degree-programme/fees-and-funding.html.

fees for international students five times higher than for domestic students.[116] Moreover, Brunei only has around 200 foreign non-exchange students, forming about 1.7% of the total number of students enrolled at its higher educational institutions,[117] in contrast to Australia, which has 418,168 overseas students, forming around 30% of the enrolments in its higher education sector.[118] The small number of international students in Brunei is unlikely to pose any serious obstacles for the universities to promote online teaching, but that might deter the public universities from generating an independent budget for updating IT facilities in a timely fashion, as discussed in section 3.2.

3.1.3. ICT in Brunei

There is no discernible investigation on the accessibility of IT facilities among students or legal professionals in Brunei. However, the Authority for Info-communications Technology Industry of Brunei Darussalam (AITI) has surveyed the use of ICT in households and business, finding that the accessibility of such facilities in Brunei is adequate but not excellent.[119] For instance, as for hardware, the survey suggests that the general proportion of household device ownership in 2018 was 88% for smartphones, 61% for laptops, 33% for tablet computers and 18% for desktop computers. The survey then studied the relationship between the monthly household income categories and the proportion of household device ownership. It found that low-income families, whose monthly income was less than 2,000 BND, had limited access to IT hardware: 87% for smartphones, 50% for laptops, 24% for tablet computers and 12% for desktop computers. In contrast, medium-income families, with monthly earnings of 2,000–6,999 BND, and high-income families, with

---

116 The University of Sydney, 'Fees, Costs and Loans', https://www.sydney.edu.au/study/study-options/fees-and-loans.html.

117 ASEM Education Secretariat, 'Consult Compendium: Brunei Darussalam' (2021), https://asem-education.org/compendiums/167-brunei/ (as of November 2018). Note that many foreign students are fully funded by the Government of Brunei Darussalam Scholarship for Foreign Students Tenable in Brunei Darussalam: Ministry of Foreign Affairs, 'The Government of Brunei Darussalam Scholarship for Foreign Students Tenable in Brunei Darussalam' (2018), http://www.mfa.gov.bn/pages/bdscholarship.aspx.

118 Australian Trade and Investment Commission, 'Monthly Summary of International Student Data: Student Data (YTD May 2021)' (2021), https://www.austrade.gov.au/australian/education/education-data/current-data/summaries-and-news; Skills and Employment Department of Education, 'Higher Education Statistics: Student Data', https://www.dese.gov.au/higher-education-statistics/student-data.

119 AITI, 'Brunei Darussalam Information Communications Technology (ICT) Business Report 2019' (2019), https://dev.aiti.labworks.digital/surveys/brunei-darussalam-ict-business-report-2019/; AITI, 'Brunei Darussalam Information Communications Technology (ICT) Household Report 2019' (2019), https://www.aiti.gov.bn/surveys/brunei-darussalam-ict-household-report-2019/.

monthly earnings of not less than 7,000 BND, had good access to such gadgets: respectively, 93% for smartphones, 80% for laptops, 44% for tablet computers and 25% for desktop computers; and 94% for smartphones, 93% for laptops, 63% for tablet computers and 37% for desktop computers.[120] Accordingly, students with lower socio-economic status have a higher chance of restricted access to online learning equipment.

In terms of household internet access, the same survey suggests that many Bruneians felt their broadband to be unaffordable and unreliable. Of the respondents, 39.4% answered that their monthly expenses on broadband were (very) expensive, while 28% evaluated the quality of broadband access speed as fair, poor or very poor.[121] Their perception may be unwarranted because Brunei maintains a high level of digital inclusiveness, thanks to its low mobile-broadband prices and affordable fixed-broadband plans. Nonetheless, Brunei has one of the lowest-quality networks in Southeast Asia, which is an underachievement given it is a developed country with a high GDP per capita.[122] Such network quality will not accelerate the introduction of online legal education in Brunei, although the low price may help students with a limited budget.

ICT usage among businesses, including law firms, shows a similar trend to that among households. In 2018, 44% of the respondents answered that they provided their employees with no computer access, probably because some employees did not require a computer in their line of work. Although 90% of respondents had access to the internet, more than 50% considered their internet quality to be in the range of fair to very poor, and 36% rated their internet subscription to be expensive or very expensive.[123] Hence, law firms in Brunei seem to have access to affordable but somewhat unreliable IT systems.

Finally, the public legal sectors have been receptive to new IT technologies. For instance, the common law courts implemented in 2015 the Judiciary Case Management System (JCMS), which consists of the Electronic Filing System (EFS), the Case Management System (CMS) and the Queue Management System (QMS).[124] The EFS is for government agencies and registered law

120 AITI, 'Brunei Darussalam Information Communications Technology (ICT) Household Report 2019' (2019), p. 13, https://www.aiti.gov.bn/surveys/brunei-darussalam-ict-household-report-2019/.

121 Ibid.

122 J. Low, D. Dujacquier and S. Kaur, *Focus: Bridging the Digital Divide: Improving Digital Inclusion in Southeast Asia*, Roland Berger GmbH, Munich 2021, pp. 12, 21, https://www.rolandberger.com/en/Insights/Publications/Bridging-the-digital-divide.html.

123 AITI, 'Brunei Darussalam Information Communications Technology (ICT) Business Report 2019' (2019), https://www.aiti.gov.bn/Shared%20Documents/ICT%20BUSINESS%20REPORT%20FA%20email%20MAR13.pdf, pp. 8–10.

124 State Judiciary Department, 'JCMS: Judiciary Case Management System' (2019), http://judiciary.gov.bn/SJD%20Site%20Pages/JCMS.aspx.

firms to file criminal and civil cases in the courts online.[125] The CMS is a computerised operation system for court officers to track case information from the registration through the EFS.[126] The QMS enables the public to obtain up-to-date information on court cases and hearings at self-service kiosks installed in the courts.[127] Moreover, the Syariah courts launched the e-Syariah system in 2017 to provide judges and registrars with simultaneous online access to case files and enable the public to make enquiries on court services and procedures.[128] In addition, the Attorney General's Chambers (AGC) have an Information and Communication Technology Unit (ICT Unit) that is responsible for the effective use of information systems, IT equipment and AGC facilities.[129]

3.2. BRUNEI'S MOVES TOWARDS ONLINE EDUCATION

Brunei detected its first confirmed case of COVID-19 on 9 March 2020.[130] The government immediately introduced social distancing measures, including the prohibition of mass gathering events. Higher education institutions were allowed to remain open and continue essential daily operations, provided that they adopted social distancing and other precautionary measures in accordance with the guidelines issued by the Ministry of Health and the Prime Minister's Office.[131] As a consequence, online teaching suddenly became the norm in universities in the country.[132]

---

125 State Judiciary Department, 'Electronic Filing System', http://efiling.judiciary.gov.bn/eFiling/index.jsp?LANG=E#; State Judiciary Department, 'JCMS FAQs' (2019), http://judiciary.gov.bn/SJD%20Site%20Pages/JCMS%20FAQs.aspx.

126 State Judiciary Department, 'JCMS: Judiciary Case Management System' (2019), http://judiciary.gov.bn/SJD%20Site%20Pages/JCMS.aspx.

127 Ibid.

128 BruDirect.Com, 'E-Syariah Officially Launched', *BruDirectCom: Brunei's No1 News Website* (22.01.2017), https://www.brudirect.com/news.php?id=21956.

129 Prime Minister's Office Attorney General's Chambers, 'Information and Communication Technology Unit (ICT Unit)' (2015), http://www.agc.gov.bn/AGC%20Site%20Pages/Information%20and%20Communication%20Technology%20Unit%20(ICT%20Unit).aspx.

130 Ministry of Health, 'Media Statement on the Current COVID-19 Infection in Brunei Darussalam: 11 March 2020', http://www.moh.gov.bn/Shared%20Documents/2019%20ncov/press%20releases/FINAL_ENG_MEDIA%20STATEMENT%20COVID-19%20INFECTION_11.03.2020.pdf.

131 Ministry of Health, 'Useful Guidelines on Covid-19', http://www.moh.gov.bn/SitePages/guidelinesCOVID-19.aspx; Prime Minister's Office, 'Guideline for Business Continuity Plan on Covid-19 for Civil Service' (2020), http://pmo.gov.bn/SiteCollectionDocuments/covid19/bcp-eng.pdf.

132 Meanwhile, the courts demonstrated adaptability to new technologies in their efforts to ensure operation continuity by utilising Microsoft Teams and Zoom to conduct remote hearings and video-conferencing. See D.S.P.S. Chong, 'Speech by the Honourable Chief Justice Dato Seri Paduka Steven Chong: Opening of Legal Year 2021' (2021), p. 3, http://www.judiciary.gov.bn/legal_year_speech/The%20Honourable%20Chief%20Justice%20Speech%202021.pdf.

3.2.1. *Achievements before the Pandemic*

Fortunately, tertiary online education has been practised in Brunei for several years.[133] The Centre for Lifelong Learning (C3L) at UBD has been offering bachelor's and master's courses, including some law-related ones such as International Legal Issues, that follow a blended learning approach, providing students with video lectures, topic notes, online discussions and assessments.[134] Web-based learning management systems such as Canvas and Moodle have been operating at UBD, UTB and other universities for a couple of years to teach law and other disciplines.[135] In contrast, continuing (post-admission) legal education mostly took place physically in and outside of Brunei. In 2019, for instance, many lawyers attended the Trial Advocacy Course by the Law Society of Brunei Darussalam held at the Supreme Court Building.[136] Judges, including those working for the Syariah courts, were sent for various capacity-building courses, such as a three-week attachment programme to the Singapore Supreme Court and Judiciary Training on Modern Secured Legal Principles in Bandar Seri Begawan.[137] Face-to-face communication appeared to be preferred in these training programmes.

3.2.2. *Achievements and Challenges after the Pandemic*

The surge of COVID-19 in March 2020 made the Prime Minister's Office order Bruneian universities to prepare Business Continuity Plans and operate based on these Plans.[138] This led the universities to shift their teaching delivery and assessment into online modes, as demonstrated in the summary table below.

---

133 M. Shahrill, N. Noorashid and C. Keasberry, 'COVID-19 and Educational Practices and Responses in Brunei Darussalam' in L.H. Phan et al. (eds), *Globalisation, Education and Reform in Brunei Darussalam*, Palgrave MacMillan, Switzerland 2021, pp. 325–354.

134 Centre for Lifelong Learning, 'Who We Are: About Us', https://ubd.edu.bn/c3l/about-c3l.html; Centre for Lifelong Learning, 'Master of Government: Programme', https://ubd.edu.bn/c3l/master-of-government.html.

135 M. Shahrill et al., 'New Norms and Opportunities from the COVID-19 Pandemic Crisis in a Higher Education Setting: Perspectives from Universiti Brunei Darussalam' (2021) 35(3) *International Journal of Educational Management* 700; W.S.H. Suhaili, 'Brunei Darussalam – Impact of COVID-19 on Brunei's Higher Education Teaching' (2020) *Higher Education in Southeast Asia and Beyond* 25.

136 F. Faisal, 'Course Leaves Lawyers More Knowledgeable on Trial Advocacy', *Borneo Bulletin* (28.07.2019), https://borneobulletin.com.bn/course-leaves-lawyers-knowledgeable-trial-advocacy/.

137 State Judiciary Department, 'Legal Year 2020' (2020), p. 94ff, http://www.judiciary.gov.bn/Publication%20Document%20Library/Legal%20Year%202020.pdf.

138 Prime Minister's Office, 'Guideline for Business Continuity Plan on Covid-19 for Civil Service' (2020), http://pmo.gov.bn/SiteCollectionDocuments/covid19/bcp-eng.pdf.

Table 1. Teaching delivery and assessment at Bruneian universities during the COVID-19 pandemic[139]

University	Teaching Delivery	Assessment
UBD	Online via Canvas	100% coursework or online examinations
UTB	Online education platforms and other non-face-to-face teaching delivery methods	No on-campus examination and all assessments converted to 100% coursework
UNISSA	Online via its learning management systems and other teaching and learning technologies	Online exams or coursework
KUPUSB	Online programmes	Online exams or coursework

UBD shifted to a fully online mode within three days of the confirmation of the first COVID-19 case in Brunei. The delivery of all lectures was done through live video, recorded video and PowerPoint presentations with narration, using online platforms such as BigBlueButton integrated into Canvas. Tutorials were converted to online assignments and discussion boards, while complex problem-solving learning sessions were conducted by video-conferencing tools such as Microsoft Teams, Zoom and Skype. Only important practical and clinical sessions continued to be in person, with social distancing majors adopted, but non-essential ones were replaced with video demonstrations on the internet.[140] The other universities appeared to adopt more or less the same approaches.[141]

Following the government's de-escalation measures, the universities in the academic year 2020/21 started transitioning from full-online modes to blended learning modes where students experience virtual and in-person classes.[142] Since then, the ratio of online teaching has been decreasing gradually, which has spared some time for Bruneian academics to reflect on the issues and challenges they faced in their virtual classrooms.

---

139 M. Shahrill and G. Hardaker, 'Country Case Report: Brunei Darussalam' in M.R. Panigrahi and B. Phalachandra (eds), *Handbook on Online Education in Commonwealth Asia: Case Studies*, Commonwealth Educational Media Centre for Asia (CEMCA), New Delhi 2022, pp. 39–41.

140 M. Shahrill et al., 'New Norms and Opportunities from the COVID-19 Pandemic Crisis in a Higher Education Setting: Perspectives from Universiti Brunei Darussalam' (2021) 35(3) *International Journal of Educational Management* 700.

141 W.S.H. Suhaili, 'Brunei Darussalam – Impact of COVID-19 on Brunei's Higher Education Teaching' (2020) *Higher Education in Southeast Asia and Beyond* 25; M. Shahrill, N. Noorashid and C. Keasberry, 'COVID-19 and Educational Practices and Responses in Brunei Darussalam' in L.H. Phan et al. (eds), *Globalisation, Education and Reform in Brunei Darussalam*, Palgrave MacMillan, Switzerland 2021.

142 For example, see UBD, 'UBD in the COVID-19 Pandemic' (2020), https://ubd.edu.bn/news-and-events/covid19.html.

First, there was the challenge of internet connectivity and accessibility, as reported by many teachers and lecturers during their remote teaching period.[143] Though inevitable, the switch to online working took place abruptly in March 2020 on a nationwide scale, involving almost all schools and higher education institutions, as well as many government agencies and companies. The sudden rise in internet traffic put pressure on internet capacity and disrupted internet connections elsewhere, as indicated by the Brunei Computer Emergency Response Team's survey, in which 69% of respondents reported they experienced internet speed and performance issues.[144] There was also the problem of pricing, as indicated by the fact that 52% answered that the cost of an internet subscription was a challenge for learning and working from home. Fortunately, however, those issues have been mitigated and improved, thanks to institutional efforts by various stakeholders. For example, UBD acquired sponsorships from its alumni and stakeholders to provide underprivileged students with laptops and internet data bundles.[145] The Ministry of Transport and Info-communications, the Ministry of Education and the AITI launched multi-sectoral initiatives to respond to the urgent and increasing demand for online education at all levels in the society.[146] The private sector has also been collaborating with the government to support students by donating devices, among other things.[147]

Second, there was the problem of students' psychological wellbeing. Teaching students online during the pandemic disconnects them from their colleagues and instructors. Even UBD students, whose typical duration of fully online study was from March to September 2020 and therefore shorter than many students outside of Brunei,[148] suffered from mental health issues due to the

---

143 N. Noorashid et al., 'Higher Education Institutions in the New Semester: Moving beyond "Pandemic" Pedagogy' in L.H. Phan et al. (eds), *Globalisation, Education and Reform in Brunei Darussalam*, Palgrave MacMillan, Switzerland 2021, pp. 355–375.

144 Brunei Computer Emergency Response Team (BruCERT), 'Survey on Learning/Working from Home: April 17–23, 2020' (2020), https://www.secureverifyconnect.info/sites/default/files/pdf/BruCERT_WFH_Survey_Report_2020.pdf?utm_source=svc&utm_medium=link&utm_campaign=wfh.

145 UBD, 'UBD Alumni & Donors Contribute Towards Students' Online Education', *UBD News* (15.04.2020), https://ubd.edu.bn/news-and-events/news/2020/04/15/ubd-alumni-and-donors-contribute-towards-students%E2%80%99-online-education/.

146 N. Noorashid et al., 'Higher Education Institutions in the New Semester: Moving beyond "Pandemic" Pedagogy' in L.H. Phan et al. (eds), *Globalisation, Education and Reform in Brunei Darussalam*, Palgrave MacMillan, Switzerland 2021, pp. 355–375.

147 Borneo Bulletin Reporter, 'Donate ICT Devices, Support Online Learning' *Borneo Bulletin* (12.04.2020), https://borneobulletin.com.bn/donate-ict-devices-support-online-learning/.

148 M. Alam and C.Y. Hoon, 'Digidemic and Students' Hysteresis during Online Learning' in L.H. Phan et al. (eds), *Globalisation, Education and Reform in Brunei Darussalam*, Palgrave MacMillan, Switzerland 2021, pp. 377–391.

lack of human-to-human interactions, cultural cues and gestures during remote learning.[149] For example, one student commented:

> It felt as if I was being entrapped in my own room ... I was left alone with my thoughts. A subtle form of depression had eaten my mind up from thinking of every bad thing that had happened before and the calamity to come in the future. It had also worsened my social anxiety, for I had become somewhat accustomed to being alone for weeks, even months.[150]

Another student stated: '[w]ith little to no social contact with my other classmates, I felt a sense of loneliness, even to the point where I missed going to the campus physically – something I had never thought I would feel before'.[151]

Because Brunei succeeded in containing the spread of the virus during the first wave of the pandemic, the universities started returning to business as usual, and face-to-face courses resumed in late 2020. Nevertheless, those challenges in online (legal) education had to be addressed for the universities to take full advantage of new opportunities[152] and to prepare for the unlikely event of the next wave of the pandemic.[153] Unfortunately, the unlikely event became a reality – the second wave of the pandemic finally arrived on Brunei's shores on 7 August 2021, which forced the country to declare another nationwide partial lockdown.[154] All universities quickly switched back to full-online mode, taking advantage of the lessons they had learned from their experience during the first wave.

---

149 C. Keasberry et al., 'Facing the Mental Health Challenges of COVID-19 in HE', *University World News: the Global Window on Higher Education* (05.12.2020), https://www.universityworldnews.com/post.php?story=20201201133134894.

150 M. Alam and C.Y. Hoon, 'Digidemic and Students' Hysteresis during Online Learning' in L.H. Phan et al. (eds), *Globalisation, Education and Reform in Brunei Darussalam*, Palgrave MacMillan, Switzerland 2021, pp. 377–391.

151 Ibid.

152 For example, the universities can be more accessible to international students without leaving the country. See, for example, UBD's approach during the pandemic: M. Shahrill et al., 'Institutional Case Report: Universiti Brunei Darussalam' in M.R. Panigrahi and B. Phalachandra (eds), *Handbook on Online Education in Commonwealth Asia: Case Studies*, Commonwealth Educational Media Centre for Asia (CEMCA), New Delhi 2022, pp. 177–190.

153 While the pandemic was at its peak in Brunei, many continuing legal education courses were cancelled, postponed or moved to online. See State Judiciary Department, 'Legal Year 2021' (2021), http://www.judiciary.gov.bn/Publication%20Document%20Library/Legal%20Year%202021.pdf. According to local practitioners, the difficulty in organising internet training sessions is fundraising, since the norm in some parts of Southeast Asia is to make webinars free of charge, and therefore some people are not happy to pay registration fees for events that do not let instructors speak in person and in front of participants.

154 S. Han, 'Brunei Extends Partial Lockdown until Sept 4', *The Scoop* (21.08.2021), https://thescoop.co/2021/08/21/brunei-maintains-covid-19-restrictions-for-two-more-weeks/.

4. SINGAPORE

The city-state of Singapore is known as a major hub for finance and shipping as well as for being a centre for cross-border dispute settlement in the Asia-Pacific region.[155] Attracted by the prosperity, there are around 6,000 practitioners, educated and trained in and outside Singapore, who work there, forming a large legal sector for a city of six million people.[156]

4.1. BACKGROUND FOR SINGAPORE

Although the origin of Singapore's legal system can be traced back to the English common law, it has evolved independently over the years into 'the common law system of Singapore'. Today, court decisions from England and other Commonwealth jurisdictions have no binding force in the country. Decisions from the Singapore Court of Appeal provide the precedents for the lower-level courts, the Singapore High Court and the State Courts.[157] Under the Civil Law Act, the Singapore courts administer the common law and equity.[158] Moreover, Muslim law is practised by the Syariah Court in accordance with the Administration of Muslim Law Act (AMLA),[159] and deals with specific personal legal matters concerning Muslims or parties married under Muslim law, including issues arising from marriages, divorces, the nullity of marriages and judicial separations.[160] Appeals from the Syariah Court's decisions are heard by the single Appeal Board only,[161] in contrast to the Muslim courts in Brunei that have three levels of appeal.[162]

---

155 For the Singapore government's recent initiatives in international dispute resolution, see L. Nottage et al. (eds), *New Frontiers in Asia-Pacific International Arbitration and Dispute Resolution*, Wolters Kluwer, Alphen aan den Rijn 2021.

156 The Law Society of Singapore, 'Statistics of Lawyers & Law Practices in Singapore: As of 31 August 2020' (2021), https://www.lawsociety.org.sg/news-media/statistics/. See also N. Teramura, *Ex Aequo et Bono as a Response to the 'OverJudicialisation' of International Commercial Arbitration*, Wolters Kluwer, Alphen aan den Rijn 2020, for the side effect of fierce competition among dispute resolution lawyers and its potential solutions.

157 Government of Singapore, 'Jurisdiction of the Supreme Court' (2021), https://www.supremecourt.gov.sg/who-we-are/the-supreme-court/supreme-court-jurisdiction; E.K.B. Tan and G. Chan, 'Ch. 01 The Singapore Legal System', *Singapore Law Watch* (2019), https://www.singaporelawwatch.sg/About-Singapore-Law/Overview/ch-01-the-singapore-legal-system.

158 Section 3 of the Civil Law Act (Cap 43, Revised Edition 1999).

159 Cap 3, Revised Edition 2009.

160 Section 35 of the AMLA.

161 Section 55 of the AMLA.

162 See section 3.1 above.

4.1.1. *Singapore's Legal Profession*

For a candidate to be called to the Singapore Bar, s/he must have obtained 'qualified person' status by earning a law degree (either LLB or JD) from the National University of Singapore (NUS), the Singapore Management University (SMU), the Singapore University of Social Sciences (SUSS) or, if s/he is a citizen or permanent resident of Singapore, one of the approved universities in the United Kingdom, the United States, Australia, Canada and New Zealand.[163] The candidate is then eligible to take the bar exam. However, different conditions apply to law graduates from the Singaporean universities (local graduates) and those from the approved foreign universities (overseas graduates). To be called to the Bar, both local and overseas graduates need to go through the full-time Preparatory Course leading to Part B of the Singapore Bar Examinations and then a six-month training period with a Singapore law practice. However, overseas graduates must undertake Part A of the Bar Examination before the Part B Examination (the Singapore equivalent of the Malaysian CPE). Overseas graduates might find their pathway more challenging because the recent Part A Exam's passing rate has been around 70%, while Part B Exam's rate has historically been close to 100%.[164] Moreover, around 90% of local graduates secured training contracts from 2012 to 2016, but only around 70% of overseas graduates managed to secure such contracts from 2013 to 2017.[165]

Accordingly, various stakeholders act as gatekeepers to the Singapore legal profession. With respect to local graduates, the three Singaporean universities are the main gatekeepers since whether the graduates can be admitted to the Bar and find employment is determined primarily by their academic record issued by the universities. As for overseas graduates, the legal job market and the existing legal profession function as the main gatekeepers because there

163 See Rules 4–6 (on the Singaporean law schools) and Rules 8–12 (on the foreign law schools) of the Legal Profession (Qualified Persons) Rules. In terms of the requirement of certain academic performance, the Rules set different criteria for different universities. For example, LLB holders from Singaporean universities must have attained at least lower second-class honours from NUS, a grade point average of at least 3.00 from SMU or a grade point average of at least 3.50 from SUSS.

164 The Committee for the Professional Training of Lawyers, 'Report of the Committee for the Professional Training of Lawyers' (2018), pp. 7 and 23, https://www.supremecourt.gov.sg/docs/default-source/default-document-library/report-of-the-committee-for-the-professional-training-of-lawyers.pdf, noting that 'the percentage of candidates who passed the Part A examinations has steadily declined in recent years (79% in 2015 and 2016, and 64% in 2017) from a consistent pass rate of over 90% from 2010 to 2014' (p. 7).

165 Ibid., also noting that, from 2012 to 2016, 98% of local law graduates found employment within six months of graduation.

are 27 approved foreign universities,[166] and whether the graduates can become qualified lawyers depends on if they can pass the Part A Exam and secure trainee contracts.

From 2023 onwards, the legal profession and the market are to play more active roles in gatekeeping. Due to the oversupply of law graduates,[167] Chief Justice Sundaresh Menon established in August 2016 the Committee for the Professional Training of Lawyers. In August 2018, the Ministry of Law accepted the Committee's reform recommendations, including: '(a) uncoupling admission to the Bar from the completion of a practice training contract; (b) lengthening the practice training period from six months to one year; and (c) raising the standard and stringency of Part B of the Singapore Bar Examinations'.[168] The implication of recommendation (c) is that the number of qualified lawyers (including non-practising lawyers) is likely to be controlled and limited by the existing legal profession.[169] Recommendations (a) and (b) may mean that the number of legal practitioners is to be decided by law firms and others eligible to offer the one-year training contracts.

4.1.2. Universities in Singapore

For aspirants to the Singapore Bar, the NUS Faculty of Law, SMU School of Law and SUSS School of Law offer different LLB and Juris Doctor (JD) programmes with different durations and components depending on students' needs.[170] The three public institutions also offer Master of Laws (LLM) and PhD in Law

---

166 As of 18 May 2021, see: Singapore Institute of Legal Education, 'Qualified Person: Approved Universities – Australia and New Zealand' (2021), https://www.sile.edu.sg/australia-and-new-zealand-approved-universities; Singapore Institute of Legal Education, 'Qualified Person: Approved Universities – United Kingdom' (2021), https://www.sile.edu.sg/united-kingdom-approved-universities; Singapore Institute of Legal Education, 'Qualified Person: Approved Universities – United States of America' (2021), https://www.sile.edu.sg/united-states-of-america-approved-universities.

167 The Committee for the Professional Training of Lawyers, 'Report of the Committee for the Professional Training of Lawyers' (2018), https://www.supremecourt.gov.sg/docs/default-source/default-document-library/report-of-the-committee-for-the-professional-training-of-lawyers.pdf; H. Loo, 'The Singapore Legal Industry: A Brief Overview and Comparison', International Immersion Program Papers (2017), https://chicagounbound.uchicago.edu/cgi/viewcontent.cgi?article=1051&context=international_immersion_program_papers.

168 Ministry of Law Singapore, 'Law Ministry Accepts Recommendations to Strengthen Professional Training of Lawyers' (30.08.2018), https://www.mlaw.gov.sg/news/press-releases/law-ministry-accepts-recommendations-to-strengthen-professional.

169 L. Lam, '"They Are Literally Raising the Bar": Changes to Singapore Bar Exams Draw Mixed Feelings', *CNA* (31.08.2018), https://www.channelnewsasia.com/news/singapore/they-are-literally-raising-the-bar-changes-to-singapore-bar-10668692.

170 NUS Law, 'Prospective Students', https://law.nus.edu.sg/prospective-students/; SMU Yong Pung How School of Law, 'Start Your Journey' (2021), https://law.smu.edu.sg/; SUSS, 'Law Programmes' (2021), https://www.suss.edu.sg/law-programmes.

degrees as well as diplomas and certificates for those who intend to deepen their expertise in a specific area of law, such as international arbitration and dispute resolution.[171] Hence, those postgraduate programmes are not designed for Bar candidates but for qualified lawyers and other international students, as discussed in this section.

According to the Singaporean government, around 10% of students at the public universities in Singapore are from overseas,[172] while certain World University Rankings suggest a significantly different percentage – 25%.[173] No discernible evidence shows the universities' revenues from international students, but typically their tuition fees are more than twice as much as domestic students' tuition fees or even higher, if they are not the recipients of the Ministry of Education's tuition grant.[174] As the government expenditure on tuition grants and scholarships for international students has fallen about 50% over the last 10 years,[175] the students' overall direct financial contribution to the universities has probably been increasing.

The law schools also generate income from foreign students. Key reasons for the NUS Faculty of Law to offer LLM courses are to attract talents from the Asia-Pacific region and 'to provide the school with a potential source of additional revenue as graduate fees can be set more flexibly compared to undergraduate fees'.[176] No official statistics show how many international students are enrolled at the Faculty of Law, but assuming many of them are learning as LLM students, their ratio to domestic students will be significant if not outstanding. During the 2020/21 academic year, 900 students in Years 1–4 pursued LLB degrees[177]

---

171 For example, see NUS Law, 'Coursework Degrees' (2021), https://law1.nus.edu.sg/admissions/coursework_deg.html.

172 Government of Singapore, 'Is It True Our Public Universities Reserve 20% of Their Places for Foreign Students?', *gov.sg* (27.01.2018), https://www.gov.sg/article/is-it-true-our-public-universities-reserve-20-of-their-places-for-foreign-students.

173 Times Higher Education, 'World University Rankings 2021' (2021), https://www.timeshighereducation.com/world-university-rankings/2021/world-ranking#!/page/0/length/25/sort_by/rank/sort_order/asc/cols/stats.

174 For example, at NUS, the tuition fees for new law students admitted in the 2021/22 academic year are 12,650 SGD for Singapore citizens, 17,700 SGD for permanent residents, 27,050 SGD for international students and 38,300 SGD for students not in receipt of the MOE's tuition grant: NUS, 'Undergraduate Students: Tuition Fees Per Annum (applicable for Academic Year 2021/2022)' (2021), https://www.nus.edu.sg/registrar/docs/info/administrative-policies-procedures/ugtuitioncurrent.pdf.

175 Y. Sharma, 'Government Pressed on Scholarships for Foreign Students', *University World News: The Global Window on Higher Education* (05.09.2019), https://www.universityworldnews.com/post.php?story=20190905133327836.

176 T.C. Han, 'NUS Law in the Noughties: Becoming "Asia's Global Law School"' (2017) *Singapore Journal of Legal Studies* 215, 220.

177 NUS, 'Summary of Undergraduate Student Enrolment 2020/2021: As at 30 Aug 2020' (2020), https://www.nus.edu.sg/registrar/docs/info/student-statistics/enrolment-statistics/undergraduate-studies/ug-enrol-20202021.pdf.

and most of them were Singaporeans.[178] In the same academic year, 143 LLM students were enrolled to complete their 'one-year' degree programmes.[179] This means that their number is somewhat comparable to that of LLB students,[180] since 518 LLM students in total were enrolled in the academic years 2017/18–2020/21.[181] Indeed, the exact number of international LLM students is unclear, but they make up the majority of students taking part in LLM courses.[182]

4.1.3. ICT in Singapore

The Infocomm Media Development Authority of Singapore's surveys in 2019 suggest that affordable and reliable ICT infrastructure is available for most university students, lectures and businesses, including legal professionals in Singapore, as follows:

- about 89% of resident households had access to a computer (like a desktop, laptop, notebook or tablet) at home, and about 10% of the respondents having no such computer access raised cost as the main reason for not purchasing a computer;[183]

---

178 NUS Law, '4-Year LLB Programme' (2021), https://law1.nus.edu.sg/admissions/4_yrs_llb_prog.html (noting that 'although most of the LLB students are Singaporeans, the Programme is also open to international students').

179 NUS, 'Summary of Graduate Student Enrolment 2020/2021: As at 30 Aug 2020' (2020), https://www.nus.edu.sg/registrar/docs/info/student-statistics/enrolment-statistics/graduate-studies/gd-enrol-20202021.pdf; NUS Law, 'Degree Requirements for Graduate Coursework Programmes' (2021), https://law1.nus.edu.sg/student_matters/grad_prog/gdc_deg_reqm.html.

180 The number of students enrolled at other courses was not outstanding: respectively, graduate LLB programmes (i.e. three-year JD programmes from 2021/22) (15) and PhD programmes (18). No discernible statistics are available for JD students.

181 NUS, 'Summary of Graduate Student Enrolment 2017/2018: As at 03 Sep 2017' (2017), https://www.nus.edu.sg/registrar/docs/info/student-statistics/enrolment-statistics/graduate-studies/gd-enrol-20172018.pdf; NUS, 'Summary of Graduate Student Enrolment 2018/2019: As at 03 Sep 2018' (2018), https://www.nus.edu.sg/registrar/docs/info/student-statistics/enrolment-statistics/graduate-studies/gd-enrol-20182019.pdf; NUS, 'Summary of Graduate Student Enrolment 2019/2020: As at 03 Sep 2019' (2019), https://www.nus.edu.sg/registrar/docs/info/student-statistics/enrolment-statistics/graduate-studies/gd-enrol-20192020.pdf; NUS, 'Summary of Graduate Student Enrolment 2020/2021: As at 30 Aug 2020' (2020), https://www.nus.edu.sg/registrar/docs/info/student-statistics/enrolment-statistics/graduate-studies/gd-enrol-20202021.pdf.

182 NUS Law, 'Frequently Asked Questions (FAQs): Admissions and Application' (2021), https://law1.nus.edu.sg/admissions/faqs_grad.html (noting '[a]ll programs are conducted on-campus', although Singaporean universities have been passionate to adopt online teaching since before the pandemic, as discussed in section 4.2). According to a senior law lecturer at NUS, 'more than 90% of LLM students are international students, while 99% of LLB students are domestic students'.

183 Infocomm Media Development Authority, 'Annual Survey on Infocomm Usage in Households and by Individuals for 2019' (2019), p. 7, https://www.imda.gov.sg/-/media/Imda/Files/Infocomm-Media-Landscape/Research-and-Statistics/Survey-Report/2019-HH-Public-Report_09032020.pdf?la=en. Note that 'resident' means Singapore citizen or permanent resident, and 'computer access' means access to desktops, laptops, notebooks and tablets.

- residential households' home internet and broadband access rates were 98.4% and 98.2%, respectively;[184]
- almost 100% of resident households reported using an internet-enabled mobile phone (i.e. internet-enabled feature phone or smartphone) to access the internet at home;[185]
- among households without internet access, 4% raised high equipment costs and 2% raised high internet subscription costs as reasons for not having internet access at home;[186]
- education services led ICT adoption in many aspects, with 99% internet and broadband usage and 96% computer usage;[187]
- business services recorded 97% usage of internet, broadband and computers;[188] and
- about 93% of businesses used virus checking or protection software, 80% used anti-spyware software, 79% had a firewall, and 77% used spam filters and anti-phishing protection.[189]

Moreover, Singapore ranked sixth in Opensignal's 2020 rankings of countries by mobile (cellular only) download speed,[190] fifth in Opensignal's 2020 rankings of countries by the quality of mobile video experience[191] and first in the March 2021 Speedtest Global Index by fixed broadband speed.[192]

Finally, the Singaporean judiciary has been active in utilising ICT in the courts for many years, to enhance its efficiency.[193] For instance, it launched in 1995 the first Technology Court equipped with, among other things, the latest audio-visual technology and video-conferencing facilities.[194] It also introduced

184 Ibid.

185 Ibid.

186 Ibid.

187 Infocomm Media Development Authority, 'Annual Survey on Infocomm Usage by Enterprises for 2019' (2019), p. 12, https://www.imda.gov.sg/-/media/Imda/Files/Industry-Development/Fact-and-Figures/Infocomm-Usage-Business/Infocomm-Usage-Survey-Public-Report-2019.pdf?la=en.

188 Ibid.

189 Ibid.

190 S. Fenwick and H. Khatri, 'The State of Mobile Network Experience 2020: One Year Into the 5G Era' (2020) p. 9, https://www.opensignal.com/sites/opensignal-com/files/data/reports/pdf-only/data-2020-05/state_of_mobile_experience_may_2020_opensignal_3_0.pdf.

191 Ibid.

192 Speedtest, 'Singapore's Mobile and Fixed Broadband Internet Speeds' (2021), https://www.speedtest.net/global-index/singapore#fixed.

193 E.K.B. Tan and G. Chan, 'Ch. 01 The Singapore Legal System', *Singapore Law Watch* (2019), https://www.singaporelawwatch.sg/About-Singapore-Law/Overview/ch-01-the-singapore-legal-system.

194 T.B. Heng, 'E-litigation: The Singapore Experience', *Focus*, https://v1.lawgazette.com.sg/2001-11/Nov01-focus2.htm; Government of Singapore, 'Court Services: Video Conference Facilities ("VC Facilities")' (2021), https://www.supremecourt.gov.sg/services/court-services/video-conference-facilities.

the Electronic Filing System (EFS) in 2000, to improve the conduct of civil litigation by enabling parties to prepare and file court documents electronically.[195] In 2013, the EFS was upgraded to e-litigation with additional functionality such as e-mail and short message services (SMS) reminder alerts for the management of case files, an online calendaring and hearing management system to select hearing dates and a form of secure access to the web-based service via Singpass – Singapore residents' digital identification.[196] Other technologies available in the courts include Mobile Infocomm Technology Facilities, comprising the Mobile Video Conferencing System, the Visualiser System, which makes it possible to project and magnify images of 3D objects or hardcopy documents, and a high-definition TV with interactive display system, allowing users to annotate and preserve multimedia contents.[197]

4.2. SINGAPORE'S MOVES TOWARDS ONLINE EDUCATION

The first COVID-19 case in Singapore was confirmed on 23 January 2020. After that, the number of imported cases and local transmissions grew exponentially, so the Singaporean government issued on 3 April 2020 the COVID-19 Control Order to implement circuit breaker measures consisting of lockdown restrictions and *cordons sanitaires*.[198] The Order came into force on 7 April 2020. The universities moved to full home-based learning mode.[199]

4.2.1. Achievements before the Pandemic

Fortunately, however, Singaporean universities have been embracing digital learning platforms since 2003, when SARS first surfaced in the country. Facing

195 Government of Singapore, 'Services for the Legal Profession: Elitigation' (2021), https://www.supremecourt.gov.sg/services/services-for-the-legal-profession.

196 Ibid.

197 Government of Singapore, 'Court Services: Mobile Infocomm Technology Facilities ("MIT Facilities")' (2021), https://www.supremecourt.gov.sg/services/court-services/mobile-info-tech-trolley-booking.

198 The COVID-19 (Temporary Measures) Act 2020: https://sso.agc.gov.sg/SL/COVID19TMA2020-S254-2020.

199 M. Mohan and A.H. Min, 'COVID-19: Singapore Makes "Decisive Move" to Close Most Workplaces and Impose Full Home-based Learning for Schools, Says PM Lee', *CNA* (03.04.2020), https://www.channelnewsasia.com/news/singapore/covid19-decisive-move-workplaces-closed-lee-hsien-loong-12606614?cid=h3_referral_inarticlelinks_24082018_cna; C.H. Min, '"Right Time" to Close Schools Now, Says Education Minister Ong Ye Kung', *CNA* (03.04.2020), https://www.channelnewsasia.com/news/singapore/schools-to-close-apr-8-ong-ye-kung-covid19-coronavirus-12606672; J. Lau, 'Asia's Cautious Restarts Offer Glimpse of Post-Covid Campus Life: The Areas Hit Earliest by the Coronavirus Are Reopening, but with Protections in Place', *Times Higher Education* (09.06.2020), https://www.timeshighereducation.com/news/asias-cautious-restarts-offer-glimpse-post-covid-campus-life.

a real possibility of campus closure, by late 2003 many universities had installed 'commercial or home grown learning management systems, content management systems, content development tools and a high bandwidth campus network'.[200] For example, NUS established a robust ICT and e-learning infrastructure: a self-developed course management system called the Integrated Virtual Learning Environment (IVLE), campus-wide licences for Adobe Presenter (Breeze), which supports content development with PowerPoint, screen-recording software called Camtasia Relay, and the recording and streaming of lectures available through the campus intranet.[201] These software facilities and hardware devices experienced major upgrades in 2009 when NUS conducted the first university-wide e-learning week requiring all faculties except the Duke-NUS Medical School to move all lectures online.[202] In 2013, NUS partnered with Coursera, a global learning platform, to offer online courses to the world and create online materials for experimenting with the 'flipped classroom' model of teaching.[203] Accordingly, Singaporean universities started preparation for teaching law and other subjects online well before the COVID-19 pandemic.

Post-admission legal education has also relied on online learning methods for several years. With effect from January 2017, all advocates and solicitors admitted to the Singapore Bar and holding Singapore Practising Certificates, and foreign lawyers registered under section 36B of the Legal Profession Act and holding foreign practitioner certificates, must satisfy the CPD requirements under Rule 2 of the Legal Profession (Continuing Professional Development) Rules 2012 (Legal Profession Rules).[204] Fulfilling the CPD requirements involves collecting CPD points by doing certain activities for the continuing professional development of advocates, solicitors and foreign lawyers, and such

---

200 R. Chandran, 'National University of Singapore's Campus-Wide e-Learning Week', *Technology in Higher Education: The State of The Art* (2011), p. 2, https://cpb-us-w2.wpmucdn.com/blog.nus.edu.sg/dist/0/119/files/2011/03/national-university-of-singapores-campus-wide-elearning-week.pdf.

201 Ibid. The NUS launched the IVLE in 1997, and the system has various functions such as discussion forums, chat rooms, online quizzes, assignment repositories, video webcasting, archiving of lectures and SMS announcements to students: M.I. Bashar and H. Khan, 'E-Learning in Singapore: A Brief Assessment', U21 Global Working Paper (2007), p. 7, https://papers.ssrn.com/sol3/papers.cfm?abstract_id=1601611.

202 R. Chandran, 'National University of Singapore's Campus-Wide e-Learning Week', *Technology in Higher Education: The State of The Art* (2011), https://cpb-us-w2.wpmucdn.com/blog.nus.edu.sg/dist/0/119/files/2011/03/national-university-of-singapores-campus-wide-elearning-week.pdf. NUS had held the e-learning week event every year until around 2016. SMU has had a university-wide e-learning day each year.

203 A. Tan, 'Zoom Is Your New Classroom: Will Online Education Become the Norm After COVID-19?', *Vulcan Post* (12.06.2020), https://vulcanpost.com/701216/university-online-education-covid-19-singapore/.

204 Singapore Institute of Legal Education, 'FAQs for Lawyers' (2021), https://www.silecpdcentre.sg/FAQs/Lawyers-FAQs/; The Law Society of Singapore, 'PC Application' (2021), https://www.lawsociety.org.sg/for-lawyers/pc-application/. Note that CPD stands for continuing professional development.

activities may consist of 'attending, or *reviewing a recording of*, any conference, lecture, seminar, workshop or discussion group' and '*reviewing any multimedia, Internet-based, audio-visual, audio or video programme or material*'.[205] Accordingly, before the pandemic, the lawyers were able to claim their CPD points without joining face-to-face events.

4.2.2. Achievements and Challenges after the Pandemic

Even though the COVID-19 pandemic forced Singaporean universities to expand their online teaching capacity abruptly in the middle of the second term of the 2019/20 academic year, they managed to handle the situation with great flexibility. For instance, SMU moved all classes online from 30 March 2020, adopting synchronous methods including Zoom and asynchronous methods like recorded lectures.[206] Many law classes were taught by using the former methods as their size was small and suitable for tutorial styles. No exams were held on campus, as they were conducted online or replaced with other assessments, such as coursework. Moreover, taking into account sudden ordeals for students caused by the pandemic, the university gave them a choice to take the grades for some or all of the courses they took in the semester or turn them into Pass/Fail grades, provided that the students were still subject to a minimum of 21 graded credits as required for graduation, as per SMU's policy.[207] Since the commencement of the 2020/21 academic year in August 2020, SMU had gradually resumed operations on campus. During the first term, the majority of courses were still conducted entirely online.[208] However, a small portion of courses adopted a mixed approach that made around half of the class attend physically, observing rigorous safe distancing measures. The other half would join online using live-streaming and other online means.[209] The university then decided on a weekly or fortnightly rotation cycle for students to alternate between physical attendance and online attendance.[210] On the commencement of the second term on 11 January 2021, SMU eased restrictions further with Singapore entering its Phase 3 post-circuit breaker, so that it started offering face-to-face classes on campus with no provision for online classes as default

205 Rule 3(1)(a)–(b) of the Legal Profession Rules (emphasis added).

206 T. Clark, 'Key Changes to UG/JD Teaching and Exams for Current Semester', *Provost's Message* (26.03.2020), https://crisisresponse.smu.edu.sg/sites/crisisresponse.smu.edu.sg/files/2020-03/Key%20changes%20to%20UG%3AJD%20teaching%20and%20exams%20for%20current%20semester.pdf.

207 Ibid. Note that SMU does not use grading curves in evaluating students' performances.

208 T. Clark, 'Update on Broad Plans for AY2020/21 Term 1', *Provost's Message* (29.05.2020), https://crisisresponse.smu.edu.sg/sites/crisisresponse.smu.edu.sg/files/2020-06/circulars_20200529.pdf.

209 Ibid.

210 Ibid.

teaching delivery methods.[211] Exceptionally, however, instructors were given the option of holding lessons online, in mixed mode, or in person with the adherence to zoning measures, when they taught some courses with an enrolment exceeding the safe capacity limit of their allocated room and other courses with an enrolment exceeding 50 students.[212]

The NUS Faculty of Law had a slightly different experience. It moved all courses online between April and December 2020, and thus lecturers taught all courses using Zoom and sometimes recorded lectures until the end of 2020.[213] Assessments were also conducted fully online in the forms of online exams and coursework, and no special consideration for plagiarism was required because open-book exams were the norm at the law school. However, unlike at SMU, students at NUS Law were not conferred special Pass/Fail grading options, and therefore the instructors gave the students grades, taking into account the adversity they faced during the pandemic. From January 2021 onwards, as was the case at SMU, face-to-face teaching was resumed for classes with no more than 50 students and no international students enrolled online from overseas.

Finally, the law schools were committed to ensuring that international students received a high-quality remote learning experience during the pandemic. Many professors offered virtual coffee hours and virtual office hours to increase their connectivity with international students and provide them with more opportunities to ask questions. Some lecturers found virtual whiteboard functions helpful in discussing complicated legal concepts with international students. Indeed, the time difference was a challenge for some students studying from foreign countries, but the universities managed to deal with the issue by providing the students with access to recorded lectures and tutorials. Probably the only real difficulty for the universities was to teach students residing in countries and regions with poor internet connectivity, which was beyond their control.

5. CONCLUSIONS

Overall, universities and the legal profession in Malaysia, Brunei and Singapore have been experimenting with online legal education since before the outbreak of

---

211 T. Clark, 'Welcome to Academic Term January 2021', *Provost's Message* (10.01.2021), https://crisisresponse.smu.edu.sg/sites/crisisresponse.smu.edu.sg/files/2021-01/Welcome%20to%20Academic%20Term%20January%202021.pdf; T. Clark, 'Plans for Academic Term Starting January 2021', *Provost's Message* (04.11.2020), https://crisisresponse.smu.edu.sg/sites/crisisresponse.smu.edu.sg/files/2020-11/Plans_for_academic_term_starting_January2021.pdf.

212 T. Clark, 'Plans for Academic Term Starting January 2021', *Provost's Message* (04.11.2020), https://crisisresponse.smu.edu.sg/sites/crisisresponse.smu.edu.sg/files/2020-11/Plans_for_academic_term_starting_January2021.pdf.

213 D. Tan, 'Teaching in Semester 1 of Next Academic Year' (20.06.2020), https://law1.nus.edu.sg/pdfs/student_matters/AY2020-21_Teaching_Advisory_for_Law_Students_20June2020.pdf.

COVID-19, offering online modules (albeit to different extents) and upgrading their ICT infrastructure. The arrival of COVID-19 in March 2020 accelerated this trend in each country with a rapid transition to online learning. The efficiency, effectiveness and impact of that transition, however, has not been felt equally.

Malaysia sits in a very different position to its neighbours in terms of its population size, geography and economic development. The pandemic has also had a greater health and economic impact than on either Brunei or Singapore. Although the federal government of Malaysia has invested substantially in ICT, significant swathes of the population have poor internet connectivity or inadequate access to equipment. This is particularly true in the rural and least developed parts of Malaysia, such as in Sabah and Sarawak. While the situation is better in the urban areas, it is the richer private universities with access to independent resources that have fared better and were more prepared for the pandemic than the public universities, which, with dwindling resources (until very recently), have had to play catch-up and rapidly train their already over-burdened staff. Malaysian students also found it difficult to cope with the transition to the online environment, with significant numbers experiencing financial hardship and psychological problems. The universities adapted and sought to address these issues, but the scale of the problems is difficult for a country to manage efficiently when the economy has been in free-fall[214] and the political situation in flux and very unstable.[215]

Brunei and Singapore are small, relatively wealthy and resource-rich. Thus, they were in a good position to weather the effects of the global pandemic. Brunei suffered from similar, if not worse, internet connectivity issues to Malaysia but had the capacity to upgrade its ICT infrastructure. It also managed the transition to online learning well through a series of public/private partnerships. Given the limited size of its legal profession, the success in containing the virus during the first wave[216] and the preference for in-person teaching, however, the universities in Brunei may be less keen to adopt further online approaches and blended learning in their legal education on a large scale. Following the earlier SARS crisis, Singapore was almost prepared for the pandemic with its universities

---

214 See Y. Ngui and S. Kamaruddin, 'Malaysia to Cut 2021 GDP Growth Outlook, Likely Close to 4%', *Bloomberg* (12.07.2021), https://www.bloomberg.com/news/articles/2021-07-12/malaysia-to-cut-2021-gdp-growth-outlook-possibly-close-to-4.

215 See R. Anand, 'Malaysia's King Says He Did Not Consent to Revoking of Emergency Laws, Regrets Govt Conduct', *The Strait Times* (30.07.2021), https://www.straitstimes.com/asia/se-asia/malaysias-king-says-he-did-not-consent-to-revocation-of-emergency-laws-regrets-govt.

216 A. Othman, 'Brunei's COVID-19 Success Story Garners Global Attention', *Borneo Bulletin* (18.07.2021), https://borneobulletin.com.bn/bruneis-covid-19-success-story-garners-global-attention-2/.

already occasionally offering blended learning well before the COVID-19 crisis. The country is efficient, technologically developed and in a strong position to lead the region by example. It has reliable ICT and almost universal internet access. The courts, legal profession and universities are well trained in online education and in a position to act as an online hub for the region.

ONLINE LEGAL EDUCATION IN THE HONG KONG SAR

From Contingency to Convention

Wilson LUI and Alice LEE

1. INTRODUCTION

This report provides an overview of undergraduate, postgraduate, qualifying (that is, the Postgraduate Certificate in Laws, PCLL) and continuing legal education in Hong Kong, and the relationship between legal education and the legal profession. It also considers the current progress and future outlook of Hong Kong in online legal education, as well as the use of information technology in legal education and within the legal sector, with a particular focus on the effects of the COVID-19 pandemic.[1]

This report observes that the development of Hong Kong online legal education had remained largely stagnant in the pre-pandemic times. During the pandemic, the resort to online legal education in law schools seems to have taken the approach of 'emergency remote teaching',[2] with a tendency to revert to face-to-face instruction and assessment whenever permitted under the pandemic restrictions. On the other hand, continuing legal education has successfully moved towards hybrid or fully online modes of delivery and is likely to remain so in the future. It is argued that the Hong Kong legal education community, and more generally the Hong Kong higher education sector, should take bold steps towards adopting well-designed and effective online pedagogies and assessment practices. As the legal profession and the judiciary in Hong Kong gradually improve their capacities and capabilities to utilise information technology and online tools, the legal education offered in the special administrative region must not shy away from responsibilities to equip aspiring legal professionals with the necessary online and technological skills in preparation for their future legal practice.

2. BACKGROUND

Hong Kong is a common law jurisdiction with its legal system and laws derived historically from the English common law as a former British colony. Following the English legal system, there are two distinct branches of the legal profession: solicitors and barristers. According to the Basic Law, the laws previously in force in Hong Kong are preserved and maintained (unless they contravene the Basic Law) since the handover of Hong Kong to the People's Republic of China in 1997,

---

1 Despite the situation of the pandemic in Hong Kong being relatively mild by global standards, Hong Kong has been imposing one of the strictest isolation and quarantine measures around the world. The cumulative total is around 13,800 cases (within a population of around 7.4 million) as of the end of January 2022. With a severe outbreak in February and March 2022, the cumulative total is around 2.6 million cases as of the end of 2022. For higher education in Hong Kong, suspensions for face-to-face classes and changes to assessments have been in place from time to time over the past two and a half years. The most recent suspension occurred from mid-January 2022 onwards and lasted for almost the whole second semester of the 2021/22 academic year. Face-to-face classes and in-person assessments were generally resumed in the semester commencing September 2022.

2 This term refers to the 'emergency' change of face-to-face delivery modes to online remote learning and is to be contrasted with online learning that has been well-planned and well-designed in advance of the course. The term is coined in C. Hodges, S. Moore, B. Lockee, T. Trust and A. Bond, 'The Difference Between Emergency Remote Teaching and Online Learning' (27 March 2020), https://er.educause.edu/articles/2020/3/the-difference-between-emergency-remote-teaching-and-online-learning. See section 3.

and the legislature may amend these laws.[3] Other laws in force in Hong Kong include new laws enacted by the legislature and a number of national laws listed in Annex III to the Basic Law.[4] The Hong Kong courts are vested with independent judiciary power, free from any interference, and have jurisdiction to adjudicate cases (except over acts of state such as defence and foreign affairs), including the power of final adjudication, and 'may refer to precedents of other common law jurisdictions'.[5] In practice, the Hong Kong courts have very frequently and consistently considered developments in other common law jurisdictions and have developed their own local jurisprudence. Therefore, legal education in Hong Kong not only involves teaching the current state of domestic law, but also requires providing multiple perspectives from other common law jurisdictions. Of course, the increasingly intertwining relationships and intensifying interactions between Hong Kong and Mainland China in terms of political, economic, social and cultural aspects mean that Hong Kong law students must also be equipped with a sufficient working knowledge of the civil law, legal Chinese and the legal system and laws of Mainland China. Legal education in Hong Kong is therefore never an easy task.

There are two main participating stakeholders in entering the legal profession in Hong Kong: law schools and legal professionals (including solicitors and barristers). The availability of places to enter the legal profession is not so much driven by the demand of the needs of the profession or the number of students willing to enter the profession, but rather by the capacity and funding of law schools and universities. Therefore, as far as undergraduate and qualifying legal education is concerned, the extent and degree of online legal education adopted in each law school is dependent on the willingness of the institution and its faculty members. The developments of (online) legal education in law schools are explored in section 3.1. On the other hand, continuing legal education has transitioned relatively smoothly into hybrid or fully online modes. Such transition is highly desirable and favoured for various reasons, including the increased convenience in attending and diversity in arranging these courses. The developments of (online) continuing legal education are explored in section 3.2.

There are many ways to qualify for legal practice in Hong Kong and this report does not intend to set them out exhaustively. The predominant route is to read a Bachelor of Laws (LLB) degree programme in Hong Kong and then to complete the Postgraduate Certificate of Laws (PCLL) programme, which is only offered in Hong Kong. Both of these programmes are offered by the three law schools in Hong Kong: the University of Hong Kong, the Chinese University of Hong Kong and the City University of Hong Kong. In Hong Kong, the PCLL programme is generally considered to be the 'gatekeeper' of the legal profession

---

3 Basic Law, Art. 8.
4 Basic Law, Art. 18.
5 Basic Law, Arts. 19, 84, 85.

in Hong Kong. This is because the PCLL programmes have relatively strict admission requirements and low admission rates (at around 55%). Moreover, unlike LLB programmes, it is far less certain that one can pass the PCLL programme, with a noticeably high failure rate (at around 25%) at first attempt. These features of the PCLL are further explained in section 2.2.

2.1. ENTERING HONG KONG LAW SCHOOLS

All three law schools offer their respective Bachelor of Laws (LLB) programmes. An LLB programme covers all the required subjects for admission to the PCLL, as well as a number of electives where students can study specific legal areas that are of interest to them. In addition to a four-year full-time programme leading to a single award of the LLB degree, there are also different joint-degree and dual-degree programmes, which allow for obtaining two degrees in usually four to five years.[6]

All three law schools offer a full-time two-year Juris Doctor (JD) programme, with the Chinese University of Hong Kong also providing a part-time option in three and a half years. The JD programme only admits students that already have a bachelor's degree in a non-law discipline, or a bachelor's degree in law from a non-common law jurisdiction. As such, despite its name, a JD programme is not a doctorate and is instead placed at Level 6 (master's level) of the Hong Kong Qualifications Framework.[7] A JD programme also covers all the required subjects for admission to the PCLL, but students can only choose a limited number of additional electives due to its intensive schedule.

All three law schools also offer various Master of Laws (LLM) programmes. Each law school provides around six to eight specialisms or streams within their respective LLM programme. Currently, the award of any LLM degrees (whether Hong Kong or overseas) do not qualify for PCLL admission or legal practice in Hong Kong.

---

6 Joint degrees that are offered in conjunction with the LLB degree include Bachelor of Business Administration (Law), Bachelor of Social Sciences (Government and Laws), Bachelor of Arts, Bachelor of Science (for the University of Hong Kong), Bachelor of Arts (Translation), Bachelor of Social Science (Sociology) (for the Chinese University of Hong Kong), Bachelor of Business Administration in Accountancy, Bachelor of Science in Computing Mathematics, Bachelor of Social Sciences in Criminology and Bachelor of Social Sciences in Public Policy (for the City University of Hong Kong). Dual degrees that are offered in conjunction with the LLB degree (in the University of Hong Kong) include LLB degree in University College London, LLB degree in Peking University, JD degree in the University of British Columbia and various LLM degrees.

7 The Chinese translation of 'Juris Doctor' is inconsistent among the three law schools. The University of Hong Kong adopted the term '法律碩士' (literally 'law master's degree'), while the other two law schools adopted the term '法律博士' (literally 'law doctorate').

We should add a word on the funding of law schools. All three law schools in Hong Kong operate as faculties (Faculty of Law or School of Law) within a university which, as with most other higher education institutions in Hong Kong, are funded and subsidised by the government.[8] However, in Hong Kong, each government-funded higher education institution is an autonomous body established under statute with its own Governing Council.[9] Therefore, the University Grants Committee (UGC) is established to ensure that these public higher education institutions are 'providing the highest possible standards of education in the most cost-effective manner'.[10] The UGC has no statutory or executive powers, but it is tasked with the important mission to allocate funding by the government to its funded institutions and to offer impartial and respected expert advice to the government on the strategic development and resource requirements of higher education in Hong Kong. According to the 2022–23 budget, an estimated amount of HK$22.59 billion is granted to the UGC.[11] The UGC promotes the understanding and mediates the interests among higher education, the government and the community at large. It also carries out research assessment exercises (through the Research Grants Council) and ensures quality assurance and enhancement (through the Quality Assurance Council).

Local students enrolled in government-funded degree programmes (including LLB degrees) in UGC-funded universities have to pay the standard prevailing rate (currently at HK$42,100 per annum), while non-local students pay a fee at around three to four times that rate (currently at around HK$140,000–171,000 per annum). Those enrolled in the joint-degree and dual-degree programmes described above may have to self-finance the additional years of study or credits taken (currently at around HK$85,000 per annum). JD programmes are self-financed and all students (local or non-local) currently pay around HK$200,000–230,400 per annum. Most LLM programmes are also self-financed and these students (local or non-local) currently pay around HK$141,120–171,000 per annum.[12] Funding is therefore generally not a problem

8 There are also a number of self-funded institutions in Hong Kong, which are irrelevant for the purposes of this report except those mentioned below.

9 The relevant statutory instruments for the three universities with law schools are University of Hong Kong Ordinance (Cap 1053), The Chinese University of Hong Kong Ordinance (Cap 1109) and City University of Hong Kong Ordinance (Cap 1132).

10 University Grants Committee, 'Roles and Functions', https://www.ugc.edu.hk/eng/ugc/about/overview/roles.html.

11 The Government of the Hong Kong Special Administrative Region, 'The 2022–23 Budget: Head 190 – University Grants Committee', https://www.budget.gov.hk/2022/eng/pdf/head190.pdf.

12 Under a UGC pilot scheme commencing from September 2020, selected local students may pursue designated taught postgraduate programmes in UGC-funded universities at the standard prevailing rate of local students for UGC-funded undergraduate programmes (currently at HK$42,100 per annum). The scheme currently includes four LLM programmes.

for universities and law schools, as the admission to all these programmes has proven to be very competitive. Moreover, given Hong Kong's position as a leading centre for international legal and dispute resolution services in the Asia-Pacific region, Hong Kong law schools are generally able to attract a considerable amount of students from Mainland China and around the world to attend. Table 1 shows the number of students admitted to selected law programmes for the 2021/22 academic year.[13] Although no statistics are available for LLM programmes, it is observed that non-local students have generally constituted a considerable proportion within the student population.

Table 1. Number of students admitted to selected law programmes for the 2021/22 academic year

Law school	LLB	Double degree with LLB	JD
Faculty of Law, University of Hong Kong	98 (53 JUPAS, 36 non-JUPAS, 9 Mainland)	160	55
Faculty of Law, The Chinese University of Hong Kong	80 (52 JUPAS, 26 non-JUPAS, 2 Mainland)	(not provided)	127 (FT) 73 (PT)
School of Law, City University of Hong Kong	54 (27 JUPAS, 17 non-JUPAS local, 10 non-local students (of which 6 Mainland))	(not provided)	85

Source: SCLET, 'Annual Report 2021', https://www.sclet.gov.hk/eng/pdf/2021e.pdf.

Some other local universities and higher education institutions also offer courses in law, especially those that offer degrees in the fields of business administration, but none of them offer programmes which qualify students for admission to the PCLL programme. There are three exceptions. First, students may take the University of London LLB examinations administered by the Hong Kong Examinations and Assessment Authority, with the option to enrol in preparatory courses offered by various self-funded higher education institutions. Upon graduating from the University of London LLB programme, students take and pass Conversion Exams (see section 2.2) in four subjects (three top-up subjects and commercial law Paper C) and become eligible to

See University Grants Committee, 'Targeted Taught Postgraduate Programmes Fellowships Scheme', https://www.ugc.edu.hk/eng/ugc/activity/targeted_postgraduate_scheme.html.

13 SCLET, 'Annual Report 2021', https://www.sclet.gov.hk/eng/pdf/2021e.pdf. Interested readers may trace the trends of these statistics by referring to other annual reports on SCLET's website. Breakdown of Mainland and international students are only available for the LLB programmes. The Joint University Programmes Admissions System (JUPAS) is a scheme and the main route of application designed to assist local students with Hong Kong Diploma of Secondary Education (HKDSE) examination results to apply for admission. Therefore, generally speaking, the majority of non-JUPAS students are international (non-local) students.

apply for the PCLL. Second, students may enrol in the Graduate Diploma in English and Hong Kong Law (Common Professional Examination) offered by the HKU School of Professional and Continuing Education (HKU SPACE) and Manchester Metropolitan University, which, through a certain progression route, gives students the eligibility to apply directly for the PCLL. There are recent calls to set up Hong Kong's own Common Professional Examination in due course. Third and most recently, students may enrol in the Advanced Diploma for Legal Executives (Graduate Level) offered by HKU SPACE, which builds on a Legal Executive course approved by the Law Society and gives students (with three years of law-related employment) the eligibility to apply directly for the PCLL. The first batch of students commenced their studies under this route in November 2021. Due to the involvement of overseas institutions and teachers and the pre-existing strict quarantine measures in Hong Kong, classes for these courses are currently delivered in two modes: face-to-face and live-streamed online. Students can choose either mode of instruction as they prefer at no extra charge.

2.2. ENTERING THE POSTGRADUATE CERTIFICATE OF LAWS PROGRAMME

The Postgraduate Certificate of Laws (PCLL), a one-year full-time programme, is the prerequisite to enter either branch of the Hong Kong legal profession. It is offered by all three law schools, with the University of Hong Kong also offering a two-year part-time option. It is an intensive programme designed to equip students with the practical skills relevant to their legal practice, including courses on, among other things, corporate and commercial transactions, civil and criminal litigation (drafting and advocacy), and professional practice and ethics. The Standing Committee on Legal Education and Training (SCLET) is established under section 74A of the Legal Practitioners Ordinance (Cap 159) and one of its functions is to keep under review, evaluate, assess and make recommendations to the system and provision of legal education and training in Hong Kong, as well as the academic requirements and standards for admission to the PCLL programme.[14]

Again, there are many ways to be eligible for admission to the PCLL. The most common route is to graduate from an LLB or JD programme in the three local law schools. Overseas law students may also be admitted to the PCLL but they must first 'demonstrate competence' in 12 subjects, including nine 'Core Subjects' (contract, tort, constitutional law, criminal law, land law, equity, evidence, business associations, commercial law) and three 'Top-Up Subjects'

14 Legal Practitioners Ordinance (Cap 159), s. 74A(2).

(Hong Kong constitutional law, Hong Kong land law and the Hong Kong legal system).[15] For those who did not meet these requirements, for example because they read or are reading an overseas LLB degree, they can take and pass the Hong Kong Conversion Examinations for PCLL admission, which is offered twice a year in January and June by the Hong Kong Conversion Examination Board. These Conversion Examinations are offered in six subjects, namely commercial law, evidence, business associations, Hong Kong constitutional law, Hong Kong land law and the Hong Kong legal system. The other six subjects must be completed as part of the student's main law qualification. Due to the intensity in preparing for these Conversion Examinations, most overseas students who intend to enter the Hong Kong legal profession will take these exams in stages, some during the first year of their law degree, in order to be eligible for PCLL admission immediately after graduation. A student can attempt a failed subject again in a later examination session.

Admission to the PCLL programme has proven to be competitive for many years. Only a limited number of PCLL places are government-funded, the tuition fee being the standard prevailing rate (currently at HK$42,100 per annum). Most are self-funded students, who have to pay a tuition fee of HK$184,500–230,400, around 4.5–5.5 times that for government-funded places. Generally speaking, the overriding criterion in determining admission and funding is academic merit, although there are different opinions as to whether and how a fair comparison can be made between single and joint degrees, between an LLB and a JD, between local and overseas students and between fresh graduates and mature graduates with legal-related work experience. Recent PCLL admission results show that an upper second class (2:1) law degree is generally required as a minimum, with government-funded PCLL places asking for a score close to a first class law degree.

Table 2 shows the statistics of the number of applications, offers and admittances to the PCLL programme in the three Hong Kong law schools for the 2020/21 and 2021/22 academic years. The admission rate is around 55% (1,513 out of 2,901, with some margin for students applying to two or more law schools) and the successful rate for government-funded places is estimated at around 15% (out of all applications) or around 27% (out of all admittances).[16]

---

15 There were 14 subjects (instead of 12) before 2021. However, in light of the recommendations of the SCLET Final Report in 2018, the three law schools have moved two procedural subjects, namely civil procedure and criminal procedure, into the PCLL programme. These two subjects are no longer prerequisites for entry to the PCLL programme. See SCLET, 'Comprehensive Review of Legal Education and Training in Hong Kong: Final Report of the Consultants' (April 2018), https://www.sclet.gov.hk/eng/pdf/final2018.pdf.

16 SCLET, 'Annual Report 2020', https://www.sclet.gov.hk/eng/pdf/2020e.pdf; SCLET, 'Annual Report 2021', https://www.sclet.gov.hk/eng/pdf/2021e.pdf. The successful rate for government-funded places has to be estimated due to the lack of publicly available statistics from the Faculty of Law of the Chinese University of Hong Kong and this is assumed to

Table 2. Number of applications and admittances to the PCLL programme for the 2020/21 and 2021/22 academic years

Law school	Academic year	Applications	Admittances		
			Total	Government-funded	Self-funded
Faculty of Law, University of Hong Kong	2020/21	667	293 (FT) 93 (PT)	117 (FT) 0 (PT)*	176 (FT) 93 (PT)
	2021/22	632	275 (FT) 88 (PT)	(statistics not provided)	(statistics not provided)
Faculty of Law, The Chinese University of Hong Kong	2020/21	324	173	(statistics not provided)	(statistics not provided)
	2021/22	287	164	(statistics not provided)	(statistics not provided)
School of Law, City University of Hong Kong	2020/21	483	221	53	168
	2021/22	508	206	53	153

* Only full-time students are eligible to be considered for government-funded places.
Source: SCLET, 'Annual Report 2020', https://www.sclet.gov.hk/eng/pdf/2020e.pdf; SCLET, 'Annual Report 2021', https://www.sclet.gov.hk/eng/pdf/2021e.pdf.

The PCLL programme is also known to have a relatively high failure rate, particularly at first attempt (at around 25%). Although the eventual number of failures is relatively low, there are implications with this figure. Most trainee solicitor contracts in Hong Kong contain a 'first attempt' clause, where students failing the PCLL programme at first attempt will have their trainee contract automatically withdrawn. These students will then have to negotiate with the solicitors' firm to resolve the issue. Aspiring pupil barristers will have to commence their pupillage later than the usual date of 1 September each year, as it is a statutory requirement to file a certificate of eligibility for pupillage no less than three weeks before the commencement of pupillage,[17] when supplementary examination results will not have been released by then. In addition to the considerable inconvenience, students also face immense pressure in attempting supplementary examinations and adapting to the short time gap before their commencement of the training contract or pupillage. Table 3 shows the number of failures of the PCLL programme for the 2019/20 and 2020/21 academic years.[18]

be similar with the other two law schools. Interested readers may trace the trends of these statistics by referring to other annual reports on SCLET's website.

17 Barristers (Qualification for Admission and Pupillage) Rules (Cap 159AC), s. 11(1).

18 SCLET, 'Annual Report 2020', https://www.sclet.gov.hk/eng/pdf/2020e.pdf; SCLET, 'Annual Report 2021', https://www.sclet.gov.hk/eng/pdf/2021e.pdf.

Table 3. Number of failures of the PCLL programme for the 2019/20 and 2020/21 academic years

Law school	Academic year	Proportion or number of students who failed to graduate at first attempt and were required to take supplementary examinations	Proportion or number of students who failed to graduate after all supplementary examinations in the same or subsequent year
Faculty of Law, University of Hong Kong	2019/20	23.9% (FT) 27.8% (PT Year 1) 16.9% (PT Year 2)	4.0% (FT) 7.2% (PT Year 1) 1.0% (PT Year 2)
	2020/21	13.1% (FT) 33.7% (PT Year 1) 38.9% (PT Year 2)	2.3% (FT) 10.0% (PT Year 1) 13.2% (PT Year 2)
Faculty of Law, The Chinese University of Hong Kong	2019/20	(statistics not provided)	0 (0.0%)
	2020/21	(statistics not provided)	0 (0.0%)
School of Law, City University of Hong Kong	2019/20	64 out of around 212 students (30.2%)	4 (1.9%)
	2020/21	70 out of around 220 students (31.8%)	10 (4.5%)

Source: SCLET, 'Annual Report 2020', https://www.sclet.gov.hk/eng/pdf/2020e.pdf; SCLET, 'Annual Report 2021', https://www.sclet.gov.hk/eng/pdf/2021e.pdf.

From the statistics above, it can be seen that the PCLL programme is relatively difficult to gain admission to, to finance and to pass, making it the major 'gatekeeper' of access to the legal profession in Hong Kong. However, most PCLL graduates are likely to find a job, with an employment rate estimated between 80% and 90%.[19] This near parity of PCLL graduates to training places is, in SCLET's view, unhealthy because smaller training providers will be fishing from a restricted pool of applicants and the Bar will also receive some weaker candidates who are unable to obtain training contracts, but eventually fall by the wayside due to insufficient available work.[20] An increase in the number of PCLL places is therefore generally favourable from competition and access perspectives. Importantly, the SCLET noted that 'restricting access to the PCLL may have unintended (negative) access and diversity consequences. Moreover, it is also not the function of a legal training (or legal services) regulator to create or control the market for lawyers.'[21] However, the 'bottleneck' will then be switched to the training contract/pupillage stage. From the US and UK

19 SCLET, 'Comprehensive Review of Legal Education and Training in Hong Kong: Final Report of the Consultants' (April 2018), https://www.sclet.gov.hk/eng/pdf/final2018.pdf, p. 81.

20 Ibid., p. 81 and n. 10.

21 Ibid., p. 82.

experience, this will mean the qualifying law exams providers will no longer be accused of an unfair admissions policy but instead of greed in taking fees from these students for whom there are no jobs. That criticism even extends to LLB and JD programmes in Australia, where law schools are accused of misleading students despite the saturated market.[22] One must therefore choose the lesser of two evils and Hong Kong (unlike many other jurisdictions) took a different path. The relatively tough admission and passing rates of the PCLL in Hong Kong are not the sole responsibility of one single stakeholder: the law schools, the legal profession and the government all have a role to play.

2.3. ENTERING THE LEGAL PROFESSION

Hong Kong maintains the divide between solicitors and barristers. Different qualifying routes and regulatory authorities apply for these two professions. As of 31 January 2022, there are around 10,800 practising solicitors and around 1,600 barristers in private practice. There are also around 1,100 trainee solicitors and around 85 pupil barristers. With a population of around 7.4 million,[23] this means around 545 people for one lawyer, or 1,835 lawyers per million in population. There is rarely any problem during the period of the trainee solicitor contract or pupillage, or during the admission process.

2.3.1. Solicitors

The Court of First Instance may admit a 'fit and proper person' to be enrolled on the roll of solicitors,[24] and the requirements for admission (and application for a practising certificate) are prescribed by the Council of the Law Society.[25] A trainee solicitor must complete a two-year trainee solicitor contract with a solicitor who is qualified to employ trainee solicitors.[26] In normal circumstances, a trainee solicitor shall apply for a certificate of eligibility for admission within 12 months after the completion of his most recent trainee solicitor contract,[27] and then proceed to apply for admission.

---

22 E. Ryan, 'Frustration grows over unis "cashing in" on law grad oversupply' (19 February 2018), https://www.lawyersweekly.com.au/sme-law/22768-frustration-grows-over-unis-cashing-in-on-law-grad-oversupply.

23 Census and Statistics Department, 'Population Estimates', https://www.censtatd.gov.hk/en/scode150.html.

24 Legal Practitioners Ordinance (Cap 159), s. 4.

25 Admission and Registration Rules (Cap 159B), s. 3 (admission); Cap 159, s. 6 (practising certificate).

26 Cap 159, s. 20.

27 Cap 159B, s. 3(3).

2.3.2. Barristers

The Court of First Instance may admit a 'fit and proper person' to be enrolled on the roll of barristers,[28] and the requirements for admission (and application for a practising certificate) are prescribed by the Council of the Bar Association of Hong Kong (the Bar Council).[29] A person is qualified for admission as a barrister if they (1) have obtained a PCLL, (2) have been admitted as a solicitor in Hong Kong for at least three years, or (3) are an overseas lawyer practising for at least three years with a currently valid practising certificate and have passed (or been exempted from) the Barristers Qualification Examination.[30] Then, they must apply for a certificate of eligibility for pupillage, and, in normal circumstances, must complete not less than six months of 'approved pupillage'.[31] After then, they can apply for a certificate of qualification for admission,[32] and obtain a limited practising certificate, and subsequently a full practising certificate.[33]

2.4. THE USE OF INFORMATION TECHNOLOGY

Hong Kong is in an advanced position in terms of technology and the government has been investing more resources in recent years to support the development of the innovation and technology industry, identifying key areas of research and development and working on various fronts. There is widespread application of information technology (IT) in the daily lives of Hong Kong citizens. According to the Network Readiness Index published by the Portulans Institute, Hong Kong is ranked first out of 130 economies in terms of international internet bandwidth and received exceptionally high scores in terms of internet access in households and schools.[34]

2.4.1. The Law Schools

Generally speaking, IT resources are not a problem for the Hong Kong higher education sector. All universities are equipped with, to various extents,

---

28 Cap 159, s. 27. For the criteria of 'fit and proper person', see *Re Youh Alan Chuen Po* [2013] 2 HKLRD 485; *Re A* [2018] 2 HKLRD 1245, [2018] HKCA 272.

29 Cap 159AC, s. 8 (admission); Cap 159, s. 30 (practising certificate).

30 Cap 159AC, s. 4(1). The Barristers Qualification Examination is held once a year which consists of five examination papers covering a wide range of subjects.

31 Cap 159AC, ss. 11–14.

32 Cap 159AC, s. 8.

33 Cap 159, s. 31(2) (limited practising certificate); Cap 159, s. 30 (full practising certificate).

34 Network Readiness Index, 'Hong Kong (China)', https://networkreadinessindex.org/country/hong-kong-china/.

IT hardware and software of good quantity and quality and that are easily accessible by staff and students. These include computers in libraries, learning commons and offices, high-speed wired and wireless internet connections, high-performance computing services for complex computational problems, as well as a range of university-wide applications for staff and students. Portable IT devices, such as laptops, tablets and smartphones are also very reliable and of good quality and are widely adopted and used within the university community. These are generally affordable to the great majority of university teachers and students, although a very limited amount of students from disadvantaged socio-economic backgrounds might encounter difficulties in terms of IT access outside the university campus. Some financial aid is in place to assist these students.

2.4.2. *The Legal Profession*

Again, the use of IT is very common in the Hong Kong legal profession. Access to both good-quality and affordable hardware and software is very easy among legal professionals. Most lawyers work on a daily basis with computers and a variety of IT tools. The legal profession has faced some challenges with the pandemic, where most employees have been working from home, and, like in many other parts of the world, requiring the use of video-conferencing tools and other online working platforms. In response to these demands, the government announced a HK$40 million LawTech Fund in April 2020, giving up to HK$50,000 for each law firm or barristers' chambers with five or fewer practising lawyers to procure or upgrade their IT systems. As of July 2020, around 400 applications were received.[35] This has supported (albeit only modestly) the turn within the legal profession to employ more online tools both for their business (for example, conferences with overseas clients and remote court hearings) and for continuing legal education.

2.4.3. *The Judiciary and the Courts*

The court processes in Hong Kong had, until the COVID-19 pandemic, remained heavily reliant on paper documents and in-person hearings. This is a rare outlier among almost all jurisdictions in the Asia-Pacific region or even globally.[36] According to the World Bank's *Doing Business 2020* survey, Hong Kong scored 1 out of 4 in 'court automation', falling behind many jurisdictions, such as

35 Department of Justice, 'Further Extension of Application Period for LawTech Fund' (24 July 2020), https://www.doj.gov.hk/en/community_engagement/press/20200724_pr1.html.

36 See further G. Lau, 'Electronic Filing and Proceedings in Courts' (28 May 2020), https://www.legco.gov.hk/research-publications/english/essentials-1920ise07-electronic-filing-and-proceedings-in-courts.htm.

Singapore and South Korea (both of which scored 4 out of 4).[37] There is an urgent need to speed up reforms in IT infrastructure.[38] The judiciary had formulated a two-stage Information Technology Strategy Plan (ITSP) and had obtained government funding of HK$684.2 million as early as May 2013. Its aims include, among other things, to provide effective and efficient services in the administration of justice and to facilitate active case management in improving access to justice.[39] One of the major outcomes of ITSP is an integrated course management system (iCMS) to support the litigation processes of courts and tribunals by enabling appropriate data sharing within a data-driven workflow and supporting the use of electronic documents. However, the implementation of both stages of the ITSP was substantially delayed and even resulted in an Audit Commission review in 2019.[40]

The COVID-19 pandemic has served as an effective catalyst for the judiciary to actively explore new ways to modernise its court processes and allow access to court services. During the first onset of the pandemic, the courts adopted a conservative approach and adjourned all court proceedings (except urgent and essential hearings) from 29 January to 3 May 2020 (known as the General Adjournment Period, GAP). As there was no comprehensive framework for remote hearings in Hong Kong before the pandemic, courts had to explore, on their own motion as a matter of case management, an appropriate framework to conduct remote hearings and take evidence from witnesses.[41] To deal with the effect on the caseload caused by the GAP, the Chief Justice issued a statement on 25 March 2020 stating that the judiciary was 'actively considering expanding the scope of hearings (beyond just urgent or essential matters) by hearing

---

37 World Bank, 'Doing Business 2020: Hong Kong SAR, China', p. 54, https://openknowledge.worldbank.org/bitstream/handle/10986/32974/Doing-Business-2020-Comparing-Business-Regulation-in-190-Economies-Economy-Profile-of-Hong-Kong-SAR-China.pdf. At that time, the initial complaint could not be filed electronically through a dedicated platform, nor was it not possible to carry out service of process electronically, or to pay court fees electronically.

38 To implement a system of e-litigation is the second among a total of six challenges of the Hong Kong judiciary suggested by Professor Anselmo Reyes in 2014, after stepping down as a Court of First Instance judge: A. Reyes, 'The Future of the Judiciary: Reflections on Present Challenges to the Administration of Justice in Hong Kong' (2014) 44(2) *Hong Kong Law Journal* 429, 436–437.

39 Legislative Council, 'Legislative Council Brief: Subsidiary Legislation Relating to the Information Technology Strategy Plan' (2 June 2021), https://www.legco.gov.hk/yr20-21/english/brief/aw275005010009_20210602-e.pdf.

40 Audit Commission, 'Judiciary Administrator's Work in Implementing Projects under the Information Technology Strategy Plan' (28 October 2019), https://www.aud.gov.hk/pdf_e/e73ch06.pdf.

41 See e.g. *Cyberworks Audio Video Technology Ltd (in compulsory liq.) v. Mei Ah (HK) Co. Ltd* [2020] 2 HKC 133, [2020] HKCFI 347; *CSFK v. HWH* [2020] 3 HKC 64, [2020] HKCA 207; *Standard Chartered Bank (Hong Kong) Ltd v. Nie Hai Yan Wendy* [2021] 2 HKLRD 425, [2021] HKCA 380. See also Rules of the High Court (Cap 4A), Order 1A and Order 1B.

submissions by telephone, by video-conferencing or similar means of visual aid and generally making use of technology'. Subsequently, the judiciary issued on 2 April 2020 a Guidance Note for Remote Hearings for Civil Business in the High Court, and appropriate hearings have been conducted using video-conferencing facilities (VCF) and telephone gradually since then. Subsequent suspension and resumption arrangements of court business due to new 'waves' of confirmed cases in Hong Kong have then seen substantial improvements. According to the latest Phase III of the Remote Hearings for Civil Business in the Civil Courts, which commenced on 2 January 2021, remote hearings can be conducted in the Court of Appeal and the Court of First Instance of the High Court, the Competition Tribunal, the District Court, the Family Court, the Labour Tribunal and the Small Claims Tribunal.[42] Hearings of the Court of Final Appeal are also occasionally conducted with the help of VCF for overseas non-permanent judges or legal representatives who are unable to come to Hong Kong. The use of a 'browser-based' VCF option has also been introduced to provide a low-cost option for court users to connect to the court for VCF hearings.

To provide a comprehensive legal framework concerning the application, operation and effect of remote hearings for court proceedings, the judiciary commenced public consultation in June 2022 on the draft Courts (Remote Hearing) Bill, together with a set of draft Practice Directions and Operational Guidelines.[43] Clause 8 of the draft Bill proposed a list of 15 non-exhaustive considerations that courts must take into account when deciding whether to hold a remote hearing. The draft Bill also includes other welcoming clarifications and amendments, notably the possibility to broadcast an open proceeding held remotely in real time (clause 23).

Another notable recent development is the new Court Proceedings (Electronic Technology) Ordinance (Cap 638), effective since 1 October 2021. Previously, the Electronic Transactions Ordinance (Cap 553), which provided recognition for electronic records and signatures with the same effect as their written counterparts, was not applicable in the proceedings of almost all courts and tribunals.[44] This created a significant gap between legal practice and the current IT trends. With the new Ordinance, Hong Kong has completed an important step of the ITSP, caught up with other jurisdictions in the electronic handling of court-related documents and demonstrated its commitment to

---

42 Judiciary, 'Guidance Note for Remote Hearings for Civil Business in the Civil Courts (Phase 3: Wider Video-Conferencing Facilities and Telephone)' (15 December 2020), https://www.judiciary.hk/en/court_services_facilities/guidance_note_for_remote_hearings_phase3.html.

43 Judiciary, 'Remote Hearing: Draft Courts (Remote Hearing) Bill, Practice Directions and Operational Guidelines' (June 2022), https://www.judiciary.hk/remote_hearing_bill/consultation_doc/eng.pdf. For a general overview of how information technology is currently used in courts, see Judiciary, 'Use of IT in Court', https://www.judiciary.hk/en/court_services_facilities/uoiic_index.html.

44 Electronic Transactions Ordinance (Cap 553), s. 13.

environmental concerns by reducing the use of paper. The key features of the new Ordinance include: (1) electronic filing or sending of documents to the court will generally be allowed; (2) documents between parties may be served electronically if there is mutual consent to serve and accept documents by electronic means; (3) signatures other than traditional manual signatures, such as digital signatures and electronic signatures, for court-related documents will generally be allowed; and (4) proper legal status is provided for printouts/copies of printouts for documents issued by the court.[45]

3. MOVING TOWARDS ONLINE LEGAL EDUCATION

Online legal education is not a new idea and has been subject to voluminous research. As reflective teachers, the challenge is to think creatively about how online teaching and learning tools can be employed to promote students' understanding of disciplinary knowledge.[46] In fact, the current technological solutions available in Hong Kong are already capable of providing high-quality and effective online legal education. However, rather than taking the lead to reform, the higher education sector has remained conservative and unresponsive. Pre-pandemic efforts to utilise online and multimedia tools for legal education are rare and scattered, with only a few enthusiastic legal educators attempting to change the largely stagnant Hong Kong legal education community. Even in the wake of the pandemic, it seems that the higher education sector is by and large resistant to changes towards a more sustainable and resilient system of teaching and learning.[47]

The situation of Hong Kong online legal education, and higher education more generally, is a clear reflection of the approach known as 'emergency remote teaching',[48] drawing a contrast from carefully planned and designed online education. Due to the unprecedented speed at which institutions and instructors were forced to move their teaching and learning online, there was a lack of preparation without comprehensive consideration of the appropriate methods of course delivery, online assessment and student support. In fact, online legal education is not simply about transferring and perpetuating (ineffective)

---

45 Judiciary, 'Subsidiary legislation related to Information Technology Strategy Plan gazetted' (4 June 2021), https://www.info.gov.hk/gia/general/202106/04/P2021060400316.htm.

46 P. Ashwin, *Reflective Teaching in Higher Education*, 2nd edn, Bloomsbury, London 2020, p. 247.

47 W. Lui and A. Lam, 'The Critical Engagement of Higher Education with Future Crises' (2021) 5(2) *Dewey Studies* 345.

48 C. Hodges, S. Moore, B. Lockee, T. Trust and A. Bond, 'The Difference Between Emergency Remote Teaching and Online Learning' (27 March 2020), https://er.educause.edu/articles/2020/3/the-difference-between-emergency-remote-teaching-and-online-learning.

approaches in face-to-face classrooms into online classrooms. Rather, it requires untangling the complexities of its design and decision-making processes. To start with, there are four fundamental dimensions to online learning: context, design, implementation and outcomes.[49] Nine further dimensions are identified in terms of online instruction design, each of which has numerous options: modality, pacing, student–instructor ratio, pedagogy, instructor's role online, student's role online, online communication synchrony, role of online assessments and source of feedback.[50] Online education also involves investing in infrastructure and other supporting resources, which inevitably take time to identify and build.

3.1. LEGAL EDUCATION

In the pre-pandemic times, legal education was largely conducted face to face. In LLB programmes, the main delivery modes are lectures (which may have a class size of over 300 students if it is a compulsory course), seminars and tutorials, which have smaller class sizes (around 10–15 students per class). The general approach of instructors in lectures or seminars is to select and deliver the teaching content unilaterally to students, with relatively limited input and feedback from students. There might be a more interactive element in tutorials, but usually tutors (who may often be practitioners teaching on a part-time basis) will continue to reinforce legal concepts through discussing texts and cases with students. There have been some successful attempts to adopt online tools and multimedia products in law classrooms, although these only occupy a very minor proportion of the overall legal education experience provided to students in Hong Kong. Some of these examples include: (1) the Optional Exploration activity and the LEAD initiative, which involves the production of multimedia outputs (which are made available online) to facilitate learning and teaching;[51] (2) the in-class optional niche (ICON), a collaborative learning and assessment activity with a student–teacher partnership where students and teachers co-create materials and co-own the learning and teaching process;[52] and (3) flipped classrooms, which involve short videos on key concepts of legal principles before a completely student-led group discussion to analyse news

---

49 B. Means, M. Bakia and R. Murphy, *Learning Online: What Research Tells Us about Whether, When and How*, Routledge, New York 2014, pp. 8–14.

50 Ibid., p. 27.

51 HKU Law Co-learning Lab, 'CoLLab at HKU Law', https://sites.google.com/view/wecollab/home.

52 A. Lee and P. Woo, 'Enlivening the Law Classroom: Let Students Speak, not Just Sit' (2021) 5(2) *International Journal for Students as Partners* 183.

articles or other relevant materials during class time.[53] Some legal educators have quoted multiple advantages of online legal education, including convenience and efficiency, increased participation and questions from students, and more effective sharing and dissemination of materials.[54]

The PCLL programme is also conducted face to face and there have been considerable difficulties in moving the learning and teaching as well as the assessments online. During the pandemic, instructors recorded the large group sessions themselves and made them available online, while small group sessions were delivered synchronously via video-conferencing tools. The majority of written exams were conducted online under controlled conditions, for example with a locked down browser and a remote proctoring system. Many performance-based assessments were also conducted and recorded via video-conferencing tools. Despite the relatively smooth operation and generally positive reception among both examiners and students, there is clearly reluctance to maintain these online delivery and assessment methods, as shown by the resumption of face-to-face classes and examinations once the situation of the pandemic was slightly alleviated. For instance, the PCLL exams in December 2021 to January 2022 were held in person, in response to a relatively stable pandemic situation during that period, while subsequent exams in February and March 2022 were held online due to the resurgence of confirmed cases. The pandemic has been treated as a transient emergency and online legal education a temporary contingency plan abandoned whenever the emergency situation eases. Face-to-face learning is still considered 'undoubtedly irreplaceable and indispensable' even in the most recent reports from the law schools.[55]

One might well ask what is in the PCLL programme that makes it impossible for it to be delivered or assessed online. In fact, as recognised in the SCLET Final Report, the option of developing an online stream of the PCLL programme to extend access to the profession is considered to be possible 'within the existing structure': it 'does not create the same level of demand on physical plant, and has cost and access advantages in enabling students to earn while they learn', citing examples of online learning in professional legal education in Australia and New Zealand, which are shorter in length and have far more generous admission and passing rates.[56] It is hesitant to make such a recommendation

---

53 The University of Hong Kong, 'Tort Law Lecture "Flipped" into an Engaging Discussion' (26 October 2015), https://tl.hku.hk/2015/10/tort-law-lecture-flipped-into-an-engaging-discussion/. There are various advantages of student-oriented models of learning and academic publishing: W. Lui, 'Advancing the Student-oriented Model of Academic Publishing: The Case of Legal Studies in Hong Kong' (2022) 35(3) *Learned Publishing* 376.

54 W. Woon, 'Why Online University Classes Herald a Better Way Forward, not a Temporary Fix' (27 January 2022), https://www.todayonline.com/commentary/why-online-university-classes-herald-better-way-forward-not-temporary-fix-1799926.

55 See e.g. SCLET, 'Annual Report 2021', https://www.sclet.gov.hk/eng/pdf/2021e.pdf, p. 44.

56 SCLET, 'Comprehensive Review of Legal Education and Training in Hong Kong: Final Report of the Consultants' (April 2018), p. 82, https://www.sclet.gov.hk/eng/pdf/final2018.pdf.

only because 'substantial upfront resourcing and development' is required. This report suggests that it is high time to consider investing in an online option for qualifying legal education given that it has been delivered quite successfully in many other jurisdictions. The perceived difficulties in implementing online legal education in Hong Kong, including both undergraduate and qualifying legal education, should now be revisited.

3.2. CONTINUING LEGAL EDUCATION

Continuing legal education has played an important role to ensure that legal practitioners are up to date with the latest developments in law and practice that have relevance to their work. The two strands of the Hong Kong legal profession have different requirements in this regard.

All solicitors with a practising certificate in Hong Kong must accumulate 15 continuous professional development (CPD) points in each CPD practice year (commencing on 1 November and ending on 31 October the following year) and trainee solicitors must accumulate 30 CPD points by the end of their two-year period of employment as a trainee solicitor.[57] One CPD point is accredited for one hour of participation in the activity. Breaches of the CPD requirement are regarded as professional misconduct and solicitors may be subject to imposition of a fine, censure, suspension or striking off, and trainee solicitors may have their training contracts cancelled or suspended.[58] Although there are a wide range of activities that can count towards CPD requirements, most Hong Kong legal practitioners will attend courses, lectures and talks for that purpose. The Law Society organises legal training courses and seminars for practitioners (and the public) which are eligible for CPD points under the auspices of the Hong Kong Academy of Law, but it is also very common for practitioners to attend courses organised by other institutions in Hong Kong (including the government, universities and external providers) where accreditation is sought for CPD points from the Law Society.[59]

Due to the COVID-19 pandemic, the Law Society granted an exemption and extension of time to solicitors such that they were only required to accumulate a total of 15 CPD points over a two-year period by 31 October 2021. During the pandemic times, most CPD events were cancelled and the remainder were no longer offered face to face but rather online. These included live webinars

---

57 Continuing Professional Development Rules (Cap 159W), s. 5(1).

58 The Law Society of Hong Kong, 'Failure to Comply with the CPD Requirement', https://www.hklawsoc.org.hk/en/Support-Members/Professional-Support/Continuing-Professional-Development-Scheme/CPD-Information-Package/Failure-to-Comply-with-the-CPD-Requirement.

59 See e.g. The University of Hong Kong Faculty of Law, 'Continuing Legal Education', https://www.law.hku.hk/knowledge-exchange-and-impact/continuing-legal-education/.

delivered synchronously or, less frequently, pre-recorded courses. According to the Guidelines of the Law Society, there must be evidence showing that these events are, among other things, '"real time" and interactive'; the interactive elements include but are not limited to question-and-answer session(s), group work, quizzes and exercises. 'A course which only requires a participant to click through a series of slides will not qualify for CPD points. Reading and reviewing cases or articles does not qualify for CPD points.'[60] Most fully online or hybrid CPD events therefore involve filling in feedback forms or answering short questions and the attendance of the participants is closely monitored. Another method to obtain CPD points that is of relevance for online legal education is to undertake certain approved distance learning courses in Hong Kong or overseas higher educational institutions.[61] Practitioners must attend classes and provide evidence by a certificate of attendance or confirmation letter issued by the relevant institution.

Pupil barristers are required to attend a programme of compulsory continuing legal education known as the Advanced Legal Education Programme (ALE), the majority of which are organised under the auspices of the Hong Kong Advocacy Training Council. They have to attend courses to obtain a minimum of 14 ALE points during the one-year pupillage, which cover areas of advocacy, drafting, professional conduct and ethics. Pupil barristers failing to attend will not be able to enter into full practice at the end of their approved pupillage.[62] In light of the pandemic, most talks traditionally held in the Jurors Assembly Room in the High Court have moved online as Zoom webinars. However, according to information online, the compulsory pupils advocacy programmes are still delivered face to face (in a larger venue), except on one occasion in September 2020 (when it was held through Zoom).[63]

The Bar Association introduced the Voluntary Scheme of Continuing Professional Development in July 2021 and will very likely introduce a mandatory programme for continuing legal education for all practising barristers in the near future. A similar CPD point system will be adopted and each member, regardless of seniority, must obtain a minimum of eight CPD points per year. There will be no accreditation system to approve courses, but members will be required to declare how a particular activity has met the CPD point requirement.

---

60 The Law Society of Hong Kong, 'Guidelines for Compliance with CPD Requirements Issued under Sections 2 and 5(3) of the CPD Rules', https://www.hklawsoc.org.hk/zh-HK/Support-Members/Professional-Support/Continuing-Professional-Development-Scheme/CPD-Information-Package/Guidelines-for-Compliance-with-CPD-requirements-issued.

61 The Law Society of Hong Kong, 'Approved Distance Learning Courses', https://www.hklawsoc.org.hk/en/Support-Members/Professional-Support/Continuing-Professional-Development-Scheme/CPD-Information-Package/Approved-Distance-Learning-Courses.

62 Barristers (Advanced Legal Education Requirement) Rules (Cap 159AB), s. 7(1).

63 Hong Kong Advocacy Training Council, 'Pupils' Courses', https://www.hk-atc.org/course.aspx.

The fulfilment of the CPD point requirement will be a prerequisite for the issue of a practising certificate in the following year.[64]

It is observed that the conversion to online modes of delivery for most CPD events for solicitors (and in the future for barristers) is and will continue to be welcomed. Most CPD events are currently offered online or in dual modes. Legal practitioners can choose to attend CPD events from the comfort of their homes or office spaces, without the need to commute to conference centres, university auditoriums or hotel ballrooms (which also incurs a substantial rental charge). The commuting time saved can be used for other tasks, whether work-related or personal. The line-up of speakers is also no longer subject to geographical boundaries, travel arrangements or visa restrictions, but perhaps only to time-zone differences. With online modes of delivery, one can also effortlessly participate in or speak at events organised in multiple jurisdictions, which all have immediate relevance to Hong Kong's legal practice. These are some of the many great benefits in continuing to organise continuing legal education through the use or facilitation of online and other technological tools.

3.3. DIFFICULTIES WITH ONLINE LEGAL EDUCATION AND THEIR SOLUTIONS

3.3.1. *Course Delivery*

As a result of the 'emergency remote teaching', teachers are given very little guidance, and therefore much discretion, in designing and delivering online courses during the pandemic. They can make it fully online through live or pre-recorded lectures, or hybrid with some form of face-to-face teaching if circumstances allow. However, regardless of the method adopted, it is general policy across universities in Hong Kong that lecture recordings must be made available in case students cannot or do not attend classes. It is particularly important during the pandemic that students are given the option of online attendance as some are 'trapped' in lockdown or quarantine as imposed by the government under the relevant regulations.

To investigate the effectiveness of fully online or hybrid teaching and learning during the COVID-19 pandemic, a survey was conducted in August 2021 by a group of teachers and students in the Faculty of Law of the University of Hong Kong under the project 'Student Engagement and Skills Training in the post-COVID World', which was funded by a Teaching Development Grant.[65]

---

64 Hong Kong Bar Association, 'Proposal for Mandatory Programme of Continuing Legal Education' (Circular No. 136/21, 31 August 2021).

65 The Teaching Development Grant is university funding for teaching-related investigations and initiatives. The survey results and recommendations of this study have been disseminated

The project also hopes to identify the way forward for higher education in the post-pandemic era. According to students' responses to the survey, even if teaching venues remain open for students to attend during the hybrid teaching period, most students have chosen not to attend classes in person for various reasons, including saving commuting time or peer influence.[66] However, many students have also indicated that the campus facilities are not up to standard, or teachers are not sufficiently familiar with their functionalities to conduct classes in hybrid mode. In other cases, there are acoustic or other technical problems (such as unreliable WiFi connections, noise or other distractions) preventing teachers and students who join Zoom in the same classroom from having meaningful communication or discussion. It might be a frustrating experience for those giving and receiving instruction. As a solution, these students have the option of participating in the in-person class (if the course is offered in hybrid mode) or participating online from a designated room in the Faculty building.

The same survey also reveals that most students are of the view that lectures can be delivered online, but tutorials and skills-based sessions, such as those on advocacy and client interviewing, should be conducted in person, for better interaction and discussion. The marked difference between lectures and hands-on activities is reflected in the survey findings: 93.6% of students agree or strongly agree that 'good use of online learning tools can facilitate the learning of disciplinary knowledge (such as lectures/tutorials/seminars via Zoom or Panopto)', while only 53.9% agree or strongly agree that 'good use of online learning tools can facilitate out-of-classroom learning'. Understandably, students are keen to practise advocacy and client-interviewing skills in a 'real', in-person setting, such as in (moot) courtrooms or offices. It also trains students to listen, understand and respond to the other parties in the conversation, such as the judge or the client. However, in view of the technological developments of the Hong Kong judiciary outlined in section 2.4.3, it is also foreseeable that these might have to be conducted in remote settings over the phone or VCF

at the International Conference on Learning and Teaching 2021 (The Education University of Hong Kong, 8–10 December 2021), the 37th BILETA Conference 2022 (University of Exeter, 12–14 April 2022), the Online Conference on Teaching and Learning in Law – Directions in Legal Education 2022 (The Chinese University of Hong Kong, 10–11 June 2022) and the 3rd HKU Teaching and Learning Festival 2022 (The University of Hong Kong, 8 November 2022). An international symposium on online teaching and learning was held on 9 December 2022 at the University of Hong Kong as a deliverable of the project.

66 Similar results are also obtained from other legal educators. In a company law seminar group at the National University of Singapore, 94% of the respondents found it (very much) more convenient to have Zoom classes: W. Woon, 'Why Online University Classes Herald a Better Way Forward, not a Temporary Fix' (27 January 2022), https://www.todayonline.com/commentary/why-online-university-classes-herald-better-way-forward-not-temporary-fix-1799926.

facilities and students will very likely come across both in-person and remote hearings in practice. As envisaged by Sir Julian Flaux, Chancellor of the UK High Court, 'as long as the pandemic remains, judges will be sensitive to medical and safety concerns and it may continue to be the case that some trials are heard remotely'.[67] Moreover, 'provided that we have up to date and robust technology, hybrid hearings may well prove to be a frequent form of hearing in the future with judge and advocates and critical witnesses in court but others such as clients or members of the media participating remotely'.[68] Effective skills to conduct advocacy and client interviews online will therefore be valuable in future legal practice. In order to learn the profession well, law schools must consider equipping students with the capability to deliver legal services online.[69]

The survey further reflects a few other constructive suggestions. Most prominently, students are almost unanimous in terms of requesting lectures to be recorded in the future, even after the pandemic, as it will help with their revision by reviewing and engaging with archived lectures at their own pace. The University of Hong Kong had once asked all teachers to continue recording all lectures and make the recordings available, unless there were specific reasons not to,[70] but later retreated and left this at the sole discretion of teachers.[71] This again shows an unexplainable reluctance to build upon the advantages and strengths of online tools and pedagogies in higher education.

In terms of supporting infrastructure, law schools and other higher education institutions should consider setting up facilities to support online legal education. The University of Hong Kong Faculty of Law has created a studio in the Faculty building and employed supporting staff to provide a dedicated space for multimedia production. It can be used to produce not only 'standard' videos that deliver course content, but also other multimedia materials that facilitate learning, such as advocacy demonstrations, career workshops, as well as more general promotional materials for the law school and its faculty members, staff, researchers and students alike. Capacity-building should also feature in these development plans, such as regular training workshops for teachers and teaching assistants to improve their IT literacy to ensure better planning and delivery of online and hybrid classes.

---

67 J. Flaux, 'Update on the Chancery Division' (14 January 2022), para. 13, https://www.judiciary.uk/wp-content/uploads/2022/01/Chancery-Bar-2022.pdf.

68 Ibid., para. 14.

69 See also D. Susskind and R. Susskind, *The Future of the Professions: How Technology Will Transform the Work of Human Experts*, updated edn, Oxford University Press, Oxford 2022; R. Susskind, *Tomorrow's Lawyers: An Introduction to Your Future*, 3rd edn, Oxford University Press, Oxford 2023.

70 I. Holliday, 'UG T&L, S1 2022–23' (8 June 2022), https://covid19.hku.hk/announcements/all/2022/06/14062/.

71 I. Holliday, 'S1 T&L arrangements' (22 August 2022), https://covid19.hku.hk/announcements/all/2022/08/14358/.

3.3.2. *Course Assessment*

While the transition to online teaching with the help of virtual learning environments (such as Moodle) and video-conferencing tools (such as Zoom) could be and was done relatively smoothly, administering online exams is much more problematic. The main concerns relate to the academic integrity of the exams, as well as the issues of cheating, collusion and plagiarism. Studies have shown that online remote proctoring is able to mitigate cheating.[72] As described in section 3.1, some PCLL exams are conducted online with a locked down browser and a remote proctoring system. While there might be various potential risks and disadvantages to certain groups of candidates (including privacy reasons, which led to the rejection of online exams in Australia), these remote proctoring arrangements are able to ensure the security and integrity of the assessments. Adequate arrangements should be in place for students requiring reasonable adjustments, and for those who are 'digitally disadvantaged' and are unable to access remote teaching and assessment.

The same reluctance about online assessments is also seen in exams for overseas students who wish to join the Hong Kong legal profession. For example, the PCLL Conversion Exams are still held in Hong Kong, where candidates must attend in person. Due to COVID-19, some students were concerned that they would be unable to do because of travel restrictions and quarantine requirements. However, following a failed discussion, none of these Conversion Exams have been held online.[73] This is in stark contrast to admission exams in other jurisdictions, such as the New York Bar Exam, with three sittings held remotely in October 2020, February 2021 and July 2021.[74] In the UK, the Solicitors Regulation Authority has authorised that assessments of the Legal Practice Course (LPC) (the UK counterpart of the PCLL) can be conducted online with remote proctoring even after the COVID-19 pandemic.[75] Remote proctoring systems enable candidates to take an examination online from their home computer, supervised remotely by the assessment provider, using the computer's audio, video, keyboard and other systems to check the candidate's identity at the start of the exam, to lock down other internet access, to prohibit

---

[72] S. Dendir and R.S. Maxwell, 'Cheating in Online Courses: Evidence from Online Proctoring' (2020) 2 *Computers in Human Behavior Reports* 100033.

[73] SCLET, 'Annual Report 2020', https://www.sclet.gov.hk/eng/pdf/2020e.pdf; SCLET, 'Annual Report 2021', p. 3, https://www.sclet.gov.hk/eng/pdf/2021e.pdf. The SCLET noted in its 2021 Annual Report 'the high possibility of a need to cater for contingencies due to the pandemic' and 'welcomed the idea of revisiting the issue regarding the feasibility of arranging online or overseas examination for future Conversion Examinations'.

[74] New York State Board of Law Examiners, 'NYS Bar Exam Reports and Press Releases', https://www.nybarexam.org/press/press.htm.

[75] K. Minns, 'Remote Proctoring of Legal Practice Course (LPC) Assessments' (27 April 2021), https://www.sra.org.uk/globalassets/documents/sra/board-meetings/2021/sra-board-item---lpc-proctoring.pdf?version=49b0f9.

cutting and pasting into the exam window, to scan the room to check that only the candidate is present, and to track eye movements and key strokes in order to pick up suspicious behaviour or cheating.[76] The Bar Standards Board (BSB) has also taken a welcoming approach towards online assessments by committing to deliver the new pupillage stage examination in professional ethics online from April 2022 onwards,[77] despite it having been under immense pressure after candidates experienced considerable difficulties with both the booking system and the remote proctoring system in the centralised exams that went online in August 2020 and led to an independent review concluded in March 2021.[78]

At a general level, it is argued that online modes of assessments should be used more frequently for any law courses. With the widespread use of computers and IT in legal practice in Hong Kong, there is now clearly a misalignment between university written examinations and actual legal practice, when computers are now adopted by students and legal practitioners alike on a daily basis.[79] To expect students to handwrite essay examinations when almost all their other work is mediated by computers is 'anachronistic'.[80] Despite all this, there is a general unwillingness in Hong Kong to hold law degree and professional examinations online. For example, some PCLL examinations still insist on students handwriting their draft pleadings and other court documents and closely following the formatting of standard templates. There is an imminent need to consider a change in practice.

For the methods and weightings of assessment, the University of Hong Kong suggested in February 2020 that 'if a course taught this semester relies heavily on a proctored final exam, it would be a good idea, where possible, to reduce the weighting for that component and boost the weighting for other assessed tasks'.[81] The institution's 'Undergraduate Teaching and Learning Strategy 2021–28' further suggested that in all undergraduate courses, no single element

---

76 Ibid., para. 10.

77 Bar Standards Board, 'The Introduction of a Professional Ethics Assessment during Pupillage' (26 November 2021), https://www.barstandardsboard.org.uk/training-qualification/becoming-a-barrister/pupillage-component/intro-of-professional-ethics-assessment.html.

78 R. Huxley-Binns and S. Kumar, 'Independent Review of the Bar Standard Board's Management of the August Sittings of the Centralised Examinations' (March 2021), https://www.barstandardsboard.org.uk/uploads/assets/d83a9e81-fd5f-4bdb-8b72396b0152185c/Final-report-of-the-independent-review-of-the-BSB-2020-exams.pdf. See also the press release and Action Plan subsequently published by the BSB in response to the Review: https://www.barstandardsboard.org.uk/resources/press-releases/bsb-publishes-independent-review-of-the-august-2020-bptc-exams.html.

79 See also A. Steel, L.B. Moses, J. Laurens and C. Brady, 'Use of E-exams in High Stakes Law School Examinations: Students and Staff Reactions' (2018) 29(1) *Legal Education Review* 1.

80 N. Mogey and A. Fluck, 'Factors Influencing Student Preference when Comparing Handwritten and Typing for Essay Style Examinations' (2015) 46(4) *British Journal of Educational Technology* 793.

81 I. Holliday, 'From Vice-President (Teaching and Learning) on Online Learning Q&As' (19 February 2020), https://covid19.hku.hk/announcements/all/teaching/general/2020/02/4750/.

should account for more than 50% of the overall course assessment, although exemptions, including for professional programmes such as law, are possible.[82] Indeed, there are no apparent changes to the assessment methods in the great majority of law courses. If one browses through the course catalogues of Hong Kong law schools, one will realise in no time that there has so far been very little progress in revolutionising the available forms of assessment for law courses in Hong Kong. In fact, such resistance to change occurs at a more general level for legal education,[83] due to the perpetuation of the doctrinal and case-based legal educational model over the generations.[84] To date, most compulsory law courses (particularly the 12 subjects that are required for PCLL admission) are conventionally assessed by in-hall examinations solely, and most law electives are conventionally assessed by way of one final research essay or take-home examination, or a combination of that with shorter essays and (less frequently) in-class presentations or class participation. Designing assessment methods and providing feedback is a vast topic in higher education,[85] with a considerable number of proponents of 'assessment for learning' where students play an active role in constructing their learning.[86] The recent rise of tools powered by artificial intelligence (such as ChatGPT) also poses new challenges for higher education. This report simply indicates that there is also a critical need to reconsider assessment designs and practices in legal education.

Since the outbreak of the pandemic, many higher education institutions, including the three law schools in Hong Kong, have provided the following options to students for several semesters in the 2019/20 and 2020/21 academic years:[87] (1) continue with letter grading for the entire course (contributing to grade point average, GPA); (2) change to Pass/Fail grading for the entire course (not contributing to GPA); or (3) opt out of the course entirely through an option to 'late drop'. Very few students exercise the 'late drop' option for law

---

82 I. Holliday, 'Delivering for our Students: Undergraduate Teaching and Learning Strategy 2021–28' (July 2021), https://tl.hku.hk/wp-content/uploads/2022/06/tl-strategy-2021-28_final.pdf.

83 S.K. Rankin, 'Tired of Talking: A Call for Clear Strategies for Legal Education Reform: Moving Beyond the Discussion of Good Ideas to the Real Transformation of Law Schools' (2011) 10(1) *Seattle Journal for Social Justice* 11.

84 R. Glofcheski, 'Rethinking Teaching, Learning and Assessment in the Twenty-first Century Law Curriculum' in C. Gane and R.H. Huang (eds), *Legal Education in the Global Context*, Routledge, Abingdon 2016.

85 See e.g. T. McConlogue, *Assessment and Feedback in Higher Education: A Guide for Teachers*, UCL Press, London 2020.

86 See e.g. K. Sambell, L. McDowell and C. Montgomery, *Assessment for Learning in Higher Education*, Routledge, Abingdon 2013; D. Carless, S.M. Bridges, C.K.Y. Chan and R. Glofcheski (eds), *Scaling up Assessment for Learning in Higher Education*, Springer, Singapore 2017.

87 This arrangement was not applicable in the 2021/22 academic year despite the resurgence of COVID-19 confirmed cases and suspension of face-to-face classes between February and April 2022.

courses as the curricula of law degrees in Hong Kong are quite packed and most of the law courses are compulsory courses for the PCLL or prerequisites for more advanced law courses. However, many students who hope to take the Pass/Fail grading option in these compulsory PCLL courses are concerned about how this impacts on PCLL admissions, which is the 'gatekeeper' of the legal profession in Hong Kong, with fierce competition for admission based on academic results in the law degree (see section 2.2). No precise guidance has been given on this despite the pandemic's continuing influence, but it is obvious that the PCLL admissions panels of the respective law schools might thus have insufficient information to assess whether the applicant possesses the required academic ability if Pass/Fail grading is opted for in a considerable amount of his/her law courses. But there are no publicly disclosed answers as to how many courses simply graded 'Pass' would be considered as problematic and how Pass/Fail grades are used (if at all) as tie-breakers in marginal cases and hence students are left at their own risk in opting for Pass/Fail grading. From the statistics of the Faculty of Law in the University of Hong Kong, the proportion of students who opted for Pass/Fail grading among the compulsory PCLL courses in the 2020/21 academic year ranged from 2.6% (The Legal System of the Hong Kong SAR) to 76.0% (Equity and Trusts).

To the best knowledge of the rapporteurs, despite the Pass/Fail option, all examination scripts in Hong Kong law schools are marked for a letter grade as usual. In this regard, there are no observable changes to the grading curves of Hong Kong law courses, even though there is experimental data (conducted among Turkish higher educators) suggesting that instructors might give out higher grades to compensate for the unforeseen negative circumstances caused by the sudden switch of the course delivery mode due to COVID-19.[88] This relative stability in terms of grades and grading curves might be attributed to the previous prevalence of 'grade inflation' (giving students higher grades than they deserve) among Hong Kong law schools,[89] which in the late 2010s resulted (in some law schools) in the adoption of internal guidelines of recommended grade distributions for larger classes (including all compulsory law courses). Instructors will have to justify grade distributions that fall outside such guidelines. This responds to some concerns over the 'inflation' in the GPA required for PCLL admissions, as well as the unfairness when comparing students across different curricula and different law schools. There are also comments from the legal profession on the difficulty in comparing between students graduating from

88 E. Karadag, 'Effect of COVID-19 Pandemic on Grade Inflation in Higher Education in Turkey' (2021) 16(8) *PLoS ONE* e02566888.

89 The occurrence of 'grade inflation' is referred to in an article of the Law Society's journal by the Faculty of Law of the University of Hong Kong: Hong Kong Lawyer, 'PCLL Admissions: Myths and Misunderstandings' (May 2014), http://www.hk-lawyer.org/content/pcll-admissions-myths-and-misunderstandings.

different law schools due to the relative leniency (or strictness) as well as the continuous 'inflation' of grades in some law schools.

3.3.3. Infrastructure

As mentioned above, access to good-quality and affordable IT hardware and software is generally not a problem for law students and teachers in Hong Kong. However, there is the need to pay attention to 'digitally disadvantaged' students who are not in the financial position to purchase suitable IT equipment. Financial aid is in place to assist these students. Relatedly, on the issue whether students should be required to switch on their camera and microphone in online classes, this has not been a mandatory requirement as a matter of policy among universities in Hong Kong, as it could be intrusive in the home environment of students. Unlike some other jurisdictions, such as Singapore, there has not been particular pressure from teachers or peers to do so. However, at the same time, teachers may have strong pedagogical reasons to encourage students to participate through an online presence, for example because the course involves active participation and discussion. In some courses (for example, in the legal context, courses involving advocacy and client interviewing), it may also be necessary for students to do so because of the nature of these tasks.[90]

4. FUTURE DIRECTIONS

The Hong Kong government had been taking a zero-tolerance approach towards COVID-19 for a substantial period of time from 2020 to 2022, with stringent measures imposed on both local residents and overseas visitors. Some are concerned that such an aggressive approach will keep the city isolated from most of the world for years to come and affect its status as an international financial and business hub.[91] Even though the direction of policies in Hong Kong has changed since December 2022, one would expect COVID-19 to impact the lives of Hong Kong people in the near future. Moreover, the pandemic is just one of the many challenges that the legal system and society of Hong Kong are currently facing. As such, Hong Kong law schools must be thoroughly

---

90 I. Holliday, 'From Vice-President (Teaching and Learning) on Online Learning Q&As' (19 February 2020), https://covid19.hku.hk/announcements/all/teaching/general/2020/02/4750/.

91 D. Strumpf, 'Foreign Executives in Isolated Hong Kong Head for Exit, Sick of Zero-Covid Curbs' (23 January 2022), https://www.wsj.com/articles/foreign-executives-in-isolated-hong-kong-head-for-exit-sick-of-zero-covid-curbs-11642950280; M.F. Cortez and I. Marlow, 'Hong Kong Covid Isolation Could Last to 2024, Euro Chamber Says' (26 January 2022), https://www.bloomberg.com/news/articles/2022-01-26/hong-kong-covid-isolation-could-last-to-2024-eu-chamber-says.

committed to engaging in the planning, implementation and delivery of online legal education. This has to be done urgently but carefully, with a detailed and practicable action plan that strikes the appropriate balance between the many significant advantages and impact it will bring, and the costs and resources it will require. Continuing legal education within the legal profession, on the other hand, has largely adapted well to the pandemic and there is reason for optimism that continuing legal education will maintain a strong online or hybrid presence after the pandemic.

More fundamentally, the current deficient state of development of online legal education in Hong Kong stems from a general lack of appreciation of key concepts and skills of teaching and learning in higher education. Despite the abundant resources for instructors to acquire these concepts and skills and to consider changes to their pedagogies, these aims have fallen outside the focus of higher education institutions in Hong Kong and around the contemporary world, which have tended to become increasingly research-oriented, metric-based and audit-driven. Higher education instructors are not encouraged sufficiently to become reflective practitioners and educators. The COVID-19 pandemic has further aggravated the deficiency in the current approaches towards online legal education. In particular, the zero-tolerance approach towards COVID-19 might be thought to have contributed towards the general attitude within the higher education sector to treat the pandemic as the exception and the 'non-pandemic' as the norm. However, quite the contrary, the pandemic has unquestionably triggered a paradigm shift, and one should embrace, not evade, new approaches and solutions.

One way to improve the situation immediately is to convene discussion groups and launch platforms across institutions and territories to share resources and experiences of online learning. This is to create a supportive environment to spark changes. The Chinese University of Hong Kong Faculty of Law has organised biennial online conferences on teaching and learning law, most recently in June 2022.[92] Enthusiastic faculty members from the Faculty of Law in the University of Hong Kong have also convened a teaching and learning discussion group where they organise regular talks and seminars, and encourage informal chats for the sharing of knowledge, skills and techniques in legal education. It is hoped that this report will serve as a reference guide for discussion and a starting point for future initiatives in this area.

This report summarises, for the first time in the academic literature, what has been done and achieved in Hong Kong in terms of online legal education and what can be done to further promote online legal education. It is now imperative

[92] The Chinese University of Hong Kong Faculty of Law, 'Online Conference on Teaching and Learning in Law – Directions in Legal Education 2022', https://webapp3.law.cuhk.edu.hk/conf/20220610/. Both rapporteurs presented papers at this conference.

for the Hong Kong legal education community, and more generally the Hong Kong higher education sector, to move away from the idea of 'emergency remote teaching' and start to take the concepts and tools of online education seriously. If there is any progress at all, these are only the very first steps. There might be many perceived challenges and difficulties for Hong Kong online legal education, exacerbated by the COVID-19 pandemic, but these can all be addressed with the appropriate methods and tools. Most importantly, there must be a fundamental change in mentality to embrace new approaches and solutions. What now needs to be done is to 'walk the talk', so that Hong Kong will be able to uphold its strong tradition of nurturing legal professionals for the region, for the country, and for the world.

ONLINE LEGAL EDUCATION IN THE MACAO SAR

Fostering Technology in a Multilingual Learning Environment

Rostam J. Neuwirth, Muruga P. Ramaswamy and Alexandr Svetlicinii*

1. INTRODUCTION

For a concise account of the status of both online and offline legal education in the Macao Special Administrative Region (SAR) of the People's Republic of China (PRC), it is first useful to provide some general background information on the many unique characteristics of the Macao SAR (MSAR). In geographical terms, it covers a small peninsula plus two connected islands located on the

* The rapporteurs are grateful to Katrine Wong, Christopher Fulton and Joan Chiang for their assistance with data collection.

shores of the South China Sea, on the western side of the Pearl River Delta across from Hong Kong. Over the past century, its size has increased from 11 to around 31 square kilometres, mainly through land reclamation from the surrounding sea.

From a macroeconomic perspective, the MSAR has experienced rapid development and a strong economic boom since the early 21st century, albeit with large fluctuations. Since then, the economy of the MSAR has generally been dominated by services, which account for over 95% of GDP, with gaming as its main economic activity, accounting for roughly half of its GDP in 2018.[1] In 2019, Macao had one of the highest per capita incomes in the world, at about US$79,977. Before COVID-19, the MSAR was expected to become the economy with the world's highest GDP per capita in 2020. However, since the World Health Organization (WHO) declared the pandemic in March 2020, revenues fell drastically due to a temporary shutdown of the casinos and the sharp decline in visitors from continuing travel restrictions imposed due to health concerns in the wake of the pandemic.[2] For instance, compared to 2019, several months in 2020 experienced a steep decline in the monthly gross revenue from games of fortune of up to 97% compared to the same month a year before.[3] Overall, the fiscal year 2020 recorded a real GDP growth for Macao of minus 56.3%.[4] In April 2021, however, the ranking from the International Monetary Fund (IMF) moved the MSAR up by 13 places from 25th in 2020 to 12th in 2021.[5]

Since substantial fiscal surpluses were posted before 2020, it was possible to mitigate the negative effects of the pandemic on the economy caused by decreased direct taxes from gaming. The government put in place several fiscal packages to offset the negative effects of COVID-19 on economic activities, including cash handouts to residents, additional health spending, transfers to eligible employees, transfers to certain services providers and utilities free of charge for residents for three months, to mention but a few.[6]

Due to improved conditions as a result of measures facilitating travel at least between the MSAR and Mainland China, the situation has gradually

---

1 WTO Secretariat, 'Trade Policy Review: Macao, China', WT/TPR/S/402 (10 November 2020), p. 7.

2 V.L. Raposo and M.T. Iong, 'The struggle against the COVID-19 pandemic in Macao' (2020) *BioLaw Journal/Rivista de Biodiritto* 747, https://www.biodiritto.org/content/download/3898/45987/version/1/file/68+Raposo+Iong.pdf.

3 Gaming Inspection and Coordination Bureau (DCIJ), 'Monthly Gross Revenue from Games of Fortune', http://www.dicj.gov.mo/web/en/information/DadosEstat_mensal/2020/index.html.

4 Knoema, 'World Data Atlas: Macau – Gross domestic product in constant prices growth rate', https://knoema.com/atlas/Macau/Real-GDP-growth.

5 IMF, 'World Economic Outlook database: April 2021', https://statisticstimes.com/economy/projected-world-gdp-capita-ranking.php.

6 WTO Secretariat, 'Trade Policy Review: Macao, China', WT/TPR/S/402 (10 November 2020), p. 7.

improved, although uncertainties remained and largely depended on the detection of new cases of COVID-19 in Macao and in Hong Kong, as well as Mainland China. In March 2022 there was still a high level of uncertainty, not only because of the pandemic, but also because of the ongoing process of restructuring the gaming industry in the context of the amendment of the gaming law and pending renewal of the casino licences, which were due to expire in December 2022.[7]

A final element that is also important to mention for online education is that as from 2019 onwards, 86.5% of the population of the MSAR had access to the internet, compared to 61.3% in 2012.[8]

Before looking more closely at the status of both online and offline legal education in the MSAR, it is useful to first highlight some of the special and unique legal features of the MSAR that are enshrined in the Macao Basic Law. Following that, the report provides a brief overview of the organisation of the legal profession and legal education in Macao. Lastly, the various concrete measures taken during the pandemic towards online legal education will be presented, before the conclusion ends with a short summary and an outlook for the future of legal education in the MSAR.

1.1. MACAO'S UNIQUE LEGAL FEATURES

From a historical perspective, Macao is special because of its former status as a Portuguese-administered territory, which lasted for several centuries until 20 December 1999, when the PRC resumed the exercise of sovereignty over Macao.[9] Legally, Macao has since then been governed by the Macao Basic Law (MBL), adopted by the National People's Congress pursuant to Article 31 of the PRC Constitution.[10] This article implements the so-called 'One Country, Two

7 P. Cortés, 'Macau Gaming Industry 8.0 – Public Policy Beyond 2022' (2021) 25(2) *Gaming Law Review* 50 and C. Wang, 'Regulations and Practice of Casino Reversion in Macao: What Further Should Be Done?' (2022) 26(1) *Gaming Law Review* 2.

8 WTO Secretariat, 'Trade Policy Review: Macao, China', WT/TPR/S/402 (10 November 2020), pp. 11 and 100.

9 See also R.L. Edmonds and H.S. Yee, 'Macau: From Portuguese Autonomous Territory to Chinese Special Administrative Region' (1999) 160 *The China Quarterly* 801; and Y. Ghai, 'The Basic Law of the Special Administrative Region of Macau: Some Reflections' (2001) 49(1) *The International and Comparative Law Quarterly* 183.

10 The Basic Law of the Macao Special Administrative Region of the People's Republic of China (MBL) (adopted at the First Session of the Eighth National People's Congress on 31 March 1993 and promulgated by Order No. 3 of the President of the People's Republic of China on 31 March 1993, and effective as of 20 December 1999); Lei Básica da Região Administrativa Especial de Macau da República Popular da China, https://bo.io.gov.mo/bo/i/1999/leibasica/index.asp.

Systems' principle, which provides the constitutional basis for the establishment of SARs, such as those of Macao and Hong Kong.[11]

The Macao Basic Law established the MSAR as 'an inalienable part' of the PRC and, as such, authorises it 'to exercise a high degree of autonomy and enjoy executive, legislative and independent judicial power, including that of final adjudication'.[12] This far-reaching autonomy also gives Macao a truly unique status of a 'glocal' (both global and local) player.[13] This is manifest, for instance in the right to use its own regional flag and emblem in addition to the national flag and emblem of the PRC.[14] It is also reflected in its right to actively participate in international organisations, including membership in the World Trade Organization (WTO)[15] and the IMF,[16] as well as associate membership in UNESCO.[17]

In practice it means that the MSAR enjoys a wide range of local and even external powers, with the important exceptions of foreign affairs and defence, which are to be exercised by the PRC government.[18] This autonomy also extends to education policy, laid down in Article 121 MBL as follows:

Chapter VI Culture and Social Affairs
Article 121

> The Government of the Macao Special Administrative Region shall, on its own, formulate policies on education, including policies regarding the educational system and its administration, the language of instruction, the allocation of funds, the examination system, the recognition of educational qualifications and the system of academic awards so as to promote educational development.

---

[11] Article 31 of the Constitution of the People's Republic of China (PRC) adopted at the Fifth Session of the Fifth National People's Congress and promulgated for implementation by the Announcement of the National People's Congress on 4 December 1982.

[12] Articles 1 and 2 MBL. At the same time, several laws apply nationwide and a list of the national laws applicable in the Macao SAR are included in the Annex III of the MBL.

[13] R.J. Neuwirth, 'Governing "Glocalisation": A View from the Macau Special Administrative Region of China' (2011) 3(1) *City University of Hong Kong Law Review* 89.

[14] R.J. Neuwirth, 'The Regional Flag of the Macau Special Administrative Region (SAR) of the People's Republic of China: A Synaesthetic Exploration' in A. Wagner and S. Marusek (eds), *Flags, Color, and the Legal Narrative – Public Memory, Identity, and Critique* (Berlin: Springer International, 2020).

[15] WTO, 'WTO Members and Observers', https://www.wto.org/english/thewto_e/whatis_e/tif_e/org6_e.htm.

[16] IMF, 'Macao Special Administrative Region of the People's Republic of China', http://www.imf.org/en/Countries/MAC.

[17] UNESCO, 'List of the 195 Members (and the 11 Associate Members) of UNESCO', http://www.unesco.org/eri/cp/ListeMS_Indicators.asp.

[18] Articles 13 and 14 MBL. While the Macao SAR enjoys a high degree of autonomy, the Central People's Government shall be responsible for the foreign affairs relating to the Macao Special Administrative Region. The application of the PRC's international treaties in Macao are decided by the Central Government on case-by-case basis in accordance with the needs of the Macao SAR and in consultation with the local government.

> The Government of the Macao Special Administrative Region shall, in accordance with law, gradually institute a compulsory education system.
>
> Community organizations and individuals may, in accordance with law, run educational undertakings of various kinds.

Furthermore, Article 122 MBL stipulates that 'all educational institutions in the Macao Special Administrative Region shall enjoy their autonomy and teaching and academic freedom in accordance with law' and enjoy further freedoms related to their activities. Finally, the Macao legal system is often described as belonging to the civil law family (or the 'Romano-Germanic' or 'continental European' tradition) due to its close historical ties with the Portuguese legal system.[19] It is further supported by its close ties to the legal system of the PRC. However, due to further influences from the neighbouring Hong Kong SAR, which is usually classified as belonging to the common law tradition,[20] as well as other factors, the legal system of Macao has also been classified as a 'mixed' or 'hybrid' legal system.[21] For instance, since the Macao legal system belongs to the civil law family, the judgments of the courts do not enjoy the status of case law due to the absence of the *stare decisis* principle. At the same time, the jurisprudence of Macao courts is not entirely irrelevant for the interpretation of the legal rules, especially in cases regarding novel legal issues and those not covered in the legislation.

A further important element contributing to the unique characteristics of the Macao legal system in general, and of great relevance to its legal education in particular, is the strong prevalence of linguistic pluralism.[22] This is first enshrined in the MBL itself, which in Article 9 states that 'in addition to the Chinese language, Portuguese may also be used as an official language by the executive authorities, legislature and judiciary of the Macao Special Administrative Region'.

The bilingual characteristic and parallel use of Chinese and Portuguese has also strongly influenced the legal system as well as the system of legal education.[23]

---

19 P. Nunes Correia, 'The Juridical System of Macau: A Comparative Law Perspective' in M. Trigo (ed.), *Report on Macau Law* (Macau/Hong Kong: University of Macau/LexisNexis, 2014), pp. 10–14; R. Ferreira Alves, 'Macau Special Administrative Region of People's Republic of China Jurisdiction' (May/June 2017), *GlobaLEX* (New York University), http://www.nyulawglobal.org/globalex/Macau.html; and A. Svetlicinii, 'Introduction to Macao Law' in *Legal Systems of Asia: A Short Guide* (Sejong: Korea Legislation Research Institute, 2016), pp. 39–51.

20 P. Cardinal, 'Fundamental Rights in Macau: From Territory under Portuguese Administration to Special Administrative Region of the PRC' in J. Godinho (ed.), *Studies on Macau Civil, Commercial, Constitutional and Criminal Law* (Hong Kong: Lexis Nexis, 2010), p. 7.

21 I. Castellucci, 'Legal Hybridity in Hong Kong and Macau' (2012) 57 *McGill Law Journal* 665.

22 A. Moody, *Macau's Languages in Society and Education: Planning in a Multilingual Ecology* (Cham: Springer, 2021).

23 S. Casabona, 'The Law of Macau and Its Language: A Glance at the Real Masters of the Law' (2012) 4(2) *Tsinghua China Law Review* 223; and T.I. Cheng, 'Linguistic Pluralism and the Legal System of Macau' (2020) 7(1) *Journal of International and Comparative Law* 183.

In fact, Macao's legal system, educational system and even daily life also have strong traits of multilingualism, given the parallel usage of Mandarin and Cantonese as well as the English language. English had already back in the 1980s been considered a significant language in Macao, but has also gained importance given Macao's role as a world casino hub and as a language of instruction in education.[24]

In sum, these different legal and other characteristics of the MSAR establish it not only as a unique glocal player in the world but also a very fruitful micro-laboratory for research in different areas, including notably law and legal education. These and other characteristics also make it a curious place to inquire into the relationship between offline and online legal education, as another final unique characteristic attributed to Macao is its reputation as a place where multiple opposites meet and eventually often become reconciled.[25]

1.2. BACKGROUND: LEGAL PROFESSION, UNIVERSITIES AND IT SYSTEMS GENERALLY

1.2.1. The Legal Profession in the MSAR

The entry to Macao legal profession has been regulated by the Statute of Lawyers 1991 as amended in 1995 (the 'Lawyers Statute')[26] and Access to Legal Practice Regulation 1999, promulgated by the Macao Association of Lawyers (AAM),[27] as updated on 16 May 2017.[28] Only the lawyers and trainee lawyers registered with the AAM are permitted to perform activities of the legal profession, including exercise of judicial mandate and provision of legal advice.[29] While the estimated number of registered lawyers is around 460, the total number of

24 W. Botha, 'English-Medium Instruction at a University in Macau: Policy and Realities' (2013) 32(4) *World Englishes* 461; and W. Botha and A. Moody, 'English in Macau' in K. Bolton, W. Botha and A. Kirkpatrick (eds), *The Handbook of Asian Englishes* (Hoboken: John Wiley, 2020), pp. 529–546.

25 B. Videira Pires, *Os extremos conciliam-se: (transculturação em Macau)* (Macau: Instituto Cultural de Macau, 1988), pp. 213–215.

26 Decree-Law No. 31/91/M as amended by Decree-Law No. 42/95/M.

27 Associação dos Advogados de Macau, https://www.aam.org.mo/.

28 See Regulation BO No. 50/1999 promulgated by the Macao Public Association of Lawyers (AAM) as updated on 16 May 2017.

29 However, the Lawyers Statute and the Access to Legal Practice Regulation recognise that university law professors may provide written legal opinions without considering themselves as practising law, and legally qualified law graduates serving as civil servant may provide legal advice as part of their duty, albeit waiving the requirement of having to formally register as a lawyer with the AAM. See Article 11(2) and (3), Decree-Law No. 31/91/M and Article 1(2) and (3), Regulation BO No. 50/1999.

trainee lawyers is projected to be around 120.[30] As part of the training, the AAM organises training courses on professional ethics and practice areas relating to litigation, registration and notarisation. Moreover, to supplement the training, attendance at seminars, conferences or other activities beneficial to practice may also be required.[31] Although the AAM is the body comparable to the bar association in other jurisdictions, it enjoys a special status in the Macao legal system as a public association.[32] The AAM not only enjoys exclusivity in registering lawyers but also is the only public sector association endowed with regulatory powers.

The Lawyers Statute and the ATA Regulation govern the entry requirements to the profession as well as various aspects of legal practice. For example, lawyers who are civil servants or administrative agents are prohibited from practising law in matters connected with their employment in public or administrative services.[33] Similarly, the activities or functions of certain vocations, which have the potential to undermine the independence and dignity of the profession, are declared to be incompatible with the practice of law.[34] Such incompatibility

[30] Associação dos Advogados de Macau, Advogados, https://aam.org.mo/os-advogados/advogados/page/47/ and Associação dos Advogados de Macau, Estagiários, https://aam.org.mo/os-advogados/estagiarios/page/12/.

[31] Article 25(1) and (3) of Regulation BO No. 50/1999. There is no specific reference or prohibition to online offering of the training courses or online attendance of the seminars and other activities. However, given the wider use of online tools in university legal education, as well as in its seminars and conferences organised online, participation in such events should gain general recognition to satisfy relevant requirements. For the scope of online legal education in neighbouring Hong Kong see the draft report of W. Lui and A. Lee, 'Online Legal Education in Hong Kong' (31 January 2022), University of Hong Kong Faculty of Law Research Paper No. 2022/03, https://ssrn.com/abstract=4019847.

[32] AAM enjoys a privileged legal status as a public association in comparison with the local bar associations in some neighbouring jurisdictions. For example, in the neighbouring Hong Kong SAR, the Hong Kong Bar Association is registered under the Societies Ordinance under which any club, company, partnership or association of persons, whatever the nature or objects, could be registered as a legal person. See section 2(1) of the Hong Kong Societies Ordinance (Cap 151).

[33] The prohibition is mandated if the civil servants or administrative agents are even in the situations of retirement or inactivity or on unpaid leave or on reserve. Similarly, the SAR Legislative Assembly (LA) members and municipality councillors are not permitted to exercise judicial mandate in certain prescribed circumstances. See Article 22 Decree-Law No. 31/91/M and Article 3 Regulation BO No. 50/1999.

[34] The vocations for which the activities or functions are declared to be incompatible with the practice of the profession include: incumbents or members of governmental bodies and certain people serving in the offices of those bodies (excluding the members of the LA); prosecutors, employees and agents of the courts; certain people serving in the municipal bodies; notaries, registrars, officials and agents of the notary and registration services; employees and agents of public services (excluding teachers in public institutions); serving members of the armed or military forces; certain brokers and auctioneers; and any vocations that by virtue of their nature or the special law governing them are considered as incompatible with legal practice as well as vocations that contractually mandate exclusive dedication. See Article 21(1) Decree-Law No. 31/91/M and Article 2(1) Regulation BO No. 50/1999.

can arise irrespective of the nature and type of rendering of the said activity, function or designation, the mode of remuneration, and the legal regime under which it is rendered.

Four key entry requirements must be satisfied by all persons seeking to enrol as a lawyer in Macao. First, enrolment requires a law degree from a university in Macao or any other law degree that is recognised in Macao. Secondly, a legal traineeship (internship or pupillage) for a prescribed period must be completed. Thirdly, a written declaration from the candidate confirming the absence of incompatibilities for the exercise of the profession shall be submitted. Fourth, the absence of any other restrictions on the right of registration should be proved by the candidate by furnishing a no-criminal-record certificate and a written declaration.

These restrictions on the right to registration are identified by the Lawyers Statute and the Access to Legal Practice Regulation, which prescribe a list of persons with certain characteristics whose registration as a lawyer can be refused. Such persons include those who are morally unfit to practise, including those convicted of a '*crime gravemente desonroso*' (seriously dishonourable crime); those who do not have full enjoyment of their civil rights; those who have lost the capacity to manage personal affairs or assets by virtue of a final sentence; those who suffer incompatibility or inhibition in legal practice due to certain prescribed activity or function that reduces the independence and dignity of the profession; those who lack the professional qualifications to practise law, and those magistrates and officials who have been dismissed, retired or placed in inactivity due to lack of moral integrity as a result of disciplinary proceedings. The process of the 'verification' and 'declaration' of moral integrity for the purpose of any of these grounds must follow prescribed procedures, including requirements of specific disciplinary proceedings and approval by the Superior Advocacy Council (SAC).[35] Criminal conviction as a bar to seeking registration is relaxed in case of rehabilitated convicted persons under certain conditions.[36]

In addition to the four standard entry requirements, candidates seeking enrolment as a lawyer with a law degree obtained from outside Macao must satisfy additional conditions. First, such candidates must complete attendance of a prescribed course on adaptation to the Macao legal system.[37] However,

[35] The Lawyers Statute recognises the SAC as the professional disciplinary body with exclusive disciplinary jurisdiction over lawyers and trainee lawyers and elaborates its characterisation, competence, composition, mandate and rules of deliberation. See Articles 2, 4, 5, 6, 9, 10, 40 and 41 of Decree-Law No. 31/91/M and Articles 4, 10 and 41 of Decree-Law No. 42/95/M.

[36] The conditions include that the relevant inquiry proves the manifest dignity of the applicant in the last three years of the five-year period and establishes that a complete moral recovery has been reached.

[37] Article 4(2) Regulation BO No. 50/1999.

the requirement of attendance at the adaptation course is waived in certain cases.[38] The objective of the adaptation course is to study the legal system of Macao, as well as specificities in relation to related legal systems. Although the AAM is endowed with responsibility for the general orientation of the course, it has the power to recognise courses offered by reputable entities in Macao with an identical value.[39] The AAM prescribes not only the duration of the adaptation course but also its structure. While requiring a general duration of a minimum of 12 months to a maximum of 15 months, the Access to Legal Practice Regulation recognises the freedom of the AAM to exceptionally reduce the duration of the adaptation course (with a guaranteed module on an introduction to the Macao legal system) for law graduates from universities in countries with similar legal systems to Macao. Regarding structure, the Access to Legal Practice Regulation mandates six specific modules, covering an introduction to the Macao legal system, private international law, administrative law, civil law, commercial law, and criminal law. In addition to prescribing specific modules, the Access to Legal Practice Regulation also provides the assessment method to be adopted at the end of each module.[40]

Second, the candidates seeking enrolment as a lawyer with a law degree obtained from outside Macao are required pass the exams for admission to an internship, and the AAM is endowed with the power to prescribe the nature and content of those exams. Failure to pass the admission test imposes a two-year waiting period before there is the possibility of repeating the test.

Specific entry requirements to the legal profession in Macao have been subjected to judicial interpretations in legal disputes challenging certain related decisions of the AAM, involving candidates seeking enrolment as a lawyer with a law degree obtained in Macao as well as candidates seeking enrolment with a law degree obtained from outside Macao. In 2013, the decision of the AAM not to permit a candidate with a law degree conferred by the Macau University

---

38 For example Macao law professors with an academic master's or higher with more than two academic years of teaching experience in a university in Macao, and former judicial magistrates, prosecutors, registrars and notaries who have served more than two years in Macao with a final classification of 'Very Good', are exempted from the adaptation course. Moreover, the AAM also has the power to grant such exemption to law graduates from universities in countries with legal systems similar to Macao who have gained more than two years of experience in exercising legal functions in Macao which in very nature and extent provides for an adequate grasp of the legal system in Macao.

39 For example, the Introduction to Macao Law programme offered by the Faculty of Law of the University of Macau is recognised by the AAM as a programme with an identical value, completion of which will satisfy the requirement of the adaptation course.

40 The assessment method for the modules is derived from the method (with necessary adaptation) prescribed for evaluation of certain other modules mandated during the internship period, which is required subsequent to the completion of the adaptation course for successful entry into the profession as a lawyer. See Article 17(4) Regulation BO No. 50/1999.

of Science and Technology to enter internship training on the grounds that the degree programme did not contain mandatory courses on Macao law was challenged by the candidate before the administrative court. The decision of the administrative court granting the challenge was subsequently appealed by the AAM in the Court of Second Instance. Although the appeal was partially granted on certain technical grounds, the Court basically held that the AAM cannot deny enrolment on the ground that the degree in question did not correspond to a degree in Macao law, especially when that degree has been duly authorised and approved by the government.[41]

Judicial challenges have also been mounted in cases of candidates seeking enrolment as a lawyer with a law degree obtained from outside Macao. In 2014, the Court of Second Instance was asked to determine a challenge against a decision of the AAM not to approve the participation of a candidate in the first phase of the internship admission test on the grounds that the candidate had completed a four-year law degree offered by Huaqiao University in China in three years instead, and that the total teaching hours in legal subjects in the qualifying degree programme were less than the total teaching hours in law courses in the law degree of the University of Macau. In addition, reasons like more than one-third of the credits in the degree programme in question being allocated to non-law subjects and a lack of any class time for studying Macao law also precipitated the decision not to approve the candidate's participation in the admission test. The Court held that the candidate's qualification could not be refused recognition on the basis that the candidate, out of their personal earnest efforts, had completed the requirements of the degree programme one year earlier than the normal study period. The Court also found that there was a mistaken belief as to the extent of the credits in non-law subjects, and that the reason of insufficient teaching hours of Macao law could not form the basis of the decision not to recognise the degree. Consequently, the Court held that the decision of the AAM not to recognise the degree of the candidate in the instant case was flawed and it was an unreasonable exercise of discretionary powers.[42]

In 2018, a candidate challenged the decision of the AAM rejecting his application for an exemption from the internship requirement for registration as a lawyer. The candidate sought an exemption under Article 19(4)(a) of the 1991 Lawyers Statute, which grants an exemption to law professors with a master's or higher degree along with university teaching experience in Macao for more

41 Case No. 664/2013, Administrative Appeal Decision rendered on 23 October 2014 by the Court of Second Instance of the Macao SAR. Irrespective of the outcome of this specific case, the decision is perceived to have recognised that the knowledge of Macao law is of decisive importance for the exercise of legal professions in the SAR.

42 Case No. 775/2014, Decision rendered on 14 April 2016 by the Court of Second Instance of the Macao SAR.

than two years. Although, the candidate had obtained a law degree from Jinan University, which is situated in Mainland China, the recognition of the degree was successfully obtained from the higher education authority of Macao in 2000. In addition, the candidate had also successfully completed the Introduction to Macao Law course and a Master of Law degree from the University of Macau. Although the candidate seemed to have satisfied all the requirements for seeking an exemption from the internship, the AAM rejected his application on the ground that the recognition of the candidate's law degree, which was approved by the education authority under the Decree Law No. 39/93/M, was subsequently revoked by the Administrative Regulation No. 26/2003 and the verification of the academic qualification under the regulation rendered the degree not suitable for registration as a lawyer due to its taught components as well as the effective teaching time of the classes not satisfying the regulation. However, the decision of the AAM was quashed by the administrative court, which held that recognition of a candidate's academic qualification is long-lasting and that such recognition is not limited only to the period in which Decree No. 39/93/M was in force. Therefore, it was held that the AAM did not enjoy the discretion to seek the verification of the academic qualifications under the Administrative Regulation No. 26/2003. Upon an appeal by the AAM, the Court of Second Instance concurred with the administrative court.[43]

1.2.2. Higher Education Institutions in the MSAR

Despite its small size and population of little more than 682,500 inhabitants,[44] Macao hosts several higher education institutions, including several universities, both public and private. Among those, three universities offer comprehensive legal education in Macao, although only the University of Macau (UM) offers legal programmes qualifying for admission to the local bar. It is the only public comprehensive university in Macao, founded in 1981.[45] At present, UM offers legal undergraduate and postgraduate programmes in Chinese and Portuguese as well as postgraduate (master's and PhD) in English. The other two universities are both private: the Macau University of Science and Technology (MUST), founded in 2000,[46] and the City University of Macau (CityU), which was originally founded as the University of East Asia in 1981 but renamed in 2011.[47]

---

43 Case No. 1097/2018, Decision rendered on 2 July 2020 by the Court of Second Instance of the Macao SAR.

44 Government of Macao Special Administrative Region, Statistics and Census Service, 'Statistics', https://www.dsec.gov.mo/en-US/.

45 University of Macau (UM), https://www.um.edu.mo.

46 Faculty of Law of the Macau University of Science and Technology (MUST), https://www.must.edu.mo/en/fl.

47 School of Law of the City University of Macau (CityU), https://sol.cityu.edu.mo/.

The University of St. Joseph (USJ) is a private Catholic university founded in 1996, which offers a master's programme in law in English as part of its Faculty of Business and Law.[48] Other higher education institutions in Macao include:[49]

- Macao Institute for Tourism Studies;[50]
- Kiang Wu Nursing College of Macau;[51]
- Macao Polytechnic University;[52] and
- Macau Millennium College.[53]

Overall and given its small size, Macao offers a great variety of higher education institutions, as the government declares:

> Macao currently has 4 public and 6 private higher education institutions, including integrated education-based and research-based universities, multidisciplinary polytechnic institutions focused on applied education, as well as professional institutions that focus on training tourism and exhibition and meeting planners, gaming specialists, paramedics, and other management professionals.
>
> Even though Macao's modern higher education institutions have a relatively short history, they have developed and flourished during the past 30 years, attracting an increasing amount of non-local students.
>
> At the same time, in recent years, over 50% of local high school graduates stay in Macao to further their education. Macao's higher education institutions are attractive to both locals and non-locals alike.[54]

---

48 University of Saint Joseph (USJ) (formerly Inter-University Institute), Master of Lusophone and International Public Law programme, https://www.usj.edu.mo/en/courses/ma-lusophone-international-public-law.

49 Education and Youth Development Bureau (DSEJ) of the Government of the Macao SAR, 'Higher Education Institutions', https://portal.dsedj.gov.mo/webdsejspace/internet/Inter_main_page.jsp?id=77748.

50 The Macao Institute for Tourism Studies (IFTM), 'General Information', https://www.iftm.edu.mo/. The IFTM was established in 1995 as a public institution of higher education in Macao that offers degree programmes and professional training in tourism and hospitality. It is under the supervision of the Secretary for Social Affairs and Culture of the Government of Macao Special Administrative Region.

51 Kiang Wu Nursing College of Macau (KWNC), founded in 1923, is a subsidiary institution of Kiang Wu Hospital Charitable Association (KWHCA), http://www2.kwnc.edu.mo/?page_id=5481.

52 Macao Polytechnic University (MPU) is a public higher education institution with an emphasis on applied knowledge and skill, https://www.mpu.edu.mo/en/mpu_introduction.php.

53 The Macau Millennium College was founded in August 2001 by well-known educators and businessmen in Hong Kong and Macao and soon recognised by the Macao SAR government as a private institution of tertiary education in Macao, https://www.mmc.edu.mo/.

54 Education and Youth Development Bureau (DSEDJ), 'Institutions' Information', https://portal.dsedj.gov.mo/webdsejspace/site/studyinmacau/en/institutions.html.

In sum, the Macao government has repeatedly expressed its intention to work to enhance the quality of tertiary education and promote its sustainable development.[55] In line with the generally strong economic data, major investments in infrastructure as well as the high internet penetration rate, the Macao government has also provided the necessary resources to achieve the goals set in the field of education. In a recent interview, the former rector of UM has also stated that 'higher education in Macau has developed fast with very good government funding'.[56]

2. MOVES TOWARDS ONLINE LEGAL EDUCATION

2.1. ANTI-EPIDEMIC MEASURES AND MOVES TOWARDS ONLINE LEGAL EDUCATION AT THE UNIVERSITY OF MACAU

The COVID-19 pandemic has been an important factor for the move towards online legal education in the MSAR. The following account summarises the experiences at UM, the only comprehensive public research university in the MSAR. The pandemic caused it considerable hardship and numerous cost-saving measures were introduced, which in particular affected the funding for a variety of research activities. Perhaps as a direct consequence, but also as part of a MSAR-wide outlook, in early 2021 UM announced it would increase its bachelor's degree tuition fees for residents and non-resident students for the 2021/22 academic year. For example, the tuition fees for local Macao resident were reported to have 'increased by 21 per cent for four-year and five-year bachelor degrees to MOP120,000 [about US$15,000], and MOP150,000 [US$18,500], respectively.'[57] The UM Five-Year Development Plan (2021–26) provides for an increase in the number of postgraduate students, which will bring the total student body from the current 12,000 to about 17,000 students.[58]

---

55 The Government of the Macao Special Administrative Region, 'Policy Address for the Fiscal Year 2021: Strengthening the foundation for consolidation Tackling challenges head on' (2021), p. 37, https://www.gov.mo/en/wp-content/uploads/sites/2/2021/01/2021_policy_e.pdf.

56 J.P. Meneses, 'Special Report – "Higher education in Macau has developed fast with very good government funding"', *Macau Business* (28 March 2021), https://www.macaubusiness.com/special-report-higher-education-in-macau-has-developed-fast-with-very-good-government-funding/.

57 N. Moura, 'University of Macau increases bachelor degree tuition fees,' *Macau Business* (10 March 2021), https://www.macaubusiness.com/university-of-macau-increases-bachelor-degree-tuition-fees/.

58 University of Macau, Five-Year Development Plan (Academic Years 2021/22–2025/26) (Outline), https://www.um.edu.mo/wp-content/uploads/2021/12/UM-Five-Year-Development-Plan_EN.pdf.

For international students, they were still subject in March 2022 to travel restrictions, which have caused a lot of hardship to the existing UM students who could not return after the holidays in early 2020. However, as most non-resident students come from Mainland China, with which travel restrictions have generally been lifted, there has been no decrease in student numbers. To the contrary, at least in terms of application numbers, it seems that the global travel restrictions imposed by various countries had the effect of diverting the applications by students from Mainland China to Macao and possibly other destinations.

While a significant part of its student body comes from Mainland China, with the outbreak of the novel coronavirus and the imposition of travel restrictions, UM was faced with a situation where many students would not be able to return to campus after the 2020 Chinese Lunar New Year holidays. On 23 January 2020, UM established the Task Force for Pneumonia Prevention and Control,[59] which began coordinating various anti-epidemic activities, including the adjustments to the teaching process. Initially, the resumption of classes after the 2020 mid-year recess was postponed to 11 February. Since the MSAR Government ordered further postponement of the resumption of classes in higher education institutions, UM has switched to online teaching and learning following the principle 'Keep Learning Amid Class Suspension'.

The university decided to resume on-site classes for the graduating bachelor's students from 20 April 2020 to allow them to complete the remaining coursework without major changes or disruptions. For all other students, including postgraduates, e-learning continued until the end of the second semester of the academic year 2019/20.[60] Master's and PhD thesis defences were allowed to resume from 4 May 2020 and graduating students were allowed to apply for return to campus in order to take part in the thesis defence.

The following learning resources were available to UM students during the e-learning period: electronic resources of the UM Library;[61] massive open online courses (MOOCs) created by UM experts and scholars on XuetangX;[62] and distance learning materials, including lectures and discussions, on the UM Moodle[63] online learning platform. The e-learning at UM was essentially based

59 University of Macau (UM), 'Task Force for Pneumonia Prevention and Control', https://www.um.edu.mo/task-force-for-pneumonia-prevention-and-control/.

60 Government of the Macao SAR, Health Bureau, 'Prevention of Novel Coronavirus Pneumonia – Advice on Class Resumption for Higher Education Institutions' (25 February 2020), https://www.ssm.gov.mo/docs/17595/17595_2a7ce23c856c4f17b9f73137d99f3269_000.pdf.

61 University of Macau, Wu Yee Sun Library, 'Databases', https://library.umac.mo/html/databases/e_databases.asp.

62 University of Macau, 'MOOC Creativity', https://www.xuetangx.com/courses/course-v1:UMX+CRT101+2018_T4/about.

63 UMMOODLE (the electronic course management system of the University of Macau), https://ummoodle.um.edu.mo/.

on the combination of using Zoom for online meetings and Moodle for out-of-class activities. The Information and Communication Technology Office (ICTO) has provided technical guidance to students and faculty members on the use of these platforms.

The MSAR Higher Education and Youth Development Bureau (DSEDJ) Guidelines on the start of the academic year 2020/21 for higher education institutions were issued on 19 August 2020 and required the universities to set out the requirements for course syllabi, assignments, teacher–student interaction, assessment, etc. Where the online teaching was carried out by means of live-streaming webinars and there was a risk of communication disruptions, the universities were required to provide the recordings of the online classes. To ensure the quality of online education, the DSES also required teaching staff to keep records of course syllabi, teaching materials, teacher–student interactions, student attendance, and assessment reports.

The academic year 2020/21 started on 7 September 2020 with on-site teaching together with observance of certain social distancing measures. Classes of up to 100 students were conducted face to face. Classes of 100–200 students were divided into two groups according to the number of students, with each group participating in face-to-face and online classes in rotation. Classes of more than 200 students were conducted entirely online. In addition, UM also offered e-learning to students who were unable to enter the MSAR due to travel restrictions imposed by the government. As a result, UM entered a phase of hybrid teaching, requiring most teaching staff to conduct face-to-face classes while allowing online participation via Zoom for students who were unable to return to campus. The hybrid teaching mode was applied in UM for the two semesters in the academic year 2020/21.

Shortly before the start of that year, however, the MSAR detected its first local cases of the COVID-19 Delta variant. Under an Executive Order, following an evaluation by Macao's Novel Coronavirus Response and Coordination Centre, the MSAR entered a state of immediate prevention, on 3 August 2021, regarding the risk of a local COVID-19 outbreak.[64] As a result, UM temporarily moved all teaching activities online from 16 August to 15 September 2021.[65] Another suspension of teaching activities occurred on 25–28 September 2021, when the local authorities organised massive testing of the population to trace a local outbreak of COVID-19.[66] In-class teaching was resumed on 7 October 2021,

---

64 Macao SAR Government, Information Bureau, 'Macao enters state of immediate prevention in relation to COVID-19' (3 August 2021), https://www.gcs.gov.mo/detail/en/N21HC4RsAt?1.

65 Macao SAR Government, Information Bureau, 'UM to resume classroom teaching on 15 Sept' (24 August 2021), https://www.gcs.gov.mo/detail/en/N21HXwTIe6;jsessionid=EA026EF0F063649034BD69E3863B69C1.app11?0.

66 University of Macau, 'Important Notice: Teaching arrangement' (25 September 2021), https://www.um.edu.mo/news-and-press-releases/press-release/detail/52554/.

while all UM staff and students were required to get vaccinated or periodically present negative COVID-19 test results starting from 25 October 2021.[67] These arrangements were again disturbed on 5–10 October 2021 for another round of massive testing, which required the resumption of online classes from 11 October 2021[68] and face-to-face classes from 25 October 2021.[69]

2.2. TECHNICAL SUPPORT FOR ONLINE LEGAL EDUCATION AT THE UNIVERSITY OF MACAU

Even before the pandemic, UM has been actively promoting blended learning,[70] i.e. traditional in-class teaching combined with the application of various e-learning technologies to enhance student engagement outside of the classroom. At the university level, the coordination of these activities was entrusted to the inter-departmental Committee on Teaching and Learning Enhancement (CommTLE). The CommTLE is composed of representatives of all faculties and institutes. It meets on a regular basis for discussions on the development and implementation of the university teaching policies.

The Centre for Teaching and Learning Enhancement (CTLE) is an academic support unit overseen by the Vice-Rector for Academic Affairs. The CTLE is charged with enhancing the quality of teaching and learning through offering specific programmes for faculty growth and development. It provides teaching evaluation and enhancement services, professional development courses, educational development projects, research and other professional services. The CTLE has been promoting blended learning through the faculty learning communities (FLCs) consisting of academics from different faculties and institutes engaging in joint professional development activities. The CTLE supported the running of two such FLCs: on teaching portfolios and on blended learning. The purpose of the Teaching Portfolio FLC is to help UM academic staff develop one of the key documents reflective of one's professional development as a university teacher. The Blended Learning FLC was aimed at helping UM

---

67 University of Macau, 'To all faculty members and students: in-person teaching at UM will resume on 7 October' (2 October 2021), https://www.um.edu.mo/news-and-press-releases/press-release/detail/52578/.

68 University of Macau, 'Important Notice: Teaching Arrangements at UM' (4 October 2021), https://www.um.edu.mo/news-and-press-releases/press-release/detail/52579/.

69 University of Macau, 'To all faculty members and students: face-to-face classes at UM will resume on 25 October' (21 October 2021), https://www.um.edu.mo/news-and-press-releases/press-release/detail/52679/.

70 K. Wong and C. Fulton, University of Macau, Centre for Teaching and Learning Enhancement, 'Implementation and design of blended learning in higher education' (20 October 2020), https://ctle.um.edu.mo/2020/10/20/implementation-and-design-of-blended-learning-in-higher-education/.

academic staff to develop their own blended learning projects for the courses they are currently teaching.

The CTLE has been helping faculty members by providing studios with equipped devices and the support of student trainees. Instructors have used the CTLE studios for producing their instructional videos, with different levels of assistance requested, ranging from standby of the CTLE's trainees to full support from the CTLE staff (video production plus post-production work, such as video editing). For this initiative, the CTLE did not recommend making recordings on Zoom, as doing so would reduce the sound and image quality of the instructional videos. Furthermore, the CTLE organised various tailor-made workshops for the Blended Learning FLC and offered different forms of resources on the Moodle platform dedicated to this initiative. The CTLE also offered personal consultations for colleagues interested in getting help with the design of their videos or blended learning courses. However, very few members requested a consultation. This could be due to the fact that professors were required within a short period of time to switch to online teaching, which did not leave much room for advanced video recording and editing.

Since development and operation of the blended learning project required additional time and resources from the faculty members involved, the CTLE has supported their efforts by organising a yearly Teaching Assistant (TA) Training Workshop Series. For example, in 2020, 440 postgraduate students completed that year's TA Training Workshop Series with a certificate. 60% of students signed up to the workshop series after being told about it by their respective faculties, while 40% were informed about the workshop series via the university bulletin (UM Today). Over 90% of respondents to a CTLE survey conducted among the workshop participants agreed that the online resources were well organised and thought that the provided videos, readings and assignments were useful and helpful in learning about teaching and learning. 76% of respondents agreed the workshop series should be mandatory for first-year doctoral students, while 63% agreed it should be required for all first-year master's students.

The ICTO provides information technology (IT) facilities for general teaching, learning and research activities, adopts or develops IT systems that facilitate the management of teaching and living facilities on campus, and explores and promotes the use of the most suitable IT systems. The ICTO is primarily responsible for the technical side of online education and offers technical support to faculty members when using Moodle[71] and Zoom[72] in blended learning or online teaching.

---

71 University of Macau, Information and Communication Technology Office, 'UMMoodle', https://icto.um.edu.mo/teaching-learning-research/ummoodle/.

72 University of Macau, Information and Communication Technology Office, 'Quick start to eLearning for teachers', https://icto.um.edu.mo/teaching-learning-research/quick-start-to-elearning-for-teachers/.

2.3. MOODLE AND ZOOM AS PRIMARY PLATFORMS FOR ONLINE LEGAL EDUCATION AT THE UNIVERSITY OF MACAU

From the outset of implementing e-learning technologies, UM opted for Moodle and Zoom as the primary platforms for online education. Even prior to the COVID-19 pandemic, which forced the move to online teaching, UM, through the CTLE, has been actively promoting the use of Moodle for sharing teaching materials and conducting various learning activities out of the classroom. Initially, the Faculty of Law was relatively slow in embracing the use of Moodle, as most professors preferred to rely on traditional in-class teaching with limited out-of-class learning activities. The outbreak of the COVID-19 pandemic accelerated the process of adopting Moodle for online and hybrid teaching. To assist teachers in using various functions of Moodle, the CTLE has provided concise guidance on collecting student feedback,[73] online assessments and exams,[74] conducting instant polls,[75] and using discussion forums.[76]

In March 2020, the CTLE conducted a survey to better understand the experiences and ways in which UM faculty members were using Zoom in their online teaching.[77] The survey was completed by 138 faculty members. 99% of respondents used Zoom for online class meetings as it was a UM requirement. 50% and 46% had moved their work meetings and supervision meetings respectively to Zoom. 42% of respondents claimed they had used Zoom for both lecturing and online activities (quizzes, discussions, feedback, etc.). Most respondents pointed to the following three resources that helped them with navigating Zoom: a CTLE step-by-step guide on how to use Zoom for online classes; video demos and blog posts on teaching with Zoom on the CTLE website; and support by the ICTO helpdesk.

---

73 University of Macau, Centre for Teaching and Learning Enhancement, 'Going paperless: Collecting student feedback using UMMoodle' (9 November 2016), https://ctle.um.edu.mo/2016/11/09/going-paperless-collecting-student-feedback-using-ummoodle-2/.

74 University of Macau, Centre for Teaching and Learning Enhancement, '3 Tips on Online Assessments and Exams' (20 November 2020), https://ctle.um.edu.mo/2020/11/20/3-tips-on-online-assessments-and-exams/.

75 C. Fulton, University of Macau, Centre for Teaching and Learning Enhancement, '3 Tips on Polls in UMMoodle' (24 August 2020), https://ctle.um.edu.mo/2020/08/24/3-tips-on-polls-in-ummoodle/.

76 C. Fulton, University of Macau, Centre for Teaching and Learning Enhancement, 'Two Takeaways from a Meet-up on Discussion Forums in UMMoodle' (7 August 2020), https://ctle.um.edu.mo/2020/08/07/two-takeaways-from-a-meet-up-on-online-discussion-forums-in-ummoodle/.

77 University of Macau, Centre for Teaching and Learning Enhancement, 'Quick Survey Results: The Ups and Downs of Teaching Online with Zoom' (7 April 2020), https://ctle.um.edu.mo/2020/04/07/quick-survey-results-the-ups-and-downs-of-teaching-online-with-zoom/.

Overall, UM faculty members considered that Zoom integration with Moodle facilitated communication and teaching. The respondents noted the following challenges: time and resources needed to refine online teaching materials and activities to align with students' preferences; unstable internet connections; issues of access to IT systems from Mainland China; poor-quality microphones, headphones and webcams; and a lack of software to edit video recordings. The CTLE has also received feedback concerning the following problems: time lags during screen sharing; disengaged students and the difficulty of tracking student participation and understanding; lack of interactivity and eye contact compared to face-to-face teaching in a classroom; lack of the necessary hardware, such as a built-in camera, microphone, writing pad or headphones to facilitate a good-quality Zoom session, and lack of software to edit video recordings of the lecture; the need to multi-task (simultaneously teach, share/switch screens and read chat discussions); lack of expertise in shooting conditions and techniques, such as lighting or presenting a pleasant appearance in front of camera; and poor applicability to practical/skill-based course teaching requiring step-by-step demonstration. The results of the CTLE survey on using Zoom and the comments provided by the respondents also demonstrate the limitations of online interaction as opposed to face-to-face contact for problem-solving and group discussion activities frequently practised in legal education.

Last but not least, the use of various online education methods must be monitored closely in line with the wider context, as for instance the COVID-19 pandemic was found to have aggravated the common mental health problems in adolescent and young adult populations known as 'problematic mobile phone use' and 'problematic internet use' or 'internet addiction'.[78] Additionally, a study tracking public opinion about online education since COVID-19 in the PRC published in February 2022 revealed that users of Weibo holding 'neutral views about online education dropped to 33.04% while those with negative views increased to 51.63%'. It concluded that while the value and benefit of online education are acknowledged, the negative views shown in the datasets should alert us to staying critical about it.[79]

78 D.-D. Xu et al., 'Internet addiction among adolescents in Macau and mainland China: prevalence, demographics and quality of life' (2020) 10(16222) *Scientific Reports* 1, https://doi.org/10.1038/s41598-020-73023-1 and H. Cai et al., 'Identification of central symptoms in Internet addictions and depression among adolescents in Macau: A network analysis' (2022) 302 *Journal of Affective Disorders* 415.

79 M. Zhou and H. Mou, 'Tracking public opinion about online education over COVID-19 in China' (2022) *Educational Technology Research and Development* 1, 10 and 18, https://doi.org/10.1007/s11423-022-10080-5.

3. CONCLUSION

The MSAR of the People's Republic of China holds a very unique position in the world not only due to its legal system, but also in historic, cultural, linguistic and economic terms. These unique legal characteristics provide great opportunities for economic development but also pose serious challenges in the area of legal education and training of future lawyers, particularly in a rapidly changing local, regional and global context. Thus, this report has provided examples of the particular challenges that legal education in the MSAR faces by looking at the programmes offered by the University of Macau. It also cast light on the developments in the specific area of online education both before and during the COVID-19 pandemic with a view of allowing for a short outlook onto a 'post-pandemic' future.

To briefly summarise, the overview of the legal profession in Macao revealed an innate link between university-level and further legal education and the conditions for seeking a licence as a legal practitioner in the MSAR. The significance of legal education in Macao law manifests not only in the minimum educational qualification requirements for entry into the profession but also for entry into the internship exam, as well as pupillage. Relevantly, although one of the basic qualification requirements for entry transcends law degrees obtained locally, any foreign law degree through which entry is sought should be locally recognised under the relevant regulations and be supplemented with an adaptation course in the local law.

The significance of local legal education in Macao law is evident from the latter requirement and the bifurcation of the relevant legal education in this regard, namely the responsibility of the AAM for the adaptation course, as well as its power to recognise courses offered by reputable entities in Macao. This enables the local higher education institutions to develop viable professional legal education programmes. The explicit recognition of the Introduction to Macao Law programme offered by the Faculty of Law of the University of Macau by the AAM evidences this fact, and the ability of the institution to align its programmes to meet the local legal profession entry standards for foreign law degree holders. This is further reinforced by the judicial decision rendered by the Court of Second Instance in Case No. 1097/2018, where the court upheld the recognition of the non-local law degree under the old Decree Law, in which one of the factors that was in favour of the plaintiff was the successful completion of the Introduction to Macao Law programme. The factual elements leading to the plaintiff's success in the case demonstrates the decisive role of professionally affiliated and well-designed law courses offered by the local legal education entities.

The analysis of the relevant regulations governing the legal profession in Macao also revealed a range of distinct features pertaining to the recognition of legal education offered by other jurisdictions. Such a recognition manifests not only with regard to the basic law degrees obtained from foreign jurisdictions but also in other contexts, like the power bestowed upon the AAM to grant exemptions from attending the adaptation course. By virtue of such a power, law degrees from universities in countries with legal systems similar to Macao receive special treatment, as the holders of such degrees (along with experience in exercising legal functions in Macao) are considered as having an adequate grasp of the legal system of Macao. Similarly, the freedom of the AAM to exceptionally reduce the duration of the adaptation course (with a guaranteed module on an introduction to the Macao legal system) for law graduates from universities in countries with similar legal systems to Macao also shows the special treatment granted to legal education from such jurisdictions.

Finally, it is pertinent to note the paramount role played by judicial review in ensuring a fine balance between the legal/regulatory recognition of various legal education components from within and outside the MSAR and the discretionary powers conferred upon the AAM, which enjoys a special legal status as the only public sector association endowed with regulatory powers. The judicial review of the various cases analysed in this report supports the inevitable conclusion regarding the indispensable role played by the Macao judiciary in ensuring that the discretion enjoyed by the AAM is not unfettered. Related jurisprudence also confirms that the decisions of the AAM relating to various elements of legal education like the local law degrees approved by the government, the duration of legal education, the balance between law and non-law courses, the sanctity of the foreign law degrees that are recognised by the higher education authority, etc. can always be subjected to judicial scrutiny.

The unique features of the Macao legal system as a mixed or hybrid jurisdiction pose challenges not only to the legal profession but also to legal education, which is expected to provide students with a comprehensive understanding of law from both a local and a global perspective. To this end, the UM Faculty of Law has recently also taken this necessity into account in institutional terms by establishing two new internal units, namely (1) the Department of Macao Legal Studies and (2) the Department of Global Legal Studies.

The Department of Macao Legal Studies covers mostly bachelor's and master's programmes in law, taught in either Chinese or Portuguese, as well as in both Chinese and Portuguese combined. This department aims to 'to respond to the increasing request from the Macao society that the Faculty of Law of UM shall serve the local need with related to legal affairs, by nurturing more students with proficient knowledge and skills of law and by acting as a think tank for the government and public entities'.[80]

80 Department of Macao Legal Studies of the Faculty of Law of the University of Macau, https://fll.um.edu.mo/department/department-of-macao-legal-studies/.

The Department of Global Legal Studies, on the other hand, offers postgraduate courses in Chinese and English in various specialised legal fields as well as in law and technology studies. It strives towards achieving 'academic excellence, particularly through the teaching of courses, the encouragement to conduct research with a view of training future lawyers capable of handling the present and future challenges of their professions through a sound understanding of law in general and global law in particular.'[81] It thus takes an inclusive but global dimension by notably 'focusing on comparative and interdisciplinary methods which allow to address the interconnections between both the different legal disciplines mutually and between domestic, regional and global law'.[82]

In addition to the institutional challenges, there are also particular challenges to legal education in material terms. Given the rapidly changing context of education and the professions, UM began before the present pandemic to actively promote new teaching methods. Some of these methods also include the use of various learning technologies which are conducive and supportive of online education. These preparatory steps were highly useful when the COVID-19 pandemic suddenly disrupted the ordinary teaching modes. The shift to online teaching after the outbreak of the pandemic also quickly transformed the format of legal education, which was focused more on classroom teaching and more reluctant to make ample use of the available e-learning tools. As was shown from the past experiences with online legal education at UM, several such electronic learning tools were encouraged to foster out-of-class engagement of the students. The experiments with online legal education were driven by individual faculty members and supported technically by UM units such as CTLE and ICTO. The blended learning format was thus encouraged but not mandated for legal education.

The experience with online legal education in the MSAR after the outbreak of the pandemic, manifested both in the local epidemic situation and regional travel restrictions, forced UM as a whole, and the Faculty of Law in particular, to shift to online legal education for one semester in 2019/20. Due the past preparatory steps, both the University and the Faculty were well prepared technically, as the relevant units (CTLE and ICTO) had offered various forms of technical support in operating Moodle and Zoom. At the same time, most of the members of the Law Faculty had little or no experience with online teaching. As a result, when the pandemic situation within Macao and Mainland China improved, UM switched back to regular in-class teaching and the use of online learning platforms (Moodle) has returned to pre-pandemic levels.

As for the future, the developments in the field of online legal education in the MSAR will therefore primarily depend on the situation of the COVID-19

81 Department of Global Legal Studies of the Faculty of Law of the University of Macau, https://fll.um.edu.mo/department/department-of-global-legal-studies/.

82 Ibid.

pandemic in Macao, in Hong Kong, and in Mainland China, as well as on the trends and travel restrictions imposed globally. So far, it is evident that the shift towards online education cannot be regarded as having been 'positive'. However, the availability of various e-learning tools allowing for legal education to continue online was a positive element in a difficult time and certainly preferable over a situation in which all educational activities were suspended. In this sense, the pandemic had an indirect positive effect on the familiarity of staff and students with the various new learning technologies. These positive effects notwithstanding, it is also important to consider the wider context of the use of modern educational technologies, such as notably the common mental health problems related to mobile phone addiction or problematic internet use. Equally, it is important to follow the opinion of users of online education.

Last but not least, it is because of the nature of law, which is strongly rooted in human interactions, that direct student–teacher contact as well as peer-to-peer learning, facilitated not only by classroom teaching but also other personal contacts on the university campus, play a crucial role in the education and training of future lawyers. For these reasons, it is also important to closely align the debate about the use of modern education technologies with the debate about the future material content of legal education.

ONLINE LEGAL EDUCATION IN JAPAN

The Postgraduate Law School Movement and COVID-19 as Cornerstones

Ken'ichi YONEDA and Luke NOTTAGE*

* This report was previously published in *Japanese Reports for the XXIth International Congress of Comparative Law* (ICCLP Publications No. 16), International Center for Comparative Law and Politics, Graduate School of Law and Politics, University of Tokyo, Tokyo 2023. We thank especially Professor Makoto Ibusuki for helpful information and feedback on earlier drafts, and Amelia Frey (through the University of Wollongong's Transnational Law and Policy Centre) for editorial assistance.

1. INTRODUCTION

This report traces the historical development of legal education based on information and communication technology (ICT) at universities in Japan. It highlights how ICT-based legal education came to be widely used through wider institutional reforms of the judicial system, the socio-economic constraints of the novel coronavirus (COVID-19) pandemic, and the support and regulations of the Ministry of Education, Culture, Sports, Science and Technology in the Japanese government (MEXT).

The degree of diffusion of ICT use in the legal education field can be measured by the degree to which the legal information database,[1] the course management system (CMS),[2] and the remote or online meeting system[3] are used in education. This depends partly on funding for them. In addition, teaching in Japanese universities must be conducted in accordance with the School Education Law (*Gakko Kyoiku Ho*) and related laws and regulations, as well as guidelines established by MEXT in line with this law. The achievement and setting of these guidelines will enable Japanese students to enjoy ICT-based legal education.

Based on the above framework, we will describe the ICT-based legal education in Japan in three major periods: before the 2004 establishment of new postgraduate law schools, after their establishment, and since the COVID-19 pandemic in 2020. Situational factors have triggered major changes in ICT-based legal education that define the circumstances of each period. By writing about the various social reactions to these changes, we can gain an

[1] This system is the equivalent of the Westlaw and LexisNexis services in American legal education. It consists mainly of a system for searching the text of Japanese court cases, with links to court cases related to the trial level of the case and court cases cited, as well as references to related legal articles. In addition, it is possible to search and display laws and regulations, as well as educational materials.

[2] This refers to a system that has functions equivalent to Blackboard or Moodle, well known for example in the United States.

[3] This refers to a system that connects different points to conduct classes. A 'remote system' refers to a meeting system using H.323 protocol and a Global IP base, like Polycom, while an 'online system' refers to a system using HTTP connections such as Zoom, Microsoft Teams, Webex, etc.

insight into how (university and other) online legal education interacted with the legal professions, university systems and ICT infrastructures in each phase, and how online legal education developed before and after the pandemic.

2. OVERVIEW OF JAPAN'S LEGAL EDUCATION SYSTEM AND PROFESSION

Japanese legal education has been traditionally conducted by a Faculty of Law (*Ho Gakubu*) at the undergraduate level, with about 36,000 students enrolling each year.[4] The curriculum includes topics useful not only for future legal professionals (especially the elite core called '*Hoso*', comprising '*bengoshi*' lawyers, who are allowed to provide all types of legal services, judges and public prosecutors). It also covers topics useful for law graduates going on to become legal professionals with a narrower scope of permitted practice, as well as national and local civil servants or corporate employees. Almost all of these law students do not go on to become '*Hoso*' or even other types of legal professionals. However, under the Justice System Reform that began in 1999, an attempt was made to increase the *Hoso* population, which led to the establishment of new law schools (*Hoka Daigakuin*) in 2004, where students study at the postgraduate level for two years (envisaged if students have already completed an undergraduate law degree) or three years.[5] Since then, the law school has become the core of the legal professional training process (*Hoso Yosei*). There were years when more than 5,500 students were enrolled in 74 law schools, but by 2022 there were only 39 law schools and about 1,700 new students enrolling each year.

To become a legal professional (*Hoso*), in principle one must study at the law school, pass the National Legal Examination, and undergo about one year of training in a programme provided by the Judicial Training Institute (*Shiho Kenshujo*) attached to the Supreme Court. The number of students has roughly corresponded to the number of those who have passed the Examination, which in the last few years has been no more than 1,500 under a 2015 decision by the government (consulting mainly with the Ministry of Justice, the judiciary

---

4 MEXT, 'School Basic Survey (Gakko Kihon Chosa 2019 nendo)'. See also generally Nottage and Ibusuki, in this volume.

5 For early quite pessimistic assessments, compare L. Nottage, 'Reformist Conservatism and Failures of Imagination in Japanese Legal Education' (2001) 2 *Asian-Pacific Law & Policy Journal* 28, manuscript at https://ssrn.com/abstract=837045l; L. Nottage, 'Build Postgraduate Law Schools in Kyoto, and Will They Come – Sooner *and* Later?' (2005) 7 *Australian Journal of Asian Law* 241, manuscript at https://ssrn.com/abstract=986529.

and the National Federation of Bar Associations).[6] Upon completion of their training, legal apprentices are employed by courts, prosecutors' offices, law firms (mostly), and so on. Since this report will focus mainly on university education, it will not discuss the use of ICT in training at the Judicial Training Institute.[7]

This report focuses on the process of diffusion of the use of ICT in legal education in Japan, using the status of undergraduate-level legal education and graduate-level professional development programmes in law schools as indicators. In Japan, there are other graduate-level education programmes that train students to be researchers or other law-related practitioners (with narrower scope of practice than *bengoshi* lawyers), but they provide approximately the same services as undergraduate-level legal education.

Regarding continuing legal education for lawyers, the Japan Federation of Bar Associations has been providing optional learning opportunities on various subjects using ICT in addition to face-to-face education since before the COVID-19 pandemic. This was mainly provided remotely, with lawyers gathering at their local-level bar association to take the course, or offered on demand. There were also two mandatory training courses: one for newcomers at the time of registration, and another on lawyer ethics to be undertaken on a regular basis. These were conducted in face-to-face group sessions in each region, but after the pandemic, on-demand classes were mobilised, with the addition of online and e-learning, and the number of classes that could be taken from lawyers' offices increased.

3. REGULATION OF ICT-BASED EDUCATION IN JAPANESE UNIVERSITIES

The Japanese universities that provide legal education must conduct classes in accordance with the Standards for the Establishment of Universities

---

6 Until the Justice System Reform, gatekeeping to the legal profession in Japan was negotiated among the courts, prosecutors' offices and bar associations. However, since the Justice System Reform, the political sector has intervened more, and the decision has been made more by the government. To increase the legal professional population (*Hoso* Jinko), the goal was to have 3,000 people pass the National Legal Examination each year, but after some confusion, the number is now around 1,500, based on a government decision in 2015. In 2021 there were 43,206 *bengoshi* lawyers, according to the Japan Federation of Bar Associations White Paper (2021, materials 1-1-2), available at https://www.nichibenren.or.jp/document/statistics/fundamental_statistics2021.html (in Japanese). For the situation until 2010, see K. Anderson and T. Ryan, 'Gatekeepers: A Comparative Critique of Admission to the Legal Profession and Japan's New Law Schools' in S. Steele and K. Taylor (eds), *Legal Education in Asia*, Routledge, New York 2009, pp. 183–212.

7 Explaining legal professionals (*Hoso*), other qualified law-related professionals and non-qualified legal specialists in Japan as part of an overview of Japanese law as a whole, see

(*Daigaku Setchi Kijun*) under the School Education Law (*Gakko Kyoiku Ho*) and the standards for the establishment of individual curricula based on these standards, as well as the methods approved by government ordinances and public notices.

The Standards for the Establishment of Universities, enacted in 1956, were based on the premise of face-to-face teaching, and basically did not envisage distance learning. However, in response to the spread of various means of communication and the internet, the Standards for the Establishment of Universities were revised in 2001 to allow for 'advanced use of a variety of media' and for classes to be held in locations other than classrooms. MEXT issued a 'Media Notice' (*Media Kokuji*) on 10 March 2001 (Notification No. 51), which sets the maximum number of credits that can be obtained and the method of conducting classes using ICT. However, teachers were not allowed to transmit lessons from home, and students were not allowed to take lessons at home. What was envisaged was for students to gather for classes in a place similar to a prepared classroom, albeit not in another university or college. In such cases, it was stipulated that the students should be given an opportunity to ask questions and exchange views on the content of the class by the teachers and assistants immediately after the class.

University education in Japan (provided by both public and private universities) is essentially subject to this regulation, and legal education is no exception. Although this regulation has now been temporarily loosened due to the COVID-19 disaster, the Media Notice remains the standard and guiding principle for the development of measures. To better understand the introduction of ICT in legal education in Japan when organised from the above perspective, the overall situation can be outlined as follows.

Figure 1. Japan's use of ICT in legal education

◎ = Everyone ○ = Almost △= Rare × = Nothing

			Internet-based Legal Information Databases	CMS (Course Management System)	Remote/Online Meeting System
After Windows 95	1995	Under-Graduate	×	×	× (△Remote)
After Law Schools	2004	Law School	◎	○	△ (△Remote)
		Under-Graduate	△	△	× (△Remote)
After Covid-19	2020	Law School	◎	◎	◎ (Online)
		Under-Graduate	○	◎	◎ (Online)

Source: Produced by the rapporteurs.

4. THE LEGAL INFORMATION ENVIRONMENT AND DISTANCE LEARNING IN LEGAL EDUCATION BEFORE THE JUSTICE SYSTEM REFORM

The reason for the establishment of law schools, a key break in Japan's legal history, came from the 'Recommendations of the Justice System Reform Council'[8] published in 2001. One of the three reform pillars was expansion of the legal profession (human resources base) to support the justice system. The future profession was to have not only specialist legal knowledge but also a professional ethics based on a broad education to play active roles in various fields of society. To achieve this goal, the reform proposed setting up new postgraduate law schools.

Before this change, we need to consider the state of legal education and ICT in universities. When Microsoft Windows 95 was released in 1995, Japanese universities as a whole, not only law faculties, installed facilities for using the internet in libraries and laboratories, set up homepages, assigned personal computers (PCs) to all faculty members, and distributed e-mail addresses to them. Gradually, students were also given e-mail addresses issued by the university too. However, except for some students who had their own PCs at home, they still had access to PCs only in certain classrooms in the university and were generally not allowed to use them.[9]

Until 2004, the Japanese legal information database in the field of Japanese legal education was not available through a network. For example, it was possible to use data stored on multiple CDs by operating a specific application on a specific PC with a five-in-one CD drive. In essence, it was a standalone environment that could only be used on a specific PC. In many cases, these were the few PCs that were shared by teachers and students in university libraries, reference rooms and classrooms designed for PC use.

M. Abe and L. Nottage, 'Japanese Law' in J. Smits (ed.), *Encyclopedia of Comparative Law*, Edward Elgar, Cheltenham 2012, pp. 157–168, with forthcoming new edition manuscript at https://papers.ssrn.com/sol3/papers.cfm?abstract_id=3672112.

8 The Justice System Reform Council, 'Recommendations of the Justice System Reform Council – For a Justice System to Support Japan in the 21st Century' (12 June 2001) (Shiho Seido Kaikaku Shingikai Ikensho), available in English at https://web.archive.org/web/20220128094617/https://japan.kantei.go.jp/policy/sihou/singikai/990612_e.html.

9 In 1995, just when Windows 95 was introduced, the Kagoshima University Research Group for Legal Information conducted a questionnaire survey of law teachers in Japan. They indicated a positive attitude toward future network use, even though even the use of existing databases was not widespread. See Kagoshima Daigaku Ho-Joho Kenkyu Kai, 'Research Report on Using Internet by Legal Scholars' (1996) 31(2) *Hogaku Ronshu (Kagoshima University)* 132 (in Japanese).

Databases on Anglo-American law (such as Westlaw) were available on the internet, but they were often subscribed to by individual researchers who had specialised in Anglo-American law and had relatively large amounts of research funds. The accounts were very expensive when subscribed to as an organisation, and when subscribed to as an individual, the cost of the account plus connecting to it was also expensive. In addition, there were restrictions on the number of accounts for simultaneous use when a university or law school made a contract. As with the Japanese Law Database, some universities were unable to introduce the system because it was for shared use by teachers and students in libraries, reference rooms and PC classrooms. In addition, although a graphical user interface for the search screen was available at the time, more advanced use was possible once the user became proficient in command line input. This meant that Anglo-American law researchers and postgraduate students who needed to use such a system were able to learn how to use it, but researchers in other fields and students in general had to overcome many hurdles to access and use it as they wished.

During this period, each university had facilities for distance learning that could be used in the field of education, but with the exception of some very advanced initiatives in legal education, they were not used at all. The distance learning system that was available at Japanese universities during this period was the Space Collaboration System (SCS). The system used satellites and radio waves to connect 100 sites, mainly national universities, and was capable of connecting multiple sites as well as one to one (all sites could be connected at the same time). However, the system needed such extensive equipment that a large parabolic antenna had to be built on the roof of the building where the classrooms were located. To use the system, it was also necessary to make an appointment with the institution that manages the whole system through the department that manages the SCS at the university, and the hourly fee for using the system was more than 70,000 yen (US$650). Furthermore, the number of classrooms was usually limited to one at each university, and the number of lines used at the same time was also limited.

The distance learning system, which combined the exchange of teaching materials and assignments by post along with some seminars, and the Open University of Japan (*Hoso Daigaku*), which opened in 1985, were the only two systems available to the general public. At the Open University, classes were held on television channels and radio broadcasts that were accessible to the general public, and students received instruction through the submission and correction of assignments, as well as some seminars. Some distance learning courses offered a bachelor's degree in law (LLB), and some courses at the Open University of Japan were taught by professors of academic authority, so the content of these courses developed a certain reputation. However, mainstream university education, the so-called full-time universities (*Zen-nichi Sei*) and universities with evening classes (*Yakan-bu*), were based on the premise that classes were held in the classrooms of the universities to which they belonged, and the implementation of distance learning was not envisaged either for law or at the university level.

At this time, law classes were conducted by teachers and students who met in classrooms with textbooks, casebooks and commentaries,[10] plus the compendium of the six main codifications and laws (*Roppo*).[11] Other teaching materials, such as summary handouts, were copied from case law books and journals in the library or reference room and distributed by the teacher when necessary for the class. The typical style of teaching was the lecture, in which the teacher was the transmitter of information, and the students were its recipients. In many cases, discussion was not included, and students were able to attend classes without having done any preparation, which was to be expected. For reports and discussions at the seminars, and for each student's research for his or her graduation thesis, each student had to go to the library or reference room to borrow or photocopy and acquire the necessary materials, read and understand them, prepare a summary handout, and print and distribute it to the participants.

During this period, all the materials and references used in the class were in paper form and the amount of them held by each university was limited, so it was physically impossible for all the students attending the class to have access to the full text of the cases dealt with in the class. For this reason, it was usual to publish a collection of precedents (like *Hyaku-sen*) with short extracts of the important parts and longer explanations required for the class, and to designate these as textbooks. Amendments to the law in the six core fields studied at university were extremely rare, so students were allowed to use the compendium (*Roppo*) they had purchased when they entered university until they graduated. Indeed, what year the students were in could be identified by the design of the cover of the *Roppo*.

Surveying the period from the popularisation of Windows 95 to the establishment of law schools in 2004, Ibusuki's 2001 report[12] shows that although the responses of legal education provider organisations showed a positive attitude toward ICT use, individual law teacher and student responses did not.

---

10 The best known of these books is the '*Hanrei Hyakusen*' (Leading Cases) series, commonly referred to as '*Hyakusen*'. Each is so named because of the original idea of compiling a collection of 100 (*Hyaku*) persuasive precedents for each sub-field.

11 *Roppo* refers to the Constitution, Civil Code, Criminal Code, Commercial Code, Criminal Procedure Code, and Civil Procedure Code as the main areas of law originally, but more generally refers to volumes (published annually) that list these plus other laws (including administrative law) that are frequently used or important for legal studies.

12 M. Ibusuki, 'Research Report on Information Technology and Legal Education' (Joho Gijutsu to Hogaku Kyoiku ni Kansuru Jittai Chosa Hokokusho) (2001) 74(3) *Horitsu Jiho* 58. Compare also M. Ibusuki and L. Nottage, 'IT and Legal Practice and Education in Japan and Australia' (2002) 4 *UTS Law Review* 31.

Thus, before the establishment of the law school, legal education had limited diffusion of ICT infrastructure. The circumstances for the provision of legal information were really appropriate for individual use, and similarly, it was mostly physically impossible to use ICT in the classroom. Therefore, institutionally, the use of ICT-based distance learning systems was not even considered, with very few exceptions.

5. CHANGES IN THE LEGAL INFORMATION ENVIRONMENT AND DISTANCE LEARNING DUE TO THE LAW SCHOOLS

5.1. DEVELOPMENT AND SPREAD OF JAPANESE LEGAL INFORMATION DATABASES

It was the establishment of law schools as a result of the Justice System Reform that triggered a drastic change in legal education, which had been conducted with teaching methods filled with such analogue methods. The policy objective of increasing the number of students passing the bar exam to 3,000 (by 2010) from around 1,500 in 2004, and the prospect of establishing postgraduate law schools in many universities accelerated this change.

The most notable impact, and one which has been carried through to the present day, is the proliferation of the Japanese legal information database via the internet. The emergence of law schools that advocated 'bridging theory and practice', as urged by the Justice System Reform Council Recommendations, created the prospect of a huge market for Japanese legal information database, as students at law schools would use the information on laws and judicial precedents for their classes, and graduates would mostly become legal practitioners who would continue to use it in the future. The need for legal information databases, which had been limited to legal practice and exceptional researchers, university units and some public libraries, was expected to increase rapidly. In the context of activities expected by graduates and the trend towards digitalisation in society as a whole, the prospect of a steady and rapid increase in the digitalisation of legal information itself in the future was also added to the development of full-text search databases of laws and judicial precedents by the companies concerned.

The databases developed by the various companies were characterised by the entry of the first search terms, such as keywords, dates of precedents, laws and articles. In addition, the databases included the option to view and print in PDF format the main law journals and publications containing commentaries on precedents frequently used as teaching materials in universities. The databases of each provider were differentiated by their content and access methods.

From the outset, there was a wide range of services available, from direct access to the vendor's server via the internet (including from home), to on-premises use where the server was located on campus, and access to the vendor's server from campus via a special proxy server. A wide variety of services were available and marketed.

In this way, the decision to establish law schools not only triggered competition among the sellers of these legal information databases, it also led to competition among the universities providing these databases for the learning environment of the new law schools. This led to the rapid spread of legal information databases.

The financial resources of each university to respond to this competitive marketing were supported by subsidies and grants from the government to each university. With the decision to establish law schools, MEXT allocated money from the national budget to each university every year for the establishment and operation of law schools. For example, a national university could aggregate all the expenses for legal information databases as part of the operating expenses for the law school and the library, and include them in its application to MEXT for university-wide operating funds. This allowed the legal information database and its costs to be included in legal education as essential costs.

In the preparations for the establishment of law schools, it was thought that all students of law schools, like their teachers, should have access to these legal information databases. To create such an environment, some universities also used government funds to lend dedicated PCs to all students. The fact that 'legal research' became a mandatory course of study at law schools also provided a boost.

In this way, the introduction and spread of legal information databases in law school education created a completely new situation in the legal information environment in Japan. Basically, the convenience was mostly enjoyed by the faculty members of law schools and their students, but the policy of each university was to set up a place to access the contracted database as part of the website of the library, and to make the legal information database available for any connection from within campus (even though there was a limit to the number of simultaneous accesses in most cases). The availability of the database to undergraduates also increased, as more and more universities made the database available to all law students. Some universities even purchased and provided accounts for all law students, including those at the undergraduate level.

Importantly, the legal information databases developed here were also sold to law firms and companies, which supported the establishment of law schools and the need to improve their educational environment. Accordingly, the spread of the legal information ICT infrastructure in the field of legal information databases progressed rapidly.

5.2. IMPACT OF THE PROJECT TO SUPPORT THE FORMATION OF LAW SCHOOLS

5.2.1. *Implementation of the 'Project to Support the Establishment of Law Schools'*

In preparing for the establishment of law schools, the policy was to allow more forms of establishment to realise the appropriate nationwide allocation of law schools as recommended by the Justice System Reform Council. For example, the government allowed establishment of a single law school in cooperation with several universities, or organisation of a curriculum in which courses are shared among several universities. In addition, to cope with the situation of some universities having their main campuses in the suburbs, which is disadvantageous for securing applicants and inconvenient for practising teachers, some universities established satellite campuses of law schools in convenient locations and organised curricula to enable students to take courses there. This was based on the use of remote meeting systems.[13]

In addition, to introduce the Socratic method and to conduct classes based on preparation and review to grant credits related to the study hours stipulated by legislation, and to deal with students who also had jobs, the introduction of ICT was expected for the CMS and the on-demand class delivery system.

Therefore, in addition to the steady supply of funds from the establishment of law schools, MEXT was able to provide a start-up programme in which the law schools would implement a completely new educational programme as a university in Japan. MEXT implemented the 'Project to Support the Establishment of Professional Graduate Schools of Law' (*Keisei Shien Jigyo*)[14] to provide the necessary funds for a certain period of time to enhance the educational system and facilities of law schools and to establish a new educational environment, by conducting a competition to select and support projects that were planned and developed through cooperation and collaboration among law schools. In this project, cooperation among multiple law schools was encouraged, and among the project plans selected for this project many introduced remote meeting systems, and many law schools, both large and small, installed such systems. In addition, projects to share teaching

13 At this time, the system was based on H.323 protocol and needed a Global IP address.

14 'Hoka-daigakuin to senmonshoku daigakuin keisei shien proguram'. See the list of supported law school projects at https://www.mext.go.jp/a_menu/koutou/kaikaku/houka.htm and the overview at https://www.kantei.go.jp/jp/singi/sihou/komon/dai17/17siryou4.pdf (in Japanese).

materials on the internet and to conduct joint academic staff development activities to improve educational cooperation between law schools were also adopted.[15]

5.2.2. Case Studies of Innovations

5.2.2.1. Remote Meeting Systems

At the Ehime University–Kagawa University United Law School, for example, students are located at Kagawa University in Takamatsu City, but faculty members affiliated with Ehime University in Matsuyama City (in a neighbouring prefecture) are also full-time faculty members of this law school, and there were times when classes or faculty meetings were held using a remote meeting (video-conferencing) system. In addition, Seikei University Law School connected its main campus in Kichijoji, a suburb of Tokyo, and its satellite campus in Otemachi, in the city centre, by a remote meeting system so that students working downtown could attend classes delivered from the satellite campus after work.

The most large-scale introduction and use of a remote meeting system was the Kyushu–Okinawa Law School Education Collaboration, in which four southern law schools (Kyushu University, Kagoshima University, Kumamoto University and the University of the Ryukyu) cooperated to organise a curriculum in which some class subjects were shared. The mainframe system of Kyushu University, Kagoshima University and Kumamoto University allowed the power to be turned on at any of the locations, even if the operator was not present in the classroom at the other university. In addition, it was very easy to operate the six cameras in the classrooms at each site, and to project any three of the images taken by the cameras on the three screens or monitors at each site, using a touch panel from any site, so that the class could be controlled.

---

15 For an example of a cross-border teaching project that involved law students from Ritsumeikan University Law School and overseas partner universities, established mainly by Professors Makoto Ibusuki and Luke Nottage and which has endured beyond the initial three-year MEXT funding, see http://www.ritsumei.ac.jp/japanese-law/kyoto-seminar/, https://japaneselaw.sydney.edu.au/2021/02/guest-blog-japanese-law-in-context-in-the-context-of-a-global-pandemic-report-on-a-podcast-series/ and L. Nottage et al., 'Beyond Borders in the Classroom – The Possibility of Transnational Legal Education' (2008) 25 *Ritsumeikan Law Review* 183, also available at https://ssrn.com/abstract=1161016. See also more generally T. Kasahara, K. Yoneda, L. Nottage and N. Inagaki, 'Hogaku Kyoiku no IT-ka – Daigaku-kan Renkei wo Shiya ni Irete' (Developing Information Technology for Legal Education: Bringing Inter-University Links Into Perspective) (2009) *Joho Netwaku (Information Network) Law Review* 191.

This enabled the smooth running of classes involving interactive and multi-directional discussions and question-and-answer sessions between classrooms able to seat up to 50 students. Teachers were also able to apply this system to hold a mock trial remotely by placing the judge on the middle screen and the lawyers on the left and right. These systems also had the ability to record video footage, which could be lent out on DVD media or provided on demand for students who were absent or for review after class.

The remote meeting systems in use at this time required a global IP address in even the simplest of configurations, which could be set up either by securing an IP address within the university network or by contracting with an external provider. The system was designed to be used in small meetings where camera operation was not required, and it was possible to see the participants' facial expressions by using the attached remote control, but when there were many students in both classrooms, it was difficult to keep up with the camera operation for interactive and multi-directional discussions where facial expressions could be seen.

At this time, Skype was the best-known PC-to-PC conferencing system, as an online meeting system, but it was not suitable for use with large groups of students. Students had to get a Microsoft account, the network bandwidth was not available for large classes, and the image quality was not good enough to be projected onto a screen via a projector. Under these circumstances, Kagoshima University Law School introduced a different online meeting system, which was developed as a product for corporate use, and added a mock trial function to the system, so that all students could bring their own PCs to the classroom for a joint class between Kagoshima University and Kyushu University Law School. In this class, all students brought their PCs into the classroom and used one of the many conference rooms provided on the system to discuss in small groups the issues raised by teachers.

The online meeting system mainly used at this time was a connection between classrooms, and it was costly in terms of equipment to accommodate large classes with many students in law school classes, where interactive and multi-directional discussions were a prerequisite. In addition, the system with the simplest configuration could not be introduced in regular classes because of the cost and the time required to operate it using remote control functions. In addition, these systems were used only in postgraduate law schools and, with few exceptions, were not used in undergraduate legal education.

However, there were quite a few cases in which remote meeting systems via the internet started to be introduced in actual legal education and used formally in classes, including the Kyushu–Okinawa Collaboration's system, as well as simpler systems of a smaller scale. The results were sufficient to prove that such systems provide video and audio of a quality that could be used in legal education.

5.2.2.2. Distribution of Video Teaching Materials

At the time of the establishment of the law schools, an attempt was made, along with the use of remote meeting systems just discussed, to create a database of internet-shared case study materials and image data (such as disputed trademarks related to intellectual property rights) for use in clinical legal education courses at the law schools.

Many law schools participated in this initiative led by Nagoya University, with more than 30 law schools at its maximum, and which is still operating.[16] Scenarios of mock trial and mock consultation cases and examples of necessary legal documents, which were prepared by participating schools for their classes or subcontracted to related organisations, were assembled scenes of mock legal consultations by professional actors were shared in the form of on-demand distribution of teaching materials used in clinical legal education courses and used in the classes of participating schools.

5.2.2.3. Introduction of the Course Management System

With the establishment of law schools, the course management system (CMS) was also introduced in legal education. In Japanese university education, Blackboard and Moodle had already appeared just before 2000, and their existence was known. There were also some commercialised CMSs that were based on corporate groupware. However, when the law schools were established in 2004, there were very few universities or faculties that had introduced a CMS and managed their educational content using such a system. Even where introduced, the use of such systems was often left to the discretion of the teaching staff and was usually dependent on their own individual skills and used on a subject-by-subject basis. For internet-based course management, individual teachers often set up a public website for the courses they needed to teach, and then restricted access to it. A similar systematic use of ICT was made by providing the syllabus of the class on the internet, where course plans and summaries were made available each term via the website before registration for classes that students took part in. However, the use of CMSs, including communication with students as individual classes progressed, was not linked to systematic activities at the faculty or university level.

In this context, the law schools were oriented from the beginning towards the systematic use of ICT for class management. There are several reasons for this. One is that, when establishing these schools, MEXT strongly demanded

[16] This initiative, called the Professional Skills Instruction Materials Consortium (PSIM Consortium), is still one of the activities of ICT-based recurrent education in legal practice and clinical legal education in Japan. See https://psimconsortium.law.nagoya-u.ac.jp/en/.

that classes be conducted on the basis of the preparation and review time stipulated in the Standards for the Establishment of Universities, and each university had to respond to this demand. In addition, the Justice System Reform, which recommended the introduction of the law school system, called for classes at law schools to be conducted through more interactive and multi-directional discussions. As a result, there was a growing need for information to be provided in accordance with the progress of the class, for information on the contents of preparatory work and review to be communicated efficiently, and for students to be provided with such information in a centralised manner. In response, some of the vendors of Japanese legal information databases offered CMSs developed for each such database, together with the legal information database as an option, and many law schools started to use such systems. In addition, some law schools developed and implemented their own CMS and used that instead.

Furthermore, the fact that accreditation was imposed on law schools had a significant impact on the spread and establishment of CMSs. To grasp the status of classes in a unified manner, such as confirming whether the class format required by the establishment standards was being implemented and whether classes were being managed appropriately, it was important and very efficient to have information on a server using ICT. In this way, CMSs became indispensable for the organisation and management of the new law schools.

5.2.3. Summary: Before the Pandemic

Overall, the establishment of law schools and MEXT funding through the 'Law School Formation Support Project' provided an opportunity and fuel for the introduction of ICT in legal education in Japan. Each university introduced a legal information database, a remote or online meeting system, and a CMS. Remote meeting systems, in particular, showed new possibilities for legal education, including the creation of cooperation that transcended university boundaries.

However, the law school system in Japan suffered a sharp decline in applicants from around 2010. The Council for the Promotion of Reform of the Legal Training System,[17] established by the government in 2015 to examine ways to deal with the problem, advocated the active use of ICT in education and tried to create an environment that would make it easier for more students to study at law schools. In addition, the Conference of Collaborators for Research and Study on the Use of ICT (Information and Communication Technology)

---

17 See 'Hosoyosei Seido Kaikaku Suishin Kaigi', with an overview available at https://www.kantei.go.jp/jp/singi/hoso_kaikaku/index.html (in Japanese).

in Law School Education[18] was established to examine the pros and cons of conducting classes in a way that goes beyond the government's earlier Media Notice. The conclusion of the meeting was to allow working students to participate in classes from any place outside the university, including their homes, as long as they could communicate with the teachers and students in the classroom in an interactive and multi-directional manner.

Against this backdrop, the number of law schools in Japan, 74 in 2006, decreased to 39 by 2022. Many of the law schools that used to offer collaborative education through remote meeting systems also closed. During this period, education at law schools in Japan substantially shifted to one in which preparation for the National Legal Examinations became the most important issue, and the breadth and richness of educational content was no longer required as much.

Under these circumstances, few law schools continued to use the remote meeting system, which relies on IP addresses to connect classrooms, because it had exceeded its depreciation period and service life, and also because of resistance at the time of use due to the complexity of operation and of securing classrooms. Remote meeting systems and on-demand delivery systems were used continuously in some exceptional cases, but they did not become widely established in general.

By contrast, legal information databases became established not only in law schools but also in research and education at the undergraduate level, and they were also widely used in legal practice in local governments and companies.

In addition, if we look at the use of CMSs at the organisational level, they have been used in law schools since 2004, and were used earlier. Around 2010, a Japanese-developed CMS appeared, and we began to see cases of its introduction at the university level or at the faculty level, including in law schools.

After 2015, the use of remote meeting systems and on-demand delivery systems was stagnant, but this was a time when university education as a whole was generally making widespread progress in using CMSs to manage classes. At this time, the use of CMSs for legal education remained sparse, as the systems of postgraduate law schools were sometimes separate from those of the university as a whole or of law faculties, and in some cases the use of CMSs was left to individual faculty members, even if they were prepared for it as an organisation. However, the use of CMSs started to steadily spread throughout legal education, thanks to the cutting-edge efforts of law schools and the promotion of their use at the undergraduate level linked to the broader trend of university education as a whole.

---

18 See 'Houkadaigakuin kyoiku niokeru ICT (Joho Tsushin Gijutsu) no Katuyou ni kansuru Chosa Kenkyu kyouryoku-sha Kaigi.' The result of discussion is available at https://www.mext.go.jp/b_menu/shingi/chukyo/chukyo4/041/siryo/__icsFiles/afieldfile/2017/05/09/1384129_08_2_1.pdf (in Japanese).

Feedback from one pre-pandemic survey was generally positive.[19] Results showed that many of the postgraduate law school students who took part in those initiatives evaluated the educational effects of remote classes and face-to-face classes to be the same as or better than those of face-to-face classes. Law school students need good marks to start their programme, but there was no selection bias in terms of teachers surveyed. The classes covered in that survey were designed to consist of teachers using ICT for the first time, as well as some of the compulsory law courses. Even though the survey was agreed upon, these were not necessarily classes in which teachers and students wanted to use ICT. Accordingly, the positive response was quite surprising to those involved in the survey. It seems that when teachers did try to use ICT, the outcomes were fairly good. This set a decent platform for the forced shift to more online education from 2020.

6. CHANGES IN THE LEGAL INFORMATION ENVIRONMENT AND DISTANCE LEARNING DUE TO THE PANDEMIC

6.1. THE COVID-19 ONSLAUGHT AND RESPONSES

At the end of 2019, the spread of COVID-19 in China was reported, and in January 2020 cases of infection appeared in Japan. On 1 February, the government of Japan issued a decree designating COVID-19 as a 'designated infectious disease', and the World Health Organization declared a pandemic on 11 March 2020. On 2 March, the Japanese government issued a directive to close all schools, including universities, for the remainder of the school year, forcing Japanese universities to deal with the effects of COVID-19.[20]

Fortunately, this was the spring holidays and time to prepare for the new academic year starting in April in Japan. During this period, various measures

---

19 'FY 2015 MEXT Commissioned Project for Promoting Leading University Reforms: Survey and Research on the Use of ICT in Law School Education: Report of Outcomes of the Commissioned Project' (Heisei 27 nendo Monbu Kagakusho Sendouteki Daigaku Kaikaku Suisin Itaku-jigyo Hoka Daigakuin Kyoiku ni okeru ICT No Katsuyo Ni Kansuru Chosa-Kenkyu Itaku-Jigyo Seika Hokokusho), https://www.mext.go.jp/a_menu/koutou/itaku/1371442.htm.

20 Despite such measures, imposed on some suppliers, Japan remains comparatively unusual in not enacting widespread mobility restrictions on citizens. See generally e.g. T. Ono and S. Matsui, 'Japan: Keeping the Death Toll to the Minimum' in V. Ramraj (ed.), *COVID in Asia*, Oxford University Press, Oxford 2021; and related webinar summary and recording available via Joseph Black, Guest Blog (27 August 2021), https://japaneselaw.sydney.edu.au/2021/08/guest-blog-pandemic-pressure-points-economics-governance-and-society-in-japan/.

were prepared by the universities, the main goal of which was realise fully remote education using ICT. This was to change the whole landscape of legal education, including law schools and undergraduate law faculties.

6.2. TRANSFORMATION IN THE FIELD OF LEGAL EDUCATION

6.2.1. Background to Introducing Fully Remote Education

In response to the outbreak of COVID-19, three major changes in the internet environment for teaching made the full deployment of remote education possible in a short period of time. The first was the increase in the speed of Internet network services used by students at home, which provided enough bandwidth for PCs and smartphones to receive video feeds and participate in online meeting systems. In some cases, the network bandwidth provided by their home was too small, or the bandwidth was insufficient for family members to use the network at the same time, but this was dealt with in different ways by the efforts of each student or with the support of their family. In addition, for contracts with data limits on smartphones, mobile phone service providers supported student learning by increasing the monthly data limits per month for students.

Secondly, PC-to-PC video-conferencing services for large numbers of participants were expanding. These systems were simple to connect to using HTTP communication, easy to operate, and provided high-quality images and sound. In particular, the fact that Zoom allowed users to join by simply providing the URL of the meeting room, and that it was free for unlimited one-on-one meetings and free for 40 minutes for multiple people, made it easy for experienced users to introduce the service to new users, and for users to try it out. Zoom also had the advantage that by this time it had implemented features for active learning, such as voting and breakout sessions for group discussion, which were becoming popular.

Thirdly, the introduction of CMSs at the university level was well underway. In addition to active learning, the use of CMS-based portfolios and rubrics was being promoted to prospective students and high school guidance counsellors as part of competition for higher education places. There was an increase in the number of cases of systematic use of this system across universities and faculties. This was partly due to the fact that MEXT had been recommending the introduction of active learning, portfolios and rubrics since around 2000. Universities that practised these methods were regarded as being at the cutting edge of the field, and were therefore more likely to win grants, which led to the introduction of CMSs that were convenient for implementing these methods, and hence their use was becoming more widespread.

6.2.2. *Widespread Use of Online Meeting Systems and Course Management Systems*

In preparation for full-scale remote education in response to COVID-19, each university proceeded rapidly with the selection of the system to be used and the contracting procedures. MEXT procured and allocated to each university the cost of the system necessary for such classes, together with the cost of equipment necessary for infection prevention, and promptly provided support for the establishment of such a system.

Amidst these efforts, an information exchange site was set up on Facebook, where very many university teachers participated in a lively exchange of information. Several tools were introduced and questions about how to use them were answered, and a wide range of information was shared, including not only teaching methods but also data on the spread of infection and the responses of each university. The number of participants on the site quickly exceeded 10,000, and as of January 2022 there were more than 20,000.

A 'State of Emergency Declaration' (*Kinkyu Jitai Sengen*) was issued almost simultaneously with the start of the new school year in April 2020. In response, the Japan Association of Law Schools (*Hoka Daigakuin Kyokai*) conducted a survey of all law schools asking whether they are able to conduct classes that met accreditation requirements. One of the questions asked what kind of educational methods would be used to conduct classes during the semester from April to August 2020. Around 86% of the schools responded that they would conduct 'online classes', and the combined total of 'face-to-face and online classes' was 100%. The survey includes the aggregate results of responses to a set of questions about operational difficulties as well as free answers at the time. It shows the perception of educational difficulties faced just prior to the implementation of classes in the wake of the COVID-19 pandemic.[21]

When classes began, some universities that had been using CMSs saw their servers and networks go down due to unprecedented simultaneous access. There were also reports of CMSs using cloud services that crashed because they could not handle the access volume. Both the service providers and the end users had no experience of this situation, but they overcame the difficulties in individual classes and implemented the entire educational curriculum by increasing the network bandwidth and adjusting access times.

University teachers acquired in a very short time the skills to use online meeting systems, record meetings, distribute recorded videos, and use the CMS

---

21 Association of Law Schools, 'Japan Association of Law Schools Survey Results' (Hoka Daigakuin Kyokai Anketo Kekka) (2020), https://www.mext.go.jp/content/20200512-mxt_senmon02-100009037_1.pdf (in Japanese).

and file-sharing system in a coordinated manner. It became a matter of course that students' learning should be based on the CMS and proceed under it.

Despite the realities already in the new postgraduate law schools, legal education had previously been seen as conservative and slow in its use and diffusion of ICT. Nonetheless, it seems to have adapted to the new environment relatively smoothly compared to other fields. This is probably due to the fact that the law schools had a good number of teachers, students and administrative staff with experience in the use of CMSs, and that information could be extended quite smoothly to undergraduate education.[22]

In any case, a system was set up for the full implementation of remote education using ICT in a university-wide response, not only in legal education at the law school, where cutting-edge initiatives were implemented, but also in legal education at the undergraduate level. The system is now firmly in place in Japan.

6.3. ESTABLISHMENT OF RULES FOR REMOTE TEACHING

As mentioned earlier, classes at Japanese universities were conducted under the constraints imposed by the School Education Law, the Establishment Standards of the Respective Curricula, and the Media Notice. However, it was clear that full remote teaching could not be carried out under the restrictions of the Establishment Standards and Media Notice.

Therefore, in parallel with the period when each university was preparing to implement full remote teaching, MEXT announced models and guidelines on how to conduct classes that could be accepted as temporary exceptions to the Establishment Standards and Media Notices under the influence of COVID-19, and MEXT asked each university to follow them. The dissemination of information on these models of teaching, together with the use of online meeting systems and CMSs, led to the spread of methods of teaching based on communication with students, which MEXT had instructed to be thorough in its models. This has also led to a change in the way students learn, with an increase in submissions of assignments and an increase in learning outside class time. This may also have been influenced by the fact that the use of CMSs made it easier for teachers to communicate information and for students to submit work and manage class information efficiently.

---

22 For example, the Japan Clinical Legal Education Association (*Rinsho Hogaku Kyoiku Gakkai*) set 'The Potential of Online Clinical Education' as one of the theme subcommittees for its 2021 annual conference, and two essay reports by law school students on the impact of the pandemic were published in volume 13 of its annual journal, *Hoso Yosei to Rinsho Hogaku* (*Lawyers and Clinical Education*).

In addition, under the Copyright Act in Japan, teaching materials used for classes could be used without permission from the author for that purpose. However, it envisaged them being distributed in paper form and not them being provided via the internet. Although the Copyright Act had been amended before COVID-19 struck and discussions were underway to enforce it, this issue was stalled because of the lack of agreement between copyright holders and educational institutions. As a result, it could have become illegal to distribute similar reference materials and teaching materials via the internet to provide education using materials that could have been provided during face-to-face teaching sessions before COVID-19. Therefore, before the May 2020 holidays, when classes were due to start at many universities, discussions between the parties concerned were hastily carried out and an agreement was reached to allow the provision of materials via the internet, and MEXT provided information on implementation.

Thus, legal measures were taken on how to conduct classes and provide teaching materials to cope with COVID-19, the environment for teaching in universities was set up, and a system for conducting university education through fully remote teaching was created and implemented.

7. FUTURE PROSPECTS

In March 2022, Japan was affected by a sixth wave of COVID-19 caused by the Omicron variant. Japanese universities have been flexible in allowing face-to-face classes or switching to remote classes according to the trends of infected students.

If we take a broad view of the relationship between legal education and ICT to date, from the time of the spread of Windows 95 until the establishment of law schools in 2004, ICT-based education was not widely used, although there were some cutting-edge initiatives. In particular, students were rarely exposed to ICT-based education and received instead an analogue-based education.

The establishment of law schools in 2004, triggered by the reform of the judicial system, led to the development and provision of a legal information database in Japan, which is available via the internet to a wide range of society, including law firms, companies and government agencies. This was the start of a 'revolution' in the way legal research is conducted in Japan, with digital technology taking centre stage. At the same time, law schools introduced CMSs, provided materials on demand, and built up a track record of education using distance learning systems. At the undergraduate level, however, the spread of distance learning remained limited.

With the spread of the internet and the increasing sophistication of the usage environment due to the progress of technological development, when COVID-19 struck, an environment was set up in which full remote education could be easily implemented as long as the system in the environment of legal education was actually used. The necessary guidelines for the teaching style were provided, and at the same time the law on the treatment of copyrighted material was amended and this knowledge was disseminated. Thus, due to the COVID-19 pandemic, since 2020 the use of online meeting systems and CMSs has become widespread and established, not only in law school education, but also in education at the undergraduate level.

At the present stage, the limitations of ICT have naturally been pointed out for the implementation of practical classes on mock trials and negotiations, and for education requiring on-site experience, such as internships. However, the recognition that ICT-based legal education is at least different from face-to-face teaching, but more than minimally adequate as an alternative, has been established. As the impact of COVID-19 becomes small enough to allow face-to-face teaching, we will get a more concrete picture of what will happen to the use of ICT, which was promoted somewhat to excess during the peak pandemic period. However, not all legal education will return to normal, but will continue to develop and evolve in some areas.

In this report, we have traced the events that took place during the long period of ICT diffusion from 1995 to the present. In doing so we described how introducing ICT in legal education in Japan did not progress much at all when it was left to the initiative of individual students and faculty members. Instead, it developed when educational organisations created a situation in which students and faculty members were forced to use ICT, by spending huge amounts of money. It is evident that this was done against a background of innovation in ICT technology and its diffusion in society. Further, when organisations had to move with new mechanisms, they were widely introduced, and this process has been repeated. Overall, Japanese society after COVID-19 is sometimes referred to as 'after corona' or 'with corona'; however, ICT in legal education will never be a case of 'after ICT', but only 'with ICT'.

ONLINE LEGAL EDUCATION IN PAKISTAN

Past and Prospects

Syed Imad-ud-Din Asad

1. INTRODUCTION

The Constitution of 1973 establishes that the Islamic Republic of Pakistan is a Federal Republic.[1] The country is comprised of four provinces – Balochistan, Khyber Pakhtunkhwa, Punjab and Sindh – as well as a federal capital.[2]

1 The Constitution of 1973, Article 1(1).

2 Ibid., Article 1(2).

In 2010, the 18th Amendment to the 1973 Constitution redefined the legislative powers of the Parliament and the Provincial Assemblies.[3] As a result, the Parliament is now empowered to make laws for the whole country or a part of it, whereas the Provincial Assemblies are empowered to make laws for the whole Province or a part of it.[4] Similarly, while the Parliament has exclusive power to legislate regarding matters enumerated in the Federal Legislative List,[5] the Provincial Assemblies have the exclusive power to legislate on matters not enumerated in the Federal Legislative List.[6] The Supreme Court has reiterated this: 'The Federal Legislature exercises its jurisdiction in respect of matters enumerated in the Federal Legislative List (FLL). All other left-over matters and subjects are secured by the Provincial Legislature in constitutional parlance referred to as residuary subjects.'[7] The 1973 Constitution provides that a Provincial Assembly may, through a resolution, ask the Parliament to enact a law for that Province.[8]

The Federal Legislative List provided in the 1973 Constitution does not mention 'education' or 'higher education'.[9] Therefore, only the Provincial Assemblies are competent to legislate on matters concerning and relating to education.[10]

2. HIGHER EDUCATION

2.1. OVERVIEW

There are over 220 public and private universities and degree awarding institutions (DAIs) across Pakistan, collectively regulated by the Higher Education Commission (HEC). The funding arrangements for public institutions entail full government funding, in contrast to private institutions, which generate funds directly through fees. As a result of their dependency on ever-changing and uncertain government funding, public universities and DAIs are

3 The Constitution (Eighteenth Amendment) Act 2010.
4 The Constitution of 1973, Articles 141 and 142.
5 Ibid., Article 142(a).
6 Ibid., Article 142(c).
7 *Federal Government Employees Housing Foundation (FGEHF), Islamabad v. Malik Ghulam Mustafa* (2021) SCMR 201.
8 Ibid., Article 144(1).
9 The Constitution of 1973, Federal Legislative List.
10 The Constitution (Eighteenth Amendment) Act 2010; *Azfar Laboratories Private Limited v. Federation of Pakistan through Secretary of Ministry of National Health Services* (2018) PLD 448.

incurring increasing losses each year. Critically, unless the government takes immediate remedial measures, these public institutions are expected to be confronted by a severe financial crisis. Between 2017 and 2021, the number of public universities and DAIs increased from 99 to 131 and the number of enrolled students increased from 1.76 million to 2.06 million. The new 32 public institutions, established primarily for political reasons, were not provided with the required funds to enable provision of adequate higher education, establish new programmes and strengthen existing programmes. The HEC's development budget should be increased to deal with these issues. It is expected that increasing this budget will also equip public institutions with the resources and capabilities to develop a proper system for the provision of online education.[11]

There is presently no right to higher education in Pakistan. In comparison to standard school education, it is more expensive to provide higher education, evinced through the extensive costs of setting up and maintaining laboratories, hiring staff and retaining faculty.[12] In 2017–18, the HEC's recurring budget was Rs 63.1 billion; in 2018–19, it was Rs 65.02 billion; in 2019–20, it was Rs 64.1 billion; and in 2020–21, it was again Rs 64.1 billion. This was insufficient to meet the demands of the public institutions.[13] In response, the government allocated Rs 81 billion in 2021–22.[14] The HEC had a total funding of Rs 108 billion for the financial year 2021–22.[15]

The insufficiency of these funds is compounded by inflation, which has had a negative impact on the provision of higher education, with faculty and staff members at public institutions demanding higher salaries. This has created a double-edged sword. Keeping staff satisfied and preventing them leaving public institutions not only requires costly expenditure to increase their salaries, but also entails re-allocating scarce resources away from education towards staff satisfaction, thus undermining the quality of higher education.[16]

---

11 J. Laghari, 'HEC in Dire Straits', *The News* (30.05.2021), https://www.thenews.com.pk/print/841797-hec-in-dire-straits.

12 F. Bari, 'Quest for Quality Education', *DAWN* (26.11.2021), https://www.dawn.com/news/1660345.

13 K. Abbasi, 'Higher Education Sector Has Remained Under-Funded, Says Stakeholders', *DAWN* (27.05.2021), https://www.dawn.com/news/1625845/higher-education-sector-has-remained-under-funded-say-stakeholders.

14 'Shafqat Terms Budget 2021–22 "Most Pro Higher Education Budget Ever"', *Pakistan Daily* (12.06.2021), https://thepakistandaily.com/shafqat-terms-budget-2021-22-most-pro-higher-education-budget-ever/.

15 K. Abbasi, 'HEC's Proposed Funding Formula in Doldrums in Absence of Chairman', *DAWN* (15.11.2021), https://www.dawn.com/news/1658124/hecs-proposed-funding-formula-in-doldrums-in-absence-of-chairman.

16 F. Bari, 'Quest for Quality Education', *DAWN* (26.11.2021), https://www.dawn.com/news/1660345.

2.2. REGULATION

The HEC was established under the Higher Education Commission Ordinance 2002 (HECO).[17] According to the Preamble of the HECO, the HEC is responsible for improving and promoting higher education, research and development in Pakistan.[18] The HECO further defines a 'university' as: 'A university established or incorporated under any law for the time being in force.'[19] A 'degree awarding institution' (DAI) is defined as: 'An institution imparting higher education and awarding degrees of its own.'[20] Both universities and DAIs impart higher education. An 'institution' is defined as: 'Any university or other degree awarding institution that offers higher education or is involved in the research and development activities.'[21] Thus, 'institution' refers to a university or a DAI.[22] A DAI can have a maximum of three departments or faculties, while a university can have four or more departments or faculties.[23]

The HEC was established in 2002 prior to the 18th Amendment to the 1973 Constitution, which occurred in 2010.[24] After this Amendment, Punjab was the first province to set up an education commission, called the Punjab Higher Education Commission (PHEC).[25] Afterwards, the Province of Sindh set up the Sindh Higher Education Commission (SHEC).[26] Unlike these two provinces, the Provinces of Balochistan and Khyber Pakhtunkhwa have not yet established their own provincial higher education commissions. However, a Higher Education Regulatory Authority has been established in Khyber Pakhtunkhwa to regulate *private* universities and DAIs, not *public* universities and DAIs.[27] Despite the changes arising from the 18th Amendment to the 1973 Constitution, the HEC still formulates standards, guidelines and policies for higher education in Pakistan.[28]

---

17 The Higher Education Commission Ordinance 2002, section 4.

18 Ibid., preamble.

19 Ibid., section 2(m).

20 Ibid., section 2(e).

21 Ibid., section 2(h).

22 Ibid., section 2(h).

23 Guidelines for the Establishment of a New University or an Institution of Higher Education, Higher Education Commission (2007), p. 7.

24 The Higher Education Commission Ordinance 2002; and the Constitution (Eighteenth Amendment) Act 2010.

25 The Punjab Higher Education Commission Act 2014; the Punjab Higher Education Commission, https://punjabhec.gov.pk/.

26 The Sindh Higher Education Commission Act 2013; the Sindh Higher Education Commission, https://sindhhec.gov.pk/.

27 The Khyber Pakhtunkhwa Registration and Functioning of Private Educational Institutions Ordinance 2001; the Higher Education Regulatory Authority, http://www.herakp.gov.pk/.

28 The Higher Education Commission Ordinance 2002, section 10(1); M. Sarmad, 'Legal Education in Pakistan: Problems & Prospects in the Context of 21st Century' (2019) 3(1) *Islamabad Law Review* 64, 74.

2.3. ACCESS TO INFORMATION TECHNOLOGY

The COVID-19 pandemic reached Karachi on 26 February 2020,[29] with cases recorded in all four provinces of the country by 18 March 2020.[30] Since then, being the fifth most populous country the world, Pakistan has experienced three different waves of COVID-19. Although the first wave subsided in July 2020, the country began to experience a second wave in November 2020, followed by a third wave in March 2021. Pakistan experienced its first lockdown from 1 April 2020 to 9 May 2020.[31] Like other countries, Pakistan enforced lockdowns and ensured strict implementation of standard operating procedures.

The COVID-19 pandemic forced public and private institutions to wrap up in-person classes, with the HEC directing higher education institutions to transition to online educative methods through the provision of online classes. Consequently, institutions stopped on-campus classes during March 2020. While private institutions possessed the resources to easily transition to online classes, many public institutions lacked the requisite infrastructure and technical and financial resources to facilitate this transition. The asymmetries in educative resourcing created issues of accessibility to higher education, worsened for millions of Pakistani students who were unable to access the fundamental tools of connected life, including smartphones, the internet and tablets to facilitate online learning. Therefore, the potential success of online education in Pakistan was greatly undermined by the 'dual-responsibility model', which not only required public institutions to expend scarce funds on transitioning to costly online education, but also made participation by students in online learning contingent on their own economic capacity to afford and access the electronic devices and services required in online models.[32]

Access to education before the pandemic presented a huge issue in Pakistan, with pre-pandemic statistics suggesting that of the over 70 million children, 22.8 million were out of school. Critically, the COVID-19 pandemic exposed these huge technological inequalities. According to the Pakistan Telecommunication Authority (PTA), outside the major cities, broadband is expensive, smartphone penetration stands at 51%, and only around one million school-age children have regular access to digital devices and the Internet. It is expected that a

---

29 N. Khan, 'Pakistan Prepares to Fight Back as Two Coronavirus Cases Emerge in Country', *Arab News* (15.03.2020), https://www.arabnews.pk/node/1633656/pakistan.

30 'Coronavirus Updates, March 18: Latest News on the Coronavirus Outbreak from Pakistan and Around the World', *GEO News* (18.03.2020), https://www.geo.tv/latest/277853-coronavirus-updates-march-18-latest-news-on-the-coronavirus-outbreak-from-pakistan-and-around-the-world.

31 R. Shehzad, 'Countrywide Lockdown Stretched Till May 9', *The Express Tribune* (24.04.2020), https://tribune.com.pk/story/2206167/1-countrywide-lockdown-stretched-till-may-9.

32 Z. Ranjah, 'Transforming Legal Education', *The Friday Times* (24.04.2020), https://www.thefridaytimes.com/transforming-legal-education/.

determined effort could almost eliminate this problem within two to three years. However, at present, an online system of education cannot be relied upon as the sole method for education delivery due to its fragility in blocking education opportunities for students unable to acquire the requisite learning resources for participation in a digital learning environment.[33]

According to the PTA, in 2012, broadband subscriptions were less than 2 million; in 2014, the figure drastically jumped to 16 million; and in 2021, it increased to 100 million. According to the Inclusive Internet Index, commissioned by Facebook and conducted by the Economist Intelligence Unit (EIU), in 2021 Pakistan ranked 90th out of 100 countries; in 2020, it ranked 89th; and in 2019, it ranked 77th. According to the EIU, in 2021 Pakistan ranked in the bottom quartile of the Index and second to last in Asia. The EIU also suggests that the gender gap in internet access between men and women is 65%, and 51% for mobile phone access.[34]

However, the increasingly competitive internet service provider environment has facilitated a decrease in mobile phone costs. Pakistan, previously ranked 67th in the world, recently recorded the highest score in the 'Affordability' category, which examined the cost of access relative to income and level of competition in the internet marketplace. Nonetheless, Pakistan ranked 79th in the 'Readiness' category, examining the capacity to access the internet, including skills, cultural acceptance and supporting policy; 91st in the 'Relevance' category, examining the existence and extent of local language content and relevant content; and 97th in the 'Availability' category, examining the quality and breadth of available infrastructure required for access and levels of the internet usage. Within the 'Availability' category, Pakistan ranked 116th in the 'Usage' class, which measured the size of the connected population in terms of the internet and mobile connectivity. Only 34% of households reported access to the internet and 2% of inhabitants had a fixed-line broadband subscription. Pakistan reported low internet quality, ranking 91st. Pakistan also faced infrastructure issues, including non-availability of public WiFi, an unlicensed spectrum policy and frequent electricity shortages, reported as one of the primary hindrances to connectivity to the internet.[35]

According to a 2021 government survey, around 12% of households owned at least one device, i.e. a computer, laptop or tablet, which highlighted both the limited access to, and equipment for, information and communication technologies in Pakistan. The Pakistan Social and Living Standards

---

33 M.Z. Malik, 'The Coronavirus Effect on Pakistan's Digital Divide', *BBC* (14.07.2020), https://www.bbc.com/worklife/article/20200713-the-coronavirus-effect-on-pakistans-digital-divide.

34 K. Ali, 'Pakistan Drops to 90th Rank on Inclusive Internet Index', *DAWN* (20.04.2021), https://www.dawn.com/news/1619250.

35 Ibid.

Measurement Survey 2019–20 (PSLMS), conducted by the Pakistan Bureau of Statistics (PBS), covered 176,790 households across rural and urban communities and collected information on a range of social sector issues, including information technology, education and health. The survey measured households with computers, laptops, tablets, mobile phones and the internet for individuals who were 10 years and older. Concerningly, the survey revealed that the percentage with ICT access was merely 19% in the urban areas and an even lower 7% in rural areas. The Province of Punjab ranked highest with 13% of households having at least one device. The Province of Balochistan ranked lowest with only 6% of households having at least one device. Although 93% of households in Pakistan reported having a mobile phone or smartphone, with 96% in the urban areas and 91% in the rural areas, these are not facilitative of online legal education and stand a testament to the issues in transitioning to an online learning environment. The Province of Khyber Pakhtunkhwa ranked highest with 95% of households having a mobile phone or smartphone, with the Province of Sindh ranked lowest with 91%. The Province of Punjab reported that 34% of households had access to the internet, the Province of Khyber Pakhtunkhwa reported 33%, the Province of Sindh reported 32%, and the Province of Balochistan reported 21%.[36]

3. LEGAL PROFESSION

3.1. OVERVIEW

The legal profession in Pakistan is comprised of a single national bar council called the Pakistan Bar Council (PBC), four provincial bar councils, and a bar council for the federal capital.[37] The Punjab Bar Council (PbBC) is the largest provincial bar council in Pakistan, with more than 100,000 registered advocates.[38] The Lahore High Court Bar Association (LHCBA) recorded 32,653 members in 2018, with the current figure yet to be published.[39] The Lahore Bar Association (LBA) has more than 25,000 members.[40] Both the LHCBA and the LBA function under the jurisdiction of the Punjab Bar Council.

There are 40,709 advocates registered with the Sindh Bar Council.[41] The total number of advocates registered with the Khyber Pakhtunkhwa Bar Council

36 M.Z. Khan, '12pc Households in Pakistan Have At Least One Facility of Digital Devices', *DAWN* (27.07.2021), https://www.dawn.com/news/1637075.
37 The Legal Practitioners and Bar Councils Act 1973, section 3(1).
38 Punjab Bar Council, https://pbbarcouncil.com/about-us/.
39 Lahore High Court Bar Association, https://lhcbar.com/bar-history/.
40 Lahore Bar Association, http://lahorebarassociation.org.pk/about.html.
41 Sindh Bar Council, https://sindhbarcouncil.org.

is not provided on its website.[42] However, a 2015 report indicated there were 6,498 advocates licensed to practise before the High Court, and 8,692 advocates licensed to practise before the subordinate courts.[43] The total number of advocates registered with the Balochistan Bar Council is not mentioned on its website.[44] The same 2015 report stated that there were 1,590 advocates licensed to practise before the High Court and 904 advocates licensed to practise before the subordinate courts.[45] This data suggests advocates do not comprise a small professional group and, given the high number, suggests it is not difficult to become an advocate in Pakistan.[46]

Pakistani lawyers have been closely allied with political parties and adopt a very active role in national politics. Because of these strong political alliances, many lawyers have been successful in obtaining prestigious appointments to the superior courts, winning elections to offices in bar councils and bar associations and obtaining appointments in the Attorney General's Office and the Advocate General's Office. Consequently, elections of bar councils and bar associations have become fierce contests between various groups of lawyers, which are supported by different political parties. Additionally, elections to bar councils and bar associations are desired not only for the political power they provide, but also to further enhance and entrench the public perception of influence, thus causing a tremendous increase in clientele for those elected.

As bar councils and bar associations have become platforms for personal career advancement, regulation of the legal profession has remained weak due to self-regulation. The number of sub-standard lawyers is increasing. The legal profession primarily comprises family law offices; children follow parents into legal practice and enjoy the benefits of inherited offices, libraries, staff and clients. A considerable number of lawyers share office spaces and divide expenses, but do not share profits. Thus, proper firms are rare.[47]

3.2. REGULATION

The PBC regulates the legal profession in Pakistan. In February 1973, the Legal Practitioners and Bar Councils Act 1973 (LPBCA) was promulgated.[48] The Preamble of the LPBCA states its purpose as: 'An Act to repeal and, with certain

---

42 Khyber Pakhtunkhwa Bar Council, https://www.kpbarcouncil.com.

43 F. Hussain, *The Judicial System of Pakistan*, Federal Judicial Academy, Islamabad 2015, p. 27.

44 Balochistan Bar Council, http://www.bbcq.org.pk/.

45 F. Hussain, *The Judicial System of Pakistan*, Federal Judicial Academy, Islamabad 2015, p. 27.

46 M. Sarmad, 'Legal Education in Pakistan: Problems & Prospects in the Context of 21st Century' (2019) 3(1) *Islamabad Law Review* 64, 80.

47 O. Siddique, 'Legal Education in Pakistan: The Domination of Practitioners and the "Critically Endangered" Academic' (2014) 63(3) *Journal of Legal Education* 505.

48 The Legal Practitioners and Bar Councils Act 1973, preamble.

modifications, re-enact the law relating to legal practitioners and bar councils.'[49] The LPBCA provides for the creation of the PBC, the Provincial Bar Councils and the Islamabad Bar Council.[50] The functions of the Provincial Bar Councils and Islamabad Bar Council include, among other things:

- admitting persons as advocates and maintaining a roll of advocates;
- admitting persons as advocates entitled to practise before the respective High Courts and maintaining a roll of such advocates;
- deciding cases of misconduct against advocates; and
- suggesting law reforms.[51]

Thus, the Provincial Bar Councils and the Islamabad Bar Council are responsible for admitting persons as advocates on their rolls.[52] The functions of the PBC include, among other things:

- preparing and maintaining a common roll of advocates;
- admitting persons as advocates entitled to practise before the Supreme Court and maintaining a roll of such advocates;
- prescribing standards of professional conduct for advocates;
- suggesting law reforms;
- exercising general supervision and control over the Provincial Bar Councils and the Islamabad Bar Council;
- promoting legal education and prescribing standards for legal education in consultation with universities, the Provincial Bar Councils and the Islamabad Bar Council;
- recognising universities whose degrees are acceptable as qualification for enrolment as an advocate; and
- organising conferences, seminars, lectures, etc., for promoting legal knowledge and learning in the legal profession.[53]

The LPBCA further provides that the PBC is empowered to make rules regarding 'uniform conditions for being eligible to apply to a Bar Council for admission as an advocate.'[54]

While the Provincial Bar Councils and the Islamabad Bar Council are responsible for admitting persons as advocates,[55] the PBC is also responsible

49 Ibid., preamble.
50 Ibid., section 3(1).
51 Ibid., section 9(1).
52 Ibid., section 9(1)(a).
53 Ibid., section 13(1).
54 Ibid., section 55(la).
55 Ibid., section 9(1)(a).

for prescribing eligibility criteria for admission as an advocate, prescribing standards of professional conduct for advocates, prescribing standards for legal education, and recognising universities whose degrees are acceptable as qualification for enrolment as an advocate.[56]

4. LEGAL EDUCATION

4.1. OVERVIEW

Some universities and DAIs offer local law programmes and some institutes offer foreign law programmes. A total of 53 institutions currently offer local law programmes.[57] In addition to offering law programmes, many institutions offer affiliation to private law colleges, requiring fee payments, registration fees and examination fees, necessary to prepare students for examinations. Thus, these affiliating institutions make additional profits. Unfortunately, statistics are not available or compiled regarding the number of private affiliated law colleges, the number of students enrolled in them, and the fee charged by them.

As for foreign law programmes, some institutes offer the University of London's external LLB and LLM programmes.[58] Unfortunately, detailed statistics are either not available or they have not been compiled for external programmes regarding the number of institutes offering them, the number of students enrolled, the career paths pursued by alumni, and the fees charged by the institutes offering the external programmes.

Although Pakistan was once a part of British India, there are many differences between Pakistani law and English law. The University of London's external law programmes do not teach Pakistani law and do not prepare students for the Pakistani legal system. Further, the University of London's external programmes are far more costly than Pakistani programmes, requiring much higher tuition fees. Consequently, only the wealthy can afford to pursue external programmes, serving as a status symbol of wealth. The high costs associated with these external programmes has meant that an overwhelming majority of Pakistanis pursue local law programmes instead.

---

56 Ibid., section 13(1).

57 The Pakistan Bar Council Legal Education Rules 2015, First Schedule and Second Schedule.

58 For instance, Universal College Lahore, https://www.ucl.edu.pk/; The Institute of Legal Studies, https://tils.edu.pk/; Pakistan College of Law, https://pcl.edu.pk/; Blackstone School of Law and Business, https://www.bsolpk.org/; Themis School of Law, https://themis.com.pk/; and Shaheed Zulfikar Ali Bhutto Institute of Science and Technology, https://www.szabist.edu.pk/.

Whether local programmes or foreign, most LLB holders or law graduates are not up to the mark. Although the PBC and the HEC are criticised as having ignored their responsibilities, it is important to recognise that universities and DAIs have not properly played their part either.[59]

The above-mentioned challenges are compounded by the following issues – reiterating that, overall, the system of legal education is in dire need of reform:

- it is overly easy to be admitted to a law programme;
- modern teaching methodologies have not yet been introduced;[60]
- the curricula for LLB and LLM programmes require improvement;
- most universities and DAIs lack proper and sufficient human resources in terms of faculty and staff;
- most law faculties and law schools are poorly administered;
- there is a severe dearth of research, both in terms of quality and quantity;[61]
- there are no law journals considered reliable;[62]
- at law faculties and law schools, there are frequent tussles between different faculty members, which is a big hindrance to improving the quality of legal education;[63] and
- members of the PBC, who are responsible for regulating legal education, are practitioners not academics, and are thus unaware of the requirements and dynamics involved in setting up and managing modern legal education programmes.[64]

---

59 R. Zahoor, 'Clinical Legal Education and its Implication on Legal Education System in Pakistan: Challenges and Prospects' (2021) 3(1) *Centre for Sustainability Research and Consultancy* 15; M. Imran, 'Role of the Bar and Bench in the Development of Legal Education' (2019) 3(1) *Islamabad Law Review* 45; M. Sarmad, 'Legal Education in Pakistan: Problems & Prospects in the Context of 21st Century' (2019) 3(1) *Islamabad Law Review* 64, 89; S. Shah, 'Legal Education in Pakistan: An Overview' (2018) 26(2) *IIUM Law Journal* 402, 403–404; A. Sial, 'Designing Legal Education to Support Social Evolution in Pakistan' (2009) 24(2) *South Asian Studies* 283, 293.

60 M. Sarmad, 'Legal Education in Pakistan: Problems & Prospects in the Context of 21st Century' (2019) 3(1) *Islamabad Law Review* 64, 78, 86.

61 R. Zahoor, 'Clinical Legal Education and its Implication on Legal Education System in Pakistan: Challenges and Prospects' (2021) 3(1) *Centre for Sustainability Research and Consultancy* 15, 16, 18; M. Sarmad, 'Legal Education in Pakistan: Problems & Prospects in the Context of 21st Century' (2019) 3(1) *Islamabad Law Review* 64, 70–71, 80.

62 M. Sarmad, 'Legal Education in Pakistan: Problems & Prospects in the Context of 21st Century' (2019) 3(1) *Islamabad Law Review* 64, 70–71.

63 R. Zahoor, 'Clinical Legal Education and its Implication on Legal Education System in Pakistan: Challenges and Prospects' (2021) 3(1) *Centre for Sustainability Research and Consultancy* 15, 18.

64 S. Shah, 'Legal Education in Pakistan: An Overview' (2018) 26(2) *IIUM Law Journal* 402, 427, 431.

4.2. REGULATION

The PBC is the main regulator of legal education. In certain matters, the PBC works in collaboration with the HEC. Regarding the role of the PBC, the LPBCA provides that it includes:

- promoting legal education and prescribing standards for legal education in consultation with universities, the Provincial Bar Councils and the Islamabad Bar Council;
- recognising universities whose degrees are acceptable as qualification for enrolment as an advocate; and
- organising conferences, seminars, lectures, etc., for promoting legal knowledge and learning in the legal profession.[65]

Thus, section 13(1)(j) of the LPBCA provides that the PBC is responsible for promoting legal education as well as prescribing standards for legal education. Further, the LPBCA provides for the creation of the Legal Education Committee (LEC), stating that: 'The Pakistan Bar Council may constitute from amongst its members … a legal education Committee … and may authorise any such Committee to co-opt as its members any other persons, not exceeding such number as the Council may determine.'[66]

Regarding those who can practise law in Pakistan, the LPBCA provides: 'Save as otherwise provided in this Act, no person shall be entitled to practise the profession of law unless he is an advocate.'[67] Thus, a person cannot practise law unless that person is enrolled as an advocate.[68] Regarding those who can be enrolled as advocates, the LPBCA provides:

> A person shall be qualified to be admitted as an advocate if he fulfils the following conditions, namely:
>
> (a) He is a citizen of Pakistan or a person deriving his nationality from the State of Jammu and Kashmir:
>
> …
>
> (c) He is a Barrister … or has obtained:
>
> (i) Before the 7th day of February 1966, a degree in law from any university in Pakistan; or
>
> …

65 The Legal Practitioners and Bar Councils Act 1973, section 13(1).
66 Ibid., section 15(2).
67 Ibid., section 22(1).
68 Ibid., section 22(1).

> (iii) A bachelor's degree in law from a university or institute recognised by the Higher Education Commission and the Pakistan Bar Council; and
>
> ...
>
> (d) He has undergone such course of training and passed such examination after the training as may be prescribed by the Pakistan Bar council.[69]

Therefore, a bachelor's degree in law, from a university recognised by the PBC and the HEC, is one of the requirements.[70] Under the LPBCA, the PBC can make rules regarding standards of legal education to be observed by Pakistani universities, as well as regarding inspection of Pakistani universities to ensure the standards are being observed.[71] The LPBCA provides:

> The Pakistan Bar Council may ... make rules to provide for:
>
> ...
>
> (f) The constitution and functions of any Committee of the Pakistan Bar Council and the term of office of the members of any such Committee;
>
> ...
>
> (la) Uniform conditions for being eligible to apply to a Bar Council for admission as an advocate;
>
> (lb) The course of practical training in law and the examination to be passed after such training for admission as an advocate;
>
> ...
>
> (q) The standards of legal education to be observed by universities in Pakistan and the inspection of universities for that purpose.[72]

In May 1976, the PBC notified the Pakistan Legal Practitioners and Bar Councils Rules 1976 (PLPBCR).[73] The PLPBCR also provides for the creation of the LEC.[74] In December 2015, the PBC notified the Pakistan Bar Council Legal Education Rules 2015 (PBCLER).[75] The notification provided: 'And whereas the existing three sets of Rules on the subject of legal education i.e. the "Pakistan Bar Council Legal Education Rules, 1978", the "Affiliation of Law Colleges Rules" and the "Pakistan Bar Council (Recognition of Universities) Rules, 2005" are to

69 Ibid., section 26.
70 Ibid., section 26(c)(iii).
71 Ibid., section 55(q).
72 Ibid., section 55.
73 Pakistan Bar Council, S.R.O. 476(I)/76 (21.05.1976).
74 The Pakistan Legal Practitioners and Bar Councils Rules 1976, Rule 86(a)(4).
75 S.R.O. 1265(1)/2015 (19.12.2015).

be reviewed and consolidated in one set of uniformed Rules.'[76] The notification further provided: 'And whereas the constant deterioration of standard and quality of legal education because of mushroom growth of law colleges and even the Universities, in private sector, necessitates strict check and control over the Universities and degree awarding Institutions, imparting legal education, and the private law colleges.'[77]

In this notification, the PBC admits the quality of legal education in Pakistan has consistently deteriorated. This admission speaks volumes about the PBC's performance, strengthening criticism levelled towards the PBC that it constantly fails to perform its responsibilities in the legal education domain. Had the PBC performed its responsibilities, the state of legal education in Pakistan would have remained satisfactory. In fact, the very bad state of both legal education in Pakistan and the legal profession has been pointed out several times.[78] The situation has even been criticised by the Supreme Court of Pakistan in many of its judgments.[79]

Further, Rule 3(vi) of the PBCLER provides: '"Recognised degree" means and includes a bachelor's degree in law awarded by a university, or a Degree Awarding Institution recognised by the Pakistan Bar Council.'[80] The PBCLER has restricted the number of LLB students in reference to the physical infrastructure and facilities available at the main campus of a university in the following words:

> (i) A Section of a Class in a Faculty of Law/Law Department/Law College shall not [exceed] more than 50 students.

---

76 Ibid.

77 Ibid.

78 S. Asad, 'Current Trends in Legal Education', *DAWN* (20.12.2009), https://www.dawn.com/news/509810/current-trends-in-legal-education; A. Cowasjee, 'Looking to the Future', *DAWN* (27.06.2010), https://www.dawn.com/news/543717/looking-to-the-future; Z. Ranjah, 'Legal Education', *DAWN* (02.10.2015), https://www.dawn.com/news/1210297; Z. Ranjah, 'Legal Education', *DAWN* (05.03.2018), https://www.dawn.com/news/1393268; Z. Khan, 'Improving Legal Education In Pakistan with Online Platforms', *Courting the Law* (22.11.2019), https://courtingthelaw.com/2019/11/22/commentary/improving-legal-education-in-pakistan-with-online-platforms/; Z. Ranjah, 'Transforming Legal Education', *The Friday Times* (24.04.2020), https://www.thefridaytimes.com/transforming-legal-education/; 'Lawyers Should Evolve with Technology', *The Express Tribune* (27.09.2020), http://tribune.com.pk/story/2261422/lawyers-should-evolve-with-technology; R. Zahoor, 'Clinical Legal Education and its Implication on Legal Education System in Pakistan: Challenges and Prospects' (2021) 3(1) *Centre for Sustainability Research and Consultancy* 15; A. Wahid, 'Seniority is Toxic', *DAWN* (16.12.2021), https://www.dawn.com/news/1664102; S. Arif, 'Changing Characteristics of Legal Education in Pakistan: Prospects and Challenges' (December 2019) 3(2) *Pakistan Social Sciences Review* 868.

79 *Pakistan Bar Council v. Federal Government* (2007) PLD 394; *Pakistan Bar Council through Chairman Legal Education Committee, PBC, Islamabad v. Federal Government through Establishment Division* (2013) SCMR 1651; *Pakistan Bar Council v. Federal Government through Establishment Division* (2018) SCMR 1891; *Pakistan Bar Council v. Federal Government through Establishment Division* (2019) SCMR 389.

80 The Pakistan Bar Council Legal Education Rules 2015, Rule 3(vi).

(ii) The total number of students admitted in 1st year LL.B. in any case shall not [exceed] 100.

However, in special circumstances, the Committee in [the] case of [the] main campus of a university, may allow admission of students to 1st year LL.B. not exceeding 150 keeping in view [the] infrastructure and facilities available in [the] main campus of the concerned University.[81]

Regarding the syllabus for the LLB programme, the PBCLER provides: 'The syllabus for [the] LL.B. programme shall include the subjects prescribed and duly approved by the Pakistan Bar Council and Higher Education Commission and as modified by them from time to time.'[82] Further, Rule 7 of the PBCLER provides that the curriculum for the LLB programme must be approved by the PBC and the HEC, thus placing it within the overlapping scope of matters in which both the PBC and the HEC may collaborate.[83]

The PBCLER provides for morning LLB classes but prohibits afternoon and evening classes.[84] Rule 13 of the PBCLER provides that LLM programmes must also be approved by the PBC. Like the LLB programme, the curriculum for the LLM programme is also prescribed by the PBC and the HEC.[85] Rule 13(iv) of the PBCLER provides that the LLM programme can only be conducted at the main campus of a university. Rule 17(i) of the PBCLER regulates the recognition of universities by the PBC, providing that a university cannot commence law programmes and admit students without its prior recognition by the PBC. Rule 17(ii) of the PBCLER provides that if a university applies for recognition by the PBC after commencing law programmes and admitting students, a monetary penalty will be imposed on it.

Rule 19(i) of the PBCLER provides that a university can only conduct the LLB classes on its main campus. Further, in relation to a university application for the recognition of its LLB programme by the PBC, the PBCLER provides:

The applicant University/Degree Awarding Institution shall have to submit an undertaking ... to the effect that it shall:

(i) Not affiliate any private law college at any place, nor itself conduct law classes anywhere else except of its main campus;
(ii) Not admit more than 100 law students in an academic year;
(iii) Abide by and adhere to the minimum standards as laid down in these Rules and instructions/directions issued by the Pakistan Bar Council from time to time

81 Ibid., Rule 5.

82 Ibid., Rule 7.

83 The latest curriculum for the LLB programme was approved in 2015. Curriculum for LLB (5 Years), Higher Education Commission, 2015.

84 The Pakistan Bar Council Legal Education Rules 2015, Rule 10.

85 The latest curriculum for the LLM programme was approved in 2006. Curriculum of LLM, Higher Education Commission, 2006.

in respect of legal education, the violation of which will render the University/ Institution to be de-recognised;

(iv) Ensure imparting of quality education strictly in accordance with the syllabus prescribed by the Pakistan Bar Council and the Higher Education Commission; and

(v) Ensure conducting and adhering only to [the] 5 years composite programme of LL.B. as per [the] standards and criteria prescribed by the Pakistan Bar Council and Higher Education Commission.[86]

Regarding infrastructure and facilities, Rule 25 of the PBCLER prescribes the minimum number of classrooms and other facilities for conducting law programmes. The PBCLER provides:

A College shall:

(i) Be located in a spacious, separate, and independent building with covered area of minimum 12000 sq. ft without any other institution or person sharing the premises;

(ii) Have at least ten classrooms, a common room, a ladies room, Committee Room, Meeting Hall, and a separate staff room;

(iii) Have adequate canteen/cafeteria, toilets and first aid facilities;

(iv) Develop/install its website also displaying [the] status of students and their attendance on [a] regular basis with intimation, through e-mail, to [the] concerned University/Institution and the Council.[87]

A university which intends to impart legal education must apply to the PBC for its recognition under Rule 16(i) of the PBCLER. The application form prescribed by the PBCLER is appended to the PBCLER under Schedule Three.[88] The application form requires a university to declare that it will impart legal education only at its main campus, not anywhere else.[89] Paragraph 3 of the application form provides that:

The aforementioned University/Institution do hereby declare that it:

(i) Is authorised and competent to impart legal education and award [an] LL.B. degree;

...

(iii) Shall introduce the syllabus of 5 years LL.B. courses which will essentially include the syllabus/courses prescribed by the Pakistan Bar Council and the Higher

---

86 The Pakistan Bar Council Legal Education Rules 2015, Rule 19.

87 Ibid., Rule 25.

88 Ibid., Rule 16(i).

89 Application for Recognition of a University or Degree Awarding Institution Imparting Legal Education, Third Schedule, the Pakistan Bar Council Legal Education Rules 2015.

> Education Commission and comply with their decisions/instructions regarding changes/amendments therein brought about by them from time to time;
>
> (iv) Shall restrict imparting of legal education to its Law Faculty/Department at its main campus only and will not impart such education anywhere else nor will affiliate any law college;
>
> ...
>
> (viii) Shall impart legal education only in morning classes.[90]

In relation to foreign law programmes in Pakistan, Rule 36 of the PBCLER provides that no institution shall offer the programmes of any foreign university without first obtaining a no-objection certificate from the PBC. This requirement also applies to the external law programmes of the University of London. Rule 40 of the PBCLER provides the PBC can request that the Provincial Bar Councils and Islamabad Bar Council refrain from issuing practising licences to the students and alumni of an institute offering a foreign law programme if it fails to comply with the PBCLER requirements. Thus, the PBC has extended its domain and regulatory scope to foreign law programmes offered in Pakistan.

4.3. SUPREME COURT AND LEGAL EDUCATION

In *Pakistan Bar Council v. The Federal Government and Others* the Supreme Court considered the matter of declining standards of legal education in the context of the growing number of private affiliated law colleges. The Supreme Court severely criticised private affiliated law colleges for focusing on making money at the expense of quality legal education. The Supreme Court observed: 'Colleges mostly have become business centers and in the name of legal education, it is a profit-making industry that they are running.' The Supreme Court further observed: 'It is these centers which produce law graduates, who are called to the Bar, some practice, some join [the] judiciary at the district level, some adorn the constitutional Courts, and some become law makers.' In short, the Supreme Court blamed private affiliated law colleges for the very bad state of the legal system in general, and the legal profession in particular. Interestingly, the Supreme Court did not discuss whether lawyers and the PBC also contributed to this sorry situation. The Supreme Court directed all law schools and colleges to comply with the rules framed by the PBC to ensure uniform quality of legal education.[91]

---

90 Ibid.

91 *Pakistan Bar Council v. The Federal Government and Others* (2007) PLD Supreme Court 394.

However, the judgment was not implemented and, in 2010, this came to the notice of the Supreme Court. Implementation proceedings were immediately initiated, which proceeded slowly. Ultimately, in 2019, the Supreme Court reiterated that 'there has been a major decline in the standard of legal education owing to various reasons.' The Supreme Court kept its focus on private affiliated law colleges only. The Supreme Court directed some private affiliated law colleges to be shut down, directed some to be disaffiliated, and allowed some to meet the prescribed requirements and standards within a period of six months. In the same 2019 judgment, the Supreme Court gave directions regarding legal education, prescribing:[92]

- a Law Graduate Assessment Test (Law-GAT) of law graduates seeking enrolment as advocates to be conducted, on a quarterly basis, by the HEC;
- a law admission test (LAT) of individuals seeking admission to the LLB programme to be conducted, biannually, by the HEC;
- eligibility criteria for full-time and visiting faculty members;
- the minimum number of full-time and visiting faculty members; and
- a ban on conducting LLB classes in the evening.

While prescribing eligibility criteria for the position of dean, the Supreme Court held:[93]

> The Dean Law Faculty/Head of Law Department/Principal of law college shall be [a] Ph.D. in law with 8 years [of] law teaching experience/practice experience in [a] High Court or [have a] Master's Degree in Law with 15 years [of] law teaching experience/practice experience in [a] High Court or [be] a retired Judge of the Supreme Court or a High Court or a retired District and Sessions Judge having 5 years of judicial service to his credit.

According to the Supreme Court, being a retired judge of a High Court or the Supreme Court, or being a retired District and Sessions Judge, having five years of judicial service, is sufficient to be appointed to the position of dean. In the case of retired judges, no doctoral degree, teaching experience or research background is required. However, these academic criteria for former judges have been perceived as a judicial attempt by the Supreme Court to create employment opportunities for retired judges.

In the 2007 and 2019 judgments discussed above, the Supreme Court's reasoning lacks both width and depth. The Supreme Court failed to notice

92 *Pakistan Bar Council v. The Federal Government and Others* (2019) SCMR 389.

93 Ibid.

trends in legal education in developed countries, including the USA, the United Kingdom, Australia and Germany. Additionally, the Supreme Court failed to notice the role of the bar councils and bar associations in these countries in regulating legal education. The Supreme Court's neglected questions of inquiry include: whether bar councils and bar associations in these countries exercise the same powers and functions regarding legal education as the PBC; whether these countries have regulators like the HEC; and how much freedom is afforded to universities in these countries regarding designing and conducting legal education. Thus, the Supreme Court took up the issue of legal education but failed to address it properly.

In April 2022, a three-member bench of the Supreme Court, headed by the Chief Justice, reiterated the above-mentioned concerns when hearing a petition regarding sub-standard lawyers contesting the elections of bar councils and bar associations. The Supreme Court 'ordered the constitution of an independent committee to make suggestions for regulating and improving the quality of legal education in the country and directed the law ministry to aid in the formation of the body.'[94] Overall, and unfortunately, the Supreme Court maintained its previous approach towards addressing the issue of legal education.

5. ONLINE, PRACTICAL AND CONTINUING LEGAL EDUCATION

5.1. ONLINE LEGAL EDUCATION

To ascertain the prospects of online legal education in Pakistan, the following must be considered:

- Rule 5(ii) of the PBCLER refers to the infrastructure and the facilities available at the main campus of a university;
- Rule 10(i) of the PBCLER provides that LLB classes can only be conducted in the morning;
- Rule 13(iv) of the PBCLER provides that the LLM programme can only be conducted at the main campus of a university;
- Rule 19(i) of the PBCLER provides that a university can only conduct the LLB classes on its main campus;
- Rule 25 of the PBCLER prescribes the minimum number of classrooms and other facilities for conducting law programmes; and

---

94 N. Iqbal, 'SC Calls For Body to Improve Quality of Law Education', *DAWN* (28.04.2022), https://www.dawn.com/news/1687202.

- The Application Form prescribed by the PBCLER requires a university to declare that it will impart legal education only at its main campus and not anywhere else.[95]

As highlighted by these provisions, the PBCLER fails to accommodate for the possibility of conducting LLB and LLM programmes online, as the PBCLER provides strictly for physical classrooms only. This inflexibility and hesitancy to adopt online learning methods created an 'educative nightmare' during the ongoing COVID-19 pandemic. When higher education institutions stopped on-campus classes, some law schools tried to conduct online courses. However, these were not very effective.[96] Unfortunately, the PBC remained silent regarding online legal education, forcing legal education almost to a standstill.

The COVID-19 pandemic has provided an opportunity for the PBC to review its priorities and create mechanisms for the provision of modern learning technologies and platforms. The PBC should survey developed countries to assess how legal education coped with the crisis. There are many examples of innovation in legal education in certain developed countries. Law schools across the world are rapidly transitioning towards online learning programmes due to the numerous advantages, such as reduced costs, flexibility and customisation of learning modules. Law schools in Pakistan should therefore be allowed to harness this opportunity to undertake legal education with the integration of technology. This opportunity is not only a necessity in a modern digital environment but could be offered beneficially as a selling point to attract increased enrolments.[97]

The PBC must acknowledge and realise the present-day needs of our technological society and update the existing provisions regarding legal education to cater to the demands of the time. The HEC should provide technical support to the PBC as well as universities to foster the provision of efficient online legal education.

5.2. PRACTICAL LEGAL EDUCATION

Practical legal education is another domain which requires significant improvement and a modern transformation in Pakistan. The latest curriculum

---

95 Application for Recognition of a University or Degree Awarding Institution Imparting Legal Education, Third Schedule, the Pakistan Bar Council Legal Education Rules 2015.

96 Z. Ranjah, 'Transforming Legal Education', *The Friday Times* (24.04.2020), https://www.thefridaytimes.com/transforming-legal-education/.

97 Ibid.

permits the LLB programme to be spread over five years and 10 semesters.[98] The curriculum provides that each LLB candidate must pursue an internship, which is seldom paid, after the conclusion of the eighth semester and before the commencement of the ninth semester. The internship must be spread over a period of 10–12 weeks, with students awarded three credits upon completion of the internship. It is pertinent to mention that the PBCLER does not currently provide for practical, experiential or clinical legal education. Consequently, the scope of the internships only encompasses legal research, maintenance of office files and performance of small tasks.[99] Once the internship ends, the supervising lawyer provides a certificate of internship to enable the university or DAI to award the student with prescribed credit points. Problematically, however, most law students approach various lawyers through a network of family and friends and obtain the certificates of internship without doing any actual work. By contrast, in the USA, the summer internships pursued by JD candidates are much more meaningful, coupled with plentiful clinical and experiential learning opportunities.

The American Bar Association and the state bars facilitate practical legal education. These issues in Pakistani legal education could be rectified by the PBC through necessary changes to the PBCLER to introduce and promote practical legal education in a meaningful way. For instance, the PBC could adopt the system of practical legal education prevalent in the USA and modify existing frameworks keeping in view the realities on the ground.

5.3. CONTINUING LEGAL EDUCATION

Continuing legal education (CLE) is not mentioned or provided for in any regulatory framework, including the LPBCA, PLPBCR and PBCLER. Contrarily, CLE is mandatory in the USA, with every lawyer required to undergo a certain number of CLE hours. Similarly, in the United Kingdom, the four Inns of Court require practising barristers to undergo continuous training. The Law Society of England conducts such training for practising solicitors to fulfil these requirements. In Pakistan, the importance of CLE cannot be emphasised enough. As mentioned above, the country has an overall poor system of legal education. The implementation of mandatory CLE would likely compel lawyers to overcome the deficiencies caused by the sub-standard LLB and LLM programmes. Thus, CLE should serve as a catalyst to improve the legal profession in Pakistan.[100]

---

[98] As mentioned above, the latest curriculum for the LLB programme was approved in 2015. Curriculum for LLB (5 Years), Higher Education Commission, 2015.

[99] Curriculum for LLB (5 Years), Higher Education Commission, 2015.

[100] Z. Ranjah, 'Legal Education', *DAWN* (02.10.2015), http://www.dawn.com/news/1210297.

In addition, CLE could be offered online. For many lawyers, it is easier to attend online CLE courses from the comfort of their homes and offices instead of attending physical classes. Online CLE courses are already being offered in many developed countries, albeit typically with fewer internet connectivity and other infrastructural challenges than those outlined above for Pakistan generally.

6. CONCLUSION

The system of legal education in Pakistan is in dire need of reform. This reform can only occur if the PBC and lawyers alike: (1) acknowledge that reforms are needed; (2) are open to learning from the positive experiences of other countries; and (3) make a sincere and determined effort to introduce and implement the reforms. These amendments will not only improve the state of legal education and the legal profession but will also open the doors for online legal education, practical legal education and continuing legal education.

The PBC is the most important player when it comes to legal education. Over the years, the PBC has assumed this significant position by giving itself numerous powers, achieved by amending the legal education rules. However, assumption of power is one thing; the ability to wield it is another. Members of the PBC, who are practitioners, are unaware of the requirements and dynamics of legal academia. Being an influential lawyer does not mean that one is well acquainted with modern trends in legal education. Similarly, being a retired judge of a High Court or the Supreme Court, or being a retired District and Sessions Judge, having five years of judicial service, does not mean one is competent or equipped to lead a law faculty. Teaching on a part-time or visiting basis does not put a lawyer or judge on a par with legal academics who have devoted themselves to legal academia, extensively designed courses and programmes, taught, conducted research, and published work, and who are abreast of the developments in legal education across the globe.

The PBC should restrict itself to regulating the legal profession, as it is ill suited to regulating legal education. The regulation of legal education must be transferred to the hands of legal academics and the HEC.

PART II

AFRICA AND EUROPE

ONLINE LEGAL EDUCATION IN SEYCHELLES

Experiences of a Small Island State

Nyasha Noreen KATSENGA

1. INTRODUCTION

The information age has changed how people live and work.[1] It has revolutionised how the legal profession operates and how legal education is conducted. For lawyers, technology has made it easier to conduct legal research and communicate with clients,[2] especially those who may be in different time zones

[1] M. Hillyer 'How has technology changed – and changed us – in the past 20 years?', *World Economic Forum* (2020), https://www.weforum.org/agenda/2020/11/heres-how-technology-has-changed-and-changed-us-over-the-past-20-years/.

[2] R.H. Bresica, W. McCarthy, A. McDonald, K. Potts and C. Rivais, 'Embracing Disruption: How Technological Change in the Delivery of Legal Services Can Improve Access To Justice' (2015) 78 *Albany Law Review* 553.

and jurisdictions. Similarly, the courts' day-to-day business has been enhanced by technology; for instance, video-conferencing has made it easier, especially for vulnerable witnesses, to attend hearings.[3] Legal education has also been revolutionised by technology over the past few years, as degrees have become more accessible online.

In the wake of the COVID-19 pandemic, access to the internet and technology has proven to be more essential than before. Public health measures such as lockdowns have been put in place, mandating the physical closure of universities, law firms and courts. At the same time, teaching must continue and it is pertinent that access to justice is not unduly limited. In Seychelles, the first 21-day lockdown was announced on 6 April 2020,[4] which included the physical closure of the University of Seychelles (UniSey). In response to this, the university moved its teaching and learning to be conducted online. Towards the end of this 21-day period, the government of Seychelles announced that UniSey, among other education institutions, could physically re-open from 11 May 2020.[5] This presented an opportunity on the part of the university to employ a hybrid approach to legal education, which has been maintained to date.

How Seychelles has fared in leveraging the use of the internet and technology against the backdrop of a raging pandemic is what the present report will consider. The report starts off by highlighting the nature of the legal profession and legal education. What one will realise is that there is a low number of lawyers in Seychelles. Moreover, there are gaps in legal education at the university and within the post-admission sphere. Owing to these gaps, leveraging the internet and technology for online legal education remains to be developed further.

In addition to the above, the report gives an analysis of information and communications technology (ICT), focusing on accessibility of the internet and the computers necessary for online legal education. Generally, Seychelles is considered a leader in ICT development among its African counterparts. However, the cost of internet access remains high for the majority of households and affects the ability of students to access online legal education. Finally, the report concludes by furnishing the key findings.

---

3 See discussion on the case for South Africa, examples from Canada, Australia, the United Kingdom and the United States of America by N. Whitear-Nel, 'Video-link testimony in civil courts in South Africa: K v Transnet LTD t/a Portnet (KZD)' (2019) 136 *South African Law Journal* 245, 252–257.

4 See http://www.health.gov.sc/index.php/2020/04/08/covid-19-coronavirus-disease-prohibition-orders-and-health-and-travel-restrictions-update/.

5 'Address by President Danny Faure on the easing of restrictions related to the COVID-19 situation' (27 April 2020), https://www.statehouse.gov.sc/news/4826/address-by-president-danny-faure-on-the-easing-of-restrictions-related-to-the-covid-19-situation.

2. BACKGROUND ON SEYCHELLES

Seychelles is an African island state off the east coast of mainland Africa. It is a small island developing state (SIDS),[6] and also a high-income country.[7] Geopolitically, it is a member state of the Southern African Development Community (SADC) and the African Union (AU).[8] This background is important to note as the report will compare Seychelles to its diverse state counterparts and draw on some of its obligations stemming from the treaties and protocols applicable to it.

The island state is considered a micro-jurisdiction,[9] which inherited its mixed legal system from colonisation by the French and British. As Twomey notes, the legal tradition of Seychelles is 'complicated by the heritage of double colonisation' by France and Britain.[10] However, the legal system and jurisprudence are still evolving, shaped by Seychellois legal tradition.[11] What this means for the legal profession and legal education is that there remain influences from the past.[12] One example to cite in this regard is that access to legal education remains limited and skewed towards only the United Kingdom, France and Mauritius. Each of these issues will be explored in the sections to follow in this report.

3. THE LEGAL PROFESSION

3.1. COMPOSITION AND MAKE-UP OF THE PROFESSION

A legal professional with the right of audience before the courts is called an 'attorney-at-law'. There is no separation of the profession between attorneys and

6 'African Development Bank Country Note on Seychelles: 2018 African Economic Outlook', https://www.afdb.org/fileadmin/uploads/afdb/Documents/Generic-Documents/country_notes/Seychelles_country_note.pdf.

7 World Bank classification available at https://data.worldbank.org/country/SC.

8 I have highlighted this in the report in order to justify why some comparisons will be made to SADC or AU member states in the report. I have also highlighted Seychelles' SIDS status and high income classification for future reference where I will compare with other similar states. Seychelles is also part of other trade and economic groupings of the Common Market for Eastern and Southern Africa (COMESA) and the Indian Ocean Commission (IOC).

9 Reference to Seychelles as a 'micro-jurisdiction' can be found in M. Twomey, *Legal Metissage in a Micro-Jurisdiction: The Mixing of Common Law and Civil Law in Seychelles*, City Print, Wellington 2017; E.J. Techera, 'Protected Area Law in Seychelles: Legal Complexity in a Micro-jurisdiction' (2019) 34 *International Journal of Marine and Coastal Law* 698.

10 M. Twomey, *Legal Metissage in a Micro-Jurisdiction: The Mixing of Common Law and Civil Law in Seychelles*, City Print, Wellington 2017, p. 3.

11 Ibid., pp. 25–29.

12 Ibid., p. 5.

advocates (solicitors and barristers) as is the case for Mauritius.[13] To qualify as an attorney-at-law, a person must have one of the qualifications set out in section 5(1)(a) of the Legal Practitioners Act (LPA).

Broadly speaking, the drafters of the LPA were cognisant of the fact that in other jurisdictions the profession is separated into advocates and attorneys. Thus, the first three subparagraphs of section 5(1)(a) recognise those legal professionals who (i) have right of audience in courts within a Commonwealth jurisdiction; (ii) are attorneys and solicitors in Commonwealth jurisdictions; or (iii) all other legal professionals admitted to practice, while simultaneously 'having professional status equivalent to an attorney-at-law in Seychelles'.[14]

The fourth subparagraph recognises law graduates. The provision states that:

> 5. (1) A person shall not be admitted as an attorney-at-law –
>
> (a) unless he –
>
> ...
>
> (iv) *holds a degree in law*, of a level prescribed by the Minister, *awarded by an institution designated by the Minister* after consultation with the Chief Justice and the Bar Association of Seychelles *and* has *successfully completed such professional or vocational examination or training* as the Minister may after consultation with the Chief Justice and the Bar Association of Seychelles by regulations prescribed; or
>
> ...[15]

The Legal Practitioners (Qualification) Regulations of 1994 (the Qualification Regulations of 1994) further specify the acceptable degrees those obtained from a university or polytechnic in the United Kingdom, a state university in France or the University of Mauritius. There are two challenges with the LPA and the Qualification Regulations of 1994.

First, listing only institutions from Mauritius, United Kingdom and France is restrictive and exclusionary for those who have LLB qualifications from other jurisdictions. Although many lawyers have been educated in these three jurisdictions, globalisation has made access to other law schools possible.[16]

---

13 As provided by the Mauritian law. See section 3 of the Law Practitioners Act, Act 55 of 1984 as amended.

14 Section 5(1)(a)(i), (ii) and (iii) of the LPA.

15 Section 5(1)(a)(iv) of the LPA (emphasis added).

16 We must understand 'globalisation' as a multifaceted concept which is not limited to international trade, but rather including the interdependence of cultures and populations owing to unprecedented levels of 'technology, and flows of investment, people, and information' – see Peterson Institute for International Economics, at https://www.piie.com/microsites/globalization/what-is-globalization.

As such, students and their sponsors may choose to study in other jurisdictions based on considerations such as economic accessibility of law schools and cultural experiences, among other things.[17]

Second, and arguably, there are inconsistencies and gaps in the LPA with respect to the qualifications for admission as provided by section 5(a) of the LPA read with the Qualification Regulations of 1994. For those with professional standing and qualifications under sections 5(1)(a)(i), (ii) and (iii), commonwealth jurisdictions suffice. It is curious, however, that there are restrictions for LLB degree qualifications to only three jurisdictions.

One may assume that the rationale to limit institutions from which LLBs are acceptable is based on the nature of Seychelles' legal system. One may also assume that since Seychelles has no home-grown law school or faculty which offers a Seychelles LLB degree, the drafters of the LPA could only work with what was possible at the time. However, the LPA appears to maintain the notion of 'journeying to London for Legal Education'.[18] Moreover, it disadvantages other law graduates, the effect of which is exclusionary and, arguably, a colonial legacy.[19]

Another inconsistency which presents itself under section 5(a)(iv) of the LPA is that in addition to a law degree (from Mauritius, the United Kingdom or France), one must have 'successfully completed professional or vocational examination or training' prescribed by the Minister. To elaborate, professional or vocational exams that are acceptable for purposes of section 5(1)(a)(iv) are those set by the Examination Board established under section 20 of the LPA,

---

17 See generally G. Magbondé, 'How Sub-Saharan African Countries Students Choose Where to Study Abroad: The Case of Benin' (2021) 9 *Social Inclusion* 278.

18 See discussion on legal education during colonial times, undertaken by S. Manteaw, 'Legal Education in Africa: What Type of Lawyer Does Africa Need' (2007) 39 *McGeorge Law Review* 915. The colonial legacy in the case of Seychelles is that since attaining independence, there was no formal legal education offered until 2010, a year after the inception of the University of Seychelles. The status quo stems from how the British were notorious for not setting up law schools in their colonies, in comparison to the French in Francophone Africa. See W. Twining, 'Legal Education Within East Africa' (1966) 12 *International and Comparative Law Quarterly Supplementary Publication* 116. Despite setting up formal legal education under the University of Seychelles, this was still centred on English law through the University of London. It remains to be seen whether this colonial legacy of journeying to London will be done away with given the development of a new Bachelor of Laws which sets a different tone for legal education in Seychelles.

19 The exclusionary stance against the proliferation of lawyers during colonial times was to ensure no one challenged the colonial system. See W. Twining, 'Legal Education Within East Africa' (1966) 12 *International and Comparative Law Quarterly Supplementary Publication* 116.

the Council of Legal Education of Mauritius, the Council of Legal Education of England, and the Law Society of England.[20]

The Qualification Regulations of 1994 only recognise four examinations from three jurisdictions (Seychelles, Mauritius and England), which do not correspond to the three designated institutions for LLBs as provided by the same Regulations. This means that those who have studied in France and undertook professional exams in France are unfairly disadvantaged. While they may still undertake the exams set by the Exam Board under section 20 of the LPA, it is still a disadvantage to them compared to their counterparts who studied and wrote similar exams in Mauritius and United Kingdom.

An additional and final qualification which is recognised by the LPA is a curious provision, which reads:

> 5. (1) A person shall not be admitted as an attorney-at-law –
>
> (a) unless he –
>
> ...
>
> (v) has passed the final examination prescribed under this Act ...[21]

For law graduates who have been unable to use section 5(1)(a)(iv), they may arguably find recourse in section 5(1)(a)(v) highlighted above. However, this a contested provision.

Some have suggested that the list in section 5(1)(a) is conjunctive for (iv) and (v). It is assumed to be an 'error' on part of the draftsperson. This argument cannot hold, mainly because it would be a transgression against principles of legislative drafting to make a list that is both disjunctive and conjunctive in one legislative paragraph. The draftsperson is aware of this as a thumb rule. As such, the list in paragraph (a) can either be disjunctive or conjunctive. It is my submission that the 'or' between subparagraphs (iv) and (v) is not only well placed, but also gives unambiguous meaning to the legislative paragraph (a).

At this juncture, rules of interpretation will be useful in understanding section 5(1)(a)(v). Three rules of interpretation come to the fore: the literal rule, the golden rule and the mischief rule. It is pertinent to give an analysis of the legislative sentence of section 5(1)(a)(v) with other rules of interpretation.

The literal rule means words take their ordinary meaning. The ordinary meaning of the words in the legislative sentence of section 5(1)(a)(v) of the LPA is clear. A person qualifies for admission if he or she has passed the admission exams prescribed by the LPA. To support this interpretation, I draw in section 14

20 Legal Practitioners (Qualification) Regulations, Statutory Instrument No. 2 of 1995.

21 Section 5(1)(a)(v) of the LPA.

of the LPA as an intrinsic aid for interpretation of section 5(1)(a)(v), which reads (emphasis added):

> A person who meets *any of the qualifications specified in section 5(1)(a)* may, subject to the rules which may be prescribed by the Chief Justice, serve as a pupil in an approved chambers.[22]

Thus, the list in section 5(1)(a) is disjunctive and subparagraph (v) is a standalone provision which, in my view, gives law graduates from 'unrecognised universities' the opportunity to access the legal profession once they pass the admission exams. Other rules of interpretation are used where the literal rule gives a meaning which is absurd or repugnant.[23] Reading the legislative sentence of section 5(1)(a)(v), the meaning is neither absurd nor repugnant.

Another suggestion is that subparagraph (v) applies exclusively to articled clerks. The proponents of this support their view with the use of section 13A(1) of the LPA, which reads (emphasis added):

> Authorisation to provide legal advice
>
> 13A. (1) The Minister may, after consultation with and receiving written confirmation that *a person satisfies any of the requirement of section 5(1)(a)(i) to (iv)* from the Chief Justice, authorise the person to provide legal advice and assistance for a fee.

According to this school of thought, section 13A of the LPA distinguishes those with formal legal education and admission to practice from those who undertake articles of clerkship. Based on this, it is assumed that the intention of the legislature is to have section 5(1)(a)(v) apply exclusively to articled clerks. There remains no merit to this argument because if the intention was to apply the provision *exclusively* to articled clerks, the provision would have expressly said so. Therefore, section 5(1)(a)(v) is a clear standalone provision which allows both articled clerks and others who may have a law degree from an 'unrecognised' university, by passing exams set under the LPA.

It would be counterproductive for section 5(1)(a)(v) to be read restrictively and exclude other law graduates for two main reasons. First, the number of lawyers in Seychelles is very low compared to other micro-jurisdictions.[24]

---

22 Section 14 of the LPA (emphasis added). This too is an interesting provision because it appears to be making pupillage optional by the use of the word 'may' – yet in section 5(1)(b) of the LPA, pupillage is compulsory.

23 M. Sanson, *Statutory Interpretation*, 2nd edn, Oxford University Press, Oxford 2017, p. 10.

24 See generally M. Barr, 'Two Tribunals and an Appeal in Seychelles: Monitoring and enforcement of legal ethics in a small jurisdiction' (2020) 3 *Small Island States & Territories* 21. A comparison of Seychelles and other micro-jurisdictions is undertaken in section 3.2 of this report.

More needs to be done for graduates to enter the profession and serve Seychelles in all its different sectors and specialised areas of the law. Second, reading section 5(1)(a)(v) restrictively and thus restricting access to the profession conflicts with the efforts the government of Seychelles has been making for at least the past 20 years. In particular, the government has sponsored studies in Australia, Cyprus, Malaysia, Reunion and South Africa.[25] For those who self-sponsor, they too will be unfairly disadvantaged if section 5(1)(a)(v) is read restrictively. It serves no purpose to restrict the entry of law graduates who have already proven their academic competencies, especially against the backdrop of a per capita figure of 0.5 lawyers per 1,000 people.

The push-back against a generous interpretation of section 5(1)(a)(v) of the LPA may include the fear that anyone can therefore become an attorney. However, this position is not only misleading but also unfounded. Admission exams remain technical and heavily rooted in the academic discipline of law, and can be passed only by those with a background knowledge in the law.[26] Assuming someone finds the law enthralling, it would not be unusual for them to undergo self-study and attempt the admission examinations. Where they are successful, they prove their competence to be admitted and must be admitted. In fact, jurisdictions such as England are good examples to cite in this regard: there, the path to becoming a barrister does not require a law degree, although non-law degrees must be accompanied by a law conversion course called the Graduate Diploma in Law.[27]

The analysis undertaken of section 5(1)(a)(v) as a recourse for other graduates is purely academic and has not been tested in the judicial system of Seychelles. Assuming there are attorneys whose qualifications are from unrecognised universities, then a few interrelated things are worth noting. Firstly, this presupposes that the Supreme Court relied on section 5(1)(a)(v) to accommodate these graduates. Secondly, if the Court has relied on the same, the precedent has been set and other graduates have this avenue available to them. Finally, if the Supreme Court has not relied on section 5(1)(a)(v) to accommodate said graduates, then the admission had no legal basis.

3.2. GATEKEEPING IN THE PROFESSION

The main gatekeeper of the legal profession is the Minister responsible for legal affairs, and this is based on what the LPA states in respect to admission under

---

25 Statistics from the Agency for National Human Resource Development on file with the author.

26 It is worth noting that pass rates for admission exams over the years has ranged between 28% and 64%, all of which were candidates holding law degrees.

27 Bar Standard Board 'Becoming a barrister: an overview' updated 15 July 2021, https://www.barstandardsboard.org.uk/training-qualification/becoming-a-barrister.html.

section 5(a). Interestingly, Seychelles does not have a designated Minister of Legal Affairs or even a Ministry with such a portfolio. This has been the status quo since independence from the British in 1976. However, the portfolio has traditionally fallen under the Office of the President or Vice President,[28] which is why some parts of the LPA refer to the President.[29]

The Minister does not act unilaterally and on a whim on matters of accessing the profession. Section 5(a) of the LPA provides that the Minister must consult with the Chief Justice and the Bar Association of Seychelles (BAS) to determine the qualifications for admission. Therefore, the Chief Justice and BAS are two additional gatekeepers of the legal profession. The Chief Justice is responsible for overseeing pupillage[30] and admission of qualified persons into the practice of law.[31] BAS is a registered association and is often referenced for consultative purposes within the LPA. However, attorneys-at-law need not register with BAS and nor does BAS undertake the role of watchdog over its members or attorneys at large. Thus, the legal profession in Seychelles does not self-regulate.[32] One will note that disciplinary actions against attorneys are lodged with the Chief Justice,[33] and therein the Supreme Court has an administrative function of supervising the profession.

It is my submission that the fourth gatekeeper of the profession is the LPA itself. It operates as a 'textual gatekeeper' to the profession because of its restrictive approach towards admission for law graduates, as analysed in section 3.1 of this report. This is mainly in respect to qualifications.

In addition to the above, the LPA makes it compulsory to undertake pupillage within approved chambers. Yet there are graduates who are unable to access chambers for pupillage because there are a limited number of approved chambers. The LPA makes no allowances for those circumstances in order for graduates to progress towards admission and earn a livelihood as legal professionals. Jurisdictions such as Mauritius do make accommodations for such instances where pupillage may be difficult to secure. The law in Mauritius provides that the Council for Legal Education may allow a person to undergo another form of training instead of pupillage where there are no facilities to accommodate a pupil.[34]

---

28 Article 64(3A) of the Constitution of Seychelles.

29 For example, section 20 of the LPA.

30 Section 17 of the LPA.

31 Section 3 of the LPA.

32 This status quo may be set to change within the coming few years through the establishing of a Bar Council geared towards self-regulation of the profession. See Speech by Chief Justice Rony Govinden on the occasion of Re-opening of the Courts in Seychelles on 10 January 2022, p. 14, http://www.judiciary.sc/wp-content/uploads/2022/01/cj-speech-2022-court-reopening.pdf.

33 Legal Practitioners (Disciplinary Measures and Reinstatement) Rules 1995.

34 Section 5A(5) of the Law Practice Act of Mauritius.

With the LPA grappling with these challenges, it is unsurprising that the number of attorneys-at-law is arguably low. Whether this number is 'low' or adequate must be assessed by factoring in the size of Seychelles and comparing this with other micro-jurisdictions. The number of attorneys licensed to practise stands at 59,[35] serving a population of approximately 98,000. This means the number of lawyers per capita is 0.5 lawyers per 1,000 people. Andorra has approximately 200 practising lawyers[36] for a population of 77,265,[37] which makes the per capita figure 2.5 lawyers per 1,000 people. Antigua and Barbuda has approximately 136 practising lawyers[38] for a population of 97,928,[39] hence a per capita number of 1.3 lawyers per 1,000 people. Thus, in comparison to other micro-jurisdictions with populations of less than 100,000 people, the number of lawyers in Seychelles is worryingly low.

4. ACCESS TO LEGAL EDUCATION AND TRAINING OF LAWYERS

One may be inclined to investigate why Seychelles has a low number of practising lawyers compared to other micro-jurisdictions. At face value, it may seem as though the profession is protectionist, a characteristic which has been previously attributed to the legal profession[40] and thus accounts for the low number of practising attorneys in Seychelles. However, there is no evidence to suggest that there is protectionism in the profession. In fact, the LPA does not limit admission as an attorney based on nationality or residency. There are other reasons which may be worthwhile to explore: (1) access to legal education; (2) training for admission exams; and (3) the financial muscle to fund the process of qualifying, to name a few. These are explored next. What is also explored below is the presence of continuing legal education, which in itself forms part of legal education for lawyers.

---

35 Licensed lawyers as provided by the Judiciary of Seychelles, https://www.judiciary.sc/legal-practitioners/licensed-lawyers/.

36 The Andorran Bar Association, https://www.cada.ad/index.php?option=com_cada&view=colegiats&task=find&Itemid=318&name=&surname=&town=&all=1.

37 World Bank 2020 estimates, available at https://data.worldbank.org/indicator/SP.POP.TOTL?locations=AD.

38 As listed by the Intellectual Property and Commerce Office, Ministry of Legal Affairs, available at https://abipco.gov.ag/lawyers/. The number may be more than 136, as this estimate takes into account the law firms listed.

39 World Bank 2020 estimates, available at https://data.worldbank.org/indicator/SP.POP.TOTL?locations=AG.

40 B.K. Smith, 'Protecting the Home Turf: National Bar Associations and the Foreign Lawyer' (2014) 21 *Indiana Journal of Global Legal Studies* 670.

4.1. FORMAL LEGAL EDUCATION AT THE UNIVERSITY OF SEYCHELLES

The University of Seychelles (UniSey) began operating in 2009 as a private university, and is a member of the Southern African Regional Universities Association.[41] Its funding comes mainly from tuition fees, research grants and rental income. There is, however, the potential for further government funding since UniSey is the only university in Seychelles and bears a name that positions it as a state university.

A year after its inception, UniSey opened its doors to a group of law students in partnership with the University of London (UOL). The purpose of the partnership was to ensure that legal education was available in Seychelles, making up part of the value chain of training legal professionals. Approximately 68 law students have graduated from the programme since 2013, with UOL as the degree-awarding institution. With this qualification, the graduates satisfy part of section 5(1)(a)(iv) of the LPA.

The UOL LLB is based on English common law. This means graduates complete the programme with a fraction of the knowledge of the legal system they are expected to operate in. As a result, the Office of the Chief Justice and UniSey undertook the teaching of the Bar Vocational Course (BVC),[42] in order to prepare students to sit admission exams as provided for by the law. The BVC was taught under the auspices of UniSey.

On the part of UniSey, the BVC was a step in a positive direction for two main reasons. First, it put UniSey on an upward trajectory in terms of legal education. Students would graduate after three years of studying for the LLB, then easily enrol for the BVC to prepare for the admission exams. Second, the BVC addressed a gap in legal education that had been apparent over the years: previously, law graduates had to prepare on their own, perhaps with little or no guidance.

Notwithstanding the availability of the legal education opportunities highlighted above, legal education is arguably costly in Seychelles. The tuition fees for the UOL LLB stand at approximately SCR 150,000 per year. In comparison with other LLB degree programmes in the SADC region, UniSey/UOL law students pay close to two or three times more per year. By contrast, in South Africa,[43] for example, the cost of formal legal education per annum is

---

41 See https://sarua.africa/sarua-members/.

42 M. Twomey, *Legal Metissage in a Micro-Jurisdiction: The Mixing of Common Law and Civil Law in Seychelles*, City Print, Wellington 2017, pp. 31–32.

43 Reference made to South Africa is based on the fact that South African academic institutes rank high in Africa – seven academic institutes in the top 10 of the top 200 universities are South African universities. See Uni Rank, Top 200 Universities in Africa – 2020 Rankings, available at https://www.4icu.org/top-universities-africa/. Other research points to nine academic

SCR 37,000–56,900.[44] In Mauritius, tuition fees for a law degree are approximately SCR 88,024 per annum at University of Mauritius.[45] While the government sponsors a good number of students to study at UniSey,[46] legal education remains expensive in comparison to Seychelles' counterparts in the SADC region.

In addition to tuition fees for an LLB degree, law graduates aspiring to have audience before the Seychelles courts must undertake the BVC, as required by section 5(1)(a)(iv). Until recently, the BVC cost approximately SCR 178,000. This is arguably exorbitant for new graduates who are unemployed or come from low-income households. The price acts as a deterrent to admission because the BVC is essential in order to perform better in the admission exams.

Some law graduates who cannot afford the BVC often undertake self-study and attempt the admission exams as a practice. This may be a more economically friendly option because the exam fee is only SCR 5,000. If a graduate attempts the admission exams three times before passing, they spend SCR 15,000 – 11 times less than what they would have spent if they had taken the BVC. While they save significantly in terms of cost, they miss out on time because the admission exams are offered only once a year. By the time a non-affording graduate passes these exams after several attempts, their affording counterparts will have long since finished the exams and will be undertaking pupillage. This presents another layer of difficulty of access to the profession by non-affording graduates.

As of 2021, the BVC has moved to be taught within the Supreme Court of Seychelles. Simultaneously, it has significantly reduced its cost, by over 50%. Notwithstanding this, it remains expensive because the alternative, which is to attempt admission exams several times, will still be cheaper.

Pass rates of admission exams have ranged from 28% to 64% between 2014 and 2020.[47] In 2015, the pass rate was recorded as 100% because only one candidate sat the exams, compared to other years, which have had six to 17 candidates per sitting. These pass rates may be taken into consideration to account for the low number of attorneys-at-law in Seychelles.

---

institutes in the top 13 African universities being from South Africa, see QS World University Rankings 2020 – Top Universities in Africa, available at https://www.topuniversities.com/university-rankings-articles/world-university-rankings/top-universities-africa.

44 Business Tech, 'University fees 2019: how much it costs to study in South Africa' (January 2019), https://businesstech.co.za/news/finance/293800/university-fees-2019-how-much-it-costs-to-study-in-south-africa/.

45 See tuition fees as provided by Admissions Office at University of Mauritius, available at https://www.uom.ac.mu/images/FILES/Admissions/2019/Undergraduate/Fees/FeePaying.pdf. For some first-year students, the fees are close to four times less. See structure of fees as provided by Admissions Office at University of Mauritius, available at https://www.uom.ac.mu/images/FILES/Admissions/2019/Undergraduate/Fees/FTPTfees.pdf.

46 Statistics provided by the School of Advanced Level Studies and on file with the author.

47 Statistics from the Registry of the Supreme Court and on file with the author.

At the end of the 2019/20 academic year, the partnership between UniSey and UOL ended.[48] With these developments, and cognisant of the need to continue with formal legal education, UniSey consulted with the Office of the Chief Justice and the leadership of BAS on the future of legal education. Both offices were of the view that legal education in Seychelles could take many forms, including UniSey developing a local LLB degree programme.

Following these consultations, UniSey embarked on developing an LLB degree programme in July 2020, and completed the development process in July 2021. In August 2021, UniSey hosted a virtual Colloquy on Legal Education where the new LLB programme was presented to key stakeholders and the legal profession for their input. It was a successful Colloquy as it garnered the necessary support from the legal profession and stakeholders. Before the end of 2021, UniSey expects to have the programme validated by the SQA. This means they may start officially offering the programme in 2022 and, presumably, change the discourse about legal education in Seychelles.

A new LLB degree based on Seychelles substantive law means that the graduates are better paced to write admission exams even without further training under the BVC.[49] Moreover, graduates are set to be equipped with ethics and professional conduct, something lacking in the current structure, yet pertinent to provide for.[50] The new LLB also presents an opportunity to take a hybrid approach to legal education between face-to-face teaching and online lectures. This is especially opportune for UniSey, given that the flexibility to control the modes of teaching and the curriculum has been limited because the LLB, currently on offer under a sunset clause, is coordinated by UOL. Furthermore, it provides an opportunity to revisit the cost of legal education, which is arguably a deterrent to accessing the profession.

4.2. FORMAL LEGAL EDUCATION OUTSIDE THE UNIVERSITY OF SEYCHELLES

Post-independence, legal education in Seychelles has traditionally been accessible outside of Seychelles. This is because there was no state or national university until 2009, nor was there any form of law school to train lawyers. The vast majority of Seychellois lawyers have been trained in the UK and Mauritius, while others have trained in France. This explains why the LPA recognises law degrees from institutions in these countries.

---

48 Although the partnership ended, previously enrolled students continue under the auspices of the previous agreement.

49 This is because the admission exams in Seychelles are substantive as opposed to being geared towards practical training.

50 See section 4.3 on ethics among lawyers in Seychelles.

With no formal legal education training in Seychelles, it meant that those families or individuals who have the financial means to pay for tuition in Mauritius, the UK or France for their adult children are able to do so. The percentage of the population that can perform this out-of-pocket sponsoring for overseas learning may be limited to high-income households. This may explain the low number of admitted lawyers in Seychelles.

Fortunately, the government of Seychelles has an ongoing scholarship scheme to improve access to higher education and increase workforces in national priority areas.[51] The scheme bodes well for meeting the constitutional obligation to realise the right to education envisaged under Article 33 of the Constitution of Seychelles. This improves access to legal education, especially in view of the fundamental principle of equal access to tertiary education.[52] Between 2000 and 2020, the government of Seychelles sponsored approximately 78 students to study law in eight countries, i.e. Australia, Cyprus, France, Malaysia, Mauritius, Reunion, South Africa and the UK.[53]

It is worth noting that Advanced Level (A-Level) education in Seychelles offered formal legal education for high school students between 2013 and 2018. Law was offered as a subject by the School of Advanced Level Studies (SALS), under the auspices of Cambridge Assessment International Education. Pass rates in these years ranged from 58% to 80%.[54]

However, since the 2019/20 academic year, law as a subject was discontinued. Three reasons were given by SALS. First, law is not considered to be one of the 10 facilitating subjects[55] that most international universities consider strongly for admission. As such, a student does not have to study A-Level law to gain admission to study at most universities. Second, there is the challenge of teaching staff. In particular, SALS found it difficult to find, attract, recruit and retain A-Level law instructors. Third, law is considered a universally difficult subject for students at A-Level. This is especially the case if students do not have a secondary school background knowledge of law at IGCSE or O-Level.

---

51 Agency for National Human Resource Development (ANHRD) 'The Government of Seychelles Scholarship Scheme' (2013), https://www.anhrd.gov.sc/uploads/downloads/GoSScholarship-Scheme-Booklet-sept2014.pdf. See also general information from Government of Seychelles, available at https://www.egov.sc/MyCitizen/TertiaryEdu.aspx.

52 ANHRD, 'The Government of Seychelles Scholarship Scheme' (2013), https://www.anhrd.gov.sc/uploads/downloads/GoSScholarship-Scheme-Booklet-sept2014.pdf.

53 This excludes those who have been sponsored to study at the University of Seychelles since its inception in 2009.

54 Statistics provided by the School of Advanced Level Studies and on file with the author.

55 Examples of facilitating subjects in this regard are: biology, chemistry, computer science, physics, mathematics, geography, history, French, English language and literature in English.

4.3. CONTINUING LEGAL EDUCATION

Continuing legal education (CLE) is a novelty which traces its roots to the US as early as 1916. The Bar Associations of New York, Cleveland, Minnesota and Wisconsin were among the first to offer CLE, and by 1937 the American Bar Association (ABA) had realised the importance of CLE.[56] At the ABA's National Conference on Continuing Legal Education in 1959, it was the general sentiment expressed there that:

> lawyers today are confronted with problems of vast and increasing complexity. No law school education can be expected to deal with all of these problems. A practicing lawyer has an obligation to continue his education throughout his professional life … The organized bar has the primary obligation to make this continuing legal education available to the members of the profession.[57]

The ABA notes the importance of lifelong learning, which is what CLE is geared to do. Most CLEs focus on a wide range of substantive and specialised areas of the law. This includes areas and skills that need to be emphasised among legal practitioners, such as legal drafting and ethics and professional conduct.

Through these trainings, legal practitioners are prepared to be competent, knowledgeable and capable to serve the requirements of the society.[58] In the South African Legal Practice Act, CLE on practice management is compulsory for those who wish to practise either alone or in partnership or as a director of a law firm.[59] Besides this, there are other areas of CLE, such as Drafting Legal Skills for Contracts, Accounts Management, Cyber Law and Electronic Transactions, among other things, offered as CLE within the Law Society of South Africa.[60] The practice of CLE acknowledges that an LLB cannot equip law graduates with all the skills needed to sustain them throughout their long careers ahead.

Notwithstanding the importance of CLE, it remains a neglected area of legal education in Seychelles. It is not referenced in the LPA nor has it made up part of customary legal tradition. Yet it is becoming more relevant in an ever-changing legal landscape since independence in 1976. An immediate example to cite in this regard is the new Civil Code, which came into force in July 2021. Since then, the legal profession has not offered training on it to keep abreast of new trends.

---

56 P. Sharma, 'Continuing Legal Education: Rethinking Professional Ethics and Responsibility in India' (2018) 5 *Asian Journal of Legal Education* 154.

57 Final Statement of the National Conference on Continuing Legal Education of the Bar (1959) *American Bar Association Journal* 139.

58 P. Sharma, 'Continuing Legal Education: Rethinking Professional Ethics and Responsibility in India' (2018) 5 *Asian Journal of Legal Education* 161.

59 Section 84(1) of the Legal Practice Act No. 28 of 2014.

60 See Training Calendar by Law Society South Africa, available at https://www.lssalead.org.za/training-calendar/.

In contrast, the Supreme Court of Seychelles has planned its own training on the new Civil Code. Through its Judicial College, the Supreme Court of Seychelles conducts CLE for judges in myriad areas of the law, including those related to technology, which supports the technological modernisation of the courts.[61] Another good example to cite with respect to CLE is the practice of South African law faculties and the Law Society. They have and continue to train legal practitioners on the Protection of Personal Information Act, which came into force in July 2021. The legal profession in Seychelles, however, lags behind in CLE, and must consider the practice of the Supreme Court of Seychelles and South Africa as worthwhile to emulate.

Ethics and professional conduct is another neglected yet pertinent area for CLE in Seychelles. As it stands, serious gaps are apparent, considering that neither the admission exams nor the UOL LLB at UniSey examine ethics and professional conduct. Recently, the Chief Justice of Seychelles voiced his concerns on the number of cases of misconduct against lawyers.[62] In a similar vein, Barr avers that there seems to be a normalisation of certain misconduct within the profession.[63] Barr further notes the need for the profession to change tolerant attitudes towards misconduct and ensure there is adequate enforcement of ethical standards.[64] Legal education can be used as a tool to respond to some of these challenges, through making CLE on ethics and professional conduct compulsory for all attorneys-at-law.

5. ICT IN SEYCHELLES

17 May is World Telecommunication and Information Society Day, which Seychelles marked with a message from the Vice President, Mr Ahmed Afif. The Vice President highlighted how COVID-19 has prepared the government, businesses and schools to adapt to new technologies, particularly to remain resilient in these times. The education system in Seychelles had to move online, and there has been an increase in the development of software for businesses and

---

61 Judiciary of Seychelles, '2020–2021 Annual Report', p. 50, http://www.judiciary.sc/wp-content/uploads/2022/01/judiciary-annual-report-2021.pdf. See also Speech by Chief Justice Rony Govinden on the occasion of Re-opening of Courts in Seychelles on 10 January 2022, p. 11, http://www.judiciary.sc/wp-content/uploads/2022/01/cj-speech-2022-court-reopening.pdf p. 11.

62 Speech by Chief Justice Rony Govinden on the occasion of Re-opening of Courts in Seychelles on 10 January 2022, p. 14, http://www.judiciary.sc/wp-content/uploads/2022/01/cj-speech-2022-court-reopening.pdf. See also Judiciary of Seychelles, 'Strategic Plan of 2021–2025', pp. 10–11.

63 M. Barr, 'Two Tribunals and an Appeal in Seychelles: Monitoring and enforcement of legal ethics in a small jurisdiction' (2020) 3 *Small States & Territories* 38.

64 Ibid., p. 39.

applications geared to assist healthcare professionals during these unprecedented times.[65]

Generally, Seychelles has been a leader in ICT development in Africa.[66] In 2017, it ranked second in Africa according to the ICT Development Index.[67] The Index considers three main factors: ICT access, ICT use, and ICT skills.[68] Access to the internet has improved over the years. In 2017, the World Bank estimated that approximately 58% of the population has access to the internet. The statistics have since improved, with a high internet penetration estimated to be over 70%.[69] Moreover, Seychelles is considered to have the highest mobile telephone penetration in Africa at an estimated 94%.[70] Leveraging its ICT development, Seychelles considers ICT as one of key sectors for investments.[71]

Internet service providers in Seychelles have responded well to the COVID-19 pandemic and subsequent demand for internet connectivity, especially among university students. Of note is that network providers have been providing extra data at no extra cost to their customers.[72] Despite these significant strides in access to the internet, Seychelles remains hobbled by the high cost compared to other African countries.[73] The high cost of internet access limits its potential for digital transformation.[74] Moreover, slow internet connectivity remains a problem.[75] These challenges pose a threat to legal education moving online and it remains to be seen how this will be remedied in future.

---

65 Message from the Vice President of the Republic of Seychelles, https://www.ict.gov.sc/documents/2021/WTISD_2021_VP_message.pdf.

66 International Telecommunication Union (ITU), 'Seychelles leads Africa in ICT development', *Country Focus by ITU News* (May 2010), https://www.itu.int/net/itunews/issues/2010/04/pdf/201004_43.pdf.

67 ICT Development Index 2017, Regional Rankings, available at https://www.itu.int/net4/ITU-D/idi/2017/index.html#idi2017byregion-tab.

68 See generally S. Teltscher, 'ICT Development Index', Presented at the ITU Regional Forum and Training Workshop on Telecommunication/ICT Indicators: Measuring the Information Society and ITU-ASEAN Meeting on Establishing National ICT Statistics Portals and Measuring ASEAN ICT targets (October 2014), https://silo.tips/download/ict-development-index-idi.

69 J. Johnson, 'Internet penetration in Africa, by country', *Statista* (2021), https://www.statista.com/statistics/1124283/internet-penetration-in-africa-by-country/.

70 ITU, 'Measuring the Information Society Report Volume 2: ICT Country Profiles' (2018), p. 160.

71 Seychelles Investment Board, https://investinseychelles.com/key-sectors/ict.

72 Message from the Vice President of the Republic of Seychelles, https://www.ict.gov.sc/documents/2021/WTISD_2021_VP_message.pdf.

73 J. Faria, 'Average price for mobile data in select African countries 2020', *Statista* (2021), https://www.statista.com/statistics/1180939/average-price-for-mobile-data-in-africa/. See also Message from the Vice President of the Republic of Seychelles, https://www.ict.gov.sc/documents/2021/WTISD_2021_VP_message.pdf.

74 Message from the Vice President of the Republic of Seychelles, https://www.ict.gov.sc/documents/2021/WTISD_2021_VP_message.pdf.

75 Ibid.

6. SEYCHELLES' MOVE TO ONLINE LEGAL EDUCATION

6.1. PRE-COVID-19 ACHIEVEMENTS

Generally, lectures and seminars for law subjects have been conducted physically on campus since the UOL LLB began to be offered at UniSey in 2010. Students did however have access to a virtual learning platform from UOL where they could access study materials such as module guides, past exam papers and a library for accessing textbooks and journals.

Similarly, the BVC has conducted its lectures and seminars physically and has made use of e-mails and Google Drive to share additional study materials since its inception in 2013. Some of the study materials essential for the BVC and admission exams, such as judgments, legislation and bills, are available via the Seychelles Legal Information Institute (SeyLII), established in 2012.[76] However, the BVC's online presence is low, which makes accessing any information on the programme difficult. In this way, the BVC has not leveraged the use of the internet and virtual platforms to share information regarding admission into the programme, the structure of the programme, or teaching and learning.

Infrastructure-wise, UniSey has provided access to the internet on campus. This means that students are able to access study materials virtually and conduct research for their studies. However, there are no computer labs to cater for students who may not have laptops or tablets.

Important to note is the use of social media by UniSey. There is a LinkedIn account, a Facebook page and a Twitter account for the university. These platforms provide a complementary service to online education in general, by offering information on registration for returning students, on applying to UniSey, and on short courses and seminars that may be running on specific thematic areas.

6.2. RESPONSES TO COVID-19: ACHIEVEMENTS AND CHALLENGES

In response to government public health measures – either the closure of academic institutions or the full lockdown announced on 6 April 2020 – UniSey moved to fully online teaching and operations of the university. Lectures and seminars were conducted virtually on Microsoft Teams and teaching staff were supported by being given an internet allowance. For the BVC, however, lectures were halted, as no similar provisions made to accommodate the public health

76 https://seylii.org/content/about-seylii.

measures. Teaching and learning only resumed when lockdown measures were relaxed. In this regard, the BVC lagged behind in comparison to the LLB at UniSey.

In 2020 and 2021, exams for the UOL LLB were changed from physical attendance in exam rooms to online. Moreover, the exams reduced the number of questions to be answered in each exam from four to two for the 2020 exams, and then an increase from two to three for the 2021 exams. When this was communicated, the mock exams at UniSey had to assimilate. In contrast, attorney admission exams remained in the traditional form of physical presence and handwritten scripts, albeit being postponed owing to lockdown measures.

Academic integrity had to be maintained during these transitions. Thus, the UniSey Assessment Policy Regulations recommended the use of Turnitin to check for plagiarism. This also assisted in the way lecturers provided further support for effective academic writing to those students who were struggling.

There are three main challenges for online legal education in Seychelles. First, the extent to which lecturers can adjust the syllabus and assessment modes is severely limited. This is mainly because the LLB programme currently taught at UniSey is the UOL one, coordinated and adjusted by UOL. Thus, adjustments of marking schemes, pass rates and syllabi were beyond the control of UniSey teaching staff.

The second challenge of moving to online legal education is the high cost of internet access. This meant that lecturers and students had to reduce their time on virtual lectures in order to save data. While lecturers were given an internet allowance, students were not provided with the same by the university or through government safety nets.

It is worthwhile to note that time is an important resource in legal education. Adequate time to teach is essential. During face-to-face lectures, there was an opportunity for in-class exercises or reading, summarising and analysing cases, among other teaching and learning techniques. However, where time on virtual lectures had to be reduced because of the high cost of internet access, the direct consequence was that less content in a module was covered or that it was rushed through. Fortunately for students, UOL also reduced the number of questions to be answered in exams, as indicated earlier, and simultaneously increased the length of time available for the exam. As such, what lecturers could cover in the limited time did end up being sufficient for students to be well prepared for the exams.

The third challenge, which is closely related to the second, is slow internet connectivity. Because of this, attendance at lectures tends to be low and lectures inconsistently taught on different days of the week. Lecturers had to reschedule lectures for another day where bandwidth would permit better connectivity.

7. CONCLUSION

There is room for improvement in the shift towards online legal education in Seychelles. UniSey responded well to the public health measures when it shifted its operations to online, including teaching and learning. However, given that UOL is the examining institution, there is not much control over changes in syllabi on the part of UniSey.

With a new LLB on the horizon for UniSey, it offers an opportunity to consider moving part of the teaching and learning online. There is scope to implement this in a way that is sustainable and at the same time maintains the quality expected in legal education. For the BVC, moving to online teaching remains an approach to be considered for future use. Lockdown measures need not halt teaching and learning. Similarly, admission exams should also consider moving online and keeping up with technological advancements. The neglected area of CLE must take its place within Seychelles' legal education, and brought in line with international and regional practices in this regard. In taking its place within legal education, CLE in Seychelles must also leverage the use of the internet and technology. To seamlessly implement these suggestions, the challenge of the high cost of internet access and slow connectivity need to be addressed by both the public and private sectors.

ONLINE LEGAL EDUCATION IN CROATIA

Convenient Responses to the Challenge of Digitalisation?

Mirela Župan

1. ROOTS AND DEVELOPMENT OF LEGAL EDUCATION IN CROATIA

The Republic of Croatia is a country situated in Central and Southeast Europe. It covers an area of 56,594 square kilometres with a population of 3,871,833.[1] The country was founded in the seventh century and had various regimes and communions (different forms of state, federation, etc) in the past. A modern sovereign state was established in 1991 as a parliamentary republic. Croatia is a member of the European Union, the United Nations, the Council of Europe, NATO and the World Trade Organization.

Legal education is one of the oldest areas of higher education (HE) with permanent continuity in Croatia. The first legal studies were conducted at the beginning of the 14th century.[2] By the middle of the 18th century, the roots of legal education were laid down by the Habsburgs.[3] Legal education in Zagreb was reformed together with the educational system in the Habsburg Monarchy and maintained its activity in various legal systems dictated by the laws and state policy on HE. In the second half of the 20th century, study programmes in law were also established in three major university centres in Croatia, i.e. Split (1961), Rijeka (1973) and Osijek (1975). These three state law schools provide legal education in Croatia to this day.[4]

Legal education in Croatia has undergone several substantial changes over the last decades, closely related to general reforms in HE and changes in the

---

1 Croatian Bureau of Statistics, 'The final results of the 2021 census', https://dzs.gov.hr/vijesti/objavljeni-konacni-rezultati-popisa-2021/1270.

2 The area of Zadar and Dubrovnik, where the first legal studies were conducted. I. Bilić, 'Neki aspekti razvoja studija prava u Hrvatskoj' (2001) 38 *Zbornik radova Pravnog fakulteta u Splitu* 19, 19–20.

3 Established first in Varaždin, while Queen Maria Theresa issued a decree in 1776 founding the Faculty of Law (Facultas iuridica) in Zagreb. The Faculty of Law later transformed into the Royal Academy of Legal Science (*Regia academia iuris*), and then to the Faculty of Legal and Administrative Sciences established under the Royal University of Franz Joseph I in 1874. D. Čepulo, 'Razvoj pravne izobrazbe i pravne znanosti u Hrvatskoj do 1776. godine i Pravni fakultet u Zagrebu od osnivanja 1776.-1918. godine' in *Pravni fakultet u Zagrebu 1776.-1996*, Pravni fakultet u Zagrebu, 1996, pp. 51–93.

4 University of Zagreb www.pravo.hr; University of Split www.pravst.hr; University of Rijeka www.pravri.hr; Josip Juraj Strossmayer University of Osijek www.pravos.hr.

Croatian legal system. It is noteworthy that the contemporary legal profession evolved in the region after World War II, when Croatia was part of the Socialist Federal Republic of Yugoslavia. With the proclamation of Croatian independence in 1991, the legal system was transformed into a parliamentary democracy founded on the three branches of government principle. This radical systemic legal transformation required significant alterations to study programmes in law. In parallel, legal studies shared the fate of the Croatian HE reforms. The most substantive change occurred in the early 2000s, with the introduction of the Bologna system. The Bologna reform refocused Croatian HE towards the standards of Western and Central European countries. This was further facilitated by the approximation to European Union law and comprehensive legal reform undertaken between 2004 and 2013 when Croatia gained full EU membership. The state of legal education in Croatia is currently dictated by the overall national HE policy, influenced by EU educational standards and imperatives.

1.1. GATEKEEPERS TO THE LEGAL PROFESSION

1.1.1. Universities

Legal HE in Croatia is offered at four state universities through similar study programmes.[5] Students attend integrated undergraduate and graduate study programmes in law (an integrated bachelor's and master's degree) for a total of five years. After fulfilling all study obligations and acquiring 300 ECTS (European Credit Transfer System) credits, a student is awarded a Master of Laws (mag. iur.). Although the curricula at these four law schools differ slightly, this does not affect the general (non-specialised) Master of Laws degree. The study programmes contain compulsory core courses, with varying lists of elective courses. As students are provided with both theoretical and practical knowledge and skills, the programme meets the requirements of the modern legal profession. The programme learning outcomes are aligned with level 7 of the national and European Qualifications Framework.[6]

Law school is the first choice for about 10% of applicants, who on average attain strong high-school educational results.[7] The total number of students

---

5 In terms of professional studies, all Croatian law schools offer an Undergraduate Professional Study Programme in Administration Studies. It is a three-year study programme for personnel qualifying to work in state administration, regional and local self-government, public services, etc. The title awarded upon completion of the study programme is Professional Bachelor of Public Administration (bacc. admin. publ.).

6 https://europa.eu/europass/en/european-qualifications-framework-eqf.

7 Agency for Science and Higher Education, https://www.studij.hr/prijave-po-znanstvenim-podrucjima.

enrolling in law schools is determined by the state quota. The total number of law students in Croatia has fluctuated slightly in the previous decades, ranging from 10,845 in the academic year 2004/05 to 11,668 in 2014/15 and 9,053 in 2019/20.[8] However, the number of graduates has tended to be rather low in recent decades, i.e. about 900 students per year.

Legal education can be continued with specialisation at the postgraduate level, i.e. by enrolling in the Postgraduate Specialist Study Programme in Law or the Postgraduate Doctoral Study Programme in Law.[9] Law schools also offer lifelong learning programmes on various topics.[10]

HE in Croatia is provided by both public and private universities. Although the number of accredited private universities is increasing, they are yet to offer a study programme in law. The four universities offering law are fully funded by the state. Each law school receives state funding, but can generate its own market revenue through tuition fees for students ineligible for state funding, postgraduate and PhD programmes, lifelong learning programmes, and other similar market initiatives. No revenue is derived from foreign students as existing law programmes are only offered and taught in Croatian.[11]

1.1.2. Legal Profession and the Market

Professional careers can be pursued in a plethora of directions, grouped into three categories. Law graduates work in the judiciary, which includes courts, state attorney's offices, the bar association, and notaries public. Graduate lawyers can choose a career path in public administration, which includes state administration, local and regional self-government units and work in the public services sector, various institutions and agencies, political bodies and diplomatic and consular services. Law graduates can alternatively work in legal affairs in companies and other legal entities, consultancy or human resources. The conditions for establishing an employment relationship differ depending on the chosen direction of professional career development.

---

8 Croatian Bureau of Statistics, Students in the academic year 2008/2009, Statistical report 1388, Zagreb, 2010, p. 21; Croatian Bureau of Statistics, Students in the academic year 2013/2014, Statistical report 1523, Zagreb, 2015, p. 21; Croatian Bureau of Statistics, Students in the academic year 2018/2019, Statistical report 1645, Zagreb, 2020, p. 22; Croatian Bureau of Statistics, Students in the academic year 2019/2020, Statistical report 1666, Zagreb, 2021, p. 22.

9 The Directory of Study Programmes lists all accredited study programmes: https://www.azvo.hr/en/preglednik.

10 For example, programmes in health/medical law, bankruptcy administrator examination, sports law, lawyer-linguist programmes, etc.

11 Foreign students enrolling in law studies are students who receive mobility funding (mostly through the Erasmus and CEEPUS programmes, or via other international or bilateral cooperation agreements).

Trainees are employed in judicial bodies through a selection procedure following a public call. The procedure for admitting trainees to traineeships occurs centrally for all judicial bodies and is performed by the Ministry of Justice in accordance with plans for determining available traineeships.[12] Traineeship lasts for two years and a trainee holds civil servant status.[13] A public call for notary public traineeships is announced centrally by the Croatian Chamber of Notaries. When selecting a notary public trainee, special attention is paid to success achieved in law studies and previous work. The qualification to practise law is acquired by registration with the Directory of Law Trainees when the person is trained for the first time and the law trainee enters into an employment relationship with a lawyer or a law firm. Trainees are eligible to take the bar examination after an 18-month internship. In addition, trainees in judicial bodies and notary public trainees must complete a programme of professional workshops at the Judicial/Notary Academy. The bar examination consists of a written and oral component taken before a five-member Bar Examination Committee. The time and place is determined by the competent Ministry of Justice. The written component consists of preparing three actions based on a specific case file in the civil, criminal and administrative law fields. The current standard curricula of the four law faculties cover the theoretical components of the substance of the bar exam well, but not the practical aspect. Graduate students currently need to both pass the traineeship, with tutoring from their supervisors, and attend additional education within the Juridical School and Croatian Judicial Academy, the Bar Association School or the Public Notary Academy. There is no limitation on the number of candidates who may pass the bar exam.

Trainees are admitted to state bodies[14] on the basis of a public call for applications in a regular procedure conducted periodically, provided funds are allocated in the state budget. Candidates applying for admission to the civil service through a public call shall, if they meet the call requirements, participate

---

12 It is noticeable that in 2021 no public call was announced for the admission of judicial trainees, while of the two calls announced for 2020, the first was finally suspended and a total of 53 trainees were selected as late as mid-2021. Javni natječaji – pravosudna tijela, Ministarstvo pravosuđa i uprave RH, https://mpu.gov.hr/pristup-informacijama-6341/zaposljavanje-ministarstvo-pravosudja-i-uprave/javni-natjecaj-pravosudna-tijela/18095.

13 Zakon o vježbenicima u pravosudnim tijelima i pravosudnom ispitu (Judicial Trainees and Bar Examination Act), Official Gazette 14/19; Zakon o odvjetništvu (Advocacy Act), Official Gazette 9/94, 117/08, 50/09, 75/09, 18/11, 126/21; Zakon o javnom bilježništvu (Notaries Public Act), Official Gazette 78/93, 29/94, 162/98, 16/07, 75/09, 120/16; Pravilnik o postupku prijema vježbenika u pravosudna tijela (Regulations governing the procedure for admission of trainees to judicial bodies), Official Gazette 106/2019.

14 Zakon o državnim službenicima (Civil Servants Act), Official Gazette 92/05, 140/05, 142/06, 77/2007, 107/07, 27/08, 34/11, 49/11, 150/11, 34/12, 38/13, 37/13, 1/15, 138/15, 102/15, 61/17, 70/19, 98/19; Zakon o službenicima i namještenicima u lokalnoj i područnoj (regionalnoj) samoupravi (Act on Civil Servants and Employees in Local and Regional Self-Government), Official Gazette 86/08, 61/11, 4/18, 96/18, 112/19.

in the selection process in which their knowledge, skills and abilities are tested. Admission to the civil service is for an indefinite period with a mandatory probationary period; in the case of trainees, the probationary period (internship) lasts 12 months, and trainees can take the state licensing examination no earlier than two months before the end of the probationary period. The state licensing examination is taken before the State Examination Commission.[15]

The legal provisions on working conditions and employment vary widely for lawyers in the public service, making it necessary to review the regulations governing their work and operation to determine the requirements for lawyers. Likewise, the conditions of employment for lawyers engaged in legal affairs in companies and other legal entities are often determined by the rules of the legal entity or its needs. However, a number of lawyers employed in companies and other legal entities will presumably take the bar examination. Specifically, only those who have passed the bar examination can act as legal representatives in litigation on property claims with a value over HRK 50,000. Likewise, when submitting a proposal to conduct an audit and when submitting an audit, proxies are required to have passed the bar examination. Lawyers employed in companies and other legal entities have the right to take the bar examination either after handling legal matters for at least two years and practising in court for at least 12 months, or after handling legal matters for at least three years.[16]

The judicial structure in Croatia includes general and specialised jurisdiction courts. The first instance courts of general jurisdiction comprise 34 municipal and 15 county courts, with the latter functioning as second instance courts. The courts of specialised jurisdiction comprise nine commercial and four administrative courts of first instance, the High Misdemeanour Court, the High Commercial Court and the High Administrative Court of second instance.[17] The Supreme Court acts as a court of both second and third instance. At the end of 2020, the Croatian judiciary consisted of 1,675 judges, 673 judicial assistants and 49 trainees.[18]

The State Attorney's Office (DORH) is an autonomous, independent judicial body that primarily acts as a prosecuting authority headed by the State Attorney General.[19] At the end of 2020, there were 25 municipal state attorneys'

15 Uredba o postupku, načinu polaganja i Programu državnog stručnog ispita (Regulation determining the procedure and the manner of taking the state licensing examination, and the Programme thereof), Official Gazette 61/06, 145/12, 1/14, 11/15, 124/15, 27/17, 70/19.

16 Arts. 91 and 91(a), para. 2, Zakon o parničnom postupku (Civil Procedure Act), SFRY Official Gazette 4/77, 36/77, 36/80, 6/80, 69/82, 43/82, 58/84, 74/87, 57/89, 20/90, 27/90, 35/91, Official Gazette 53/91, 91/92, 112/1999, 129/00, 88/01, 117/03, 88/05, 2/07, 96/08, 84/08, 123/08, 57/11, 25/13, 89/14 and 70/2019.

17 Zakon o sudovima (Courts Act), Official Gazette 28/13, 33/15, 82/15, 82/16, 67/18.

18 Report of the President of the Supreme Court (Izvješće Predsjednika Vrhovnog Suda Republike Hrvatske o stanju sudbene vlasti za 2020. godinu), Zagreb, 2021, p. 26, www.vsrh.hr.

19 Zakon o državnom odvjetništvu (State Attorney's Office Act), Official Gazette 67/2018.

offices, 15 county state attorneys' offices, and one Office for the Suppression of Corruption and Organised Crime (USKOK), employing 638 state attorneys, 166 state attorney councillors and 25 trainees.[20]

The Croatian Bar Association is an independent, self-governing professional organisation comprised of 4,943 lawyers and 1,516 trainees.[21] Notary public services are provided by 327 offices, where lawyers work as notaries public, notary public assessors, notary counsellors and notary public trainees.[22]

Fewer employment opportunities in the judiciary and public administration have contributed to declining interest in the legal profession. Despite legal services offered on the European market with open mobility options,[23] few Croatian lawyers have taken the opportunity to register their services.[24] Fierce competition creates a monopoly of work for larger firms, with small, non-specialised firms struggling to find a place in the market.[25] Corporations have further operationalised their businesses and concentrated management and legal services to minimise costs.

A Croatian degree and legal qualifications are recognised on the EU territory, allowing lawyers to move freely on the EU labour market. Positions within EU institutions, agencies and other international organisations are preferred. However, the requirements for these positions are very high, especially considering requisite language skills. English, the most popular language among Croatian law students, does not fully correspond to desired jobs on the labour market, which require professionals with German and French language skills.

---

20 Report for 2020 of the State Attorney's Office (Izvješće Glavnog državnog odvjetnika Republike Hrvatske o radu državnih odvjetništava u 2020. Godini), p. 10, www.dorh.hr.

21 Croatian Bar Association, *Directory of lawyers*, https://www.hok-cba.eu/imenik/?naziv=&tip=odvjetnik&adresa=&mjesto=&jezici=.

22 Croatian Notaries Chamber, *Search engine for notary public offices in the Republic of Croatia*, https://www.hjk.hr/Uredi.

23 Directive 98/5/EC of the European Parliament and of the Council of 16 February 1998 to facilitate practice of the profession of lawyer on a permanent basis in a Member State other than that in which the qualification was obtained, OJ L 077, 14.03.1998.

24 Two in 2016, five in 2018, and 16 in 2020. CCBE Lawyers' Statistics 2016, https://www.ccbe.eu/fileadmin/speciality_distribution/public/documents/Statistics/EN_STAT_2016-_Number-of-lawyers-in-European-countries.pdf; CCBE Lawyers' Statistics 2018, https://www.ccbe.eu/fileadmin/speciality_distribution/public/documents/Statistics/EN_STAT_-2018_Number-of-lawyers-in-European-countries.pdf; CCBE Lawyers' Statistics 2020, https://www.ccbe.eu/fileadmin/speciality_distribution/public/documents/Statistics/EN_STAT_2020_Number-of-lawyers-in-European-countries.pdf.

25 V. Smokvina, M. Mrakovčić and M. Tonković, 'Suvremeni izazovi zapošljavanja mladih pravnika u odvjetništvu, javnom bilježništvu i pravosuđu' in L. Belanić and, D. Dobrić Jambrović (eds), *Unaprjeđenje kvalitete studiranja na pravnim fakultetima u Hrvatskoj – Zbornik koautorskih radova nastavnika i studenata sa znanstvene konferencije*, Sveučilište u Rijeci, Pravni fakultet, 2021, p. 110.

The total number of judges is very high, with more than 40 per 100,000 inhabitants,[26] compared to 10–30 professional judges per 100,000 inhabitants in most EU member states. A reason for this high number is that Croatia is a legal system influenced by law and institutions in Germany, which traditionally has a very high per-capita rate of judges and civil servants.[27] Croatian judges must attend lifelong training at least once a year.[28] The satisfaction of that duty should be stated in the periodic evaluation report that is conducted for each judge. However, it is doubtful that this obligation meets the needs and expectations of current judges.

1.2. ONLINE STUDY PROGRAMMES IN CROATIA

In the Croatian HE system, the approval of any study programme, including an online programme, is subject to procedures prescribed by the Agency for Science and Higher Education (AZVO).[29] Initial accreditation is regulated by the Act on Scientific Activity and Higher Education (SAEH Act), the Act on Quality Assurance in Science and Higher Education and other regulations.[30] Initial accreditation of the proposed study programme is conducted by the Ministry of Science and Education and AZVO. The proposal undergoes external evaluation to determine whether the quality standards (related to learning outcomes, the study programme, the teaching process, student support and resources) are met. Pursuant to the SAEH Act, a study programme can be delivered online through a distance learning system (Article 79(4)). Final approval for accreditation of an online study programme is granted by the National Council for Science, Higher Education and Technological Development. The standard accreditation procedure also applies to online study programmes. However, if the proposed study programme is to be delivered online, additional evaluation criteria and

26 https://public.tableau.com/app/profile/cepej/viz/CEPEJ-Explorerv2020_1_0EN/Tables.

27 Council of Europe, 'European judicial systems: CEPEJ Evaluation Report', 2020 Evaluation cycle (2018 data), https://rm.coe.int/evaluation-report-part-1-english/16809fc058.

28 Zakon o sudovima (Courts Act), Art. 93 para. 3.

29 https://www.azvo.hr/en/evaluations/evaluations-in-higher-education/initial-accreditation-of-study-programmes.

30 Act on Quality Assurance in Science and Higher Education (Zakon o osiguravanju kvalitete u znanosti i visokom obrazovanju) Official Gazette 45/09; Ordinance on the Content of a Licence and Conditions for Issuing a Licence for Performing Higher Education Activity, Carrying out a Study Programme and Re-Accreditation of Higher Education Institutions (Pravilnik o sadržaju dopusnice i uvjetima za izdavanje dopusnice za obavljanje djelatnosti visokog obrazovanja, izvođenje studijskog programa i reakreditaciju visokih učilišta) Official Gazette 24/10, www.azvo.hr.

procedures apply.[31] These criteria apply to study programmes in which at least 50% of the courses are taught online. An online course is a course in which at least 50% of the teaching hours are delivered online.

The students' rights, responsibilities, status and academic degrees earned upon completion of a study programme delivered partially or fully online are equivalent to traditional forms of instruction at HE institutions. The learning outcomes and competencies acquired after completing the course should be based on standards that apply in traditional forms of study programmes. However, the defined learning outcomes must be achievable in online teaching and learning modes. A detailed schedule of weekly online activities must include an estimated student workload. The teacher must include a list of learning materials and other freely available resources (either freely available books and papers or materials prepared for students by a teacher of the course) that are appropriate for students to work independently. Online class instructions for students must be clear and concise. Knowledge assessment criteria must be clear and transparent, and students should be either self-assessed or assessed by means of appropriate online methods available through an online learning tool.[32] Institutions seeking accreditation for an online study programme must demonstrate they have sufficient infrastructural, technical, administrative and human resources to deliver the study programme.

Although distance learning platforms were used for law faculty course delivery before the pandemic, and law faculties conducted online teaching during the pandemic,[33] there is still no accredited permanent online study programme in law resulting in fully online law degrees.

2. MOVING TOWARDS ONLINE EDUCATION

Digital education is also known as technology-enhanced learning or e-learning, comprising innovative digital tools and technologies used in teaching and learning processes. It refers to an educational delivery model based on digital technology or the internet, and thus includes two modes: online and blended learning.

E-learning is not necessarily an invention of the modern era, as it has been systematically developing over the past decades across the world, including

31 Kriteriji i postupci za vrednovanje online studija, Nacionalno vijeće za znanost, visoko obrazovanje i tehnološki razvoj (Criteria and procedures for the evaluation of online study programmes, National Council for Science, Higher Education and Technological Development), Zagreb, 07.04.2016, available at www.azvo.hr.

32 Ibid., p. 6.

33 See sections 2.3 and 2.6.

in Croatia. In the 1980s, computers entered the field of education and were supplemented by the internet in the 1990s. This development continued with social networks and Google Scholar in the 2000s, cloud computing in the 2010s,[34] and open educational resources in the 2020s. However, e-learning in Croatia has affected neither levels of education nor areas of HE. Hence, the development of achievements in HE in the field of law is seemingly dictated by general e-learning and HE strategies. Considering lifelong learning, e-justice strategies are markedly important.

2.1. STRATEGIES SUPPORTING ONLINE EDUCATION IN HIGHER EDUCATION

The strategic foundations of EU e-higher education are found in the Digital Education Action Plan 2018–2020.[35] The European Digital Education Action Plan 2021–2027 later reset education and training for the digital age by prioritising: (1) fostering the development of a high-performing digital education ecosystem; and (2) enhancing digital skills and competencies for the digital transformation. Digital competencies are an inevitable ingredient of HE legal education. Therefore, the plan goes hand in hand with the European Skills Agenda.[36]

Croatian strategic planning surrounding the use of information and communication technologies (ICT) for educational purposes has been closely linked to the regional European Union and Council of Europe policies since the early 2000s.[37] The first impetus for e-learning can be traced to the e-Croatia Programme of 2007.[38] The 2014 National Strategy for Education, Science and Technology aims to expand and enhance the application of ICT in education

34 B. Cope and M. Kalantzis, 'Pedagogies for Digital Learning: From Transpositional Grammar to the Literacies of Education', in M.G. Sindoni and I. Moschini (eds), *Multimodal Literacies Across Digital Learning Contexts*, Routledge, 2021, available at https://www.researchgate.net/publication/344876961_Pedagogies_for_Digital_Learning_From_Transpositional_Grammar_to_the_Literacies_of_Education.

35 Communication from the Commission to the European Parliament, the Council, the European Economic and Social Committee and the Committee of the Regions on the Digital Education Action Plan, COM(2018) 022 final, Brussels, 17.01.2018.

36 https://ec.europa.eu/social/main.jsp?catId=1223&langId=en.

37 The Information and Communication Technology Strategy – Croatia in the 21st century relies on e-Europe 2003. Strategija 'Informacijska i komunikacijska tehnologija – Hrvatska u 21. stoljeću', Official Gazette 109/02, 18.09.2002.

38 Operativni plan provedbe Programa e-Hrvatska 2007. za 2004. godinu (Operational Plan for the Implementation of the e-Croatia Programme 2007 for 2004), https://vlada.gov.hr/UserDocsImages//2016/Sjednice/Arhiva//027-01.pdf.

and learning.[39] The strategy highlights the benefits of e-learning for all stakeholders. For students, it implies fast and flexible access to multimedia and interactive learning materials and the opportunity to adapt to personal learning styles, learn collaboratively and acquire skills for project work and teamwork. E-learning puts learners at the centre of the learning process, encouraging them to take an active role in and responsibility for their educational outcomes. For universities, it provides access to a wider range of learners. However, teaching staff employed in HE must adopt new responsibilities regarding the creation, development and review of instructional content and educational resources. The programme calls for the creation, organisation, collection, preservation and permanent availability of open repositories of knowledge and teaching resources. The concept of massive open online courses has been introduced for the first time, defined as 'large-scale free repositories of academic and other educational content' that change the approach to education delivery. The strategy develops didactic knowledge for future e-contents and resources, and emphasises the need to develop teachers' digital competence at every educational process level. To ensure compliance with didactic standards, the strategy encourages the development of free content funded by public or EU funds, or peer-reviewed commercial content.[40]

Ambitious measures have been proposed in developing digital educational content, tools and methods for ICT use in teaching and learning,[41] and establishing a digital system for assessing and monitoring achievement of learning outcomes.[42]

The strategy addresses e-infrastructure as a fundamental common infrastructure system for science and HE, facilitating an environment where scientists, researchers, students and other academic and research community members share access to distributed and/or common research resources, advanced computing tools, communications and data. The strategy announces the establishment of the Croatian Scientific and Educational Cloud (HR-ZOO).[43]

The 2014 Strategy identifies digital competence as a core aspect of the lifelong learning process.[44] In accordance with its third mission, HE institutions, especially universities, must adopt new obligations regarding lifelong learning and adult education, creation and implementation of new programmes and training of teachers for these programmes, creation and implementation of

39 See Objective 5, New Colours of Knowledge, Strategy for Education, Science and Technology, Official Gazette 124/14, 24.10.2014, p. 18, https://mzo.gov.hr/UserDocsImages//dokumenti/Obrazovanje//Strategy%20for%20Education,%20Science%20and%20Tehnology.pdf.
40 Ibid., pp. 36–37.
41 Ibid., pp. 72–73.
42 Ibid., p. 142.
43 Ibid., p. 252.
44 Ibid., p. 24.

part-time study programmes, career guidance and counselling, development of e-tools, and the organisation and design of open digital educational content, knowledge and tools. The section of the strategy related to HE therefore proposes the establishment of lifelong learning centres.[45]

In the latest 2021–2027 General National Strategy, the 'Digital Transformation of HE' is recognised as a top priority.[46] Insufficient digital maturity and effectiveness of HE in Croatia is attributed to a lack of digital teaching infrastructure, teaching tools and empowerment of teachers to teach in a digital environment.[47]

2.2. BIRTH OF ONLINE EDUCATION IN CROATIAN HIGHER EDUCATION

2.2.1. Infrastructure, Capacity and Early E-Learning Initiatives

The ICT infrastructure in HE has developed in Croatia over the last decades. Its main pillar is the University Computing Centre (SRCE), founded in 1971 at the University of Zagreb. SRCE is the principal computing centre, architect of e-infrastructure for all Croatian HE institutions, competence centre for ICT, and training and support centre in ICT application.[48]

The services established and offered by SRCE provide a solid platform for the qualitative development of e-learning and open science resources at HE institutions. The E-learning Centre plays a central role in the systematic implementation of e-learning in Croatian HE and provides training and support for teachers, students and institutions in the use of e-learning technologies. Merlin is a virtual learning environment established at SRCE, nationally recognised as a stable and highly useful platform used by numerous teachers and students in Croatia.

In 1991, the Croatian Academic and Research Network (CARNET) was established under the Ministry of Science and Technology of the Republic of Croatia. In November 1992, CARNET established the first Croatian internet connection to the world. Today it is responsible for e-learning in education and hosts the Loomen platform. Although Loomen is also available for HE, it is not used that frequently.

E-learning was first introduced in Croatia in the 1990s at the University of Zagreb. At that time, teachers professionally involved in various aspects

45 Ibid., p. 220.

46 C3.1. R2-I1 Digitalna preobrazba visokog obrazovanja (The Digital Transformation of Higher Education).

47 Ibid., pp. 873–875.

48 https://www.srce.unizg.hr/en/about-srce.

of technology were engaged in digitalisation. The systematic introduction of e-learning started in 2007[49] at the universities of Zagreb, Rijeka and Dubrovnik. Despite strategic[50] and operational documents prepared for e-learning and the establishment of e-learning support centres, the evaluation of e-learning progress showed a rather poor result in a 2013 survey conducted by Zagreb University.[51]

2.2.2. *Internet and ICT Penetration in Croatia*

Internet and ICT penetration across the Croatian population generally is promising. The proportion of individuals using the internet in 2019 was 56.7% globally,[52] 87% in the EU, and 80% in Croatia.[53] The share has increased somewhat since then. The proportion of households with computers in 2017 was 74% in Croatia and 83% in the EU.[54] The percentage of Croatian households with broadband internet access in 2021 was 86%.[55] Broadband internet speed in 2022 was 69.09 Mbps for download in Croatia,[56] higher than the average broadband internet speed globally (59.75 Mbps).[57]

2.3. CROATIAN ONLINE LEGAL EDUCATION BEFORE THE PANDEMIC: FACTS AND FIGURES

Croatian HE distance learning services were used at four law schools before the pandemic, primarily in the form of blended online education. The Moodle platforms of Merlin and Loomen were principally used to store learning materials and assignments for students, especially in smaller intensive seminar groups. The didactic skills of HE teachers were left to individual preferences, so the use of the available tools depended on personal engagement and skills of teachers.[58] A Merlin courses review reveals that some Croatian law schools did not offer

49 International Tempus project EQIBELT – Education Quality Improvement by E-learning Technology, http://eqibelt.srce.hr/.
50 University of Zagreb, E-learning Strategy 2007–2010, http://www.unizg.hr›e-ucenje›e-ucenje_strategija.
51 http://www.unizg.hr/studiji-i-studiranje/studiji/e-ucenje/povjerenstvo-za-e-ucenje-2010-2014/.
52 https://data.worldbank.org/indicator/IT.NET.USER.ZS.
53 https://ec.europa.eu/eurostat/databrowser/view/isoc_ci_ifp_iu/default/table?lang=en.
54 https://ec.europa.eu/eurostat/databrowser/view/isoc_ci_cm_h/default/table?lang=en.
55 https://ec.europa.eu/eurostat/databrowser/view/ISOC_CI_IT_H__custom_2016270/default/table?lang=en.
56 https://worldpopulationreview.com/country-rankings/internet-speeds-by-country.
57 https://www.speedtest.net/global-index.
58 https://katalog-e-kolegija.srce.hr/izvjestaji.

e-courses before the pandemic. The number of courses increased rapidly in the first year of the pandemic and has remained relatively high to date. However, due to the current Ministry's policy of in situ teaching, distance learning platforms have largely ceased from their pre-pandemic role as a substitute tool in the teaching process.

The overall national and EU strategy was not systematically implemented in HE prior to the pandemic. Online education at HE institutions has lagged far behind other compulsory education levels, especially the centralised primary and high school systems.[59] The autonomy of the university and its faculties is a decisive factor for multispeed e-learning at Croatian HE institutions. This autonomy can be an advantage or a burden. In a post-pandemic context, it will allow more flexibility and experimentation, but only if utilised, raising two aspects for attention. First, the nature of the occupation for which education is provided largely affects the use of technology. STEM occupations have an advantage over social sciences as they are strictly dependent on ICT and have to keep pace with their progress. It is unsurprising that information and computer science students have the most positive attitude towards e-learning and its possibilities. The statistical significance of the differences in student attitudes depending on their academic field of study was confirmed in two-thirds of the variables analysed. It is expected that further introduction of e-learning in Croatian universities will be reflected in increasing popularity among students.[60] When focusing on law, the academic approach was largely dictated by the legal system of the state. Indeed, in the civil legal system (such as the Croatian one), the demands for dynamic education and up-to-date information were not at the forefront. When Croatia expanded international cooperation and became an active partner of international organisations and, most critically, a full member of the EU, this perspective changed. Croatian legal education became part of the European and international community, where the competencies of lawyers are aligned with standards. Legal norms are no longer national and are changing rapidly. They are interpreted by supranational courts with decisions reflecting sources of law. All of these changes have dramatically changed Croatia's legal landscape and affected legal education. Students are expected to find accurate and timely information and develop into resourceful lawyers. The EU accession has reinvigorated the Croatian judicial system. ICT has affected the methodology of work and cooperation with other judges and authorities, case management,

---

59 Akcijski plan za provedbu nastave na daljinu: Model nastave na daljinu (Action plan for the implementation of distance education: Distance education model), Zagreb, 07.2020, p. 6, https://mzo.gov.hr/UserDocsImages//dokumenti/Obrazovanje/NastavaNaDaljinu//Akcijski%20plan%20za%20provedbu%20nastave%20na%20daljinu%20-%20Model%20nastave%20na%20daljinu.pdf.

60 D. Dukić, 'E-Learning: Perceptions of Students at the Josip Juraj Strossmayer University of Osijek' (2011) 44(2) *Informatol* 94, 99.

usage of artificial intelligence (AI), remote systems for witness hearings, taking of evidence and other facets.[61]

Other aspects also affect the rhythm of modernising of education. HE institutions are central academic career pillars for conducting research and teaching; however, from the standpoint of HE teacher qualifications in Croatia, they are perceived primarily as research institutions. Specifically, the requirements for HE teachers are consistently set high in terms of research and publications, compared to the rather vague and weak standards around pedagogy and teaching methodology.[62] Therefore, pedagogy was not conceived as a priority for HE teachers.[63] Pedagogical requirements of HE teachers are checked at the level of individual universities according to their own rules and criteria. Notably, in Croatian legal education only the Faculty of Law in Osijek makes the appointment of teachers conditional on their enrolling in a one-year programme in methodology, pedagogy and didactics, and passing the examination. Digital competence of HE teachers is also considered part of this programme.

2.4. SCHOLARLY APPROACH TO THE MODERNISATION OF LEGAL EDUCATION

Over time, Croatian scholars have addressed educational problems[64] and possible reforms for legal education.[65] However, the efforts of law professors in conceptualising the modernisation of legal education in Croatia are rather scarce. The reason is that Croatian law teachers are primarily scholars rather than teachers, and hence are under the pressure of high standards of publishing and research. The elevated numbers of students in previous decades also affected their workload, shifting concern to handling student overload and

---

61 See section 2.5.

62 See the introduction to this report.

63 S. Kučina Softić, 'Praćenje provedbe strategija e-učenja', http://higherdecision.foi.hr/sites/default/files/D12.1.%20Pra%C4%87enje%20provedbe%20strategija%20e-u%C4%8Denja.pdf.

64 I. Padjen, 'Internationalisation of Legal and Political Studies in Yugoslavia: Croatian University System as a Model' (1990) 40(4) *Zbornik Pravnog fakulteta u Zagrebu* 505; I. Pađen, 'Nezavisnost sudova, pravno rasuđivanje i pravno obrazovanje' (1992) 42(2) *Zbornik Pravnog fakulteta u Zagrebu* 797; I. Pađen, 'Uloga pravnih fakulteta u izobrazbi odvjetnika' (2001) 38 *Zbornik radova Pravnog fakulteta u Splitu* 37; Z. Jelinić, 'Izgradnja modernog i konkurentnog studija prava kao odgovor na zahtjeve tržišta sutrašnjice (u cilju promocije interesa studenata, društva i ekonomije) – između zadržavanja postojećeg stanja i aktiviranja raspoloživih potencijala' (2016) *Zbornik Pravnog fakulteta Sveučilišta u Rijeci* 1349.

65 J. Barbić (ed.), *Reforma pravnog obrazovanja*, HAZU, 2007; B. Smerdel and M. Ajduković (eds), *Razvoj modela unaprjeđivanja kvalitete studija na Pravnom fakultetu Sveučilišta u Zagrebu*, Pravni fakultet, Nacionalna zaklada za znanost, visoko školstvo i tehnologijski razvoj RH, 2006, https://www.pravo.unizg.hr/rmuks/dokumenti.

ensuring the smooth of running programmes. They have only dealt with the digitalisation of law and legal education sporadically. The reluctance of legal education to adopt the changes brought about by ICT was first emphasised decades ago[66] and remains an issue in the discourse on the modernisation of legal education.

Insufficient clinical legal education has been raised as a core issue of legal education.[67] This aspect currently affects the competence of lawyers in the application of EU law, which is largely based on the interpretation of the CJEU. Moreover, the skills in modern technologies as sources of information for the application of EU law can often only be found in databases and online.[68] The worldwide phenomenon of a return to the moot court can be observed in Croatian legal education. The interaction between legal practice and law students and teachers, considered a rediscovery of old, valuable methods of legal education, is reflected in foreign moot court participation and organisation of moot courts by law schools.[69] Opportunities to participate in moot court competitions increase with advancements in technology as many competitions are held online.[70]

The underestimated value of language skills[71] is emphasised. This can affect the use of ICT, where English is a common language. The need for generic/transversal skills is further highlighted.[72] A lack of generic skills is even more problematic in an online environment, as it affects the capacity to carry out tasks and communicate at an appropriate level. The rise of ICT raises the issue of digital literacy among students and lecturers as a neglected aspect of legal education, relating to many specific and unique aspects of the legal field.[73] The use of electronic resources, e-learning tools and the internet is a *conditio sine qua non* for the daily work of lawyers. Most sources of information on laws,

---

66 I. Bilić, 'Neki aspekti razvoja studija prava u Hrvatskoj' (2001) 38 *Zbornik radova Pravnog fakulteta u Splitu* 19.

67 Z. Jelinić, 'Integrirano kliničko obrazovanje studenata prava i ekonomije – prikaz projekta pravno-ekonomske klinike Pravnog i ekonomskog fakulteta u Osijeku' (2014) 30(3–4) *Pravni Vjesnik* 285.

68 The same problem has been noted in Slovenian practice, with almost identical legal education to Croatian. S. Ivanjko, 'Slovenian Legal Profession Meets European Union' (2014) 5 *Croatian Academy of Legal Sciences Yearbook* 54, 70.

69 J. Snape and G. Watt, *The Cavendish Guide To Mooting*, Cavendish Publishing, 2000, p. 235.

70 A. Ivancan and D. Petric, 'Moot Court as Method of Practical Education at Law Schools' (2019) *Zbornik Pravnog Fakulteta Zagrebu* 277.

71 I. Kunda, M. Bajčić and D. Nikolla, 'Strani jezik u pravnom obrazovanju: dokad ćemo se praviti Englezi?' in L. Belanić and D. Dobrić Jambrović (eds), *Unaprjeđenje kvalitete studiranja na pravnim fakultetima u Hrvatskoj – Zbornik koautorskih radova nastavnika i studenata sa znanstvene konferencije*, Sveučilište u Rijeci, Pravni fakultet, 2021, pp. 35–50.

72 I. Padjen, 'Hrvatski pravni studiji: izazovi i izgledi' (2007) 44 *Zbornik radova Pravnog fakulteta u Splitu* 532.

73 D. Golenko and Lj. Siber, 'Information Literacy of Lawyers in Their Working Environment' in S. Kurbanoğlu et al. (eds) *Information Literacy in the Workplace*, Springer, 2018.

legal provisions, regulations, directives and court decisions are available online or in specialised databases. 'Law students must learn to find, use, evaluate and cite different legal sources, recognise the peculiarities of legal bases, but also learn to analyse and critically approach a legal problem, recognise the normative framework for a legal problem, compare different legal systems available in legal databases or other sources of information.'[74] Legal education must develop not only generic information literacy skills, but contextual (professional) information literacy skills in the field of law.

The fact that current curricula are not market-oriented was universally addressed in the 2012 Madrid Resolution on Legal Education and Professional Life: Adapting to Current Challenges of the European Law Faculties Association (ELFA).[75] Research on the future of legal education in Croatia and the directions of change are based on the needs of the labour market.[76] Major research assessing whether legal employers were satisfied with their employees who were educated at law schools in Croatia before the pandemic revealed that 31% believed their computer skills were lacking.[77]

2.5. E-LIFELONG LEARNING EDUCATION IN LAW

Croatian scholars dealing with educational problems were concerned about the need to develop permanent and systematic education to meet the needs of the modern judiciary.[78] At the regional EU and CoE level, the need for judicial training is systematically addressed, with ICT use in the lifelong learning process considered a concern.[79] Considerable challenges in the design of judicial training can be overcome through informed and tailored use of available distance learning methods and training formats, with electronic tools

---

74 K.H. Ryskey, 'On Solid Legal Ground: Bringing Information Literacy to Undergraduate-Level Law Courses' (2007) 7(2) *Journal of Effective Teaching*, 21, according to D. Golenko and E. Arh, 'Information Literacy Programmes (Theoretical Framework in the Field of Law and Medicine)' (2020) 25 *BOSNIACA* 17.

75 http://elfa-afde.eu/legal-education/.

76 Z. Jelinić, 'Izgradnja modernog i konkurentnog studija prava' (1991) 37(3) *Zbornik Pravnog fakultet Sveučilišta u Rijeci* 1349, 1350; V. Kregar, 'Teorijski i društveni kontekst modernizacije pravnog obrazovanja' in J. Barbić (ed.), *Reforma pravnog obrazovanja*, HAZU, 2007.

77 IURISPRUDENTIA – Improving the Quality of Education at Faculties of Law in Osijek, Rijeka and Split, 2016, p. 50, https://www.pravos.unios.hr/pravo-arhiva/iurisprudentia.

78 M. Dika, 'Marginalije uz problem reforme pravosuđa, Hrvatska – kako dalje: zadanosti i mogućnosti' in J. Kregar, V. Puljiz and S. Ravlić (eds), *Hrvatska – kako dalje: zadanosti i mogućnosti*, Pravni fakultet Sveučilišta u Zagrebu, Centar za demokraciju i pravo Miko Tripalo, 2004, pp. 119–133.

79 Art. 10 of the Declaration of Judicial Training Principles, International Organisation for Judicial Training, 08.11.2017, https://www.unodc.org/res/ji/import/international_standards/declaration_of_judicial_training_principles/declaration_of_judicial_training_principles.pdf.

and new technologies providing additional support in achieving efficiency and/or accessibility of training. ICT-supported training is attractive from all stakeholder perspectives, i.e. funding institutions, organising agencies, trainers and trainees, because it is time-saving, cost-effective, flexible and enables expanded participation. The design of distance lifelong learning modules should consider the typical properties judges have due to their profession and specific characteristics of adult education.[80]

A recent EU survey of the use of ICT in the Croatian judiciary indicates that development of digital skills is needed at the levels of HE and lifelong learning education. The use of electronic communication and electronic case management systems in Croatian courts remains limited. Although figures relating to digitalisation and ICT in the courts are not specifically addressed by national surveys of the state of the judiciary, the use of ICT for case management and electronic communication between courts and parties is among the least developed in the EU.[81] However, the annual Supreme Court President's report reveals that when using tools and instruments of modern technology to manage and review the work of the court as a whole and the judge as an individual official, the judiciary must ensure dispute resolution is of the highest possible quality at all stages of the trial.[82] To address low levels of e-communication system adoption, the Ministry of Justice launched a project titled 'Support to the implementation of e-communication in the Croatian judiciary'.[83]

Examples are useful. Workshops on basic and advanced use of European legal databases are organised within the framework of science popularisation events.[84] An Online Translation Tools and EU Vocabulary course has been carried out as part of the Lifelong Learning Programme for Lawyer-Linguists at the Faculty of Law in Osijek. The content of this course is taught by using computer technology (translation tools and databases that are accessible online), which is used as a medium for teaching translation. The main objective of this course is to teach students how to use this media properly and skilfully.[85]

---

80 M. Župan, I. Kunda and P. Poretti, 'Judicial Training in European Private International Law in Family and Succession Matters' in T. Pfeiffer, Q.C. Lobach and T. Rapp (eds), *Facilitating Cross-Border Family Life – Towards a Common European Understanding: EUFams II and Beyond*, Heidelberg University Publishing, 2021, pp. 122–124; K.A. Thomas, *Attorneys' Experiences with Continuing Legal Education Delivered Online: A Holistic Single Case Study*, Liberty University, 2019, pp. 95–101.

81 2020 EU Justice Scoreboard, 2020 Rule of Law Report Country Chapter on the rule of law situation in Croatia, SWD(2020) 310 final, Brussels, 30.09.2020, p. 5.

82 Report of the President of the Supreme Court of Croatia for 2020 (Izvješće Predsjednika Vrhovnog Suda Republike Hrvatske o stanju sudbene vlasti za 2020. godinu), Zagreb, 2021, p. 6, www.vsrh.hr.

83 Support requested through the Structural Reform Support Programme – 2020; the project is implemented with the Council of Europe (CEPEJ).

84 https://www.pravos.unios.hr/katedra-za-europsko-pravo/program-2018.

85 Lj. Kordić, Ž. Rišner and D. Papa 'New Media in Formal and Non-formal Higher Education in Social Sciences' (2018) 10 *European Journal of Interdisciplinary Studies* 109.

2.6. OUTBREAK OF THE PANDEMIC

With the outbreak of the pandemic, the Ministry of Science worked with universities and stakeholders[86] to organise online classes at HE institutions to ensure classes were held in some form. Guidelines for the implementation of distance education were supported by SRCE. HE institutions decided how to implement instruction in practice. On average in the first weeks, it took more time for HE institutions to adapt to new circumstances than schools due to process management, with schools being more centralised than HE institutions. In the transition to distance learning, where it was important to respond quickly and in a coordinated manner, central coordination was more efficient.[87] In the academic year 2020/21, mainly hybrid lectures were held at HE institutions (some students on-site and some online). When classes started in the winter semester of 2020/2021, the policy shifted towards traditional classes instead of online classes.[88] This was justified by results obtained in research conducted by AZVO indicating that online classes were not delivered properly. The fact remains that there are hardly any accredited online study programmes in Croatia.[89] One of the main problems with online HE during the pandemic is the assessment of knowledge.[90]

During the pandemic, recommendations for the delivery of courses at HE institutions were formulated by the universities themselves, then transposed to classrooms by each teacher individually. An example of successful crisis management and the transition from online learning to a new normal at the level

---

86 Croatian Academic and Research Network (CARNET), University Computing Centre (SRCE), Agency for Education (ETTA), Agency for Vocational Education and Training and Adult Education (AVETAE), and Agency for Mobility and EU Programmes (AMEUP).

87 Akcijski plan za provedbu nastave na daljinu: Model nastave na daljinu (Action plan for the implementation of distance education: Distance education model), Zagreb, 07.2020, https://mzo.gov.hr/UserDocsImages//dokumenti/Obrazovanje/NastavaNaDaljinu//Akcijski%20plan%20za%20provedbu%20nastave%20na%20daljinu%20-%20Model%20nastave%20na%20daljinu.pdf.

88 On 31 August 2020, at the request of the Ministry of Science and Education of the Republic Croatia and in cooperation with the University of Zagreb, the Croatian Institute of Public Health issued Recommendations for teaching at HE institutions during the pandemic caused by COVID-19 with the application of anti-epidemic measures: https://mzo.gov.hr/UserDocsImages/dokumenti/Obrazovanje/VisokoObrazovanje/Preporuke%20za%20odrzavanje%20nastave%20na%20visokim%20ucilistima%20u%20razdoblju%20pandemije%20bolesti%20COVID-9%20uz%20primjenu%20protuepidemijskih%20mjera.pdf.

89 https://www.azvo.hr/hr/azvo-vijesti/2616-predstavljeni-rezultati-istrazivanja-studenti-i-pandemija-kako-smo-pre-zivjeli.

90 Akcijski plan za provedbu nastave na daljinu: Model nastave na daljinu (Action plan for the implementation of distance education: Distance education model), Zagreb, 07.2020, pp. 11–12, https://mzo.gov.hr/UserDocsImages//dokumenti/Obrazovanje/NastavaNaDaljinu//Akcijski%20plan%20za%20provedbu%20nastave%20na%20daljinu%20-%20Model%20nastave%20na%20daljinu.pdf.

of HE in law is found in Croatia. During the pandemic, online legal education continued at the universities of Zagreb, Osijek and Rijeka.[91]

The Faculty of Law in Zagreb quickly moved to online classes in an environment of complete lockdown in 2020, so students did not lose the opportunity to attend classes. Toward the end of the pandemic, in the academic year 2021/22, teaching was conducted entirely live, respecting epidemiological measures on site but with scope for students to also follow online lectures.[92]

After the outbreak of the pandemic in the summer semester of 2019/2020, the Faculty of Law in Rijeka moved all classes to a virtual environment without any delays or mishaps. Lectures were recorded and made available to students for later examinations. The examinations were mostly conducted online. The methodology of virtual legal education changed slightly in the academic year 2020/21. Respecting health measures, compulsory courses were held on campus,[93] while electives were largely held online as supervised classes. Classes were held as full-class sessions with online contact with the teacher, with online materials and self-assessment assignments available as well. In the academic year 2021/22, all classes were delivered directly through Merlin, Microsoft Teams or Cisco Webex for students unable to attend classes in person (e.g. due to self-isolation).

Another example of quality management is found at the Faculty of Law in Osijek, which moved classes online and ensured their smooth operation during the pandemic. All compulsory classes were conducted using teaching materials on Merlin and video-conferencing or recorded lectures via Zoom. In the 2021/22 academic year, teachers had the option of livestreaming on-site lectures.[94] The management of the Osijek and Rijeka law schools guarantee to

---

91 A high rate of law students without online classes was recorded at the Faculty of Law in Split. N. Matković, *Stavovi i percepcije studenata splitskog sveučilišta o provedbi online nastave za vrijeme trajanja epidemije Covid-19*, Split, 2021, p. 28, https://zir.nsk.hr/islandora/object/ffst:3173.

92 Interview with Prof. Iris Goldner Lang, Vice-Dean at the Faculty of Law in Zagreb.

93 'Classes were held in large weekly modules, i.e. 4 or 5 hours of classes in one course a day (to prevent mixing of students between cohorts), then the lecture room was disinfected and aired, and after that another group of students was able to enter the lecture room. We used multiple entrances and exits, and the classes were scheduled such that classes in different groups started and finished with a 15-minute interval (e.g. the classes in years 1, 2 and 3 started at 8 a.m., 8:15 a.m. and 8:30 a.m., respectively) to prevent contact with other students (a bubble approach). In addition, large classes were divided into smaller groups to meet the physical distancing requirement, which meant that we taught the same lesson content several times. This resulted in slightly higher teacher workload because, due to limited capacity (spatial and teaching), this could have been applied only to the first and the second year of law and administrative studies'. Interview with Prof. Ivana Kunda, Vice-Dean at the Faculty of Law in Rijeka.

94 T. Petrašević and P. Poretti, 'Svaka je prijetnja prilika: kako je PRAVOS postao E-PRAVOS' (2020) 57 *Sveučilišni glasnik* 11.

comply with rules and procedures,[95] and to amend accordingly. In Osijek, the rules of procedure for final examinations allow for an online public defence.[96] Exams were conducted through distance learning platforms in combination with video-conferencing. At the Osijek Law Faculty, each department set its own procedural rules for written exams, while students had to ensure a stable internet connection, log in at least 15 minutes before the start of the exam for identification purposes, and turn on their camera and microphone but remain silent. For oral exams, a video-conferencing platform was used. Students had to join the meeting in breakout rooms and identify themselves. Students were upset about privacy issues and were unhappy with exams during the pandemic. As soon as epidemiological measures were relaxed in the summer of 2020, exams returned to on-site environments at faculty facilities.

Another step towards online legal education was taken during the pandemic within the framework of international cooperation consortiums. For example, four Croatian law schools participated in the development of the e-course 'Key Issues in Commercial and Investment Arbitration'.[97] Complex learning machines are, among others, the subject of research of a consortium led by Zagreb Law School.[98] During the pandemic, law schools also shifted their academic activities online, such as the Science Festival, a science popularisation event, which took place online. There were also positive effects at the PhD level. The Faculty of Law in Rijeka organised a PhD conference with the greatest globally recognised academics.[99] In terms of non-formal learning during the pandemic, seminars and trainings (national[100] and international events)[101] were held online. Several European law schools organised online seminars hosted by the Faculty of Law in Osijek. They attracted prominent EU speakers and participants and resulted in freely accessible learning materials.[102] Academic conferences were also organised.[103] The impact of digitalisation on law and legal education is

95 https://www.pravri.uniri.hr/hr/component/content/article/7-hr/1813-panika.html.

96 Interview with Prof. Paula Poretti, Vice-Dean at the Faculty of Law in Osijek.

97 An advanced master's level course created by the consortium of Europa-Institut Saarbrücken, South East European Law School Network (SEELS) and its member faculties (Split, Osijek, Zagreb, Rijeka, Zenica, Sarajevo, Belgrade and Nis): https://ei-mag.eu/global/ecourse-introduction-to-arbitration.

98 Project AFAR: Algorithmic Fairness for Asylum Seekers and Refugees, https://www.pravo.unizg.hr/EJP/afar_algorithmic_fairness_for_asylum_seekers_and_refugees.

99 https://pravri.uniri.hr/en/study-programmes/postgraduate-doctoral-study.html.

100 https://research.abdn.ac.uk/poam/events/croatian-training-workshops-2021/; https://www.pravos.unios.hr/seels/nacionalni-seminar-24-05-2021-01.

101 http://www.prafak.ni.ac.rs/158-force-migration-project-seels.html; https://pf.um.si/en/acj/projects/pr09-eu-en4s/results/first-conference/conference-01/.

102 https://www.pravos.unios.hr/katedra-medunarodnog-privatnog-prava/nova-pravila-za-prekogranicne-obitelji-uredba-brussels-iiter; https://youtube.com/channel/UCglXo1_dWcdjWEadtt-Xzhg.

103 https://www.pravos.unios.hr/eclic-2021/conference-programme.

acknowledged by a series of conferences held by the Scientific Council for Legal Affairs of the Croatian Academy of Sciences and Arts, most of which were also held entirely online.[104]

2.7. ACHIEVEMENTS AND CHALLENGES TOWARDS THE END OF THE PANDEMIC

2.7.1. Assessment of Pandemic Online Courses

The health crisis of the COVID-19 pandemic is accelerating digital transformation in HE. Although HE institutions demonstrate different levels of digital capacity, most are eager to show high-level readiness to guarantee educational processes. Data on active courses at Croatian law schools on the Merlin national e-learning platform indicate that online education was mostly seen as an intermediate stage in an emergency situation rather than a possible permanent option for the future.

During the pandemic, several surveys were conducted to investigate aspects of online education to be implemented in Croatian HE during the 2020–21 health crisis. The surveys reveal students have a positive attitude toward online learning, with perceptions of teaching quality and acquired knowledge unlikely to significantly exceed traditional course delivery. However, well-established rules, good quality tool choices with purposeful application and equal (high-quality) engagement of teachers ensure distance learning is not worse than classical education. If conducted properly, it can provide the same level of quality as on-site classes. Students felt they had sufficient computer skills for online classes.[105] However, caution must be exercised regarding the overall positive attitude to online education in light of the extreme situation students were experiencing at the time. Hence, the above student reasoning may have been due to a lack of reasonable alternatives at the time of full lockdown.

Although students appreciate the availability of their teachers and personal contact, the prevailing student opinion is that distance learning, in its current form, has little positive impact on the speed of knowledge acquisition and even a slightly negative impact on the quality of knowledge acquired and grades achieved. The problematic aspect relates to knowledge assessment, as it was difficult to strike a fair balance between the need to eliminate cheating and to

---

104 A. Bačić, 'Pedeset i pet knjiga edicije Modernizacija prava – doprinos Hrvatske akademije znanosti i umjetnosti razvoju pravne teorije i prakse u Republici Hrvatskoj, Zagreb, 2006. – 2020' (2021) 55=545 *Rad Hrvatske akademije znanosti i umjetnosti. Razred za društvene znanosti* 197.

105 Results of research on student satisfaction with online classes, 05.2020, p. 15, https://www.pravos.unios.hr/~marijan/pdf/uzuokvo/on-line_nastava_web_2020.pdf.

preserve student dignity.[106] Therefore, the strong tendency towards introducing ever more online components should be justified in a different way. The only truly positive remarks refer to reducing the cost and time of travel for non-resident students.

2.7.2. The Way Forward: The Development of MOOCs in Law

The impact of the pandemic on fostering e-learning has had some positive effects. The availability of EU funding, particularly through the Erasmus+ platform, is one of them. The Time to Become Digital in Law (DIGinLaw) project is the most prominent example of a progressive, thorough and well-established approach to online legal education.[107] The project aims to address aspects of digitalisation in legal education and law. It addresses the development of digital competencies of HE teachers for innovative teaching practices, which are the backbone of the module on knowledge, skills and competencies for T-shaped lawyers. As part of this, 12 massive open online courses (MOOCs) have been developed via collaboration between four participating universities.[108] Digital competencies for lifelong learning for law students are also being developed. In addition to digital skills, the promotion of research and publication on the topic of 'digitalisation in legal education and law' lies on the foundation of open science.

2.8. FUNDING POLICY AND ONLINE LEGAL EDUCATION

Spending on education in Croatia is close to the EU average (4.6% of GDP); in 2017, Croatia spent 4.7%. The share of spending on tertiary education is 21.5%, above the EU average (15.0%).[109] The criteria for the allocation of budgetary funds for scientific activity and HE are determined by the National Council for Science, Higher Education and Technological Development. Taking into account the established criteria, the Minister prepares the budget proposal for the financing of science and HE on the basis of the collected budgetary proposals of scientific organisations, universities, polytechnics and colleges.[110] Additional

---

[106] Ibid., p. 15.

[107] https://diginlaw.com/.

[108] Josip Juraj Strossmayer University of Osijek (UNIOS) (coordinator), University of Aberdeen (UNIABD), University of Milan (UNIMI) and University of Zagreb University Computing Centre (SRCE) as partners.

[109] Pregled obrazovanja i osposobljavanja za 2019, Hrvatska, Europska komisija, https://education.ec.europa.eu/sites/default/files/document-library-docs/et-monitor-report-2019-croatia_hr.pdf.

[110] Decision on program financing of public higher education institutions in the Republic of Croatia in academic years, Art. 108 para 2 of the Scientific Activity and Higher Education Act (Zakona o znanstvenoj djelatnosti i visokom obrazovanju) Official Gazette 123/03, 198/03, 105/04, 174/04, 02/07, 46/07, 45/09, 63/11, 94/13, 139/13, 101/14, 60/15, 131/17. The financing model

funds are allocated for HE. For 2022, the amount planned for programme funding is HRK 430 million, with significant funds for STEM, and smaller funds for social sciences and humanities.[111] Only state universities offer law programmes, and are fully funded by the state. The Croatian budget finances the regular activities of the law faculties. On average, 60.15% of the total revenues of the Faculty of Law in Osijek comes from the central state budget.[112]

Although the 2014 National Strategy promotes digitalisation and appropriate use of ICT for educational purposes, it is unclear from strategic plans whether HE has been allocated significant funds for these purposes.[113] This was confirmed by the 2020 Action Plan for the implementation of distance education, which reveals that a small part of the funds for e-learning (equipment, facilities, education, communication, support) come from the state budget, whereas the largest part comes from EU funds.[114] The EU and other international funds are used to assess and develop digitalisation of HE in Croatia. The ongoing Assessment of the Digital Maturity of Higher Education institutions in the Republic of Croatia project[115] is a prerequisite for the digital transformation of HE in Croatia. It is one of the priorities of the National Recovery and Resilience Plan 2021–2026, funded by the EU in the amount of HRK 633 million.[116] The purpose of the investment is to provide the necessary teaching infrastructure and open digital teaching resources for quality HE, development and implementation of e-learning, online learning, and active learning. This investment will help to overcome the crisis and support the long-term and sustainable development of HE. A sudden transition to distance learning provides

has now been amended. Each public university is financed according to multi-year financing determined by a signed contract, Art. 99 of the Higher Education and Scientific Activity Act (Zakon o visokom obrazovanju i znanstvenoj djelatnosti) Official Gazette 119/2022.

111 Odluka o programskom financiranju javnih visokih učilišta u Republici Hrvatskoj u akademskim godinama 2018./2019., 2019./2020., 2020./2021. i 2021./2022., Official Gazette 87/18, point XV.

112 Prijedlog financijskog plana za 2022. godinu i projekcija financijskog plana za 2023. i 2024. godinu Pravnog fakulteta Osijek, https://www.pravos.unios.hr/financijski-izvjestaji-i-financijski-planovi.

113 https://mzo.gov.hr/pristup-informacijama/planovi-i-izvjesca/provedbeni-program/184.

114 Akcijski plan za provedbu nastave na daljinu: Model nastave na daljinu (Action plan for the implementation of distance education: Distance education model), Zagreb, 07.2020, p. 37, https://mzo.gov.hr/UserDocsImages//dokumenti/Obrazovanje/NastavaNaDaljinu//Akcijski%20plan%20za%20provedbu%20nastave%20na%20daljinu%20-%20Model%20nastave%20na%20daljinu.pdf.

115 Procjena digitalne zrelosti visokih učilišta u Republici Hrvatskoj (Assessment of digital maturity of higher education institutions in the Republic of Croatia), https://www.srce.unizg.hr/vijesti/zapoceo-projekt-procjena-digitalne-zrelosti-visokih-ucilista-u-rh/objav2021-11-08. The project is funded by the EU and the Organisation for Economic Co-operation and Development (OECD).

116 Nacionalni plan oporavka i otpornosti (National Recovery and Resilience Plan) 2021–2026, p. 875, https://planoporavka.gov.hr/UserDocsImages/dokumenti/Plan%20oporavka%20i%20otpornosti%2C%20srpanj%202021.pdf?vel=13435491.

an opportunity and incentive to develop high-quality digital tools and resources. This investment includes development of open digital teaching resources and the purchase of active equipment (equipping classrooms with a projector, a computer, a sound system, a video-recording studio) and improvement of passive networks (lighting, optics, electrical installations, switchboards, connectors, etc.).

The availability of EU funds is subject to EU rules and procedures. It is noteworthy that state universities benefit from the infrastructure developed for all levels of education. Online teaching platforms are created and maintained by state-funded resources. However, in the period of intensive online teaching, they were unable to meet the needs of HE, so tools for video-conferencing were funded by each university. The University of Rijeka has allocated resources for the optimisation of e-courses.

3. CROATIAN PERSPECTIVES ON ONLINE LEGAL EDUCATION

3.1. PROS AND CONS OF ONLINE HIGHER EDUCATION

Digitalisation is fuelling profound changes in every aspect of society. Legal education, and law generally, are no exception. Drivers for the digitalisation of HE include internationalisation, mobility and collaboration, availability of digital teaching tools, and development of new teaching methods to address the needs of new generations. The pandemic has normalised the online environment. It has promoted ICT usage in all facets of our lives, especially in the educational process. Rapid technological advances are contributing to more complex digital environments in HE. The impact of technologies on HE is highlighted by the expansion of online and blended learning, the development and availability of digital services that have become irreplaceable (such as Big Data and HE Management Information Systems), and the transformation of educational patterns. Teachers working at HE institutions are faced with changing roles and demands for new qualifications. Innovation in digital teaching is not of a technical nature, but reflects structural changes in academic attitudes and mental shifts. The increasing competitiveness of the model is forcing universities to reshape their business models.

Digitalisation in HE has many strengths. Potential students have access to educational offerings irrespective of their location. The learning process is individual and flexible. Students in online courses can access educational content 24/7 and control their self-directed learning. Digital content is more tailored to Generations Y and Z. Teachers at universities demonstrate greater flexibility when structuring their engagement and allocating time to teaching and research. They receive new IT professional development opportunities that improve their competitiveness. Universities have opened an avenue for new income as they are able to reach new audiences.

In this context, one must consider a specific feature of legal education which justifies additional consideration of digitalisation in legal education. ICT acceleration and digitalisation have many implications not only for legal education, but for the content of legal rules and legal practice, which must be reflected in legal education through curriculum reforms. The University of Zagreb has the only law school in Croatia with a chair in legal informatics, which offers several courses.[117] The Information Technology Law course is an integral part of the curriculum,[118] although its content is insufficient to cover the broad intersection of law and technology. The impacts of AI and blockchain technology are felt in areas of law. Digitalisation in business is widely accepted. Digital assets are creating new legal dilemmas across private law. New dispute resolution methods are emerging, such as online dispute resolution tools, smart courts and various technology-driven solutions used in the digitalised administration of justice.[119]

However, there are drawbacks of HE digitalisation in HE and law. The reduction of social chains of less connected professors and fellow students can lead to isolation. ICT changes rapidly and requires constant updating of IT skills. The capital-related costs of e-learning require new computers and other infrastructure. There is great potential for cheating and plagiarism not easily eliminated with software.

It remains uncertain whether online HE, boosted by the pandemic to be one of the top EU priorities, will lead to a real digitalisation of legal education in Croatia. This area requires additional research and a novel approach to implement strategies.[120] The changes must be driven by the fact that technology is educationally neutral. It does not contribute to growth in the educational sector if used improperly.[121] Thus, adherence to permanent post-pandemic online legal education must address specific features of e-learning.

Legal education should consider impacts of changing roles in law firms and demands of the labour market, guided by the vision of the T-shaped lawyer.[122]

---

117 https://www.pravo.unizg.hr/PI/predmeti.

118 https://www.pravo.unizg.hr/PI/predmet/pit/literatura.

119 R. Susskind, *Online Courts and the Future of Justice*, Oxford University Press, 2019, p. 4.

120 P. Isaias, D.G. Sampson and D. Ifenthaler (eds), *Online Teaching and Learning in Higher Education*, Springer Nature, 2021.

121 B. Cope and M. Kalantzis (eds), *E-Learning Ecologies, Principles for New Learning and Assessment*, Routledge, 2017, p. 1.

122 E. Mak, *The T-shaped Lawyer and Beyond: Rethinking Legal Professionalism and Legal Education for Contemporary Societies*, Eleven International Publishing, 2017.

3.2. PATHWAYS FOR DEVELOPING E-LEARNING IN CROATIAN LEGAL EDUCATION

A number of new educational technologies are emerging in both traditional and modern learning venues.[123] The concept, cost and benefits of online HE have occupied academia during the last decade, with recent academic assessment dealing with online HE in general[124] and in law.[125] However, Croatian legal education theory has so far not critically addressed basic underlying features of online education, referred to as phenomena of e-learning ecologies.[126] The well-established strategies previously described do not resemble HE in law.

At Croatian law schools, online legal education is offered in the form of updated traditional legal education, active blended learning and MOOCs. Regardless of what form online legal education takes, acceptance of the changing role of the teacher and the learner is a prerequisite for each.

3.3. REVERSAL OF THE TRADITIONAL TEACHER–LEARNER ROLE CALLS FOR A NEW PEDAGOGICAL APPROACH

There is a high risk involved in delivering online classes without appropriate methodology.[127] Some data indicate that the rate of satisfaction with online classes reflects the attitudes of students towards online teaching in HE. Online education requires a change in pedagogical approaches that accompany e-learning and the use of computers. Digitalisation promotes the interaction and knowledge exchange between teachers and students. However, it can lead to reservations or barriers and result in insufficient usage.[128]

---

123 B. Cope and M. Kalantzis (eds), *E-Learning Ecologies, Principles for New Learning and Assessment*, Routledge, 2017.

124 K.J. Fandl and J.D. Smith, *Success as an Online Student: Strategies for Effective Learning*, Elsevier, 2013; P. Isaias, D.G. Sampson and D. Ifenthaler (eds), *Online Teaching and Learning in Higher Education*, Springer, 2020; S. McKenzie, F. Garivaldis and K.R. Dyer, *Tertiary Online Teaching and Learning: TOTAL Perspectives and Resources for Digital Education*, Springer, 2020; J. McDougall, *Critical Approaches to Online Learning*, Critical Publishing, 2021; S. Kučina Softić, M. Odak and J. Lasić Lazić, *Digitalna transformacija – nove prilike i izazovi u obrazovanju*, Nakladnik Sveučilište Sjever, 2021, p. 207.

125 E. Jones and F. Cownie, *Key Directions in Legal Education: National and International Perspectives*, Routledge, 2020.

126 B. Cope and M. Kalantzis (eds), *E-Learning Ecologies, Principles for New Learning and Assessment*, Routledge, 2017.

127 R. Bennett and M. Kent (eds), *Massive Open Online Courses and Higher Education: What Went Right, What Went Wrong and Where to Next?*, Routledge, 2017.

128 G.D. Constantino and J.E. Raffagheli, 'Online teaching and learning, going beyond the information given' in M.G. Di Gesú and M.F. González (eds), *Cultural Views on Online Learning in Higher Education: A Seemingly Borderless Class*, Springer Nature, 2021, p. 4.

Teachers must develop digital competencies in methodology and didactics. The overall positive attitude towards ICT and e-learning in teaching, which accounts for 90.1% of respondents at the University of Zagreb, should be seen as a promising starting point.[129]

All over the world, under pressure due to the COVID-19 pandemic, countries have combined high-tech and low-tech approaches to help teachers support student learning.[130] The implementation of e-learning in the educational process enables a paradigm shift from the teacher being at the centre of the process to the student being the centre of the process. The teacher is thus afforded a new role of mentor and coordinator, with students becoming active participants and taking responsibility for their results, in both the transfer and creation of knowledge and research.

The number of law students in law schools or graduating in a typical year must be taken into account. In the academic year 2019/20, 9,053 students (all years of study, full- and part-time) were enrolled in university studies at law faculties in the Republic of Croatia, and in the same academic year 525 teachers and associates were employed. However, in 2019, only 920 students graduated from university studies at law faculties.[131] The number of enrolled students is still high, though the number of graduates is poor. Law teachers are not afforded enough time to focus on developing skills and a student-centred approach, in comparison to the time in which they are expected to deal with their everyday workload. However, there are several factors that have reduced the numbers of enrolling law students over the years, including a reduced number of children in schools, fostered by family migration to other countries, and constant new tertiary education programmes for vocations that the legal market cries out for.[132]

Technology interventions have improved teacher engagement with students. Effective teachers rely on improved access to content, data and networks to better support student learning. The positive outcomes should be used as a starting point for building inclusive education systems. This is acknowledged

---

129 S. Kučina Softić, 'Teachers' digital competencies for E-learning application in higher education' in *Towards Personalized Guidance and Support for Learning*, EDEN Research Workshop, Barcelona, 2018, p. 206, https://www.eden-online.org/proc-2485/index.php/PROC/article/view/1679.

130 M. Barron, C. Cobo, A. Munoz-Najarinaki and S. Ciarrusta, *The changing role of teachers and technologies amidst the COVID 19 pandemic: key findings from a cross-country study*, https://blogs.worldbank.org/education/changing-role-teachers-and-technologies-amidst-covid-19-pandemic-key-findings-cross.

131 Državni zavod za statistiku, Statističko izvješće br. 1665, Visoko obrazovanje u 2019., pp. 28 and 98; Statističko izvješće br. 1666, Studenti u akademskoj godini 2019./2020., p. 43.

132 See above section 1.1.1.

by the Croatian national strategy.[133] Policymakers should thus support the application of the models that have proven to be effective and integrate them into the regular education system. This requires investment in the development of didactic-methodological resources and capacities to exploit the full potential of remote and blended learning.

There is growing focus on learning processes, with students becoming active participants responsible for their learning achievements, and teachers using innovative teaching methods, encouraging students and motivating them to get involved, explore, reflect, build new knowledge and acquire new skills. Traditional teaching methods, primarily with the teacher at the centre of the educational process, are insufficient for today's students and do not meet their needs as students learn differently. Technology has enabled and encouraged a paradigm shift in focus from teaching to learning, and provides a model for student placement at the centre of the educational process. Digital technologies in teaching and learning are changing the skills teachers must have and shifting the focus from teaching design to learning design, changing the teacher's perspective from a sage on the stage to a guide and tutor.[134] The role of the teacher is changing from a synthesiser of disciplinary content to a digital content curator who designs learning activities.[135]

3.3.1. MOOCs: Self-Paced and Active Blended Learning

The most prominent form of online education is the creation of MOOCs. However, existing leading MOOC platforms are outside the EU. In Europe, there is a diverse range of online courses offered, but very few MOOCs.

MOOCs can be self-paced, fully online or guided.[136] The digital environment calls for a new approach to defining student activities and achieving desired

---

133 The Strategy of Education, Science and Technology of the Ministry of Science and Education, 2014, states similarly: 'The role and importance of teachers as mentors, coordinators and promoters of the educational process is growing with the spread of e-learning and education. E-learning enables the student to be at the centre of the educational process, taking an active role and responsibility for educational outcomes.'

134 T.L. Dysart and T. Norton, *Law Teaching Strategies for a New Era: Beyond the Physical Classroom*, Carolina Academic Press, 2021.

135 M.G. Sindoni and I. Moschini (eds), *Multimodal Literacies Across Digital Learning Contexts*, Routledge, 2021; B. Cope and M. Kalantzis, 'Pedagogies for Digital Learning: From Transpositional Grammar to the Literacies of Education' in M.G. Sindoni and I. Moschini (eds), *Multimodal Literacies Across Digital Learning Contexts*, Routledge, 2021, p. 7, https://www.researchgate.net/publication/344876961_Pedagogies_for_Digital_Learning_From_Transpositional_Grammar_to_the_Literacies_of_Education.

136 A. Armellini and B.C. Padilla Rodriguez, 'Active Blended Learning: Definition, Literature Review, and a Framework for Implementation' in *Cases on Active Blended Learning in Higher Education*, IGI Global, 2021, https://doi.org/10.4018/978-1-7998-7856-8.ch001.

learning outcomes.[137] Students must be provided with adequate learning materials. Adequacy is measured by several criteria. In terms of availability, it is necessary to create digital materials[138] or use open access.[139] Complexity and quantity of learning materials depends on the education level. In line with the EQF guidelines, the number of pages for any given reading material should be calculated on the basis of the time a student is expected to spend reading and learning. Law teachers should develop digital competencies. This know-how is available for Croatian law professors through an open-access MOOC on digital competence for law teachers.[140]

3.3.2. *Online Components Penetrating Traditional Legal Education*

Existing curricula should be updated. Initially, at least one general course on law and technology should be established. Computer literacy should be promoted as part of each course. An in-depth assessment of the course content should be carried out, as technology does not affect all aspects of legal education equally, but is innate to some. For instance, litigation and dispute resolution courses should be delivered in a manner that enables students to resolve disputes using both online dispute resolution (ODR) and traditional means.[141] EU private international law courses should refer to online methodology addressed by regulations and the Hague Conventions advocating ICT for cross-border cooperation. Students should be taught how to handle EU regulations and Hague conventions.

Further, the concerns described earlier raised by Croatian scholars about legal education should be addressed.[142] For example, Croatian legal education has been concerned with the introduction of the moot court learning model in law schools. Problem-based learning relies on learning theories which state that students who learn through facilitated problem solving can master the

137 I. Gil-Jaurena and S. Kučina Softić, 'Aligning learning outcomes and assessment methods: a web tool for e-learning courses' (2016) 13 *International Journal of Educational Technology in Higher Education*, Art. 17, https://doi.org/10.1186/s41239-016-0016-z.

138 E. Rubin, *Legal Education in the Digital Age*, Cambridge University Press, 2012.

139 S. Kučina Softić and S. Rako, 'Otvoreno obrazovanje i otvoreni obrazovni sadržaji. Otvorenost u znanosti i obrazovanju' in I. Hebrang Grgić (ed.), *Otvorenost u znanosti i visokom obrazovanju*, Školska knjiga, 2018, https://repozitorij.srce.unizg.hr/islandora/object/srce%3A142/datastream/FILE0/view.

140 www.mod.srce.hr.

141 G. Grant and E. Lestrell, 'Bringing ODR to the Legal Education Mainstream Findings from the Field' in C. Denvir (ed.), *Modernizing Legal Education*, Cambridge University Press, 2019, pp. 92–108.

142 See sections 2.4 and 2.5 above.

content and strategies required.[143] Another prominent example is the legal clinic on law and technology.[144] Although educational theories find suitable ways to apply in online environments,[145] such approaches have not been evaluated in Croatia.

However, the rise of AI has changed the concept of technological literacy. Therefore, online legal educational patterns should go beyond low-level assessment, as future lawyers must learn to deal with AI.[146] A prototype of an upgraded model can be found in experiments in legal education: an interdisciplinary method derived from design schools and human–computer interaction programmes.[147]

4. CONCLUDING REMARKS

Legal education at the four Croatian law schools is primarily conducted using traditional in situ teaching methods. However, the pandemic has shifted teaching to a virtual environment, although the methodology essentially remains traditional. Lectures are recorded or livestreamed, and distance learning platforms are mostly used to supplement stored learning materials. E-learning modalities, their advantages and disadvantages, and the opportunities and threats they represent for legal education are the talk of the town among Croatian legal scholars. The Croatian reality is that online education has been introduced without developing the digital competencies of teaching staff. The post-pandemic open online course numbers may indicate that the legal HE system has been slow to adopt effective digital education practices. The high number of students is keeping law professors busy with teaching activities. In addition, the career development criteria put more emphasis on their research activity than teaching excellence.

---

143 C.E. Hmelo-Silver, 'Problem-Based Learning: What and How Do Students Learn?' (2004) 16 *Educational Psychology Review* 235; A. Carpenter, 'Developing "NextGen" Lawyers through Project-Based Learning' in C. Denvir (ed.), *Modernising Legal Education*, Cambridge University Press, 2020, p. 126.

144 F. Ryan, 'Rage against the machine? Incorporating legal tech into legal education' (2021) 55(3) *The Law Teacher* 392, 395, https://doi.org/10.1080/03069400.2020.1805927.

145 M. Moallem and E. Igoe, 'Problem-Based Learning and Computer Based Scaffolds on Online Learning', 15th International Conference on Cognition and Exploratory Learning in Digital Age (CELDA 2018), https://files.eric.ed.gov/fulltext/ED600595.pdf.

146 J.O. McGinnis and R.G. Pearce, 'The Great Disruption: How Machine Intelligence Will Transform the Role of Lawyers in the Delivery of Legal Services' (2014) 82 *Fordham Law Review* 3041, 3042.

147 M. Hagan, 'Design Comes to the Law School' in C. Denvir (ed.), *Modernising Legal Education*, Cambridge University Press, 2020, pp. 109–125.

E-learning strategies are generally not systematically implemented in Croatian HE in general, including in law. Although the University Computing Centre offers free courses on various e-learning topics, they are attended depending on the individual preferences of HE teachers. Digital competencies are a formal requirement for teacher appointments at only one Croatian university offering law.

To date, no formal study programme in law has been accredited for online teaching. However, online teaching and learning are employed in both formal and non-formal education, and are becoming increasingly important due to the e-digitalisation impetus of the EU. Several international consortium initiatives have addressed the issue of e-learning and developed a corresponding approach. Taking into account the basic features and nature of e-learning, the digital competencies of HE teachers are developed, MOOCs are created and the digital competencies of students are improved. Open Merlin courses indicate that most teachers have adopted a blended learning approach.

The focus of these initiatives resides in the fact that emerging technologies offer new opportunities for teaching and learning. However, the teacher must not only be an expert in their subject area, but also follow and become familiar with the development of ICT. The teacher must build on their pedagogical background and properly use ICT in the educational process.

Considering the desired T-shaped lawyer as a product of the educational process, Croatian legal education requires a profound change in attitude, mindset and pedagogic methodology. Law professors should develop their digital competencies by default to use ICT in both online and blended teaching. This will shift the focus from teaching to learning. Teachers should incorporate the pedagogical characteristics of Generations Y and Z and adult learning into decisions relating to student activity. In addition to utilising ICT to support traditional teaching, teachers should be encouraged to create MOOCs and partake in national and international communities for open and inclusive education. Digital literacy of law students should be emphasised in study programmes. Where courses rely on digitalisation in their subject matter, students should be taught to work through material in a virtual environment.

ONLINE LEGAL EDUCATION IN CYPRUS

An Era of Change?

Demetra Loizou and Lida Pitsillidou

1. INTRODUCTION

This report considers the position of online legal education and the legal profession in Cyprus, both before and after the COVID-19 pandemic. The outbreak of the pandemic substantially impacted not only the global economy and public health, but also the way legal education institutions operate in Cyprus. Indeed, due to the imperative urgency to prevent the spread of

COVID-19, the Cypriot government was asked to deal with an unprecedented challenge through imposing massive restrictions and lockdown measures to ensure social distancing. Following the announcement made by the Minister of Education, Culture, Sports, and Youth (MOEC) on 10 March 2020 to suspend face-to-face operations of all higher educational institutions in Cyprus,[1] this resulted in the temporary physical closure of Cypriot universities,[2] accelerating the transformation of legal education from traditional in-classroom teaching into 'emergency remote teaching'.[3]

Emergency remote teaching is defined by Hodges and others as the 'temporary shift of instructional delivery to an alternate delivery mode due to crisis circumstances'.[4] In comparison to online teaching, this does not aim 'to re-create a robust educational ecosystem but rather to provide temporary access to instruction and instructional supports in a manner that is quick to set up and is reliably available during an emergency or crisis'.[5] With emergency remote teaching, Cypriot law schools witnessed an evolution to online teaching, a teaching delivery mode which was nearly absent due to the reluctance of law schools and accredited/professional bodies to recognise distance-learning LLB degrees in Cyprus.

Although Cypriot universities smoothly adjusted to the transition of online teaching due to their digital infrastructures and development of new technologies, this was not the case with the legal profession. The lack of information communication technologies (ICT) across Cypriot courts

1 MOEC, 'Προληπτικά μέτρα που αφορούν στα Ιδρύματα Ανώτερης Εκπαίδευσης έναντι του νέου κορωνοϊού (COVID – 19)' (10.03.2020), https://enimerosi.moec.gov.cy/archeia/1/ypp10528a; MOEC, 'Διευκρίνιση για τα Ιδρύματα Ανώτερης Εκπαίδευσης όσον αφορά στην ανακοίνωση του Υπουργείου Παιδείας, Πολιτισμού, Αθλητισμού και Νεολαίας για τη λήψη μέτρων πρόληψης της εξάπλωσης του ιού COVID-19, ημερομηνίας 11.03.2020' (12.03.2020), https://enimerosi.moec.gov.cy/archeia/1/ypp10547a; see also CYQAA, 'Εξ αποστάσεως συνέχιση των μαθημάτων, Επ' Αόριστον λόγω του COVID-19' (10.03.2020), https://www.dipae.ac.cy/index.php/en/news-and-events/announcements/13-dipae-el/dipaeel/anakoinoseis/498-10-03-2020-anavoli-episkepseon-distance-learning.

2 CYQAA, 'Εξ αποστάσεως συνέχιση των μαθημάτων, Επ' Αόριστον λόγω του COVID-19' (10.03.2020), http://www.dipae.ac.cy/index.php/en/news-and-events/announcements/13-dipae-el/dipaeel/anakoinoseis/498-10-03-2020-anavoli-episkepseon-distance-learning; CYQAA, 'Διαδικτυακή διδασκαλία/εξέταση και προσωπικά δεδομένα (Αρ. 2)' (30.09.2020), http://www.dipae.ac.cy/index.php/el/nea-ekdiloseis/anakoinoseis-el/546-30-09-2020-diadiktyaki-didaskalia-exetasi-kai-prosopika-dedomena-2; see also T. Farnell, A.S. Matijević and N.Š. Schmidt, 'The Impact of COVID-19 on Higher Education: A Review of Emerging Evidence' (Publications Office of the European Union, 17.03.2021), https://op.europa.eu/en/publication-detail/-/publication/876ce591-87a0-11eb-ac4c-01aa75ed71a1/language-en.

3 C. Hodges et al., 'The Difference Between Emergency Remote Teaching and Online Learning' (EDUCAUSE, 27.03.2020), https://er.educause.edu/articles/2020/3/the-difference-between-emergency-remote-teaching-and-online-learning.

4 Ibid.

5 Ibid.

has been a critical weakness of the justice system, as courts are based almost entirely on manual and paper-based systems, which led to excessive delays in resolving disputes. It was not until the outbreak of COVID-19 that we saw the implementation of an electronic justice system in Cyprus (the 'iJustice' system) in July 2021, aiming to change the operational norms of the legal profession by moving to the digitalisation of the Cypriot justice system. As a result of the shift to an electronic justice system, the need has been acknowledged to further enhance the lifelong training of judges and the continuing professional development of lawyers.

This report aims to provide an overview of the legal profession in Cyprus, both before and after the pandemic, and evaluate the impact of COVID-19 on the digitalisation of the Cypriot justice system. It also aims to examine the evolution of online legal education in Cyprus by exploring the challenges and opportunities presented to reshape legal pedagogy, accelerating the transformation of a contemporary legal education that embraces the use of digital technology in the law curriculum.

2. BACKGROUND: LEGAL PROFESSION, UNIVERSITIES AND IT SYSTEMS GENERALLY

2.1. LEGAL EDUCATION AND PROFESSIONAL RECOGNITION REQUIREMENTS

The accreditation of LLB degrees delivered by Cypriot universities is determined by the Cyprus Agency of Quality Assurance (CYQAA), the quality assurance and accreditation body for academic programmes in Cyprus. 'Regulated professions', including the legal profession, are subject to conditions of practice determined by applicable legislation.[6] For lawyers, the relevant legislation is the Advocates Law (Cap 2). Thus, the (re-) accreditation of law degrees by the CYQAA does not automatically guarantee their professional recognition. According to the Advocates Law, the sole 'gatekeeper' to the legal profession is the Legal Council (LC). According to CYQAA legislation, a degree can be accredited based on conventional[7] or non-conventional modes of delivery (distance learning or a combination of both methods).[8] While the CYQAA can

6 Law on Quality Assurance and Certification of the Higher Education and on the Establishment and Function of an Institution for Pertinent Issues (Law 136(I)/2015), section 2.

7 According to the CYQAA, attendance with physical presence is compulsory for conventional programmes of study. See CYQAA Announcement (27.07.2016), http://www.dipae.ac.cy/index.php/el/nea-ekdiloseis/anakoinoseis-el/86-ypochreotiki-parousia-programmata-spoudon.

8 Law on Quality Assurance and Certification of the Higher Education and on the Establishment and Function of an Institution for Pertinent Issues (Law 136(I)/2015), section 24.

accredit an online LLB degree, the LC has not recognised any distance learning LLB degrees to date.[9]

Interestingly, the provision of legal education in Cyprus is quite recent. The first law school was only established on the island in 2006 at the University of Cyprus.[10] Until then, prospective law students had no alternative but to undertake legal studies abroad. This was a general characteristic of higher education in Cyprus beyond the field of law. The University of Cyprus, as the first university of the island, was established in 1989 and admitted its first students in 1992.[11] Today, there is one public and six private universities[12] accredited by the CYQAA to deliver LLB degrees. These are the University of Cyprus, the only public university, followed by the private universities, namely the European University, Frederick University, Neapolis University, University of Central Lancashire Cyprus, University of Nicosia, and Philips University.[13]

The vast majority of law graduates come from British and Greek universities.[14] The former choice accords with the fact that Cyprus, as a former British colony, has a legal system which is principally founded on the principles of common law and equity.[15] Hence, studying law at a British university is an attractive choice in terms of pursuing a career in law. At the same time, the shared culture and language between Greece and Greek Cypriots renders Greek universities a natural choice for studies in higher education, whether in law or another field. This also explains the fact that even though Cyprus has among the highest number of lawyers per capita in the EU, law schools in Cyprus generally have small classes.[16] This state of affairs is expected to be redefined in the next few years because of Brexit and its financial implications for tuition fees.[17]

---

9 The sole exception is the distance learning LLB of the University of London, which has been recognised by section 4 of Advocates Law (Cap 2) almost since the independence of Cyprus (Advocates (Amending) Law (Law 42/1961)).

10 University of Cyprus, Department of Law, https://newdev.ucy.ac.cy/law/.

11 Cyprus Ministry of Education, Culture, Sport, and Youth, 'Historical Background' (Higher Education), https://www.highereducation.ac.cy/index.php/en/dae/istoriki-anadromi.

12 The Cyprus Council of Recognition of Higher Education Qualification (KY.S.A.T.S.), 'Private Education', https://www.kysats.ac.cy/index.php/en/genikes-plirofories/idiotiki-ekpaidefsi.

13 Public universities are founded as public corporate bodies which are funded by the Cyprus government, though they can obtain funding from other sources, such as EU projects. On the other hand, private universities are founded as private corporate bodies (as provided by the Private Universities (Establishment, Operation and Control) Law 109(I) of 2005, section 6) which are funded through private sources, such as student tuition and fees and funding through EU projects (see Ministry of Education and Culture, 'Higher Education in Cyprus' (2012), https://www.kysats.ac.cy/archeia/pdf/highereducation-vivliaraki.pdf).

14 Statistical Service, Education Statistics – 2018–2019 (31.03.2021), https://www.cystat.gov.cy/en/PublicationList?s=33.

15 N. Hatzimihail, 'Cyprus as a Mixed Legal System' (2013) 6(1) *Journal of Civil Studies* 37.

16 See sections 2.3 and 3.1.1 below.

17 Press and Information Office, 'Cyprus and Brexit', https://brexit.com.cy/students.html.

2.2. ENTRY REQUIREMENTS

The powers of the LC are set out in section 3 of the Advocates Law.[18] The LC is responsible for the admission to practice and enrolment of advocates. It decides whether individuals satisfy the legal requirements for their initial registration as trainee lawyers. The qualifications necessary to be admitted to the bar are provided in section 4 of the Advocates Law. An individual seeking admission to practice must hold a law degree recognised by the LC, whether obtained in Cyprus, another EU member state or a third country.[19] Additionally, a trainee lawyer must complete a 12-month legal practice period and successfully pass the examinations set by the LC.[20] Significantly, the LC organises the trainee lawyers' lectures and conduct of exams.[21] Every advocate qualified to practise must enrol in the Register of Practising Advocates maintained by the Cyprus Bar Association (CBA) Council.[22] The CBA Council issues the advocates' annual licence to practise upon satisfaction of specific requirements,[23] including the requirements for continuing professional development.

2.3. SIZE OF THE LEGAL PROFESSION

The legal profession in Cyprus is large both in absolute numbers and in proportion to the population. Since the commencement of the European Justice Scoreboard (EJS) in 2013, Cyprus has consistently ranked among the countries with the highest number of lawyers per capita in the EU. According to the 2021 EJS, Cyprus had the highest number of lawyers in 2020, with over 450 lawyers per 100,000 inhabitants.[24] Almost 500 new lawyers are registered each year

---

18 Advocates Law (Cap 2), section 3. See also Legal Council, *Powers of the Legal Council*, https://www.legalcouncil.org.cy/the-powers-of-the-council/?lang=en.

19 Advocates Law (Cap 2), section 4(d)(i)–(ii).

20 Ibid., section 4.

21 Ibid., section 5.

22 Ibid., section 6A.

23 Ibid.

24 European Commission, *European Justice Scoreboard 2021*, figure 34, https://ec.europa.eu/info/sites/default/files/eu_justice_scoreboard_2021.pdf. A similar picture is reflected in the previous years: EU Justice Scoreboard 2020, figure 37 (second); EU Justice Scoreboard 2019, figure 35 (first); EU Justice Scoreboard 2018, figure 43 (first); EU Justice Scoreboard 2017, figure 38 (fourth); EU Justice Scoreboard 2016, figure 33 (fourth); EU Justice Scoreboard 2015, figure 42 (fourth); EU Justice Scoreboard 2014, figure 25 (fifth); EU Justice Scoreboard 2013, figure 21 (fifth). More the latest statistics see: European Justice Scoreboard 2022, figure 38 (second).

in a country with a population of around one million.[25] As of October 2022, there were more than 4,400 active members on the CBA's website.[26] However, only a proportion of new lawyers elect to remain in the profession as practising lawyers. Many seek employment elsewhere after the 12-month legal practice and LC examinations. Thus, the actual number of law graduates is much higher than the number of practising lawyers. The reason why so many people decide to study law but only a portion of them eventually end up working as practising lawyers is because a law degree is regarded as a strong and versatile option for career development, in both the public and private sectors.[27]

2.4. CONTINUING PROFESSIONAL DEVELOPMENT

2.4.1. Advocates

Section 24 of the Advocates Law allows the CBA Council to provide for the continuing legal training of lawyers. However, compulsory continuing professional education (CPE) for lawyers was only introduced as recently as 2017.[28] The CBA determines the number of hours, which may vary accordingly. The renewal of a lawyer's licence is contingent upon successful completion of CPE, unless certain exceptions apply (e.g. if a lawyer is over 60 years of age, provided they have been practising for 30 years).[29] CPE programmes include 'seminars, lectures or other educational activities delivered face to face or via the web or other electronic means, including audio-visual material prepared by approved providers'.[30] Notably, a lawyer will not be considered to have

---

25 A.C. Emilianides, 'How Did the Number of Registered Lawyers Increase During British Rule' (*Dikaiosyni portal*, 02.12.2019), https://dikaiosyni.com/katigories/arthra/pws-avxithike-o-arithmos-twn-eggegrammenwn-dkikgorwn-stin-agglokratia/. According to the latest demographic statistics, at the end of 2019, the population in the areas of the Republic of Cyprus which were under the effective control of the government of the Republic of Cyprus was estimated at 888,000: https://www.mof.gov.cy/mof/cystat/statistics.nsf/All/55FC039F275B7049C225862D003ACD70?OpenDocument&sub=1&sel=1&e=&print.

26 Lawyers – Members (Cyprus Bar Association), https://www.cyprusbar.org/CypriotAdvocateMembersPage.aspx.

27 According to the Cyprus Statistical Service, law and business administration are the most popular choices for undergraduate studies of young adults aged 25–34. See Statistical Service, Infographics – Young Adults and Education – 2nd Quarter 2019 (06.11.2019), https://www.cystat.gov.cy/en/PublicationList?s=33&p=1.

28 Continuing Professional Education (Regulatory Administrative Act 386/2017), http://www.cylaw.org/KDP/data/2017_1_386.pdf.

29 Continuing Professional Education (Regulatory Administrative Act 386/2017) as amended by Regulatory Administrative Act 80/2020, http://www.cylaw.org/KDP/data/2020_1_80.pdf.

30 Ibid., para. 5(a).

attended more than four CPE hours by merely watching audio-visual material.[31] This ensures quality standards, with lawyers' continuing education focusing primarily on synchronous learning.

In March 2020, as a result of the emergency government measures to address the COVID-19 pandemic, all scheduled courses were postponed by the CBA until late April.[32] In June 2020, the CBA Council waived the requirement for mandatory CPE units/hours to renew lawyers' licences for the year 2021; this requirement ultimately recommenced on 1 January 2021 with 12 CPE units/hours required by the end of 2021 to renew licences for 2022.[33] Both the CBA and local bar associations made an effort to organise online courses to count towards lawyers' CPE obligations.[34] More recently, the CBA decided that, as of 2022, approved international seminars could count towards the total number of teaching hours.[35]

While the CBA was initially slow in responding to the challenges created by COVID-19, its eventual reaction demonstrated an ability to adapt to ensure the uninterrupted continuing professional education of practising lawyers through online legal education. Online seminars and workshops are now well established and have remained even though COVID-19 restrictions have been eased or lifted. The addition of international seminars has positively broadened the scope and variety of knowledge and training available to practising lawyers.

2.4.2. *Judges*

The functional needs and operations of the Cypriot courts have been the subject of internal reports for several years, the most recent being the 2016 report by George Erotocritou, former Judge of the Supreme Court and Director of Reform and Training.[36] The lifelong training of Cypriot judges was among the key issues

31 Ibid., para. 5(b).

32 CBA Announcement (18.03.2020), http://www.cyprusbarassociation.org/index.php/el/news/2385-2020-03-18-07-29-41.

33 CBA Announcement (16.06.2020), https://www.cyprusbarassociation.org/index.php/el/news/3840-2020-06-16-06-45-02; CBA Announcement (08.12.2020), https://www.cyprusbarassociation.org/index.php/el/news/8340-2020-12-08-11-24-09.

34 CBA Announcement (08.12.2020), https://www.cyprusbarassociation.org/index.php/el/news/8340-2020-12-08-11-24-09.

35 CBA Announcement (24.09.2021), https://www.cyprusbarassociation.org/index.php/en/news/15070-2021-09-24-10-17-47.

36 Supreme Court Report on the Functional Needs of the Courts and Other Related Matters (06.2016), http://www.supremecourt.gov.cy/judicial/sc.nsf/All/58D9022CA52B670BC225839A00300FA8/$file/final%20inside%20PAGES.pdf.

identified by the Erotocritou report. The report recommended establishing a training department for judges, legal officers, registrars and court staff. In 2017, Professor Jeremy Cooper and Judge George Erotocritou developed a more comprehensive study and action plan, subsequently approved by the Supreme Court of Cyprus and facilitating the establishment of a judicial college.[37] In January 2017, the Supreme Court created the Office of Reform and Judicial Training, requiring newly appointed judges to undertake a rigorous 10-day training course before embarking on their roles. A legislative framework was introduced in 2020 with the adoption of the Law on the Establishment and Operation of the Judicial College.[38] Section 3 of the Law provides that the Judicial College is responsible for issues regarding the professional training and education of judges, based on the needs that arise from time to time, including training in the development of skills, information technology, case management and professional development.

Cyprus was one of the last EU member states to introduce a formal system for the continuing training of judges, in contrast to EU law and policy.[39] Although the objective is to train all legal professionals, the European Commission placed particular emphasis on the training of judges and professionals responsible for the enforcement and respect of EU law.[40] Judicial training is perceived as a means of improving the efficiency of the justice system and cross-border cooperation. The European Commission thus called upon all actors to bolster this by requesting that 'budgets must be allocated; time must be made available, incentives developed, and clear commitments taken.'[41]

The EU judicial training strategy for 2021–24 further strengthens judicial training. Emphasis is placed on the upscaling of the digitalisation of justice considering the lessons learned during the COVID-19 pandemic and the need

---

37 J. Cooper, 'Creating the Cyprus School for Judicial Training'. The content of the report is not publicly available but its adoption is mentioned in the Functional Review Report (p. 19) and in public speeches (e.g. 'Speech for the Ceremony of the Official Delivery of the Final Report on the General Reform of the Courts', G. Erotocritou, Former Judge of the Supreme Court and Director of Reform and Training (27.03.2018), http://www.supremecourt.gov.cy/judicial/sc.nsf/All/4F4B016078A6DA93C22583BD003D9CDB?OpenDocument). See also Functional Review Report of the Courts System of Cyprus, Technical Assistance Project 2017/2018, IPA, Ireland (Supported by the Structural Reform Support Service (SSRS) of the European Commission) (03.2018) https://www.cyprusbarassociation.org/files/publications/Functional_Review_of_Courts_System_of_Cyprus_IPA_Ireland_-_Final_Report.pdf; N. Mouttotos, 'Reform of Civil Procedure in Cyprus: Delivering Justice in a More Efficient and Timely Way' (2020) 49(2) *Common Law World Review* 99, 123–124.

38 Law on the Establishment and the Operation of the Judicial College (Law 101(I)/2020).

39 Consolidated version of the Treaty on the Functioning of the European Union (TFEU), OJ C 326, 26.10.2012, pp. 47–390, Articles 81(2)(h) and 82(1)(c).

40 European Commission Communication, 'Building Trust in EU-Wide Justice a New Dimension to European Judicial Training' (COM(2011) 551 final, 13.09.2011), p. 4.

41 Ibid., p. 12.

to shift from face-to-face to online proceedings.[42] In this regard, judicial training should encourage utilisation of new technologies to reach wider audiences and support quality training.[43]

Cyprus still lags behind other EU member states. The annual EJS often highlights the lack of and/or inconsistent provision of judicial training in Cyprus. However, key steps and significant progress have been achieved in the last few years regarding the lifelong training of judges. According to the 2019 EJS, more than 80% of Cypriot judges undertook continuing training activities in EU law or the law of another member state.[44] However, the progress of judge craft, IT skills, court management and judicial ethics is less clear and consistent.[45] On balance, the establishment of the Judicial College ushered in a new era in the continuing and professional development of judges.

During the pandemic, the newly established Judicial College remained active, continuing the provision of judicial training in an uninterrupted manner. International training sessions, originally scheduled to take place face-to-face, were moved online.[46] While the Judicial School tried to organise its own webinars and online courses, because of its limited capabilities it also relied on the assistance of its European and international partners to provide regular training courses to judges on a weekly basis, such as the European Judicial Training Network, the European Research Area and the United Nations Office on Drugs and Crime and other national Judicial Colleges.[47] In 2021, most judicial training seminars continued online, not only because of COVID-19 restrictions but also because many trainings involved training partners from abroad.[48]

---

42 European Commission Communication, 'Ensuring Justice in the EU – a European Judicial Training Strategy for 2021–2024' (COM(2020) 713 final, 02.12.2020), p. 9.

43 Ibid. See also types of actions provided in Article 8 of Regulation (EU) 2021/693 of the European Parliament and of the Council of 28 April 2021 establishing the Justice Programme and repealing Regulation (EU) No 1382/2013, OJ L 156, 05.05.2021, pp. 21–38, in particular subparagraph 8(e).

44 EU Justice Scoreboard 2019, figure 36, https://ec.europa.eu/info/sites/default/files/justice_scoreboard_2019_en.pdf.

45 There was evidence of such training in the EU Justice Scoreboards of 2020 (figure 38), 2018 (figure 45), 2017 (figure 41), and 2016 (figure 36), but not in the other reporting periods.

46 Judicial Training School Announcement, 'Speech for the Judicial Deontology Ethics Seminar for New Judges', G. Erotocritou, Former Judge of the Supreme Court and Director of Reform and Training (06.10.2020), http://www.supremecourt.gov.cy/Judicial/SC.nsf/All/1CE0617FB333794DC22585FA002C32C0?OpenDocument.

47 Judicial Training School Announcement, 'Online Judicial Training in Times of COVID-19' (22.04.2020), http://www.supremecourt.gov.cy/Judicial/SC.nsf/All/CC1C1897F2BE70E8C22585520037C833?OpenDocument.

48 E.g. Judicial Training School Announcement, Online Seminars on 'Briefing the Trainers' for Judges, Registrars and Lawyers on the New Civil Procedure Rules (19.07.2021), http://www.supremecourt.gov.cy/Judicial/SC.nsf/All/B605A36A7801B9A3C2258717002E4BDE?OpenDocument.

2.5. LEGAL PROFESSIONALS

The lack of information communication technologies (ICT) across Cypriot courts has fostered chronic issues affecting the administration of justice, including excessive delays and weak case management. Notably, the courts rely almost entirely on manual and paper-based systems.[49] The lack of ICT presents challenges at all stages of a case, from its initiation, its progression and the hearing and judgment stages, through to the completion of an appeal.[50] The Functional Review Report therefore recommended the introduction of digital audio recordings in court proceedings.[51]

The use of ICT in court proceedings has been a key feature of the annual EJS assessments. Cyprus' performance is one of the poorest across the EU. According to the 2018 EJS, the use of ICT between courts and lawyers was one of the lowest in the EU, accounting for less than 5% of correspondence.[52] Significantly, in 2018 the Council of the European Union characterised the 'low digitalisation of courts and the lack of lifelong training for judges'[53] as being a critical problem in the Cypriot justice system, recommending the implementation of an e-justice system.[54] The linked digitalisation of the courts with judicial training is illustrative of the mutually reinforcing relationship between IT systems (in court proceedings) and IT skills (of judges and court staff) and the necessity of online legal education in advancing these aims. More broadly, the engagement of legal professionals with ICT is reflective of Cyprus' performance so far towards digitisation. According to the 2021 edition of the EU's Digital Economy and Society Index (DESI), Cyprus has improved its performance in almost all DESI categories. Most of the progress achieved concerns connectivity. That said, Cyprus still ranks 21st among the 27 EU member states. Hence, the country is still one of the poorest performers, with a score of 43.5 compared to the EU average score of 50.7.[55]

---

49 Functional Review Report of the Courts System of Cyprus, Technical Assistance Project 2017/2018, IPA, Ireland (Supported by the Structural Reform Support Service (SSRS) of the European Commission) (03.2018) https://www.cyprusbarassociation.org/files/publications/Functional_Review_of_Courts_System_of_Cyprus_IPA_Ireland_-_Final_Report.pdf, pp. 5–7.

50 Ibid., p. 225.

51 Ibid., recommendation 14, 147. See also Feasibility Study on the Introduction of Digital Audio Recording (DAR) in Court Proceedings in Cyprus, Technical Assistance Project 2019, IPA Ireland (Supported by the Structural Reform Support Service (SSRS) of the European Commission) (04.07.2019), p. 5, http://www.supremecourt.gov.cy/Judicial/sc.nsf/All/A47FDB9DC8E6F7B5C2258480003AC7C4/$file/Feasibility%20Study%20on%20the%20Introduction%20of%20Digital%20Audio%20Recording%20(DAR).pdf.

52 EU Justice Scoreboard 2018, figure 30.

53 Council Recommendation of 13 July 2018 on the 2018 National Reform Programme of Cyprus and delivering a Council opinion on the 2018 Stability Programme of Cyprus, OJ C 320, 10.09.2018, pp. 55–59.

54 Ibid.

55 Digital Economy and Society Index (DESI) 2021 – Cyprus, https://digital-strategy.ec.europa.eu/en/policies/countries-digitisation-performance.

More recently, the 2021 EJS accorded special attention to the digitalisation of the courts, which proved crucial for keeping the courts functional during the COVID-19 pandemic, and more generally as a means of promoting efficient and accessible justice systems. Cyprus had consistently ranked among the lowest-performing countries vis-à-vis all indicators.[56] These poor findings accord with the Supreme Court's approach during the months-long lockdowns imposed by the Cypriot authorities in response to the COVID-19 pandemic.[57]

Initially, the Supreme Court suspended adjudication and further promotion of cases between 16 March 2020 and 30 April 2020, except for urgent cases.[58] This reaction demonstrates an implicit acknowledgement on the part of the Supreme Court of the existence of systemic limitations affecting the administration of justice in Cyprus, exacerbated by the COVID-19 pandemic. Therefore, the Supreme Court's approach was one of prudence and reserve. When restrictions eased in May 2020, the Supreme Court decided courts would reopen in line with the decrees of the Ministry of Health.[59] The operation of the courts and progress of cases were subject to the specific needs and particularities of each jurisdiction, including the condition of the court premises and buildings. To avoid overcrowding, the Supreme Court rescheduled first appearances. In the absence of digital trials, the progress of a substantial number of court cases was hampered by postponements and delays. To alleviate the situation, in September 2021 the Supreme Court adopted a new procedural regulation, enabling courts to handle cases in the absence of the parties, provided it was deemed appropriate and the parties consented.[60] Furthermore, the courts now have power to use e-mail for the issuance of directions and notification of decisions (interim and final) to the parties. This reflects the first step towards some form of 'asynchronous' court proceedings.[61]

---

56 EU Justice Scoreboard 2021, 'Digitalisation', figures 39–47.

57 See also D. Loizou and D. Christofi, 'The Impact of the COVID-19 Pandemic on the Operation of the Cypriot Courts: Technological Challenges and the Maintenance of Rule of Law – A Comparative Analysis with Other Common Law Jurisdictions' in the Rule of Law Monitoring Mechanism, School of Law, UCLan Cyprus (11.06.2020), https://ruleoflawmonitoringmechanism.eu/posts/the-impact-of-the-covid-19-pandemic-on-the-operation-of-the-cypriot-courts-technological-challenges.

58 Supreme Court Announcement (16.03.2020), http://www.supremecourt.gov.cy/judicial/sc.nsf/All/CABFC161B80C9E6BC225852D00465B6E?OpenDocument.

59 Supreme Court Announcement (30.04.2020), http://www.supremecourt.gov.cy/Judicial/sc.nsf/All/00E7188B24D219A7C225855A00391080?OpenDocument.

60 Electronic Justice (Electronic Communication) Procedural Regulation of 2021 (17.09.2021), http://www.supremecourt.gov.cy/judicial/sc.nsf/All/2AF4BC3788347815C2258753002E6CB1?OpenDocument.

61 Term taken from 'Online Hearings in Cyprus – A Midsummer Night's Dream or a Possible Step for Solving Our Problems' (Softline, 18.05.2020), https://softline.com.cy/educational/diadiktiakes-akroaseis-stin-kypro-oneiro-therinis-nyktos-i-efikto-vima-epilysis-ton-provlimaton-mas/.

The introduction of an electronic justice system had long been seen as a decisive turning point towards the digitalisation of justice in Cyprus. The iJustice system, otherwise referred to as the 'Intermediate Electronic Justice Solution', was adopted as an intermediate step to pave the way for the implementation of the final and integrated system of electronic justice, called eJustice.[62] iJustice was formally introduced on 21 July 2021.[63] However, its introduction was hampered by delays and compromises. Moreover, data aggregated during the first two months of its launch suggested electronic justice had not yet been embraced by most lawyers. At first, the new system applied only to new cases; the option for hard-copy submissions was maintained with respect to external users. Nevertheless, external users were encouraged to opt for electronic submission.[64] This signified a marked departure from previous positions, which provided for compulsory use of the system, with no option for hard-copy submissions.[65]

The introduction of the iJustice system was the culmination of a long process that commenced in 2017.[66] The system was developed and designed by the Deputy Ministry of Research Innovation and Digital Policy, in cooperation with the Supreme Court and CBA. The kick-off meeting in October 2020 signified the official launch of the system.[67] New procedural rules on electronic justice were adopted by the Supreme Court judges on 13 January 2021.[68] The pilot phase was initially delayed and was extended on various occasions.[69] In January 2021, the

---

62 For an overview of the eJustice project see: Supreme Court Announcement (30.08.2022), http://www.supremecourt.gov.cy/judicial/sc.nsf/All/1B2710564D0079F1C22588AE001851B2?OpenDocument.

63 The pilot phase of the system ended on 20 July 2021. The new system became fully operational with respect to all the courts, except the International Protection Administrative Court, and with respect to all jurisdictions, except the criminal jurisdiction of the District Courts, Assize Courts, and the Supreme Court. See Supreme Court Announcement, Pursuant to Regulations 6 and 40 of the Electronic Justice (Electronic Submission) Procedural Regulation of 2021 (20.07.2021), http://www.supremecourt.gov.cy/Judicial/SC.nsf/All/1937F86A1A56A42CC2258718003BD623?OpenDocument.

64 Ibid. External users are to be distinguished from courts officers. External users may be lawyers or non-lawyers.

65 CBA Announcement (09.12.2020), Pilot Implementation of the System for the Interim Solution of Electronic Justice, https://www.cyprusbarassociation.org/index.php/en/news/announcements-ijustice/8421-2020-12-09-14-11-02.

66 Functional Review Report, pp. 84–85.

67 Press Release, Press Office of the Supreme Court (09.10.2020), http://www.supremecourt.gov.cy/judicial/sc.nsf/All/726D21115686F9CCC22585FC003FD59E/$file/%CE%94%CE%95%CE%9B%CE%A4%CE%99%CE%9F%20%CE%A4%CE%A5%CE%A0%CE%9F%CE%A5%20kick%20off%20meeting.pdf.

68 Electronic Justice (Electronic Submission) Procedural Regulation of 2021 (13.01.2021), http://www.supremecourt.gov.cy/judicial/sc.nsf/All/B9D7949A6A0318A5C225865E002E5C48/$file/4131%2015%201%202021%20PARARTIMA%202o%20MEROS%20I.pdf.

69 Supreme Court Announcement (15.01.2021), http://www.supremecourt.gov.cy/judicial/sc.nsf/All/46437B2DAF1CCCC3C225865E002B9EB5/$file/%CE%94%CE%95%CE%9B%CE%A4%CE%99%CE%9F%20%CE%A4%CE%A5%CE%A0%CE%9F%CE%A5%20

Supreme Court, following a request by the CBA, afforded more time to lawyers to undertake training to get familiarised with the system before making its use compulsory.[70] Lawyers were trained on using the system so they could aid other colleagues.[71] There were technical difficulties on the part of the contractor company regarding fully integrated and uninterrupted access to the system.[72] Full access to the system revealed that trainers and lawyers were not comfortable with the system. In response, the Supreme Court extended the virtual use of the system, postponing its launch.[73] The system's pilot phase was ultimately launched on 14 April 2021, lasting until 20 July 2021.[74]

Over 840 lawyers participated in the first online training seminar organised by the CBA. During the seminar, more than 130 questions were answered.[75] The seminar recording was made available on the CBA website.[76] Despite some delays by the contractor company, a user manual was prepared and made available on the iJustice platform.[77] The Deputy Ministry of Research Innovation and Digital Policy disseminated videos with guidelines outlining processes for submission of a new case, updating a current case, and studying cases.[78] The CBA website has an FAQs page for iJustice on its website.[79]

---

iJustice%2015.1.21.pdf; Supreme Court Announcement (04.02.2021), http://www.supremecourt.gov.cy/Judicial/sc.nsf/All/B39F705F13B5B8D9C22586720043574E/$file/ANAKOIN%CE%A9%CE%A3%CE%97%20AN%CE%A9%CE%A4%CE%91%CE%A4%CE%9F%CE%A5%20%CE%94%CE%99%CE%9A%CE%91%CE%A3%CE%A4%CE%97%CE%A1%CE%99%CE%9F%CE%A5%20-%20%CE%99-JUSTICE%204-2-2021.pdf.

70 Supreme Court Announcement (15.01.2021), http://www.supremecourt.gov.cy/judicial/sc.nsf/All/46437B2DAF1CCCC3C225865E002B9EB5/$file/%CE%94%CE%95%CE%9B%CE%A4%CE%99%CE%9F%20%CE%A4%CE%A5%CE%A0%CE%9F%CE%A5%20iJustice%2015.1.21.pdf.

71 CBA Announcement (06.12.2020), https://www.cyprusbarassociation.org/index.php/el/news/announcements-ijustice/8268-e-justice.

72 CBA Announcement (15.01.2021), http://www.cyprusbarassociation.org/index.php/en/news/announcements-ijustice/9165-i-justice0.

73 Supreme Court Announcement (04.02.2021), http://www.supremecourt.gov.cy/Judicial/sc.nsf/All/B39F705F13B5B8D9C22586720043574E/$file/ANAKOIN%CE%A9%CE%A3%CE%97%20AN%CE%A9%CE%A4%CE%91%CE%A4%CE%9F%CE%A5%20%CE%94%CE%99%CE%9A%CE%91%CE%A3%CE%A4%CE%97%CE%A1%CE%99%CE%9F%CE%A5%20-%20%CE%99-JUSTICE%204-2-2021.pdf.

74 Supreme Court Announcement, Pursuant to Regulations 6 and 40 of the Electronic Justice (Electronic Submission) Procedural Regulation of 2021 (12.04.2021), http://www.supremecourt.gov.cy/Judicial/sc.nsf/All/BB10733C2D6C3F00C22586B5002A5D2A?OpenDocument.

75 CBA Announcement (27.01.2021), https://www.cyprusbarassociation.org/index.php/en/news/announcements-ijustice/9461-i-justice-4k.

76 CBA Announcement (04.02.2021), https://www.cyprusbarassociation.org/index.php/en/news/announcements-ijustice/9578-ijustice-questions-2.

77 iJustice, https://ijustice.judicial.gov.cy/#/login/:b94dn7hfjj.

78 Deputy Ministry Research Innovation Digital Policy, https://www.youtube.com/channel/UCwRFBklCzdlmTbC5wOjfUBQ.

79 CBA, iJustice – FAQs, https://www.cyprusbarassociation.org/index.php/el/for-lawyers/ijustice/faqs1.

Support and training of users on the new system has also been undertaken by the local bar associations. In preparation for the court commencement period in 2021–22, the Nicosia Bar Association appointed a responsible person to assist lawyers – members of the Nicosia Bar Association – during the month of September. Lawyers/firms who were not previously supported were prioritised to explain and train lawyers on the system and submission process, especially colleagues lacking knowledge of computer operations.[80]

A prevalent feeling among members of the legal profession was that the training and preparation provided were inadequate. The early use of the system vividly demonstrates that lawyers have yet to embrace electronic justice. In late October 2021, data presented to the Cyprus House of Representatives revealed that only 10–15% of lawyers (700) chose to use the iJustice platform and submit documents electronically, suggesting resistance to change on the part of civilians and lawyers.[81] Despite delays and compromises, the electronic system of justice dramatically changed the way legal professionals had worked for decades. Moreover, it was undertaken during a politically charged and highly contested reform of the whole Cypriot legal system. Hence, an in-depth assessment of electronic justice, including training, may not yet be appropriate, as further significant developments are expected in the short term. The Supreme Court recently decided that all new cases are to be submitted electronically, as of 1 February 2022, except for courts indicated in its announcement.[82]

2.6. UNIVERSITIES AND STUDENTS

In March 2020, the CYQAA announced that all universities in Cyprus could switch to distance learning mode to curb the spread of COVID-19. In parallel, they were obliged to abide by necessary quality standards in terms of maintaining a full record of their actions (e.g. video-conferences, student activities, attendance, communication with the teachers at prescribed times, etc.).[83] The CYQAA also provided a list of tools for online classes from which each

---

80 Nicosia Bar Association Announcement (28.07.2021), https://www.nba.org.cy/anakoinosi-dikigorikou-syllogou-lefkosias-2/.

81 '15% of lawyers submit the documents electronically' (*Philenews*, 26.10.2021), https://www.philenews.com/oikonomia/kypros/article/1320940/15-ton-dikigron-katachoroyn-ilektronika-ta-engrafa.

82 Supreme Court Announcement (21.12.2021), http://www.supremecourt.gov.cy/judicial/sc.nsf/All/42C8E4A5B6258385C22587B2004247C4?OpenDocument. The exemption from electronic submissions concerns the International Protection Administrative Court, the courts exercising criminal jurisdiction, including the Assize Courts, the Military Court and the Supreme Court.

83 CYQAA Announcement (10.03.2020), http://www.dipae.ac.cy/index.php/el/nea-ekdiloseis/anakoinoseis-el/498-10-03-2020-anavoli-episkepseon-distance-learning.

institution could choose.[84] On 20 March 2020, the Cyprus Rectors' Conference recognised the full compliance of universities with the emergency government measures in addressing the pandemic, including their high-quality adoption and implementation of distance learning for study programmes and online digital tools and techniques. This reflected the investments universities made in their digital infrastructures and development of new technologies.[85] Alternative forms of assessment were similarly adopted for final exams, including online written exams.[86]

Alternative forms of teaching and assessment continued throughout the academic years 2020/21[87] and 2021/22.[88] Universities proceeded with blended teaching, relying on conventional and online teaching, to support the attendance of students unable to attend in-person classes.[89] The CYQAA clarified that students registering for conventional programmes of study for the winter semester of 2021 could return face-to-face.[90] However, it also enabled the continuation of blended teaching and learning methods as an ancillary means to facilitate the education process, and assist students who belong to vulnerable groups and for reasons of force majeure.[91] More recently, the CYQAA called on all universities to undertake appropriate planning and actions so that students on conventional programmes of study could physically come to class for the winter semester 2022/23. Significantly, the CYQAA pointed out that the delivery

84 CYQAA Announcement (17.03.2020), http://www.dipae.ac.cy/index.php/el/nea-ekdiloseis/anakoinoseis-el/501-17-03-2020-ergaleia-tilemathima.

85 CYQAA Announcement (20.03.2020), http://www.dipae.ac.cy/index.php/el/nea-ekdiloseis/anakoinoseis-el/505-20-03-2020-psifisma-sinodou-pritaneon.

86 CYQAA Announcement (31.03.2020), http://www.dipae.ac.cy/index.php/el/nea-ekdiloseis/anakoinoseis-el/511-31-03-2020-final-exams-koronoios.

87 CYQAA Announcement (05.11.2020), http://www.dipae.ac.cy/index.php/el/nea-ekdiloseis/anakoinoseis-el/552-5-11-2020-endiameses-kai-telikes-exetaseis-cheimerinou-examinou-2020-2021-sta-idrymata-anoteris-ekpaidefsis-kai-asfalistikes-diklides-poiotitas; CYQAA Announcement (27.04.2021), http://www.dipae.ac.cy/index.php/el/nea-ekdiloseis/anakoinoseis-el/582-27-04-2021-endiameses-kai-telikes-exetaseis-ypo-synthikes-pandimias.

88 CYQAA Announcement (03.01.2022), https://www.dipae.ac.cy/index.php/el/nea-ekdiloseis/anakoinoseis-el/628-03-01-2022-exetaseis-xeimerinou-earinou-examinou-2021-2022-2.

89 CYQAA Announcement (13.05.2020), http://www.dipae.ac.cy/index.php/el/nea-ekdiloseis/anakoinoseis-el/527-13-05-2020-leitourgia-idrymaton-xeimerino-examino-20-21.

90 CYQAA Announcement (24.08.2021), http://www.dipae.ac.cy/index.php/el/nea-ekdiloseis/anakoinoseis-el/604-24-08-2021-engrafi-neoeiserchomenon-foititon-gia-to-cheimerino-examino-2021-2022.

91 CYQAA Announcement (27.07.2021), http://www.dipae.ac.cy/index.php/el/nea-ekdiloseis/anakoinoseis-el/598-28-07-2021-programmata-spoudon-kai-poiotiki-leitourgia-tis-anoteris-ekpaidefsis-kata-to-cheimerino-examino-2021. See also CYQAA Announcement (16.09.2021), http://www.dipae.ac.cy/index.php/el/nea-ekdiloseis/anakoinoseis-el/617-16-09-2021-programmata-spoudon-kai-poiotiki-leitourgia-tis-anoteris-ekpaidefsis-kata-to-cheimerino-examino-2021.

of conventional programmes of study should be in line with pre-COVID-19 conditions.[92]

While universities in Cyprus have invested in digital infrastructure and registered students with access to hardware and software on campus, the pandemic forced some students to rely on their own or their families' resources, which were not necessarily equipped for educational purposes. In April 2020, the CYQAA obliged universities to ensure that all registered students had a computer appropriate for facilitating education processes.[93] There is no evidence to indicate whether such an obligation was implemented (or not) in practice.

3. MOVES TOWARDS ONLINE EDUCATION: AN ERA OF CHANGE?

Amid the COVID-19 pandemic, the implementation of emergency remote teaching in the legal educational system in Cyprus has posed technological, pedagogical and social challenges.[94] With the COVID-19 pandemic changing the operational norms of higher educational institutions, it is more important than ever to ensure the effectiveness and stability of legal education in Cyprus through robust practices and innovative teaching and learning approaches.[95] As Emilianides stated, 'in an era of globalisation, liberalisation and unprecedented technological change, law schools need to be as open-minded and innovative as possible, in order to effectively address the challenges and opportunities that these developments present'.[96] Therefore, this portion of our report examines the challenges and opportunities identified both before and after the outbreak of the pandemic, including the impact of COVID-19 on legal education in Cyprus and its future.

---

92 CYQAA Announcement (26.09.2022), https://www.dipae.ac.cy/index.php/el/nea-ekdiloseis/anakoinoseis-el/673-26-09-2022-mathimata-cheimerinou-examinou-2022-2023-sta-symvatika-programmata-spoudon-ton-idrymaton-anoteris-ekpaidefsis-3.

93 CYQAA Announcement (07.04.2020), http://www.dipae.ac.cy/index.php/el/nea-ekdiloseis/anakoinoseis-el/519-07-04-2020-distance-learning-computer.

94 F. Ferri, P. Grifoni and T. Guzzo, 'Online Learning and Emergency Remote Teaching: Opportunities and Challenges in Emerging Situations' (2020) 10(4) *Societies* 1, 4.

95 L. Pitsillidou, 'Legal Education in An Era of Change: The Impact of Covid-19' (Rule of Law Monitoring Mechanism Blog, 12.08.2021), https://ruleoflawmonitoringmechanism.eu/posts/legal-education-in-an-era-of-change-impact-covid19-lida-pitsillidou.

96 A.C. Emilianides, 'A Post-Pandemic Legal Education' (Gold: The Business Magazine of Cyprus, 18.07.2021), https://www.goldnews.com.cy/digitaledition/#/reader/39983/1486800.

3.1. PRE-PANDEMIC LEGAL EDUCATION

3.1.1. Universities

Until recently, the option to study for an online LLB degree seemed impossible, as degrees offered in Cyprus were taught exclusively face-to-face,[97] with the only exception being distance learning offered by the University of London through a local Recognised Teaching Centre in Cyprus.[98] A person seeking admission to the CBA as a practising lawyer must hold a recognised LLB degree either from a university of an EU member state, or any other university, whether in the Republic of Cyprus or a third country.[99] Section 4 of the Cyprus Advocates Law (Cap 2) provides that any qualifications recognised before the amendment of Cap 2 in 2020 are still recognised, including the distance learning law degree offered by the University of London. A distance learning LLB degree has neither been validated nor approved by the CYQAA or the LC.[100]

With the traditional method of teaching being prevalent in law schools, the LLB degree is predominantly delivered and taught through face-to-face lectures and seminars. However, this teaching method has been criticised for its failure to provide enough opportunities for students to participate in the classroom, as 'except for the student who happens to be sitting on the hot seat, no one else actively participates in the dialogue'.[101] This is compounded as lectures encourage passive learning through surface, rather than deep, approaches to student learning.[102] Students are required to listen and take notes for the majority of their classes and, therefore, no sufficient opportunities arise for student engagement and participation. As Hess argues, 'students do not learn much just sitting in classes and listening to teachers, memorising pre-packaged assignments, and spitting out answers. They must talk about what they are learning, write about it, relate it to past experiences, and apply it to their lives'.[103]

---

97 Ibid.

98 Cyprus Advocates Law (Cap 2) 83(I) 2020, section 4; see also Cyprus Advocates Law (Cap 2) 124 (I) 2005.

99 Cyprus Advocates Law (Cap 2) 83(I) 2020, section 4(d).

100 CYQAA, 'Bachelor Degree Accredited Programmes' (2022), https://www.dipae.ac.cy/index.php/en/accreditation-en/accredited-programmes-bachelor-en; Cyprus Legal Council, 'List of Approved Degreed' (2022), https://www.legalcouncil.org.cy/list-of-approved-degrees/?lang=en.

101 P.L. Caron and R. Gely, 'Taking Back the Law School Classroom: Using Technology to Foster Active Student Learning' (2004) 54(4) *Journal of Legal Education* 551, 554.

102 J. Biggs and C. Tang, *Teaching for Quality Learning at University* (4th edn, McGraw-Hill Education 2011); see also P. Ramsden, *Learning to Teach in Higher Education* (2nd edn, RoutledgeFalmer 2003).

103 G.F. Hess, 'Heads and Hearts: The Teaching and Learning Environment in Law School' (2002) 52 *Journal of Legal Education* 75, 85.

However, enrolments in Cyprus law schools are very low, which eliminates the challenges of engaging many students during classes. Lectures usually comprise 30–40 students, whereas seminars usually comprise 10–15 students. Due to this small number, students are provided with opportunities to actively interact in discussions with their teachers and peers, thus helping to enhance their knowledge and understanding of the subject matter.

The rapid development of technology has revolutionised practices of teaching and learning in legal education in Cyprus. Law lecturers have re-considered their current teaching practices by adopting more innovative e-learning approaches to enhance traditional methods of teaching in law schools. Indeed, law schools have witnessed an increasing growth in the use of technology over the last decade, as lecturers have been given the opportunity to deploy a wide array of e-learning technologies to enhance student learning and participation. While the LLB by distance learning is not offered as an option, virtual learning platforms, such as Blackboard and Moodle, are at the forefront of recent technological advances in legal education in Cyprus. Virtual learning platforms have been adopted by all universities to provide access to various online teaching and learning materials, including PowerPoint slides, lecture and seminar handouts, audio and video clips, online quizzes, and online discussion groups.

Nevertheless, although it has been accepted that the adoption of virtual learning platforms has 'revolutionised the traditional teaching system' through acting as an aid to pedagogy,[104] it has also been recognised that many of these platforms tend to focus on the delivery of information rather than the improvement of teaching and learning practices.[105] Indeed, prior to COVID-19, virtual learning platforms were primarily used for downloading and accessing module materials, with few lecturers using them to engage students with e-learning activities.

This is mainly due to the unwillingness of lecturers to use e-learning technologies to enhance student learning, primarily due to their preference for using traditional teaching methods. Although e-learning technologies offer a variety of pedagogical benefits, many are not convinced their implementation could help improve their teaching delivery and make their classes more interactive and engaging. Another reason is the fact that, prior to the pandemic, it was not necessary to offer trainings on the available e-learning technologies and their pedagogical benefits. Even if such trainings were offered in the past,

---

104 J.A. Alokluk, 'The Effectiveness of Blackboard System, Uses and Limitations in Information Management' (2018) 10 *Intelligence Information Management* 133, 134.

105 Ibid.; see also A. Heirdsfield, S. Walker, M. Tambyah and D. Beutal, 'Blackboard As An Online Learning Environment: What Do Teacher Education Students and Staff Think?' (2011) 36(7) *Australian Journal of Education* 1, 1; J. Herrington, T.C. Reeves and R. Oliver, 'Online Learning as Information Delivery: Digital Myopia' (2005) 16(4) *Journal of Interactive Learning Research* 353.

they were non-mandatory and therefore only those who were interested in learning more about new technologies were willing to attend such trainings. Indeed, many of the universities in Cyprus are offering non-mandatory trainings, especially to new members of staff as part of their induction training.[106] By contrast, UCLan Cyprus requires that all members of staff undergo mandatory training on teaching and learning, through obtaining the Fellowship of the UK's AdvanceHE.

In addition, implementing e-learning technologies in theory-based modules, such as jurisprudence, may be seen as counterproductive, as students are mainly required to enter into debates with their teachers and peers on various theoretical aspects, such as justice and fairness. This makes the use of e-learning technologies challenging and difficult. Finally, lecturers see the implementation of e-learning technologies as time-consuming, as it requires a great amount of time to learn and implement new technologies in the curriculum. Although the number of students in law schools is small, the pressure of academia is still present. This is also evidenced by the fact that the student–teacher ratio in Cyprus is relatively high as compared to other EU countries, with a ratio of 22 students per member of staff.[107]

3.1.2. *Legal Profession*

Even prior to the pandemic, the CBA offered its bar training online, undertaken to provide flexibility to trainee lawyers to attend lectures either synchronously or asynchronously without the need to travel to the capital city, Nicosia, to physically attend lectures. The fact the bar training initially occurred in Nicosia made it difficult for those living in distant provinces to attend lectures physically. Offering the bar training online has given them the flexibility to organise their time more effectively, as they can access training materials online at any time and place. In addition, the increase in the numbers of law trainees in the last decade[108] has made it difficult to host face-to-face lectures as it is impossible to fit everyone within the same class.

On the other hand, the bar exams have always been conducted in person. The Cyprus Advocates Law (Cap 2) requires a trainee lawyer to hold a recognised university law degree to join the CBA and sit the exams of the LC. A trainee

---

106 See University of Cyprus, 'Workshops and Seminars for UCY Instructors', http://www.ucy.ac.cy/ctl/en/activities/for-instructors/workshops-seminars; UNIC, 'Training and Development for Faculty', https://www.unic.ac.cy/psu/training-and-development-for-faculty/.

107 Eurostat, 'Tertiary Education Statistics', https://ec.europa.eu/eurostat/statistics-explained/index.php?title=Tertiary_education_statistics&oldid=552003%20%20https://ec.europa.eu/eurostat/statistics-explained/index.php?title=Tertiary_education_statistics&oldid=552003#Teaching_staff_and_student-academic_staff_ratios.

108 CBA, https://www.cyprusbar.org/CypriotAdvocateMembersPage.

lawyer is required to sit 10 modules, eight of which are compulsory and two optional. The exam covers a range of areas of law, such as constitutional law, contract law, criminal law, company law, tort law, law of evidence, civil and criminal procedure, property law, wills and succession law, advocates law and deontology, and family law.[109] In light of the COVID-19 pandemic, no significant changes were made to the operation of the exams and the bar training remained unchanged as before the pandemic.

3.2. POST-PANDEMIC LEGAL EDUCATION: OPPORTUNITIES AND CHALLENGES

Amid the COVID-19 pandemic, the Cyprus legal educational system has witnessed an increasing growth in the use of e-learning technologies. The announcement made by the MOEC on 10 March 2020 to suspend face-to-face operations of all universities spurred the urgent use of e-learning technologies, accelerating the transformation of all law schools from in-classroom teaching to emergency remote teaching.[110] The sudden move to emergency remote teaching has transformed the way teaching occurs in law schools. Although online legal education previously seemed impossible due to the resistance of law schools, technological changes in the operation of the legal educational system have made this necessary.

However, the transformation to emergency remote teaching has posed significant challenges to Cypriot law schools. As no further research has been conducted regarding the legal educational challenges resulting from the pandemic, further examination should be conducted of the identified challenges to fill the gaps, using the UCLan Cyprus experience as a case study. Despite emergency remote teaching posing significant challenges for legal education in Cyprus, the pandemic has offered opportunities to cultivate the potential benefits of online education and explore new means of teaching and learning. Indeed, 'emergency remote teaching has given a significant boost to online teaching, opening up new opportunities and reflections for the educational

109 Cyprus Legal Council, 'Exam Schedule' (2022), https://www.legalcouncil.org.cy/exam-schedule/?lang=en.

110 MOEC, 'Προληπτικά μέτρα που αφορούν στα Ιδρύματα Ανώτερης Εκπαίδευσης έναντι του νέου κορωνοϊού (COVID – 19)' (10.03.2020), https://enimerosi.moec.gov.cy/archeia/1/ypp10528a; MOEC, 'Διευκρίνιση για τα Ιδρύματα Ανώτερης Εκπαίδευσης όσον αφορά στην ανακοίνωση του Υπουργείου Παιδείας, Πολιτισμού, Αθλητισμού και Νεολαίας για τη λήψη μέτρων πρόληψης της εξάπλωσης του ιού COVID-19, ημερομηνίας 11 Μαρτίου 2020' (12.03.2020), https://enimerosi.moec.gov.cy/archeia/1/ypp10547a; see also CYQAA, 'Εξ αποστάσεως συνέχιση των μαθημάτων, Επ' Αόριστον λόγω του COVID-19' (10.03.2020), https://www.dipae.ac.cy/index.php/en/news-and-events/announcements/13-dipae-el/dipaeel/anakoinoseis/498-10-03-2020-anavoli-episkepseon-distance-learning.

system'.[111] As a result, this report aims to explore not only the challenges but also the opportunities that have been presented to reshape legal pedagogy in Cyprus in light of the COVID-19 pandemic.

3.2.1. *Technological Challenges and Opportunities*

The proliferation of the COVID-19 pandemic has sparked some of the greatest technological developments in the 21st century. With e-learning technologies gaining prominence in law schools, many lecturers have re-considered their teaching and learning practices towards adopting more innovative e-learning approaches. As a response to the inescapable emergence of the pandemic, the need for technology has induced law schools to explore different learning options through video-conferencing applications and platforms, such as Zoom, Microsoft Teams, Skype, Blackboard and Moodle.[112] For example, Microsoft Teams has become an integral e-learning platform at UCLan Cyprus, creating a supportive remote learning environment which allows law students to connect to online classrooms in real time and engage with teachers and peers on various e-learning activities.

Although e-learning technologies existed before COVID-19, 'the unprecedented situation created by the pandemic provided the impetus for their further development and enhanced use', as law schools have been forced to 'adopt newer e-learning technologies and use old modalities in more innovative and inventive ways'.[113] Law schools have smoothly adjusted to the technological changes imposed to transform in-classroom teaching to emergency remote teaching. A key reason for the smooth transition is the fact many universities already had IT infrastructure in place with access to video-conferencing and online platforms. The transition to emergency remote teaching was successfully achieved due to the collaborative efforts of all law schools to adjust to the rapid changes imposed on legal education in response to the pandemic, including cooperation with the CYQAA to ensure implementations were as smooth as possible.[114]

Although the COVID-19 pandemic has given a significant boost to online teaching, it has also exposed technological challenges in law schools, including

---

111 F. Ferri, P. Grifoni and T. Guzzo, 'Online Learning and Emergency Remote Teaching: Opportunities and Challenges in Emerging Situations' (2020) 10(4) *Societies* 1, 6.

112 CYQAA, 'Εργαλεία για τηλεμαθήματα' (17.03.2020), https://www.dipae.ac.cy/index.php/el/nea-ekdiloseis/anakoinoseis-el/501-17-03-2020-ergaleia-tilemathima.

113 L. Pitsillidou, 'Legal Education in An Era of Change: The Impact of Covid-19' (Rule of Law Monitoring Mechanism Blog, 12.08.2021), https://ruleoflawmonitoringmechanism.eu/posts/legal-education-in-an-era-of-change-impact-covid19-lida-pitsillidou.

114 A.C. Emilianides, 'A Post-Pandemic Legal Education' (Gold: The Business Magazine of Cyprus, 18.07.2021), https://www.goldnews.com.cy/digitaledition/#/reader/39983/1486800.

the lack of internet connectivity and access constraints.[115] Although many students have smoothly adjusted to online teaching, others have struggled due to poor internet connectivity which prevented them from harvesting the fruits of online teaching. Over the last two years, access to a reliable internet connection has become vital, as students regularly use the internet to access online classes and teaching materials. The increased use of the internet during the pandemic has caused significant disruptions and delays, which has impacted students' capacity to attend and participate in online classes.[116]

Aside from the lack of internet connectivity, students were prevented from accessing electronic devices, such as computers, laptops and tablets, normally available via their university library. The library is an important resource for students as it provides access to electronic devices and various research and study materials, a resource which was not considered available during lockdown restrictions.[117] Due to access constraints, some students, especially those from disadvantaged backgrounds residing in countries and regions with poor internet connectivity, were forced to use mobile phones to attend online classes and access teaching and library materials.[118] This had a detrimental effect on their performance as many students struggled to properly conduct their research to complete assignments on time. As a result, law schools witnessed an increased number of applications for extensions and mitigating circumstances, as students were unable to cope with their studies due to the uneven access to necessary technologies, such as a fast internet connection and computer devices.[119]

The technological challenges have unmasked digital inequalities among students from more socially deprived and economically challenged backgrounds. Digital poverty has become a major issue in legal education, as the transition to emergency remote teaching has 'exposed technology's weakness to support students from disadvantaged backgrounds, including those with disabilities. Indeed, the inequality gaps between students in legal education have been exposed during the pandemic because of the uneven access to technology'.[120]

---

115 F. Ferri, P. Grifoni and T. Guzzo, 'Online Learning and Emergency Remote Teaching: Opportunities and Challenges in Emerging Situations' (2020) 10(4) *Societies* 1, 6.

116 M. Smith, 'Integrating Technology in Contemporary Legal Education' (2019) 54(2) *The Law Teacher* 209, 211–212.

117 L. Pitsillidou, 'Legal Education in An Era of Change: The Impact of Covid-19' (Rule of Law Monitoring Mechanism Blog, 12.08.2021), https://ruleoflawmonitoringmechanism.eu/posts/legal-education-in-an-era-of-change-impact-covid19-lida-pitsillidou.

118 F. Ferri, P. Grifoni and T. Guzzo, 'Online Learning and Emergency Remote Teaching: Opportunities and Challenges in Emerging Situations' (2020) 10(4) *Societies* 1, 7.

119 Ibid., p. 6.

120 L. Pitsillidou, 'Legal Education in An Era of Change: The Impact of Covid-19' (Rule of Law Monitoring Mechanism Blog, 12.08.2021), https://ruleoflawmonitoringmechanism.eu/posts/legal-education-in-an-era-of-change-impact-covid19-lida-pitsillidou.

Another technological challenge is the lack of adequate training on the use of video-conferencing applications and online platforms.[121] Due to the well-known resistance of law schools to online teaching,[122] it was not previously essential to provide training on available e-learning technologies. This did not happen until the outbreak of COVID-19, which has imposed an urgent need to put in place trainings and technical support to enhance the digital skills of both lecturers and students. However, although guidance has been provided to students on e-learning technologies, such as Microsoft Teams, it was identified that many students have found it difficult to adjust to the rapid technological changes. By contrast, students who were 'born into a world that has embraced technology' and had been using the internet since childhood have smoothly adjusted to those changes.[123]

3.2.2. Pedagogical Challenges and Opportunities

Aside from the technological challenges, COVID-19 has also induced the implementation of innovative methods of teaching, helping in the development of new pedagogical approaches.[124] As a result of the paradigm shift to online teaching, an opportunity was provided for all lecturers to reconsider current methods of teaching by exploring innovative e-learning technologies to enhance student learning. As Pistone argued, 'technological innovations are not only changing the ways that students learn, communicate, and interact, but they are also allowing educators to do things that were not possible without technology'.[125] According to Shavers, there are several reasons why lecturers should consider using e-learning technologies, including 'the recognition of different learning styles (for example, the use of classroom computer projections may help the student who learns best through visual cues), the incorporation of new learning experiences, accommodation of disabled students, the ability to access information that is not readily available at the researcher's location, the possibility of multiparty discussions with colleagues around the world,

---

121 See A.M. Johnson et al., 'Challenges and Solutions when Using Technologies in the Classroom' in S.A. Crossley and D.S. McNamara (eds), *Adapting Educational Technologies for Literacy Instruction* (Routledge 2016).

122 C. Easton, 'An Examination of Clicker Technology Use in Legal Education' (2009) 3 *Journal of Information, Law, and Technology*, https://warwick.ac.uk/fac/soc/law/elj/jilt/2009_3/easton/.

123 M. Pistone, 'Law Schools and Technology: Where We Are and Where We Are Heading' (2015) 64(4) *Journal of Legal Education* 586, 586.

124 A.W. Shavers, 'The Impact of Technology on Legal Education' (2001) 51(3) *Journal of Legal Education* 407, 409–410.

125 M. Pistone, 'Law Schools and Technology: Where We Are and Where We Are Heading' (2015) 64(4) *Journal of Legal Education* 586, 589.

communication with students outside of the classroom, and the provision of courses to students in distant locations'.[126]

Since the onset of COVID-19, the implementation of innovative e-learning activities in law curricula has become vital, as they could transform the law classroom into a supportive active-learning environment for all students to engage and participate in discussions with teachers and peers.[127] For example, at UCLan Cyprus e-learning activities, such as online multiple-choice questions, mini quizzes, online discussions, blogs and virtual field trips, have been used to tackle the challenges of the pandemic. Implementing these e-learning activities has helped students receive adequate formative feedback on their modules, allowing them to identify gaps or misconceptions that could be improved before taking their summative assessments, such as written assignments and exams. With the help of digital technology, law lecturers provided prompt formative feedback to their students, helping them 'to take control over their own learning by obtaining necessary remediation for identified deficiencies in their understanding, and to adjust their approaches to future learning tasks'.[128] E-learning activities present a unique opportunity to transform law students from passive to active learners, as the learning process involved not only the 'usual suspects' but also students who are usually reluctant to participate during classrooms.[129]

Recent technological developments have also induced the use and implementation of recorded lectures in law schools. In comparison to other countries, such as the UK, where recorded lectures are a common phenomenon in legal education,[130] the law schools in Cyprus implemented recorded lectures for the first time after the outbreak of the pandemic. Following the announcement made by the CYQAA in March 2020,[131] all universities were

126 A.W. Shavers, 'The Impact of Technology on Legal Education' (2001) 51(3) *Journal of Legal Education* 407, 409–410.

127 L. Pitsillidou, 'Legal Education in An Era of Change: The Impact of Covid-19' (Rule of Law Monitoring Mechanism Blog, 12.08.2021), https://ruleoflawmonitoringmechanism.eu/posts/legal-education-in-an-era-of-change-impact-covid19-lida-pitsillidou.

128 R.A. Lasso, 'Is Our Students Learning? Using Assessments to Measure and Improve Law School Learning Environment' (2010) 15(1) *Barry Law Review* 73, 75.

129 L. Pitsillidou, 'Legal Education in An Era of Change: The Impact of Covid-19' (Rule of Law Monitoring Mechanism Blog, 12.08.2021), https://ruleoflawmonitoringmechanism.eu/posts/legal-education-in-an-era-of-change-impact-covid19-lida-pitsillidou.

130 M. Smith, 'Integrating Technology in Contemporary Legal Education' (2019) 54(2) *The Law Teacher* 209, 212; see also M.J. Draper, S. Gibbon and J. Thomas, 'Lecture Recording: A New Norm' (2018) 52(3) *The Law Teacher* 316.

131 CYQAA, 'Διαδικτυακή διδασκαλία/εξέταση και προσωπικά δεδομένα' (10.04.2020), https://www.dipae.ac.cy/index.php/el/nea-ekdiloseis/anakoinoseis-el/516-10-04-2020-distance-learning; see also CYQAA, 'Διαδικτυακή διδασκαλία/εξέταση και προσωπικά δεδομένα (Αρ. 2)' (30.09.2020) https://www.dipae.ac.cy/index.php/el/nea-ekdiloseis/anakoinoseis-el/546-30-09-2020-diadiktyaki-didaskalia-exetasi-kai-prosopika-dedomena-2.

required to implement recorded lectures in their curricula in compliance with EU Regulation 2016/679[132] and the provisions of the Cypriot Law for the Protection of Natural Persons about the Processing of Personal Data and for the Free Movement of such Data of 2018 (Law 125(I)/2018).

The shift to recorded lectures benefited students vastly as they were given the opportunity to return to the recordings and re-watch the lectures at any time and place, allowing them to make their own notes and pay closer attention to the material taught. Embedding the recorded lectures into the law curriculum could also support an inclusive education with flexibility for all learners to access the materials taught.[133] Informal discussions with students at UCLan Cyprus have shown great satisfaction with the implementation of this new feature, with students advising that they would like to see recorded lectures permanently added and used throughout their LLB studies. However, the introduction of the recorded lectures has caused much controversy and debate, with some lecturers expressing their concerns over the impact on teaching.[134] Concerns were mainly based on the negative impact of recorded lectures on the students' performance, as students tend to considerably rely on recordings, thus preventing them from paying attention during the lectures, with some students very often missing their classes.

The pandemic also induced the development and promotion of open access to various online courses and webinars, providing the opportunity for all learners to attend previously unavailable and non-accessible online courses, such as trainings and summer schools. Due to the lockdown measures, which prevented students accessing hard-copy research materials, the use of online resources thrived significantly, as students were able to access a variety of online research materials, such as e-books and journals, which were made available online to tackle the challenges of the pandemic and its impact on higher education, 'thus heading towards a more inclusive learning environment'.[135]

---

132 Regulation (EU) 2016/679 of 27 April 2016 on the protection of natural persons regarding the processing of personal data and on the free movement of such data, and repealing Directive 95/46/EC (General Data Protection Regulation), OJ L 119, 04.05.2016, pp. 1–88.

133 J.R.D. MacKay, 'First Year Undergraduates Make Use of Recordings to Overcome Barriers in Higher Education: Evidence from a Survey' (2020) 28 *Research in Learning Technology* 1, 2–3.

134 J.R.D. MacKay, E. Nordmann, L. Murray, A. Browitt, M. Anderson and J. Hutchison, 'The Cost of Asking: "Say that Again?": A Social Capital Theory View into How Lecture Recording Supports Widening Participation' (2021) 6 *Frontiers in Education* 1; N. Skead, L. Elphick, F. McGaughey, M. Weson, K. Offer and M. Montalto, 'If You Record, They Will Not Come – But Does it Really Matter? Student Attendance and Lecture Recording at an Australian Law School' (2020) 54 *The Law Teacher* 349; M.J. Draper, S. Gibbon and J. Thomas, 'Lecture Recording: A New Norm' (2018) 52(3) *The Law Teacher* 316.

135 L. Pitsillidou, 'Legal Education in An Era of Change: The Impact of Covid-19' (Rule of Law Monitoring Mechanism Blog, 12.08.2021), https://ruleoflawmonitoringmechanism.eu/posts/legal-education-in-an-era-of-change-impact-covid19-lida-pitsillidou.

Furthermore, open access helped facilitate research and knowledge transfer, as academics around the world were able to attend and participate in online conferences, research seminars, workshops and trainings. Open access has provided an opportunity for academics to actively contribute to the dissemination of new knowledge and research across the world. This 'provides significant pedagogical benefits to the students, as by being actively involved in research, educators could support their teaching by keeping students up to date with the new legal developments'.[136] As Smith argues, open access could 'provide the opportunity to increase the efficiency of legal education and offer greater access to knowledge of the law'.[137]

Although the pandemic has induced the development of new pedagogical approaches, it also highlighted various pedagogical challenges. One of the key challenges is student engagement, as the shift to online teaching has made it difficult to engage students in classrooms. This is because, with the sessions being fully online, students often find themselves easily distracted, preventing them from engaging in discussions with teachers and peers. It is even challenging to identify whether students are attending online sessions, as most of them have their cameras off. This is because during the academic year 2020/21 it was not mandatory for students to turn their cameras on. Although with the new academic year 2021/22 this became mandatory, most students were still unwilling to turn their cameras on, preventing them from being fully engaged.

The lack of human interaction that exists in traditional face-to-face teaching makes it difficult to assess student performance and identify any misconceptions or gaps in their learning. In an era of change, increasing student motivation to engage throughout their LLB studies was found to be challenging. Indeed, 'making students engage in their learning during such an increasingly complex world that places high demands on students, is one of the biggest struggles that educators have been asked to deal with during the pandemic'.[138] Further, as many law students are used to the traditional method of teaching, many perceive online teaching as burdensome.

The pedagogical challenges of online learning were also exposed when the universities were asked to shift their attention to hybrid approaches to teaching (also known as the 'blended learning approach') in September 2020,[139] requiring

136 Ibid.

137 M. Smith, 'Integrating Technology in Contemporary Legal Education' (2019) 54(2) *The Law Teacher* 209, 213.

138 L. Pitsillidou, 'Legal Education in An Era of Change: The Impact of Covid-19' (Rule of Law Monitoring Mechanism Blog, 12.08.2021), https://ruleoflawmonitoringmechanism.eu/posts/legal-education-in-an-era-of-change-impact-covid19-lida-pitsillidou.

139 CYQAA, 'Λειτουργία Ιδρυμάτων Ανώτερης Εκπαίδευσης κατά το Χειμερινό Εξάμηνο 2020–21' (13.05.2020), https://www.dipae.ac.cy/index.php/el/nea-ekdiloseis/anakoinoseis-el/

lecturers to simultaneously deliver classes in person and online at the same time. The main reason behind the implementation of the hybrid approach to teaching is to provide flexibility to a diverse range of students, as most students coming from abroad were facing difficulties in travelling to Cyprus due to COVID-19-related reasons and visa restrictions, thus preventing them from attending their classes physically.

Although the hybrid approach to teaching enhances inclusivity in law schools,[140] it also poses significant challenges. Although many students at UCLan Cyprus have shown their satisfaction with the implementation of a hybrid approach to teaching, others have expressed concerns about not receiving the same quality of teaching compared to on-campus students. Many students have felt left out from various teaching and learning opportunities, as more focus was given to on-campus students. This is because law lecturers struggled to deliver a hybrid mode of teaching that simultaneously engaged on-campus and online students, especially in circumstances where online students demonstrated little or no interest in participating in discussions with teachers and peers. The hybrid approach to teaching also had a negative impact on the physical attendance of students, as many preferred to continue attending classes remotely. Due to the small number of law students, this makes the use of a hybrid approach to teaching challenging. Irrespective, it seems that hybrid approaches to teaching are here to stay, as they offer the flexibility to deliver the LLB in a more innovative way.

Following the announcement made by the CYQAA on 31 March 2020, all universities were instructed to use alternative assessment methods to eliminate challenges posed by social distancing restrictions.[141] Although the shift to alternative assessment methods has not caused any significant issues for traditional written coursework, it affected the operation of the final written exams as universities were instructed to carry out exams remotely. Using an alternative assessment exam was challenging, as the traditional on-campus exam was swapped with a 24-hour online exam. Although many students at

527-13-05-2020-leitourgia-idrymaton-xeimerino-examino-20-21; CYQAA, 'Λειτουργία Ιδρυμάτων Ανώτερης Εκπαίδευσης κατά το ακαδημαϊκό έτος 2020–2021' (07.09.2020), https://www.dipae.ac.cy/index.php/el/nea-ekdiloseis/anakoinoseis-el/540-07-09-2020-leitourgia-idrimaton-2020-2021.

140 M. Castan and R. Hyams, 'Blended Learning in the Law Classroom: Design, Implementation and Evaluation of an Intervention in the First Year Law Curriculum Design' (2017) 27(1) *Legal Education Review* 1, 2.

141 CYQAA, 'CYQAA Statement on Covid-19 Pandemic' (2020), https://www.dipae.ac.cy/archeia/anakoinoseis/CYQAA%20STATEMENT%20ON%20COVID.pdf; CYQAA, 'Τελικές εξετάσεις σε καταστάσεις έκτακτης ανάγκης λόγω κορονοϊού: Πρότυπα Ποιότητας και Κατευθυντήριες Γραμμές για Εναλλακτικές Μορφές Αξιολόγησης' (31.03.2020), https://www.dipae.ac.cy/index.php/el/nea-ekdiloseis/anakoinoseis-el/511-31-03-2020-final-exams-koronoios.

UCLan Cyprus have found that shift beneficial, instances of malpractice, such as plagiarism and collusion, have been identified. Due to the difficulties in invigilating a 24-hour seen exam, it was impossible to identify whether the exam paper was wholly written by the student or by a third party.

It is worth noting that since September 2022, all universities have been asked to shift back to the pre-COVID-19 face-to-face teaching delivery, requiring students registered on conventional programmes to attend their classes physically, as per the instructions provided by the CYQAA.[142]

3.2.3. *Social Challenges*

The biggest challenge of emergency remote teaching was not physical but psychological. Students were prevented from physically communicating with teachers and peers during the pandemic, and thus mental health issues such as anxiety and depression surfaced among students. The lack of social and cognitive presence has affected the motivation of students to participate and engage during their studies, with many performing worse in their coursework and final exams. Further, not all students have 'a reliable working environment … with some finding themselves working in bedrooms they share with their siblings or in busy communal areas.'[143] Indeed, 'working in such an environment makes it difficult for students to concentrate, with many struggling to cope … [T]he shift to online teaching has forced many law students to be working from home where there are enormous distractions and other domestic issues'.[144] Therefore, most students find it challenging to maintain focus during online teaching.

Despite this, the hybrid approach has helped eliminate some social challenges. It has offered an opportunity for all learners to collaborate and communicate with teachers and peers via electronic means, which can reinforce the feeling of community belonging.[145]

---

142 CYQAA Announcement (26.09.2022), https://www.dipae.ac.cy/index.php/el/nea-ekdiloseis/anakoinoseis-el/673-26-09-2022-mathimata-cheimerinou-examinou-2022-2023-sta-symvatika-programmata-spoudon-ton-idrymaton-anoteris-ekpaidefsis-3.

143 L. Pitsillidou, 'Legal Education in An Era of Change: The Impact of Covid-19' (Rule of Law Monitoring Mechanism Blog, 12.08.2021), https://ruleoflawmonitoringmechanism.eu/posts/legal-education-in-an-era-of-change-impact-covid19-lida-pitsillidou; F. Ferri, P. Grifoni and T. Guzzo, 'Online Learning and Emergency Remote Teaching: Opportunities and Challenges in Emerging Situations' (2020) 10(4) *Societies* 1, 10.

144 L. Pitsillidou, 'Legal Education in An Era of Change: The Impact of Covid-19' (Rule of Law Monitoring Mechanism Blog, 12.08.2021), https://ruleoflawmonitoringmechanism.eu/posts/legal-education-in-an-era-of-change-impact-covid19-lida-pitsillidou; F. Ferri, P. Grifoni and T. Guzzo, 'Online Learning and Emergency Remote Teaching: Opportunities and Challenges in Emerging Situations' (2020) 10(4) *Societies* 1, 10.

145 F. Ferri, P. Grifoni and T. Guzzo, 'Online Learning and Emergency Remote Teaching: Opportunities and Challenges in Emerging Situations' (2020) 10(4) *Societies* 1, 10.

4. CONCLUSION

The outbreak of the COVID-19 pandemic has served as a catalyst in reshaping the operation of contemporary legal education and legal professions in Cyprus. With regard to legal education, the immediate transition from in-classroom to emergency remote teaching has posed significant technological, pedagogical and social challenges. This has led universities to reconsider various aspects of legal pedagogy, such as accessibility, equality and inclusivity. The lack of internet connectivity and access constraints have unmasked digital inequalities between students in accessing the materials taught to harvest the fruits of online teaching, with many struggling to cope with their studies due to their incapacity to attend and participate in online classes. One of the problematic areas highlighted by the pandemic is the inequality gap and digital poverty, as 'socio-economic inequalities are still a current problem in legal education nowadays.'[146] The COVID-19 pandemic has therefore highlighted the need to support students 'in their learning activities by mitigating the risks of inequality and uneven access to education through embedding activities that support wider participation and inclusivity.'[147]

Reconsidering current pedagogical approaches and practices to assess student performance and enhance student learning could support the transformation of a contemporary legal education in Cyprus that embraces digital technology and supports innovative practices to enhance participation and inclusivity. Although the use of online legal education was nearly absent before the pandemic, COVID-19 has led law schools in Cyprus to experiment with online teaching, leading to the implementation of digital technology in the law curriculum.

Therefore, the recent technological developments are not a 'panacea' for legal education,[148] but rather an opportunity to explore a wide array of new innovative methods of teaching. Indeed, the implementation of innovative e-learning technologies has become a necessity, as they could transform the law classroom into a supportive and inclusive environment for all students to participate and engage in. The rapid technological developments have induced the need to implement recorded lectures in law schools in Cyprus for the first time, leading towards a supportive and inclusive legal education with flexibility for all learners to access the materials taught as well as participate in law classrooms. The development of open access to various online materials and courses has also played a catalytic role in supporting all learners during their learning journey,

146 L. Pitsillidou, 'Legal Education in An Era of Change: The Impact of Covid-19' (Rule of Law Monitoring Mechanism Blog, 12.08.2021), https://ruleoflawmonitoringmechanism.eu/posts/legal-education-in-an-era-of-change-impact-covid19-lida-pitsillidou.

147 Ibid.

148 F. Ferri, P. Grifoni and T. Guzzo, 'Online Learning and Emergency Remote Teaching: Opportunities and Challenges in Emerging Situations' (2020) 10(4) *Societies* 1, 6.

helping to mitigate the challenges students have been asked to deal with as a result of the COVID-19 pandemic.

Aside from legal education, the COVID-19 pandemic has also posed unprecedented obstacles to the legal profession in Cyprus, as legal professionals and the courts have been asked to deal with operational changes during what were already challenging times for the administration of justice in Cyprus. In an era of change, a shift to online continuing professional education was seen to be essential, as it has provided opportunities to legal professionals to access CPE workshops and seminars remotely. This change has embraced a new format of professional development for legal professionals in Cyprus. In an increasingly globalised and competitive society, the importance of the shift to online CPE cannot be overstated as it has improved access to professional development in a more flexible way. With the demands of the legal profession rapidly evolving, online CPE has become a hallmark for legal professionals in Cyprus, as it helps them maintain and improve their legal knowledge and skills, ensuring that high standards are maintained in legal professionals' practice.

The legal profession in Cyprus also saw the establishment of the first Judicial College in 2020, which aims to provide lifelong training for judges in Cyprus. Although this can be seen as a significant development in the legal profession, aiming to improve the efficiency of the Cypriot justice system, further improvements are needed to strengthen the resources for continuing education of judges, especially with regard to the digitalisation of justice and the shift from face-to-face to online proceedings, leading towards an alignment with other EU member states.

The implementation of the iJustice system in Cyprus was a first step towards revolutionising the traditional court system and the way legal professionals have been working for decades. Although iJustice has been in the works since 2017, COVID-19 prompted the need for its official implementation in 2021 to address the difficulties posed in the operation and functioning of the courts during the pandemic. COVID-19 has exposed the low level of digitalisation of the Cypriot courts as well as the limitations that exist in the administration of justice due to enormous delays and disruptions that litigants face to obtain justice in Cyprus. The introduction of iJustice system aimed to usher the Cypriot legal system into a new age of speedy and effective justice that embraces the use of digital technology in the legal profession. As iJustice is still at its early stages, more remains to be seen in the future as to what gaps need to be filled in order to improve the Cypriot justice system. Ultimately, the implementation of eJustice is expected to complete the long-overdue digital transformation of the Cypriot courts.

As a result of the pandemic, the recent technological developments have therefore transformed the legal profession and legal education in Cyprus and will likely continue to do so in the coming years. COVID-19 has highlighted the importance and power of online education in helping students acquire the knowledge, skills, values and attitudes they need to contribute constructively to society, as well as in creating a stable and effective legal profession through enhancing the digitalisation of the Cypriot court system, the lifelong training of judges and the continuing professional development of legal professionals in Cyprus.

ONLINE LEGAL EDUCATION IN ITALY

Previous Experiences and the Pandemic's 'Creative Destruction'

Rossella Esther CERCHIA and Barbara VARI*

1. INTRODUCTION

This report focuses on online legal education in Italy before the COVID-19 pandemic and after the first lockdown. Italy was one of the first European countries affected by the pandemic. In late January 2020, two cases of coronavirus were identified in Chinese tourists visiting Rome. On 21 February, what was

* In July 2021, e-mails were sent to most Italian universities requesting a series of information relevant for this report. Unfortunately, only a few responded. Our thanks to those who did. This report is up to date as of 20 December 2022.

mistakenly referred to as 'patient zero' was found, and within days, northern Italy was hit by a first devastating wave of the virus. Authorities attempted to contain the spread of the contagion by imposing a national lockdown. At the beginning of March 2020, a decree of the Prime Minister suspended on-site lectures in all Italian universities but allowed the 'possibility of carrying out distance learning activities'. Although online legal education previously existed, it was limited to distance learning universities (called 'telematic universities') or other niche experiences. Due to the pandemic, all universities that followed a traditional in-person model until then switched to online distance learning in a matter of days. Online education thus became the daily reality of all professors and students.

The 'emergency teaching' phase began. Within days, the transmission of knowledge and the relationship between professors and learners shifted online without an adequate period for rethinking or adapting teaching methods and styles. Consequently, all academic players were required to deal with new teaching methods and utilise technologies that had not yet entered their classrooms. The relationship between teaching and new digital technologies has come to the forefront of online legal education, raising concerns over the inherent limitations in its application: primarily the exacerbation of the so-called 'digital divide' for those lacking the requisite hardware or high-speed internet connection, or simply the knowledge to operate new technologies.

This report first briefly outlines the Italian framework for legal education and access to legal professions, provides an overview of information and communication technologies and finally highlights the impact of the pandemic on online legal education. The outcomes of this complex process remain uncertain. The fourth wave of the virus underway in Europe at the time of writing makes it difficult for academics to both design education plans that are truly post-pandemic and set the foundation of what will be 'the new normal'. These are the challenges universities must face.

2. BACKGROUND

2.1. LAW SCHOOLS

2.1.1. Overview

Italian universities offer two types of law degrees: a three-year first-level degree intended to prepare students for prompt access to the labour market (labour consultants, in-house legal advisors, law clerks, etc.) and a five-year course (*laurea magistrale*) required for students to access traditional legal professions (attorney, magistrate, notary) but not primarily oriented toward professional training.[1] Both degrees are undergraduate courses, which suggests why the *laurea magistrale* offers 'virtually all-encompassing and, above all, mainly preparatory, institutional teaching.'[2]

Law school remains rooted in 'the legacy, dating back at least to the middle of the nineteenth century, of its perception as a school of higher education providing generic training to the ruling class rather than as a real "school of law" aimed at preparing its pupils for legal professions, such as lawyers and magistrates.'[3] Traditionally, public university law programmes do not set barriers to entry: there are no entrance tests,[4] course attendance is not compulsory, and students take exams when they themselves feel ready and prepared. Students essentially remain enrolled until they have completed the core curriculum and attained the requisite credits for graduation (if they pay tuition). This structure explains why there has not been any real necessity or sense of 'need' to provide forms of distance learning that cater to working or non-resident students unable to attend in-person lectures.

In the 1970s, Merryman noted a profound difference between American and continental universities regarding the 'degree of self-consciousness about the objectives and methods of university education', which he perceived as marked in the United States. By contrast, he argued: 'Most who teach in civil law universities are, by comparison, totally unconcerned' about such objectives and methods; 'this characteristic is particularly marked in the law schools'.[5] The portrait he sketched is outdated and less true today.[6] There is now significant

---

1 V. Barsotti and V. Varano, 'Legal education in Italy' (2010) 1 *Opinio Juris in Comparatione* 1, https://www.opiniojurisincomparatione.org/articles/legal-education-in-italy/.

2 A. Dondi, 'Qualche considerazione comparata in tema di educazione giuridica istituzionale' (2013) 1–2 *Politica del diritto* 105, 120.

3 Ibid., p. 121, referring more generally to law schools in continental Europe.

4 There are some law schools that require an entrance test, failure of which may entail additional educational obligations for students who wish to confirm their choice, generally to be fulfilled in the first year (as in the case of the University of Milan), while others have a set number of students (for example, the University of Trento). The Single Annual Form of Study Courses (SUA – CDS) of all law schools, containing this and other information, can be read on the portal https://www.universitaly.it/index.php/cercacorsi/universita.

5 J.H. Merryman, 'Legal Education There and Here: A Comparison' (1975) 27 *Stanford Law Review* 859, 864.

6 Merely as an example, we note the 'Collana per l'osservatorio per la formazione giuridica', which includes numerous contributions on the subject (conducted according to different points of view) and, more recently, the essays collected in B. Pasciuta and L. Loschiavo, *La formazione del giurista. Contributi a una riflessione*, Romatrepress, Rome 2018, at https://romatrepress.uniroma3.it/wp-content/uploads/2020/02/La-formazione-del-giurista.-Contributi-a-una-riflessione.pdf. Italian scholars are involved in a broader European dialogue, which takes place within the European Law Faculties Association. The International Association of Comparative Law has always shown interest in the topic, see the volume on the internationalisation of legal education, where the Italian report was edited by R. Sacco and A. Gianola (C. Jamin and W. Van Caenegem (eds), *The Internationalisation of Legal Education*, Springer, Switzerland 2016) and the surveys on comparative law and multicultural

debate on educational objectives, teaching methodology and offering e-learning across Italian universities (as attested, for example, by the existence of Teaching Learning Centres, University E-learning Centres, courses for the training of young academics, and innovative teaching projects such as online teaching), albeit not yet widespread nor encompassing all academic players.

Conversely, it is necessary to remember the rather high average age of Italian professors,[7] who belong to the group Eric Prensky terms 'digital immigrants [not] digital natives',[8] and the fact that online courses, especially in their first edition, require significant investments of time and money – two scarce resources. Further consideration is required regarding the little weight teaching has in a professor's career progression in Italy,[9] and the allocation of fewer funds towards academia and research compared to other European countries – funds that have seen further cuts in recent years.[10] These issues are compounded by the requirement for all university courses (as well as all universities) to be accredited by ministerial structures, which leads to a certain rigidity.

In Italy, there are state universities and non-state universities. This is a traditional distinction, although it has been observed that non-state universities are quite varied, including universities of a public nature linked to local authorities

---

legal classes and bilingual legal education presented at the 2018 Congress (C. Varga (ed.), *Comparative Law and Multicultural Legal Classes: Challenging or Opportunity?*, Springer, Switzerland 2020; N.E. Estrazulas (ed.), *Bilingual Study and Research*, Springer, Switzerland 2022).

7 This aspect is characteristic of the entire university system, as has recently been reported in the Ministry of Universities and Research's focus on the academic year 2020/21: 'the classic pyramid structure of teaching and research staff is confirmed, as well as the high age of almost all qualifications, including those for access to academic careers.' At state universities, the average age is 52, ranging from 58 for full professors and 52 for associate professors to 46 for researchers. If we also include research fellows (*assegnisti di ricerca*, generally the first post-doc temporary position), the overall average age drops to 48. Specifically for legal sciences, the average age (also considering *assegnisti di ricerca*) is 49.3 years (56.6 for full professors, 49.7 for associate professors, 39 for temporary assistant researchers and 34.1 for *assegnisti di ricerca*). See the Ministerial 'Focus on "Teaching and non-teaching staff in the Italian university system – Academic Year 2020/2021"', September 2021, http://ustat.miur.it/media/1208/focus_pers_univ2020.pdf.

8 M. Prensky, 'Digital Natives, Digital Immigrants' (2001) 9 *On the Horizon* 1 https://www.marcprensky.com/writing/Prensky%20-%20Digital%20Natives,%20Digital%20Immigrants%20-%20Part1.pdf.

9 M. Vogliotti, 'Per una nuova educazione giuridica' (2020) XX *Diritto & Questioni pubbliche* 229, http://www.dirittoequestionipubbliche.org/page/2020_n20-2/00-DQXX-2020-2_02-6_studi_Vogliotti.pdf.

10 In 2019, public spending on Italian universities reached 0.5% of GDP, much lower than not only France (1.1%) and Germany (1%), but also the EU average (0.9%); see OECD, 'Public spending on education' (indicator), https://www.oecd-ilibrary.org/education/public-spending-on-education/indicator/english_f99b45d0-en. The distance with respect to European benchmarks is also recorded on other important parameters, see *Research training and university recruitment*, document approved by the assembly of the Italian University Rectors' Conference (Conferenza dei Rettori delle Università Italiane, CRUI) on 22 April 2021.

and others that depend entirely on private initiatives.[11] There are so-called 'telematic universities' within the sphere of non-state universities that are subject to less rigid rules[12] but have been reported to provide a poorer quality of education compared to traditional universities.[13] Further, the Italian university model (based on the model established in Germany in the 19th century) combines didactics and scientific research. The importance of university libraries is highlighted in this model as they are necessary to carry out research activities and guarantee continuously updated teaching. The low prestige that has characterised telematic universities can also be explained by the fact that they separate teaching from research,[14] generally resulting in inadequate libraries and databases, particularly foreign ones.

2.1.2. Funding

The primary source of funding for public universities comes from the Ministry of Universities and Research (MUR)[15] through the Ordinary Financing Fund (FFO). Money from the FFO is distributed among universities according to criteria that are subject to continual adjustments. In particular, the FFO is mainly composed of the basic quota, which primarily depends on the number of students enrolled,[16] the bonus quota, which concerns the quality of research and teaching, and the equalisation quota, which is intended to rebalance the situation among state universities. After the 2008 financial crisis, the FFO was eroded and returned to the nominal 2008 level only in 2019, albeit with a reduction in real value, and increased also in 2020. The National Recovery and Resilience

---

11 A. Sandulli, 'L'arcipelago delle università non statali' (2015) 3 *Munus* 609, https://www.rivistamunus.it/wp-content/uploads/2020/04/Munus-3-2015.pdf.

12 Report of the Study Commission on Issues Pertaining to Telematic Universities established by D.M. No. 429 of 3 June 2013, p. 14, https://www.istruzione.it/allegati/relazione_conclusiva_commissione_studio_universita_telematiche.pdf.

13 V. Barsotti and V. Varano, 'Legal education in Italy' (2010) 1 *Opinio Juris in Comparatione* 1, 2, http://lider-lab.sssup.it/opinio. On this point, the same evaluation was given a few years ago by the National University Council (CUN), which noted 'less preparation possessed by graduates from telematic universities than that achieved by graduates from conventional universities' (as reported in Report of the Study Commission on Issues Pertaining to Telematic Universities established by D.M. No. 429 of 3 June 2013, p. 15).

14 See National Committee for the Evaluation of the University System, Analysis of the Situation of the Telematic Universities, January 2010, p. 9, http://www.cnvsu.it/_library/downloadfile.asp?id=11682; Report of the Study Commission on Issues Pertaining to Telematic Universities established by D.M. No. 429 of 3 June 2013, https://www.istruzione.it/allegati/relazione_conclusiva_commissione_studio_universita_telematiche.pdf.

15 For an overview of the financial aspects of the management of the universities, with data from recent years, see the Report on the University System, issued by the Corte dei Conti in May 2021, pp. 95 ff., https://www.corteconti.it/Download?id=5078c35f-a683-482b-821c-33e05f1ac3e5.

16 The criterion currently used is the so-called 'standard cost per student'.

Plan (NRRP)[17] played an important role in the growth Italy experienced in 2021, through the provision of extraordinary European funds.[18]

The second most significant source of funding for public universities comes from student tuition fees. Universities have discretion to determine tuition fees (which must reflect progressive principles with graduated fees based on the student's tax bracket), but student tuition cannot exceed 20% of the amount of the FFO.[19] The accredited private universities (including telematic ones) rely on private tuition fees, but also receive annual state funding in accordance with Law No. 243/1991.

2.2. LEGAL PROFESSIONS: ATTORNEY-AT-LAW, NOTARY AND MAGISTRATE

2.2.1. Access to Legal Professions

Graduates from a five-year law degree who wish to pursue a traditional legal profession must continue their legal training.[20] To become an attorney, a notary or a magistrate, graduates must follow different paths that conclude with a different examination. To become a lawyer, it is necessary to both complete an 18-month apprenticeship in a law firm[21] and sit and pass the bar exam.[22] The bar exam is held annually in December and consists of a written component

---

17 Many of the increases for 2021 are linked to specific provisions, which provide for allocation constraints. The criteria for the distribution of the FFO for the year 2021 were defined by Ministerial Decree No. 1059 of 9 August 2021, which distributes over €8,383 billion. The text is available at https://www.mur.gov.it/it/atti-e-normativa/decreto-ministeriale-n-1059-del-09-08-2021.

18 The budget for the three-year period 2021–23 confirms these values, with forecasts of the item (Chapter 1694) of €8,402,986,950 for 2022 and €8,399,292,950 for 2023: see D.M. of 30 December 2020, available at https://www.rgs.mef.gov.it/_Documenti/VERSIONE-I/attivita_istituzionali/formazione_e_gestione_del_bilancio/bilancio_di_previsione/bilancio_finanziario/2021-2023/LB/RIC/LB_2021_LB-04-DRC-110-MUR.pdf.

19 See Article 5 of D.P.R. No. 306 of 25 July 1997, concerning university fees.

20 83% of graduates have participated in at least one postgraduate educational activity (including internships and apprenticeships) within one year after graduation. The percentage increases to 88% if the timeframe is extended to three years after graduation. See Almalaurea data for 2020. These and other interesting data can be found at https://www2.almalaurea.it/cgi-php/universita/statistiche/tendine.php?config=occupazione.

21 It is possible to fulfil up to one year of the apprenticeship period by attending (and receiving a diploma from) a school of specialisation for the legal professions. Additionally, up to 12 months of the apprenticeship period may be carried out at the State Legal Service, the legal department of a public entity or at a court, and up to six months may be spent in another European Union country, under the supervision of an attorney. Lastly, students regularly enrolled in law school may begin the apprenticeship period early, in the last six months of their degree programme.

22 From 2022 onwards, the apprenticeship, in addition to practice in a law firm, will also consist of compulsory attendance (for a period of at least 18 months) at professional training courses held by legal professional associations, as well as by some other entities.

comprising of three written works and an oral component.[23] The written exams are corrected over a period of several months, with those who pass going on to sit the oral component. After passing both sections of the exam, it is necessary to join the local bar association and take the oath to practise law.

The career paths to become a notary or magistrate present considerable challenges, including a highly competitive national competition organised by the Ministry of Justice with a limited number of seats available. The notary is a socially prestigious figure and has traditionally been a very lucrative profession. The Ministry of Justice determines the number of notaries and almost always annually announces a national public competition. Eligibility to participate in the competition is conditional on an 18-month training period in a notary's office.[24] The exam to become a notary consists of drafting three deeds, and undertaking an oral component after passing the written exam. Like the bar exam, the written element of the notary exam is corrected over a period of several months, with those who pass ranked by the Ministry of Justice, who subsequently assigns the available seats.

Eligibility to enter the competition to become a magistrate depends on the possession of additional qualifications, such as a diploma from a school of specialisation for the legal professions, being an attorney-at-law, having completed an 18-month apprenticeship at judicial offices, or holding a doctorate in law.[25] The public competition to become a magistrate also consists of three written essays and an oral exam, with several months required to correct the written portion. Thus, many months tend to pass between the two sittings. The number of candidates who pass both tests is generally less than the number of posts to be filled. Newly appointed magistrates then commence an 18-month training period.[26]

2.2.2. Gatekeepers of the Legal Professions

Most Italian law schools do not present barriers to enrolment. However, the postgraduate path to the legal professions is long and not without obstacles. This is compounded by the increasingly limited absorption capacity of the

---

23 For the written part, the prompts, or legal problems, which are the same throughout the state, are prepared by the Ministry of Justice and the bar examinations take place concurrently at each Court of Appeal in their respective district. The Minister appoints the members of the commissions that evaluate the candidates. According to Article 47 of Law No. 247 of 31 December 2012, each commission consists of five full members (and an equal number of substitute members), of whom three are lawyers designated by the National Bar Council (one of whom chairs it), one is a magistrate (retired as a priority, and only in the second instance still in service), and one is a university professor or assistant professor in legal matters.

24 It is possible to begin the notary apprenticeship as early as the last semester (i.e. six months) of the final year of law school.

25 For the complete list see D.lg. of 5 April 2006, No. 160, Article 2 as amended. During the publishing process, the legislation was reformed: access to the competition will be open to graduates with at least a four-year degree in law (D.L. No. 144 of 23 September 2022, Article 33).

26 The path to becoming a notary or magistrate tends to be long and uncertain, so many aspiring notaries or magistrates become lawyers in the meantime.

market (also because of the recent economic crisis), which has contributed to the decline in matriculation rates in law courses.[27]

While there is a significant barrier to entry and only a limited number of graduates can aspire to become a notary or magistrate, the difficulties for attorneys arise even after passing the bar examination. It is worth considering, in fact, that the bar exam is not a competition; it is a qualifying exam without an established quota of candidates that can pass. Moreover, eligible candidates can take the exam an infinite number of times. Despite a long period where the annual increase in the number of lawyers registered with the bar association (i.e. the difference between new members and outgoing members) was between 4,000 and 5,000, the increase in the number of members has gradually attenuated to only 48 more units between 2019 and 2020.[28] This testifies to the fact that the legal profession has lost its appeal in recent years. The extremely high number of Italian lawyers[29] (one of the highest in Europe) and periods of economic crisis have collectively resulted in a 'proletarianisation' of the legal profession,[30] with a contraction in turnover and income for lawyers.[31] In 2019, the average annual income declared by practising lawyers was €40,180, an increase of 1.8% compared to the previous year. The figure remains unaffected by the pandemic crisis, as the income data for 2020 is not yet known.[32]

The exams to become a notary or a magistrate entail public competitions with a limited number of available positions – announced by the Ministry of Justice based on the number of seats deemed necessary to fill. Both competitions

27 For a comprehensive analysis of the crisis in legal studies, see A. Banfi, 'Fine di un amore? A proposito del crollo delle iscrizioni nei corsi di giurisprudenza' in B. Pasciuta and L. Loschiavo (eds), *La formazione del giurista. Contributi a una riflessione*, Romatrepress, Rome 2018, pp. 15–30, https://romatrepress.uniroma3.it/wp-content/uploads/2020/02/La-formazione-del-giurista.-Contributi-a-una-riflessione.pdf; and R. Caso, 'The law does not live here anymore: the legal education crisis between data and questions', Trento Law and Technology Research Group Paper series 25 (2016), https://iris.unitn.it/retrieve/handle/11572/133900/59285/LTRP_25_Caso.pdf.

28 The data are from D. Monterisi, 'Rapporto Censis – Cassa Forense sull'avvocatura 2021: molte ombre, pochissime luci' [2021] *La Previdenza Forense* 1, https://www.cassaforense.it/riviste-cassa/la-previdenza-forense/avvocatura/rapporto-censis-cassa-forense-sull-avvocatura-2021-molte-ombre-pochissime-luci/.

29 In 2020, there were 231,295 active attorneys enrolled in the Pension Fund for Attorneys (Cassa Forense), which corresponds to approximately four active attorneys for every 1,000 inhabitants. See ibid.

30 The expression, here translated, is from A. Banfi, 'Fine di un amore? A proposito del crollo delle iscrizioni nei corsi di giurisprudenza' in B. Pasciuta and L. Loschiavo (eds), *La formazione del giurista. Contributi a una riflessione*, Romatrepress, Rome 2018, p. 24, https://romatrepress.uniroma3.it/wp-content/uploads/2020/02/La-formazione-del-giurista.-Contributi-a-una-riflessione.pdf.

31 Ibid.

32 D. Monterisi, 'Rapporto Censis – Cassa Forense sull'avvocatura 2021: molte ombre, pochissime luci' [2021] *La Previdenza Forense* 1, https://www.cassaforense.it/riviste-cassa/la-previdenza-forense/avvocatura/rapporto-censis-cassa-forense-sull-avvocatura-2021-molte-ombre-pochissime-luci/.

are considered very challenging in terms of difficulty and duration. Candidates may only sit the exam to become a magistrate three times, compared to five times for the notary exam. Many candidates who are unsure of their papers in the written exam prefer not to submit them to avoid wasting one of the (few) opportunities to access the profession. Many aspiring notaries and magistrates attend preparatory courses to increase their chances of passing the exam. A competitor's socio-economic background may play an important role in the choice to pursue these careers and persevere, since both competitions require much preparation and aspiring notaries and magistrates may remain in limbo for years before achieving their goal, considering how long it may take to finally pass the competition.

The extent of these challenges is illuminated by the following examples. In the 2018 competition, 6,682 candidates applied and competed in the first written test for 330 ordinary magistrate positions. Many aspiring magistrates withdrew, and only 3,091 delivered their essays. Only 301 candidates were admitted to the oral part, of whom only 285 were successful.[33] The ranking list of those who passed the competition was not published until 31 March 2021. Likewise, in the 2019 competition for 310 ordinary magistrate positions (whose written tests, due to the pandemic, were held on 15 and 16 July 2021), only 3,797 of the 5,827 who sat the exam submitted their written tests. At the time of writing corrections are still in progress.[34] Similarly, the last notary competition to be completed was announced in 2018 for 300 notary positions: 1,585 candidates submitted their exams for the session held in April 2019, and only 244 participants were admitted to the oral part. In November 2021, the ranking list of the 199 who ultimately passed the competition was published.[35]

2.3. ACCESS TO IT AND ADOPTION OF TECHNOLOGY

The use of new information and communication technologies (ICT) by individuals and families represents one of the fundamental goals of social and cultural inclusion policies.[36] Internet access and broadband are some of the

33 See https://www.mgiudiziario.it/mgiudiziario/notiziario-concorsi-magistratura-ordinaria-3/.

34 For a critical perspective on the current system of magistrate recruitment, see a recent resolution of the self-governing body of the Italian judiciary (CSM), welcoming the idea of allowing law graduates to directly access the competition, as provided for in a bill of 2020 (D.D.L. No. 2681, presented on 28 September 2020). See CSM, 7 December 2021, https://www.csm.it/web/csm-internet/-/risoluzione-sulla-normativa-in-materia-di-concorso-per-il-reclutamento-di-magistrati-ordinari. During the publishing process, the reform was finally implemented (see D.L. No. 144 of 23 September 2022, Article 33).

35 For more information, see https://www.giustizia.it/giustizia/it/mg_1_6_1.page?facetNode_1=5_2&facetNode_2=1_2(2018)&facetNode_3=5_2_2&contentId=SCE153339&previsiousPage=mg_1_6.

36 See the report of the National Institute of Statistics (ISTAT), https://www.istat.it/it/files//2019/12/Cittadini-e-ICT-2019.pdf.

prerequisites for the diffusion of ICT among the population. Over the preceding decade in Italy, the number of people connected to the internet has significantly increased. Yet the 'digital divide' is still present.[37] Pre-pandemic data from the National Institute of Statistics (ISTAT) paints the following picture. In 2019, 76.1% of Italian households had internet access and 74.7% had a broadband connection.[38] However, there were wide disparities between regions, with central and northern Italy at an advantage. There were also asymmetries between municipalities of different demographic sizes. In metropolitan areas, broadband access rates reached 78.1%, while in municipalities of up to 2,000 inhabitants this figure dropped to 68.0%. Among households, a strong digital divide remained, primarily due to generational and cultural factors. Almost all households with at least one minor had a broadband connection (95.1%); among households composed exclusively of persons over 65 years of age, this share dropped to 34.0%. Most households without home internet access indicated lack of capacity as the main reason (56.4%), while 25.5% did not consider the internet a useful or interesting tool. Economic reasons were also reported, related to the high cost of connections or of the necessary tools (13.8%), while 9.2% did not surf the Net at home because at least one member of the family accessed the internet from another place.

As a result of the COVID-19 pandemic, a race has emerged to access the new technologies essential for 'smart working', distance learning (employed from primary school through to university), and other needs. Over one million people connected to the internet for the first time during 2020 (an increase of 2.2%).[39] 97% of the population reported owning a smartphone, and three out of four people reporting using a desktop or laptop computer.[40]

During the emergency phase, various measures were launched to ensure adequate economic, technological and cognitive support for distance teaching. In 2020, €85 million was added to the budget to finance the National Plan for Digital Schools.[41] Other initiatives to bridge the digital divide caused by economic reasons also emerged. For instance, ADSL technology was installed and activated, free of charge, in some areas of the country, free cloud services for distance teaching were offered, as well as web hosting for e-commerce, students

---

37 On the digital divide, see P. Zuddas, 'Covid-19 e digital divide: tecnologie digitali e diritti sociali alla prova dell'emergenza sanitaria' (2020) 3 *Osservatorio Costituzionale* 285, https://www.osservatorioaic.it/images/rivista/pdf/2020_3_17_Zuddas.pdf.

38 The framework and related data are taken from ISTAT Report, https://www.istat.it/it/files//2019/12/Cittadini-e-ICT-2019.pdf.

39 The data are those of the Report 'Digital 2021' by We Are Social, in collaboration with Hootsuite, https://wearesocial.com/it/blog/2021/02/digital-2021-i-dati-italiani/.

40 Ibid.

41 P. Zuddas, 'Covid-19 e digital divide: tecnologie digitali e diritti sociali alla prova dell'emergenza sanitaria' [2020] 3 *Osservatorio Costituzionale* 286, 298, https://www.osservatorioaic.it/images/rivista/pdf/2020_3_17_Zuddas.pdf.

without personal computers received them on loan, and free internet was offered – for a period – in areas particularly affected by the pandemic.[42]

The European Commission has monitored member states' digital progress and published annual Digital Economy and Society Index (DESI) reports. The DESI 2021 report, based primarily on 2020 data concerning the state of the digital economy and society in the first year of the pandemic, ranks Italy 20th out of 27 EU member states.[43] It reveals that during 2020, Italy made some progress in both coverage and uptake of connectivity networks, with a particularly notable increase in connectivity services offering speeds of at least 1 Gbps. However, the pace of fibre deployment slowed between 2019 and 2020, and efforts are still required to increase the coverage of very high-capacity networks and 5G and to encourage uptake.[44]

Italy lags significantly behind its EU counterparts on human capital. Compared with the EU average, it records lower levels of basic and advanced digital skills.[45] However, these issues do not apply to lawyers and notaries. In recent years, lawyers have had to equip themselves and learn to interact with new technologies to fulfil the requirements of the 'telematic civil process',[46] while notaries have computerised their offices. By contrast, judicial offices are still lagging behind in the process of computerisation and the use of new technologies. Therefore, among the objectives of the NRRP, digitalisation and computerisation of judicial offices are essential to reducing the duration of the justice process.[47]

The Italian Recovery and Resilience Plan is the largest in the EU, accounting for a total of about €191.5 billion, of which 25.1% (i.e. approximately €48 billion) is devoted to the digital transition.[48] The reforms and investments contributing to the digital transition cover the digital transformation of the public administration and justice system and the strengthening of the healthcare system through digital

42 Ibid., p. 303.

43 See Digital Economy and Society Index (DESI) 2021 – Italy, https://digital-strategy.ec.europa.eu/en/policies/countries-digitisation-performance.

44 Ibid.

45 Ibid.

46 The telematic civil process consists of a fixed series of procedural activities that are carried out telematically (i.e. remotely) and therefore requires the possession of some computer skills.

47 One of the major innovations brought about by the health emergency is undoubtedly the launch of the telematic criminal process, introduced in forced stages during 2020 to counterbalance the measures that restricted access to the registries and secretariats of judicial offices, thus preventing physical access. The Ministry of Justice intends to replicate in the criminal sector the model already introduced in the telematic civil process to improve the efficiency of the criminal process in all its phases, guaranteeing the transfer of information between the various offices and making the elements necessary for decisions available more quickly.

48 Digital Economy and Society Index (DESI) 2021 – Italy, https://digital-strategy.ec.europa.eu/en/policies/countries-digitisation-performance.

technologies, the modernisation of businesses through the uptake of advanced technologies (Transition 4.0), and the deployment of gigabit connectivity across the country.[49] The plan also addresses digital skills development, with measures aimed at improving the basic digital skills of the general population, increasing the offer of training on advanced digital skills, and upskilling and reskilling the workforce.[50]

3. MOVES TOWARDS ONLINE LEGAL EDUCATION

3.1. ACHIEVEMENTS BEFORE THE PANDEMIC: TELEMATIC UNIVERSITIES AND DISTANCE LEARNING

In the most generic sense, the term e-learning refers to the application of new information technologies to teaching. These technologies were previously adopted by Italian universities, for example by using platforms to make materials available, to exchange documents or to create forums. However, the provision of online degree courses was a field left primarily to telematic universities. Before the pandemic, online education in traditional universities was used in some 'experimental' projects, left to the initiative of individual universities and/or teachers.[51] In the legal field,[52] for example, there were massive open online courses (MOOCs)[53] and other select courses[54] available via distance learning.

There was also a significant online offering related to continuing legal education, which is required of attorneys. Although the flexibility and time

49 Ibid.

50 Ibid.

51 From the academic year 2015/16, for example, the University of Turin has provided that students of the five-year degree in Law can attend some courses online (up to a maximum of 200 university credits (CFUs), out of the total 300 CFUs). Students who make this choice can take advantage of all the services offered to 'traditional' students, plus the possibility of being included in online classes, upon payment of an additional contribution to university fees. The University of Turin already offered the entire three-year degree course in Administrative Sciences in online mode.

52 It should be noted that a survey conducted in 2013 showed that e-learning appears to be relatively uncommon in law (M. Gaebel, V. Kupriyanova, R. Morais and E. Colucci, 'E-learning in European Higher Education Institutions', EUA Publications (2014), p. 33, https://www.eua.eu/downloads/publications/e-learning%20in%20european%20higher%20education%20institutions%20results%20of%20a%20mapping%20survey.pdf).

53 See, for example, the offer of free courses (also) in the legal area of the telematic University Uninettuno, partner of the OpenupEd project.

54 The University of Milan, for example, already in 2017 allowed online participation in the postgraduate course in 'Diritti e inclusione delle persone con disabilità in una prospettiva multidisciplinare' (Rights and Inclusion of People with Disabilities in a Multidisciplinary Perspective).

efficiency of online education is particularly suited to the needs of professionals, the use of such technologies faces a series of limitations. Indeed, the National Bar Council[55] (CNF) establishes a limit of 40% of continuing education credits to be obtained through accredited online courses in a three-year period,[56] and such courses are only allowed to the extent it is possible to verify participation.[57]

Before the pandemic, online legal education at the undergraduate level was primarily provided by telematic universities. Indeed, Italy contains both traditional (public and private) universities and telematic universities, which are specifically designed according to an e-learning model. Legislative initiatives towards distance learning date back to the last century,[58] but the growth of telematic universities took place from 2003.[59] Since then, there have been numerous regulatory actions, albeit rather piecemeal and chaotic.[60] The initial permissive legal framework led to the creation of various universities, whose educational offerings and quality, however, were considered inadequate. Therefore, the establishment of new telematic universities was prohibited and the quality criteria were defined with greater precision and rigour. In the end, these universities (which are recognised by the MUR) issue degrees that have the same legal value as those issued by traditional universities.

---

55 The National Bar Council (Consiglio Nazionale Forense, CNF) is the highest institution of Italian attorneys-at-law. It is a public institution and the governing and regulatory body of the Italian legal profession. For more information see both the Professional Law, adopted in 2012 (L. No. 247/12) and https://www.consiglionazionaleforense.it/.

56 Lawyers must acquire 60 credits over a period of three years and at least 15 credits each year. The number of credits depends on the activity carried out. For refresher activities (mainly aimed at adapting and deepening the acquired experience and knowledge gained in initial training): half-day events are attributed between one and three credits; one-day (or more) events receive two to 12 credits. Training initiatives may be organised and promoted not only by the CNF and by local bar associations, but also by other associations, institutions, public or private organisations, including for-profit organisations. See CNF, *Regulations for Continuing Education* (Reg. 16 July 2014, No. 6), https://www.consiglionazionaleforense.it/documents/20182/182382/Regolamento+16+July+2014,+n.+6+-+Continuing+Education.

57 See CNF, *Nota tecnica sull'accreditamento delle attività di formazione a distanza (FAD)*, https://www.consiglionazionaleforense.it/documents/20182/182382/Nota+tecnica+sulle+procedure+di+accreditamento+delle+attivit%C3%A0+di+Formazione+a+distanza+(FAD).

58 See D.P.R. 382/1980, Article 92 ('Experimentation of new teaching methods') and L. 341/1990, which provides for 'financial support for university distance learning initiatives implemented by universities, including in consortia with other public and private entities.'

59 D. interm. of 17 April 2003, containing 'Criteria and procedures for the accreditation of distance learning courses of state and non-state universities and university institutions authorised to issue academic titles as per Article 3 of Decree No. 509 of 3 November 1999', which also took into account the requests coming from Europe (see National Committee for the Evaluation of the University System, 'Analysis of the Situation of Telematic Universities', January 2010 at http://www.cnvsu.it/_library/downloadfile.asp?id=11682).

60 Report of the Study Commission on Issues Pertaining to Telematic Universities established by D.M. of 3 June 2013, No. 429, 3, https://www.istruzione.it/allegati/relazione_conclusiva_commissione_studio_universita_telematiche.pdf.

In an annex to a 2016 ministerial decree on accreditation,[61] degree courses were divided into four categories: (1) conventional courses (delivered in person or combined with limited online activities, not exceeding 10%); (2) mixed mode (with online activities not exceeding two-thirds of the total educational activity); (3) predominantly distance learning (online activities exceeding two-thirds); and (4) entirely distance learning. Telematic universities may only establish type (3) and (4) courses, but exams and final dissertations must be conducted on site, in a traditional setting.[62] There are currently 11 accredited telematic universities; 10 of these offer degree programmes in the legal field; eight offer the five-year degree in law.

The national agency for the evaluation of universities and research institute (Agenzia di Valutazione del Sistema Universitario e della Ricerca, ANVUR) provides criteria for calculating university credits (CFUs) for online courses, where CFUs represent the student workload and educational activities aimed at passing exams. For traditional, on-site courses, one CFU corresponds to 25 hours of learning activities, six to 10 hours of which are dedicated to face-to-face teaching (lectures) with the rest comprising of individual study. Regarding online teaching, a distinction has been made between *didattica erogativa* (like face-to-face teaching in the classroom, focused on the presentation of content by the teacher) and interactive teaching. For each CFU, the teaching must reach the minimum threshold of six hours, ensuring at least one hour for each of the two forms of teaching.[63] The ANVUR therefore clarifies the importance of didactic interaction, which must be ensured in the context of courses held through telematic means. Faced with initial unflattering evaluations received by telematic universities, ANVUR has fortunately intervened, following the indications of the scientific literature on online education.[64]

---

61 Annex 3 of Miur D.M. of 8 August 2016, No. 635 (General guidelines for university planning 2016–2018 and indicators for periodic performance assessment); this distinction is found reiterated in Annex 3 of D.M. 989/2019 and Annex 4 of D.M. 298/2021.

62 The telematic university Pegaso proposed to amend its regulation, to make permanent the possibility of taking the exams remotely (as had been allowed during the emergency), but the Minister rejected the amendment and that decision has been considered legitimate by the Administrative Court (Tar Lazio, Roma, 17 May 2021, Bo. 5797, in *database Pluris*).

63 See ANVUR, 'Guidelines for pre-activation evaluations of Courses of Study (CdS) in telematic mode by the Commission of Evaluation Experts (CEV)', 23 December 2013, https://www.unite.it/UniTE/Engine/RAServeFile.php/f/presidioateneo/03_LGPreattivTelematiche_Def231213.pdf. The distinction between the two different teaching methods can be found also in documents published in subsequent years.

64 See A.R. Formiconi, 'La tortuosa via della didattica online nell'università' (2016) 1 *Studi sulla formazione/Open Journal of Education* 105, 127, https://oajournals.fupress.net/index.php/sf/article/download/9121/9119/.

3.2. THE PANDEMIC'S 'CREATIVE DESTRUCTION'

3.2.1. *Emergency Teaching*

On 8 March 2020, a decree of the Italian Prime Minister suspended in-person lectures in all Italian universities but allowed them to continue through distance learning activities. Therefore, all Italian universities have transitioned from a traditional model of face-to-face teaching to distance learning (*didattica a distanza*, DAD). This transition can be defined as an emergency phase of teaching: in just a few days, the transmission of knowledge had to shift online. Academics, with the support of their universities (who provided e-learning platforms), have been generally independent in choosing their modalities. For instance, some provided live video lectures while others made recorded video lectures available or opted for slides with audio commentary.[65] Most law professors also accompanied online lectures with additional, supplemental teaching material, such as texts, diagrams, slides, images, videos, bibliographies or suggestions for supplementary readings or exercise materials.[66] There were those who delivered the courses with modifications and adaptations related to the methods and times of delivery and those who kept them identical.[67]

On the positive side, roll-out delays were limited to a few days, class schedules did not depart from those previously established, most professors managed to carry out their teaching programmes in full, the number of 'attending' students did not decrease, and exams were held regularly.[68]

Professors interacted with the students by appointment through the digital platforms, by e-mail or by phone. For the most part, examinations for law schools continued in the same way as before the pandemic, mainly through the provision of (online) oral examinations.[69]

---

65 These indications are taken from the survey carried out by ANVUR, on universities' teaching experiences during the COVID-19 health emergency. The results of the questionnaires on the management of the emergency and on distance learning (intended for teachers), cited here as the 'ANVUR survey', are available at https://www.anvur.it/attivita/ava/didattica-a-distanza/.

66 Ibid.

67 These are the results of the national survey on emergency teaching accomplished in June 2020 through interviews with 3,398 teachers, by an online questionnaire highlighting that 67% of faculties have modified somewhat both the content and structure of their teaching, 24% have kept it unchanged and 9% have taken the opportunity to significantly rethink their teaching. See F. Ramella and M. Rostan, 'Universi-DaD, Gli accademici italiani e la didattica a distanza durante l'emergenza Covid-19', Working Papers CLB-CPS 1 (2020), p. 1, https://www.dcps.unito.it/do/documenti.pl/ShowFile?_id=gfk5;field=file;key=4G3PLidHy8YQAwy46cnWQSzYCxRhjocgmo6f2vGxXL03D8js7D6;t=3283.

68 Ibid.

69 See ANVUR survey, available at https://www.anvur.it/attivita/ava/didattica-a-distanza/.

Depending on their computer skills, preferences and possibilities, each academic tried to cope with the new reality of distance learning. ANVUR research shows most of them felt they had both the ability to adapt to DAD and an adequate internet connection to carry it out.[70] More negatively, professors have also highlighted the difficulties encountered. They lamented the lack of direct interaction with students,[71] the difficulty in keeping students' attention, the significant organisational effort involved, and an excess of time spent in front of a screen.[72]

Some universities have conducted internal surveys on emergency teaching. For example, the University of Trento carried out a survey aimed at collecting information on the experiences, evaluations and opinions of students with respect to distance learning delivered in the second semester of the academic year 2019/20.[73] Among other data, it is interesting to highlight how online teaching for almost all students represented an absolute novelty: only 14.9% had some experience, generally quite limited, with online classes. Based on their experience, the comparison between online teaching and classroom teaching shows an overwhelming preference for the latter over the former. However, the data indicates students appreciated DAD as an alternative mode of learning and continuing their studies in a particular situation, which did not allow for alternative solutions. For the rest, other positive aspects do not undermine the primacy of traditional teaching. The major problems encountered by students were difficulty in concentration and motivation and lack of involvement.

Other interesting insights are those provided by a University of Pisa survey,[74] among them that DAD can be very advantageous for students with certain types of disabilities (especially physical) but exacerbates the difficulties of those with certain learning disabilities. On the one hand, there has been a proliferation of written materials not designed for students with learning disabilities, and on the other, there is less direct interaction with teachers and classmates, a fundamental element for overcoming the obstacles related to understanding concepts and student learning.[75]

---

70 Ibid.

71 Ibid.

72 Ibid.

73 The survey, to which over 5,100 students responded (31% of the student body), was conducted between 28 May 2020 and 25 June 2020. The questionnaire collected information on attendance levels, the assessment of the different forms of online education (synchronous and asynchronous) compared to that in person and the difficulties encountered (technical, psychological and relational problems). See https://www.unitn.it/alfresco/download/workspace/SpacesStore/415c1950-9d02-4312-8c93-802d29661d36/Studenti%20e%20DOL.pdf.

74 See the survey 'Evaluation report on the distance learning model adopted by the University of Pisa during the lockdown' by Human Foundation Do&Think Tank per l'Innovazione Sociale, Pisa University Press, Pisa 2020, open access e-book available at https://store.streetlib.com/it/aavv/limpatto-sociale-della-dad-di-unipi?product=6184f070ea9042c7bb03a3ea.

75 Ibid.

While traditional universities have adapted quickly to DAD, they have been unable to rapidly increase their stock of digital libraries and develop necessary library services for academics and students alike. While paper libraries have been partially replaced by databases, this replacement is not complete and many law libraries remain undigitised, unlike in France and other European countries.

3.2.2. *The Pandemic Continues: Dual Teaching*

September 2021 marked the start of the first semester in which a return to 'relative' normality was possible. However, while at the beginning of the semester the curve of COVID-19 cases had dropped considerably, at the end of the semester Europe was hit by the so-called 'fourth wave'. The format adopted in this semester entailed the so-called 'mixed' or 'dual' delivery approach, where face-to-face lectures were also available online, via streaming and/or as video recordings. The capacity of classrooms was reduced to allow adequate distancing and ensure safety, and, for the same reasons, physical access to the classrooms was possible mostly through a reservation system, whereby students reserve their spot in class. Access to university facilities also requires a 'COVID-19 Green Certificate'.[76]

The adoption of dual teaching catered to different needs. It allowed for the participation of students who were unable to reserve a seat in the classroom or could not participate in in-person activities for health reasons, and simultaneously proved a useful tool for other students who, for whatever reason, preferred not to attend on-site lectures and for non-resident students unwilling or unable to travel in such uncertain times.

3.2.3. *Other Pandemic Effects*

The suspension of in-person teaching has had an impact on all postgraduate courses, from the schools of specialisation to master's courses and continuing legal education generally. Given this exceptional period, the National Bar Council has removed the 40% limit on credits that can be earned through distance learning, at first only for 2020 but since extending through to 2021 and 2022.

Distance learning – via e-learning, streaming, webinars and video-conferencing – has spread like wildfire. The compulsory shift online has made it possible to appreciate the advantages of online education, including the freedom to follow

---

76 The Green Certificate is a document that attests to one of the following criteria: vaccination against COVID-19, a negative antigen or molecular swab test taken within the past 48 hours, or recovery from infection. As of 1 February 2022, university staff are subject to compulsory vaccination (D.L. No. 1 of 7 January 2022), for which a 'super green pass' is issued.

courses regardless of one's physical location or the cities in which they are held. The greater difficulty in networking is, on the other hand, one of the negative aspects.

The pandemic has impacted access to the legal professions. Due to the emergency, some changes were introduced concerning apprenticeships and the bar exam:[77] the 2020 session was postponed to May 2021. The format was also amended: the written component was abolished, and candidates instead took two oral exams. This new approach was also adopted for the 2021 exam (which, due to the delay of the 2020 exam, did not take place until 2022).

The 2019 competition for 300 new notary positions could not be held due to the pandemic and was only held, with the addition of 100 seats, in late November/ early December 2021. Finally, the competition for 320 ordinary magistrate posts, scheduled for November 2019, was also delayed until July 2021 and the written part was modified such that candidates were required to complete only two tasks (in civil and criminal law) instead of three. At the time of writing both national competitions are still in progress, and many aspiring lawyers have also yet to complete the bar exam.

4. ONLINE LEGAL EDUCATION: ACHIEVEMENTS AND CHALLENGES

Although considerations on the didactic methodologies for legal studies were present in the Italian debate, they were not central, and e-learning experiences carried out by the universities (more developed in other disciplinary fields) were still limited, except for telematic universities. However, the pandemic (still underway) has accelerated the process which had already begun: all professors have had to acquire new technological skills, which has opened up possibilities that were previously inconceivable. The debate regarding online education has emerged from the niches where it was taking place, acquiring greater centrality and renewing enthusiasm but also raising concerns.

Online teaching (not entailing lectures simply held in front of the camera or livestreamed or dual teaching methods provided by universities this year for pandemic reasons) offers important opportunities and specific affordances different from those of face-to-face teaching. To transform the difficulties in higher education caused by the pandemic into a valuable learning opportunity, it is important not to solely view online teaching from the perspective of the pandemic experience.[78] In fact, there are a multitude of studies, knowledge

---

[77] See D.L. No. 22 of 8 April 2020, converted with amendments by L. of 6 June 2020, No. 41.

[78] There seems to be a broad consensus on this observation, which is also expressed by the Commission in its recent communication 'Digital Education Action Plan 2021–2027.

and experiences in the field that can be exploited. On this basis, it should be possible to design innovative educational solutions that are more widespread, accelerating the existing trend towards online and hybrid learning.[79]

Consider MOOCs, for example: after gaining the attention of the *New York Times* in 2012 (which called that year 'The Year of the MOOC'), MOOCs have proven to be an interesting training ground for educational innovation.[80] However, MOOCs are characterised by heterogeneous experiences in terms of methodological choices and the possibilities of didactic interaction of learners, in terms of the business model followed, of the type of students and target, and of the objectives pursued. At an institutional level, as well as in scientific literature, there is a lively discussion on the state of the art and the most promising pathways, the practical advantages, and the possible risks and strategies to pursue, considering different contexts. The European context is distinct from the North American one. In Europe, discussions are carried out, projects are launched and funding is offered.[81] Italy actively participates in this debate,[82] with interest extending well beyond just a few universities and

---

Resetting education and training for the digital age', COM(2020) 624 final, https://eur-lex.europa.eu/legal-content/EN/TXT/?uri=CELEX%3A52020DC0624. The Commission concludes that '[t]he COVID-19 pandemic is impacting heavily on education and training systems. In highly difficult circumstances it has accelerated the digital transformation and triggered rapid, large-scale change. Developments that could have taken years happened in just a few weeks. We are now faced with both challenges and opportunities. This means we need to use the lessons of recent months to step up our efforts and gradually evolve from temporary, emergency-focused remote education to more effective, sustainable, and equitable digital education, as part of creative, flexible, modern, and inclusive education and training. This process should be informed by contemporary teaching practices and research.'

79 See for example the Unitutor project of the University of Foggia, which calls for each department to create at least one course of study in blended mode (for that of Law, the course in 'Investigative Sciences'). The new three-year degree course at the University of Turin in 'Agricultural and Food Law' was created in 2020–21 with lectures held entirely online, also to meet a demand from students from all over Italy.

80 L. Pappano, 'The year of the MOOC', *The New York Times* (2 November 2012).

81 See for instance the EMMA platform, born from a pilot project funded by the European Union called Emma European Multiple MOOC Aggregator, launched in 2015 and coordinated by the University of Naples Federico II. Here it is also possible to find several lessons related to the EulawinEN project, coordinated by the Fondazione Italiana del Notariato and aimed at providing blended and integrated content and language training for European notaries and magistrates. See http://project.europeanmoocs.eu/deliverables/D2.1_Aggregator_UNINA.pdf and R. De Rosa, 'Emma: una piattaforma Mooc che parla europeo' (2015) 6 *Universitas* 67, https://www.researchgate.net/publication/304115056_EMMA_Una_piattaforma_MOOC_che_parla_europeo.

82 Italy, with Spain and France, is a leader in absolute numbers in the EU (cf. the Commission Staff working document accompanying the Communication on 'Digital Education Action Plan 2021–2027. Resetting education and training for the digital age', COM(2020) 624 final, p. 37, and the various studies cited here). An indication of this interest is also the fact that some important international conferences have been hosted by Italian universities, such as the eMOOC19 Conference hosted by the University of Naples Federico II, and the OEGlobal Conference 2019 hosted by the Polytechnic of Milan.

scholars (consider the work done at the Italian University Rectors' Conference, CRUI).[83] A recent survey on the offering and characteristics of Italian MOOCs has depicted the Italian MOOCs ecosystem as 'rather dynamic both in terms of scientific debate and actual offering'.[84]

In recent years, MOOCs have not only increased in number but have new potentials to be exploited (and may be further exploited in the future) following what has been achieved in other experiences. MOOCs can, for example, be used as an orientation tool (as well as a recruitment tool) for high school students, who can follow courses on some of the qualifying subjects for the various university degree courses and are thus able to explore the educational offering and assess their interest and predisposition[85] (this is also the goal of the lessons freely accessible on platforms such as YouTube).[86] MOOCs can further be integrated into curricular courses[87] or courses recognised directly in the student's curriculum. The possibility of earning credits to be applied toward one's degree by following MOOCs from other universities is gaining increasing attention.

In Italy, the experience of Federica and EduOpen is particularly illustrative. In 2007, the University of Naples Federico II launched a web-based learning project called 'Federica', which evolved from the Federica.eu platform. Federica Web Learning is the University Centre for innovation, experimentation and

83 See S. Paleari, F. Corradini, A. Perali, F. Porta and E. Breno, *MOOCs Massive Open Online Courses. Prospettive e opportunità per l'Università italiana*, Fondazione CRUI, Rome 2015, https://www.crui.it/images/demo/crui_web/pubblicazioni/crui_mooc_2015.pdf, which was followed by the elaboration of National Guidelines for the preparation of quality MOOCs delivered by Italian universities (https://www.crui.it/images/1-_LineeGuidaMOOCsItalia_aprile2017.pdf). The discussion continued in the context of the 2018 meeting on the National Digital University Plan; see in particular the report by M. Calise, 'MOOCs: sfide e opportunità', I Magnifici Incontri CRUI 2018 (2018), https://www.pisauniversitypress.it/news-news-i-magnifici-incontri-crui-2018-6252.html.

84 See V. Goglio and F. Nascimbeni, 'Moocs in Italy: an open and fragmented landscape' (2021) 30(2) *Italian Journal of Educational Technology* 82, https://ijet.itd.cnr.it/article/view/1233/1110.

85 The orientation of high school students is an objective pursued for example by the start@unito project of the University of Turin, where students can also attend courses that will be recognised in their university career plan. See https://start.unito.it/; for an overall analysis of the project, see M. Marchisio, S. Rabellino and M. Sacchet, 'Start@unito as Open Educational Practice in Higher Education' (2020) 16 *Journal of e-Learning and Knowledge Society* 46, https://www.je-lks.org/ojs/index.php/Je-LKS_EN/article/download/1135354/1240/.

86 See for example the video cycle 'The first lesson of', on the YouTube channel of the Ca' Foscari University of Venice.

87 See for example the experience of the MOOC on 'Human Rights and International Criminal Law', by C. Dal Bon and C. Ferranti, 'MOOC non curriculari @Unipd: tra diffusione nazionale e internazionalizzazione' in M. Fedeli, D. Mapelli and C. Mariconda, *L'innovazione didattica all'Università di Padova. Teorie, Ricerche e Pratiche*, Unipd, Padua 2020, http://www.padovauniversitypress.it/system/files/attachments_field/9788869382185.pdf.

dissemination of multimedia teaching of the University of Naples Federico II.[88] It presents a rich educational offering[89] where courses from other universities can also be found thanks to its established partnerships.[90] The FedericaGo project was launched at the outbreak of the pandemic to allow all professors, even those who did not already participate in existing partnerships, to use the format and assistance offered by Federica to (quickly) prepare a MOOC.

Further, a MOOC platform called EduOpen was created in 2016 by a consortium of Italian universities and other partners, coordinated by the University of Foggia, within a project funded by the Minister of Education, University and Research.[91] The EduOpen platform also initiated master's modules and advanced courses, but not yet in legal subjects.[92] Participants who completed the required activities were awarded an attendance certificate and open badge,[93] and certain courses also offered the opportunity to obtain a verified certificate or receive CFUs upon completion of the course and passing an exam.[94]

Transmissive (content-oriented) education based on formal lectures has proved unsuitable for developing a series of skills required in the labour market.[95] Online education – suitably designed as student-centred – can also teach the

---

88 The University of Naples has also begun offering degree courses in the MOOC format in 'fremium' mode; there are not currently any degree courses in legal studies, but there are law courses included in the available online curricula.

89 Federica.eu is Europe's leading platform for open access multimedia education.

90 At the same time, Federica's MOOCs can be found on EdX, and a deal with Coursera was reached in 2021.

91 See http://learn.eduopen.org/.

92 See A. De Santis, K. Sannicandro, B. Fazlagic, C. Bellini, C. Tedeschi and T. Minerva, 'I MOOC per l'alta Formazione: I Master su EduOpen Attivati dall'Università di Modena e Reggio Emilia' in A. Volungeviciene and A. Szűcs (eds), *European Distance and E-Learning Network Annual Conference (EDEN 2018). Exploring the Micro, Meso and Macro: Navigating between Dimensions in the Digital Learning Landscape*, European Distance and E-Learning Network Budapest 2018, p. 673, https://www.researchgate.net/publication/335830713_I_Mooc_per_l'alta_formazione_i_master_su_EduOpen_attivati_dall'Universita_di_Modena_e_Reggio_Emilia.

93 An open badge is a digital certificate; it is verifiable, portable and contains metadata of the skills and achievements of the person displaying it. See https://openbadges.org/.

94 For an analysis of the outcomes of a survey conducted after two years of activity, see A. De Santis, K. Sannicandro, B. Fazlagic, C. Bellini, C. Tedeschi and T. Minerva, 'Gli Open Learners di EduOpen: Numeri e Prospettive' in A. Volungeviciene and A. Szűcs (eds), *European Distance and E-Learning Network Annual Conference (EDEN 2018). Exploring the Micro, Meso and Macro: Navigating between Dimensions in the Digital Learning Landscape*, European Distance and E-Learning Network Budapest 2018, p. 887, https://www.researchgate.net/publication/335830790_Gli_open_learners_di_EduOpen_numeri_e_prospettive.

95 On the soft skills required for the legal professions, of which the university system designed by the Bologna process should take charge, see G. Pascuzzi, *Giuristi si diventa*, 3rd edn, Il Mulino, Bologna 2019. The author has also long emphasised the potential of new technologies in legal education; see the experiments and possible trajectories reported in G. Pascuzzi, 'L'evoluzione dell'e-learning: l'apprendimento delle abilità' (2008) *Journal of e-Learning and Knowledge Society* 129, and updates in G. Pascuzzi, *Avvocati formano avvocati*, Il Mulino, Bologna 2015.

necessary soft skills. E-learning can also become a tool for opening international experiences up to a greater number of students, and it could be integrated into agreements between professors, universities and within the Erasmus programme,[96] including through blended mobility formats.

Distance learning is also a tool that can be very attractive to those who are already in the labour market. Beyond the continuing education required of lawyers, the lifelong learning sector assumes a crucial role in a society affected by increasingly rapid change, and universities have an interest in carving out a greater space for themselves in this market. In this context, so-called 'micro-credentials' could take on increasing importance, also stimulated by European policies and the intention to develop a European approach to such micro-credentials (a Council Recommendation on micro-credentials for lifelong learning and employability scheduled for the end of 2021, was finally adopted in June 2022).[97]

5. CONCLUSIONS

While the COVID-19 pandemic remains ongoing or recent, it is difficult to make predictions about the future. The opportunities offered by new technologies and the arrival of new education market players (not only universities but also private companies) pose important challenges for our university system. In order to face those challenges, imagining the future of higher education and the new pedagogical possibilities for universities, we must first of all accept the challenge, and face it with cultural awareness and an open mind.[98] Law professors have partially considered these issues, although with less pressure, as the five-year law degree remains compulsory to access the traditional legal professions and ministerial regulations and associated rigidity limits the possibility of carving out innovative paths within this degree. These issues have not prevented

96 See Erasmus+ 2021–2027 programme, Key Actions 1, https://ec.europa.eu/programmes/erasmus-plus/sites/default/files/2021-erasmusplus-programme-guide_en.pdf, which provides for blended mobility. In the Commission's Communication on 'Digital Education Action Plan 2021–2027', COM(2020) 624 final, it is stated that '[a]s digitalisation advances, the Action Plan provides the policy context and strategic guidance to increase the digital impact of the Erasmus programme. Blended mobility will be "mainstreamed" (i.e., integrated) into the Erasmus programme by introducing a "virtual learning" component to Erasmus'.

97 See https://ec.europa.eu/education/education-in-the-eu/european-education-area/a-european-approach-to-micro-credentials_en and the Council Recommendation of 16 June 2022 on a European approach to micro-credentials for lifelong learning and employability (2022/C 243/02).

98 See P. Limone, 'Towards a hybrid ecosystem of blended learning within university contexts', CEUR Workshop Proc. 2817, Foggia 2021, http://ceur-ws.org/Vol-2817/paper26.pdf.

changes in legal education[99] and emergence of a didactic style that is not only transmissive.[100] However, innovative online teaching experiences are quite limited, also because of an inadequate knowledge of the necessary technologies and their potential.

The Italian background was not particularly helpful, since, on the one hand, expertise in a certain subject has been considered sufficient to be able to teach it for too long and, on the other, quality of teaching is not valued for the purposes of academic career progression. The Italian university system does not encourage teachers to invest in their own training as instructors and is reluctant to valorise the efforts required to prepare innovative courses. This aspect – irrespective of the nostalgic phase 'in which the need for a return to presence and forms of socialisation of knowledge is accentuated'[101] – could mean missing out on the opportunities offered by online education.

In Italy, there have been innovative experiences that have exploited e-learning and pilot projects aimed at paving the way for the education of the future where universities can maintain a central role and guarantee quality teaching at affordable costs.

The debate about online education concerns the entire university system and its future. Law schools cannot avoid it. For some time now, legal scholars, not only in Italy, have been discussing the future of legal education, currently said to be under fire.[102] The time, the consistency and the quality of the response depend on many variables (recovery fund interventions could provide important support), as well as on the commitment of academics. Professors must receive the necessary technical and didactic knowledge and incentives to exploit them and be part of a vision in which they are conscious actors making valuable contributions to the future of legal education. Appropriate funding, cultural and pedagogical awareness, and commitment of academics are certainly needed if we want the 'new normal' to be a better one.

---

99 See M. Graziadei, 'Eppur si muove: la rivoluzione silenziosa in corso nell'educazione giuridica' (2021) 1 *Diritto & questioni pubbliche* 67, http://www.dirittoequestionipubbliche.org/page/2021_n21-1/index.htm.

100 See, for example, the spread of so-called legal clinics.

101 G.A. Toto and P. Limone, 'From Resistance to Digital Technologies in the Context of the Reaction to Distance Learning in the School Context during COVID-19' (2021) 11 *Education Sciences* 163, https://www.mdpi.com/2227-7102/11/4/163.

102 S. Cassese, 'Legal Education under Fire' (2017) 25 *European Review of Private Law* 143.

APPENDIX
QUESTIONNAIRE

PART A. BACKGROUND: LEGAL PROFESSION, UNIVERSITY AND IT SYSTEMS GENERALLY

- Who are the main 'gatekeepers' to the legal profession?[1] Does its corresponding size and nature make it generally harder or easier to move (university/qualifying or continuing) legal education online?
  - The existing legal profession (e.g. like Japan: *bengoshi* lawyers, negotiating with the Ministry of Justice and courts): tends to result in smaller legal profession, but still many other LLB graduates (not qualified as lawyers)
  - Universities (e.g. like Australia previously or now NZ: LLB and JD graduates can almost all qualify as lawyers, as they need to just complete a short easy practical training course, so the numbers of law students allowed into universities – by the government as in NZ, or by universities themselves since 2011 in Australia – determines the size of the legal profession): tends to result in a larger legal profession
  - The market (e.g. like USA: as there are so many accredited law schools, and state bar exams are easily passed at least after a few attempts, so the number of lawyers is really determined only by whether students think they will be able to get a job as lawyer after graduating): tends to result in the largest legal profession
- How are universities (and law schools) generally funded? Does this make it harder or easier to move legal education online?
  - E.g. universities in Australia: growing dependence on international student revenues, including more recently in law – many are non-native English speakers (e.g. from China), so may be more difficult to move effectively their legal education online
  - Cf. universities in Japan: still much lower international student proportions, especially in law; correspondingly more emphasis on research, so maybe easier to move online

---

1 Cf. K. Anderson and T. Ryan, 'Gatekeepers: A comparative critique of admission to the legal profession and Japan's new law schools', in S. Steele and K. Taylor (eds), *Legal Education in Asia: Globalization, Change and Contexts*, Routledge, London 2009, pp. 45–67.

- How widespread is access to good-quality and affordable IT hardware (computers etc.) and software (including internet access), among university students/teachers and legal professionals?
  - E.g. in Australia: quite good for both groups, making it again easier to move university/qualifying and continuing legal education online
  - Cf. in Japan: quite good for lawyers but less so for judges/courts, variable for university teachers, quite bad for many university students

PART B. MOVES TOWARDS ONLINE EDUCATION

- Summary achievements before the pandemic, in light of the above background
  - University and/or qualifying legal education
  - Continuing (post-admission) legal education
- Achievements and challenges after the pandemic
  - Briefly re continuing legal education
  - Details for university and/or qualifying legal education
  - Course/programme goals (any revisions needed?)
  - Course assessment methods (fewer exams, more assignments and/or essays? Changes to grading curves?)
  - Delivery methods (purely online e.g. live and/or pre-recorded, hybrid with some face-to-face teaching?)
  - Other administrative challenges (e.g. more plagiarism?)
  - Student welfare and extra-curricular activities?

PART C. CONCLUSIONS

- Overall, has the shift to more online education been positive?
- With (big!) assumptions of similar structure for legal profession, university funding and IT systems, what are the prospects for further online legal education as the pandemic abates?

QUESTIONNAIRE

PARTIE A. CONTEXTE : PROFESSION JURIDIQUE, UNIVERSITÉS ET SYSTÈMES INFORMATIQUES EN GÉNÉRAL

- Qui sont les principaux « gardiens » de la profession juridique ?[1] La taille et la nature de la profession rendent-elles généralement plus difficile ou plus facile la mise en ligne de l'enseignement juridique (universitaire/qualifiant ou continu)?
  - La profession juridique existante (par exemple, comme au Japon: avocats ou *bengoshi*, négociant avec le ministère de la justice et les tribunaux): tend à réduire la profession juridique, mais il y a toujours de nombreux autres diplômés de LLB (non qualifiés en tant qu'avocats)
  - Les universités (par exemple, comme l'Australie auparavant, ou maintenant la Nouvelle-Zélande : les diplômés de LLB et de JD peuvent presque tous se qualifier en tant qu'avocats, car ils n'ont qu'à suivre un cours de formation pratique court et facile, de sorte que le nombre d'étudiants en droit admis dans les universités – par le gouvernement comme en Nouvelle-Zélande, ou par les universités elles-mêmes depuis 2011 en Australie – détermine la taille de la profession juridique): tend à entraîner une profession juridique plus grande
  - Le marché (par exemple, comme aux États-Unis, où il existe un grand nombre d'écoles de droit accréditées et où les examens du barreau de l'État sont facilement réussis, du moins après quelques tentatives, de sorte que le nombre d'avocats n'est réellement déterminé que par le fait que les étudiants pensent pouvoir obtenir un emploi d'avocat après l'obtention de leur diplôme): tend à donner lieu à la plus grande profession juridique
- Comment les universités (et les facultés de droit) sont-elles généralement financées ? Cela rend-il plus difficile ou plus facile l'enseignement juridique en ligne ?
  - Par exemple, les universités australiennes dépendent de plus en plus des revenus des étudiants internationaux, y compris, plus récemment, en droit – beaucoup d'entre eux ne sont pas des locuteurs natifs de l'anglais (par exemple, de Chine), il peut donc être plus difficile de transférer efficacement leur enseignement juridique en ligne

1 Cf. K. Anderson and T. Ryan, 'Gatekeepers: A comparative critique of admission to the legal profession and Japan's new law schools', in S. Steele and K. Taylor (eds), *Legal Education in Asia: Globalization, Change and Contexts*, Routledge, London 2009, pp. 45–67.

  - Cf. les universités japonaises : la proportion d'étudiants internationaux est encore beaucoup plus faible, surtout en droit; en conséquence, l'accent est davantage mis sur la recherche, ce qui facilite peut-être le transfert en ligne
- Dans quelle mesure l'accès au matériel informatique (ordinateurs, etc.) et aux logiciels (y compris l'accès à Internet) de bonne qualité et abordables est-il répandu parmi les étudiants et enseignants universitaires et les professionnels du droit?
  - Par exemple, en Australie: assez bon pour les deux groupes, ce qui facilite à nouveau le transfert en ligne de la formation universitaire/qualifiante et de la formation juridique continue
  - Cf. au Japon : assez bon pour les avocats, mais moins pour les juges et les tribunaux, variable pour les enseignants universitaires, assez mauvais pour de nombreux étudiants universitaires

PARTIE B. ÉVOLUTION VERS L'ENSEIGNEMENT EN LIGNE

- Résumé des réalisations avant la pandémie, à la lumière du contexte ci-dessus
  - Formation juridique universitaire et/ou qualifiante
  - Formation juridique continue
- Réalisations et défis après la pandémie
  - Brève description de la formation juridique continue
  - Détails de la formation juridique universitaire et/ou qualifiante
  - Objectifs du cours/programme (révisions nécessaires ?)
  - Méthodes d'évaluation du cours (moins d'examens, plus de devoirs ou de dissertations ? Modification des courbes de notation ?)
  - Méthodes d'enseignement (purement en ligne, par exemple en direct ou préenregistré, hybride avec un enseignement en face à face ?)
  - Autres défis administratifs (par exemple, plus de plagiat ?)
  - Le bien-être des étudiants et les activités périscolaires ?

PARTIE C. CONCLUSIONS

- Dans l'ensemble, le passage à un enseignement plus en ligne a-t-il été positif ?
- Avec des hypothèses (importantes !) de structure similaire pour la profession juridique, le financement des universités et les systèmes informatiques, quelles sont les perspectives pour la poursuite de l'enseignement juridique en ligne alors que la pandémie s'atténue ?

INDEX

O

P

Q

R

S

T

U

ABOUT THE EDITORS

LUKE NOTTAGE (PhD VUW, LLD Kyoto) is Professor of Comparative and Transnational Business Law at the University of Sydney, Associate Director of its Centre for Asian and Pacific Law (CAPLUS) and founding Co-Director of the Australian Network for Japanese Law (ANJeL). He is Honorary Professor at the University of Wollongong, Special Counsel with Williams Trade Law and a titular member of the International Academy of Comparative Law. Professor Nottage has published 19 books and taught law in Australasia, Southeast Asia, Japan, North America and Europe.

MAKOTO IBUSUKI (LLD Hokkaido) is Professor of Law at Seijo University in Tokyo and ANJeL-in-Japan Program Convenor for the Australian Network for Japanese Law. His major areas of research, teaching and writing are in cyberspace law and criminal procedure. He was a founding director of the Hojohogakkai (Association for Legal Informatics) and a key member of a study group promoting IT issues in Japan's major reforms to criminal and civil justice. Professor Ibusuki formerly taught at Kagoshima University in Kyushu (1990–2002) and at Ritsumeikan University in Kyoto (2002–2008).

ABOUT THE SERIES

As globalisation proceeds, the significance of the comparative approach in legal scholarship increases. The IACL / AIDC with almost 800 members is the major universal organisation promoting comparative research in law and organising congresses with hundreds of participants in all parts of the world. The results of those congresses should be disseminated and be available for legal scholars in a single book series which would make both the Academy and its contribution to comparative law more visible. The series aims to publish the scholarship emerging from the congresses of IACL / AIDC, including: 1. of the General Congresses of Comparative Law, which take place every 4 years (Brisbane 2002, Utrecht 2006, Washington 2010, Vienna 2014, Fukuoka 2018 etc.) and which generate (a) one volume of General Reports edited by the local organisers of the Congress; (b) up to 30 volumes of selected thematic reports dealing with the topics of the single sections of the congress and containing the General Report as well as the Special Reports (national and non-national) of that section; these volumes would be edited by the General Rapporteurs of the respective sections; 2. the volumes containing selected contributions to the smaller (2–3 days) thematic congresses which take place between the International Congresses (Mexico 2008, Taipei 2012, Montevideo 2016 etc.); these congresses have a general theme such as "Codification" or "The Enforcement of Law" and will be edited by the local organisers of the respective Congress. All publications may contain contributions in English and French, the official languages of the Academy.

More information about this series at: www.larcier-intersentia.com/en/series/ius-comparatum.html

Académie Internationale de Droit Comparé
International Academy of Comparative Law

www.ingramcontent.com/pod-product-compliance
Ingram Content Group UK Ltd.
Pitfield, Milton Keynes, MK11 3LW, UK
UKHW051846100926
8556IPUK00005B/485